APOCALYPSE AND POST-POLITICS

APOCALYPSE AND POST-POLITICS

The Romance of the End

Mary Manjikian

LEXINGTON BOOKS
Lanham • Boulder • New York • Toronto • Plymouth, UK

Excerpts from *World Made By Hand*, copyright © 2008 by James Howard Kunstler. Used by permission of Grove/Atlantic, Inc.

Published by Lexington Books
A wholly owned subsidiary of
The Rowman & Littlefield Publishing Group, Inc.
4501 Forbes Boulevard, Suite 200, Lanham, Maryland 20706
www.rowman.com

10 Thornbury Road, Plymouth PL6 7PP, United Kingdom

Copyright © 2014 by Lexington Books

All rights reserved. No part of this book may be reproduced in any form or by any electronic or mechanical means, including information storage and retrieval systems, without written permission from the publisher, except by a reviewer who may quote passages in a review.

British Library Cataloguing in Publication Information Available

Library of Congress Cataloging-in-Publication Data

The hardback edition of this book was previously cataloged by the Library of Congress as follows:

Manjikian, Mary.
Apocalypse and post-politics : the romance of the end / Mary Manjikian. p. cm.
1. American fiction—History and criticism. 2. Apocalypse in literature.
3. End of the world in literature. 4. Exceptionalism—United States. I. Title.
PS374.A65M36 2012
813'.009353—dc23

2012000555

ISBN: 978-0-7391-6622-2 (cloth : alk. paper)
ISBN: 978-0-7391-9066-1 (pbk. : alk. paper)
ISBN: 978-0-7391-6624-6 (electronic)

∞™ The paper used in this publication meets the minimum requirements of American National Standard for Information Sciences—Permanence of Paper for Printed Library Materials, ANSI/NISO Z39.48-1992.

Printed in the United States of America

CONTENTS

Introduction   1

PART 1: APOCALYPSE AS PREDICTION

1   Apocalypse and National Security   41

2   Catastrophe Novels and Prediction   77

3   Utopian Novels and Forecasting   105

4   The Romance of the World's End   125

PART 2: APOCALYPSE AS CRITIQUE

5   Apocalypse and Epistemology   145

6   Exceptionality and Apocalypse   185

7   Going Native   227

8   The Traveler   255

PART 3: APOCALYPSE AS ETHICS

9   Encountering the Other   285

Bibliography	305
Index	319
About the Author	337

INTRODUCTION

In recent years, the United States of America has undergone major challenges and trials in the area of foreign policy, domestic politics, and the economy. Since the beginning of this new century, citizens have watched as their nation became the subject of a terrorist attack on their own soil, as a devastating natural disaster in New Orleans crippled large sections of America, and as economic problems have had very real impacts on their lives. To most Americans who are used to living in what was ostensibly the safest country in the world, these threats seem to defy logic and comprehension.

At the same time, Americans developed a fascination with apocalyptic scenarios. Hollywood profited from the release of films like "I Am Legend," "The Book of Eli," and "The Road" while television shows like "Survivor" became popular as well. In literature, there were a number of bestselling novels written—all of which rest on the premise that America has been destroyed frequently due to errors committed by its own government. In each case (film, literature, and television), America's citizens are described as at sea in a world which is virtually unrecognizable. In this new world, the state no longer exists, citizenship and rule of law have been forgotten, and America's sense of historic destiny and role as a world leader and beacon of progress are only distant memories.

But how do we explain the sudden rise of interest in this type of imagining? What accounts for increased production and reader demand for this literature and what does it say about how Americans feel about their nation's position in the world today? Man has always been fascinated by tales of disaster and terror, and has always been drawn to theorize about his own final end or the demise of the world.[1] As long as we could conceptualize of our world as having a history, we have—understandably—wondered about how it would end. Indeed, the first epic ever written, the ancient Sumerian *Epic of Gilgamesh* (believed to date from 2000 BC) rests on the myth of a flood which overtakes the world and destroys everyone except for a chosen few. (The story shares many similarities thus with the story of Noah and the flood.) More recently, the author Justin Cronin has assured us in his novel *The Passage* that: "It happened fast. Thirty-two minutes for one world to die, another to be born."[2]

However, historians tell us that for most of history, religious apocalyptic theorizing was largely the province of the weak and the disenfranchised. Individuals who lacked education and an understanding of the modern world saw an event like a plague or a flood as a type of divine judgment. Thus we can understand and explain the growth of apocalyptic theorizing during the outbreaks of plague in Europe in the 1500s.[3] The disenfranchised subject in particular may be drawn to the fact that an apocalypse affects all alike, from the poorest to the wealthiest member of society, and the poor member of society might be comforted to think that the wealthy will be punished while he himself might profit from divine favor.

But all sorts of people are drawn to apocalyptic theorizing—of both the secular and the religious variety. And the more citizens begin to know about the natural world, the more they are fascinated about sources of disaster. Increasing education has not led us to explain away disaster and cease to find it a subject of interest. Rather, educated citizens living in relatively safety are frequently not reassured when they hear about disaster. They are not comforted. They are merely intrigued—desiring to know more and to explore disaster in all its facets.

In modern times, one can point to the huge swell of popular interest around the world which followed the devastating Lisbon earthquake in 1755. The earthquake, which registered the equivalent of 8.5 on the Richter scale, took place while citizens were packing Portugal's churches to celebrate All Saint's Day. Hundreds of thousands died of crush injuries as the churches collapsed upon them while others perished in the fires that soon followed. Still more died in the tsunami produced by the earthquake which came ashore in short succession with thirty-foot waves. As the historian Nicholas Shrady tells us, newspaper readers around the world—from the American colonies to England and throughout Europe—devoured lithographs and drawings of the devastation which occurred and organized scientific roundtables to learn about and study the phenomenon. Indeed, Voltaire's literary work *Candide*, written at the same time, included an earthquake as one of its seminal events.[4]

Approximately 130 years later, in August 1883, amateur scientists and current-events watchers around the world were fascinated by news of a volcanic explosion in Krakatoa, Indonesia. That event produced what the historian Simon Winchester calls "the loudest sound ever experienced by man on the face of the earth."[5] The geography of the whole Indonesian region was changed and climactic effects were felt in Europe and the United States, as dust clouds blotted out the sun and caused an unusually cold summer and crop failures. In the aftermath of the explosion which killed approximately 35,000, lectures and scientific projects were again organized around the world to study the phenomena, and at least one Victorian children's book includes the event as a subject of the story.

At the same time historic audiences were fascinated by genuine disasters, they were equally drawn to experiencing what the analyst Ted Steinberg terms "faux disaster." He argues that from a position of relative safety in the United States, it has been easy for Americans in particular to regard disaster as a form of entertainment. He describes a range of disaster-related amusements available to the average New Yorker in the early 1900s—with rides and exhibits at Coney Island which simulated Mount Pelee erupting and even the 1889 Johnstown storm and flooding incident.[6] Even today, visitors at U.S. amusement parks can experience the Last Days of Pompeii at Busch Gardens in Williamsburg, Virginia—as well as having the opportunity to ride on amusements with names such as the Tornado, the Earthquake, and the Tsunami.

However, despite our outward fascination with disaster and our desire to experience and explore terror, the world is actually safer today than it has ever been before. In most of the developed world, individuals enjoy longer lifespans and lower mortality rates that at any time in history. Individuals today are much less likely to die in an industrial accident, a plane crash, or an auto accident than they might have a decade or a century ago. Those proponents of the High Reliability school of industrial technology argue that today's safety mechanisms, training programs, and redundancy procedures can safely check the likelihood of unforeseen events like a reactor breach, an accidental nuclear strike, or the accidental release of toxic chemicals into the atmosphere.[7]

On both an individual and a corporate level, Aaron Wildavsky's statement that "richer is safer" appears to hold true. Even when the event that one fears is categorized as an unpreventable natural disaster or Act of God—like a large-scale hurricane, tornado, or tsunami—technological advances make it much more likely that analysts will be able to predict and prepare for disasters and avert tragedies. This is particularly true in wealthy nations with strong, stable, and functioning governments.[8] This leads to the following puzzle: Those who appear to be most fascinated by the study of and imagining of disaster are those who actually have the least to worry about. They are the least likely to actually suffer the consequences which they fear.

However, one might argue that it is *because* disaster seems so unlikely that citizens are fascinated by it. As Clarke points out, citizens today feel very different about every kind of danger than they might have hundreds of years ago. Previously, citizens were much more willing to accept that their lives were precarious and that at any time a child might die, a crop might fail or a team of foreign invaders might arrive to take possession of one's land. Clarke tells us to:

> Imagine the poor fellow in thirteenth-century Asia. He farms and occasionally enjoys a piece of meat for supper. But he's regularly subject to the vagaries of nature and marauders. Floods come and he runs for his life. Genghis Khan comes and everyone is subject to a death sentence. Nowadays these might be worst cases, but our hapless peasant probably did not judge them so. He did not expect the government . . . to protect him. Destruction was just part of the natural order.[9]

Today, however, we expect to feel safe and are therefore particularly surprised when we are not. As Boin and 't Hart express the matter, "Citizens expect to be safeguarded by their state; the idea that wholesale crisis cannot be prevented comes as a shock."[10] Thus, what today's citizens really want to know (and what they seek to find out in reading apocalyptic fiction) is how and why a "modern" society is *not* immune to devastating acts of destruction, how it is that "modern" people and their leaders behave in times of great danger, and whether there are lessons and opportunities one's society may draw from danger.[11] We want to know how it is that we are safe, but not invulnerable.

However, perhaps we are drawn to the study and imagination of disaster not because of its probability (or rarity) but because of its scope. Perhaps the fact that the end of the world is extremely unlikely is irrelevant. Instead, what is relevant is the magnitude of the loss which we as citizens are both capable of sustaining and inflicting upon ourselves. We were fascinated by September 11 simply because of the scope and scale of the suffering, which was unprecedented in our nation's history. We experienced not rational fear, but irrational dread—an emotion which mimics fear but is much more complex in its genesis and explication.[12]

Lindgren has labeled Americans' fascination with bad news of all types as "pessimism porn"—a type of voyeurism in which the relatively fortunate stand and watch like spectators while others lose jobs and homes.[13] Some have argued that our fascination with the disaster spectacle is therapeutic because it allows for a conversation about fears. In addition, some viewers might be experiencing *schadenfreude* if they believe that some types of victims "deserve it."[14] However, Lindgren suggests that the motive for embracing apocalyptic scenarios is not actually one of hoping to see justice meted out—in, for example, rejoicing when a Wall Street baron loses his home to foreclosure. Rather, Lindgren argues that the impetus for creating and studying such scenarios is one of control—in which citizens learn all they can about the impending doom in hopes of surviving it.

What Lindgren terms "pessimism porn" goes by the more academic term "eschatological anxiety" in the work of Frank Kermode. Writing in the late 1960s, Kermode argued that there was "nothing at all distinguishing about eschatological anxiety"[15] which had been around since Mesopotamian culture. He argued that worrying about the apocalypse is actually a feature of societies undergoing significant technological and social transitions. The shift in life as we know it—in the current case, occasioned by increased globalization and reliance on technology—leads the individual to feel that life is precarious and that they are dependent on events which they do not fully understand. This is the argument made by Charles Perrow as well in his discourse about "normal accidents." Perrow argues, in opposition to those of the High Reliability School, that in an increasingly complex world, the probability of accidental destruction through technological failure is actually higher, rather than lower.[16] Thus, Perrow would argue that it is normal for people to worry more as society advances. Life hasn't become safer, but rather more dangerous.

Thus, to summarize, worrying about apocalypse, death, and destruction is caused simultaneously by insufficient education and too much education, relative poverty and relative wealth, a desire to view other's misfortunes and the desire to preserve one's own, and it is both an entirely irrational activity and a highly rational one. In short, there is little consensus regarding the propensities of individuals to theorize about the end times, the motivations of those who do so, the meaning of such an activity, and ultimately, its utility.

However, there is a consensus that apocalyptic theorizing is both on the increase and an activity which now appeals to mainstream Americans—rather than being exclusively the province of such fringe groups as religious fundamentalists or survivalists who have always been drawn to this type of theorizing. Works about apocalypse are now published by mainstream publishing houses and frequently wind up on best-seller lists. (A search for the term "apocalypse" under books in Amazon.com brings up nearly eight thousand titles, while the popular website goodreads.com counts nearly two thousand apocalyptic titles on its virtual shelves. Netflix offers a selection of over forty apocalypse films to its viewers, with 90 percent of these produced in the last five years.)

One simplistic explanation for this phenomenon would involve pointing to September 11 and suggesting that as Americans became aware of the precariousness of their state's leading position in the world, they have been drawn to the creation of this type of end times culture. One can find precedent for this type of explanation in looking at the explosive growth of literary imagining and theorizing about the aftermath of nuclear explosions during the 1950s and 1960s. Booker argued that America's "nuclear anxiety" was made manifest in much of the literature of the time.[17] Thus, it is not surprising that a present-day post-apocalyptic novel like James Howard Kunstler's *World Made by Hand* features a "jihadist" attack as part of the narrative, while works like Jim Crace's *The Pesthouse* and Justin Cronin's *The Passage* both focus on a pestilence or pandemic which wipes out most of America's population.

INTRODUCTION

When I began reading post-9/11 apocalyptic literature, I thought that one could easily describe the ways in which the world seemed precarious today. One could point to the rise of phenomena like globalization which in a sense render even superpowers more vulnerable since they require them to depend on their neighbors. Thus, one could build a theory to explain the output of apocalyptic literature today.[18] However, as I began to explore more deeply, I began to sense that there was something both brand new and also deeply familiar about the American stance at present—towards itself and towards the international system. I also began to ask a more nuanced question—namely, why it is that writers and readers from nations which appear to be world leaders would choose to engage in speculation about the end of their state at all? While one can argue that nuclear anxiety led to the creation of apocalyptic scenarios in the 1960s (and not, say, in the 1920s) and that 9/11 anxiety led to the creation of jihadist scenarios (such as those that appear in Tom Clancy novels) in the 2000s,[19] in doing so, one has merely answered a sort of *when* question as in "why were they written at this time period and not that?" One still has not satisfactorily explored the genesis of these scenarios altogether. It seems oddly counterintuitive that wealthy nations would create apocalyptic scenarios rather than poor ones, and that societies where citizens feel safe would create survival narratives while societies where citizens feel unsafe would not. As I thought more deeply about these questions, I found myself intrigued by the parallels between the sorts of speculative fiction created in Victorian Britain and that created in the present-day United States. I began to wonder why strong nations seemed to have a monopoly on the creation of this type of literature, and what, if anything, citizens of these dominant nations might learn from a closer reading of this literature.

Ultimately, I concluded that apocalyptic and utopian fiction have always been uniquely beguiling to those writers and artists who worked within the context of power—whether in Victorian Britain or in the contemporary United States. The current flowering of American apocalyptic and dystopian literature and the attendant demand for it are both products of unipolarity and an imperial foreign policy. Imagining the demise of one's empire serves both psychological and political ends and is a useful way for moving beyond the situatedness of one's own experience and coming to a broader understanding of the hegemon's significance (or lack thereof) in the international system. Throughout this work, I draw parallels between the apocalyptic appetite in Victorian Britain and the United States—suggesting that the circumstances which created the literature itself and the attendant demand for it—are similar and logical.

In addition, I argue that writers from the two states have both consciously and unconsciously sought to use speculative fiction in general and apocalyptic fiction in specific as the basis for a critique of imperial foreign policy and the discourse of exceptionalism. Both Britain and the United States are highly ideological societies with a strong, dominant narrative which serves to build national identity. Within that discourse, it is often difficult to establish a counternarrative which rests on different assumptions. Here, we might briefly consider the remarks by President Barack Obama in April 2009, when he stated that:

> I believe in American exceptionalism, just as I suspect that the Brits believe in British exceptionalism and the Greeks believe in Greek exceptionalism. . . . Now, the fact that I am very proud of my country and I think that we've got a whole lot to offer the world does not lessen my interest in recognizing the value and wonderful qualities of other countries.[20]

President Obama's remarks were widely described by political analysts as a mistake and one which he was not likely to make again. Instead, analysts like Monica Crowley of Fox News suggested that the glorious myth of American exceptionalism had prevailed for longer than Obama was likely to, and that questioning this mythology was a good route to political oblivion for an American politician.[21]

In contrast, in both positing the existence of other "exceptional" nations (as one does in a utopian novel), and in positing the erasure of one's own exceptional nation (as one does in an apocalyptic novel), the writer can raise questions about how and why the state's identity has come to be seen as both immutable and unquestionable in the first place. The novel can thus serve as a means for exploring the narrative of the nation's identity, as well as for raising ethical, moral, and political questions about it.

CHOICE OF NOVELS AND METHODOLOGY

My decision regarding which apocalyptic literature to analyze in this work is not merely haphazard. Instead, I used a number of criteria to winnow all of the apocalyptic literature currently available down to a representative sample. First, I chose to analyze only those novels which could be regarded as "mainstream" publications. For that reason, I eliminated apocalyptic novels published by boutique publishing houses, such as those devoted to Christian literature or survival-type literature.[22] In addition, I chose only novels which had sold at least one hundred thousand copies, and which were either best-sellers or award-winners. In addition, I considered whether a book had been excerpted in the popular press and whether a "book club" edition of the book had been created for large-scale distribution to subscribers of a book club.

Thus, among present-day apocalyptics I have chosen to examine James Kunstler's 2008 novel *World Made by Hand*; Cormac McCarthy's 2006 novel *The Road*; Jim Crace's 2007 novel *The Pesthouse*; and Justin Cronin's 2010 novel *The Passage*.

Table I.I. Six Modern Novels to Be Considered

Novel	Author	Date	Subject Matter
World Made by Hand	James Kunstler	2008	Writer and reader travel to a future America in which the Industrial Revolution and interdependence have been reversed.
The Road	Cormac McCarthy	2006	Writer and reader travel to a future America which has been destroyed by nuclear winter. Americans turn to cannibalism.
The Pesthouse	Jim Crace	2007	Writer and reader view America from a perspective of 1,000 years later. America has gone the way of Rome and all that remains are a few archeological remnants of American civilization.
The Passage	Justin Cronin	2010	Writer and reader travel to a future America which has been destroyed by technology gone mad. Anthropologists consider post-apocalyptic America from a distant future.
Falling Man	Dom DeLillo	2007	Martin Neudecker experiences the events of 9/11 and the ways in which the world changes as a result.
The Second Plane	Kingsley Amis	2008	Amis narrates the events of 9/11 from the perspective of the hijacker, a time-traveler who "visits" the United States and offers a unique perspective on it.

Each of these novels takes place in the geographic space which was formerly known as America, and each features a devastating man-made event which has led to the end of the state known as the United States. Here, I distinguish between man-made events—such as war (including nuclear war and biological warfare), assassinations, and invasions—and natural events such as a tsunami or a meteorite. Since we are interested in exploring American anxiety related to the end of the state, it seemed important to focus on only those events which were both scientifically and socially plausible, as well as those which were seen as having causes located within that state. For this reason, I also draw a line in my work between the apocalyptic novel and the apocalyptic horror novel. I do not analyze novels which depict a future which can only be 'believed' if one relaxes what one knows about hard science. In a true apocalyptic novel, the emphasis is on human relations, on community, and on how citizens come to understand their changed circumstances—both in relation to one another and in relation to their new environment. In contrast, in an apocalyptic horror fiction, like Max Brooks' *The Zombie Survival Guide: Complete Protection from the Living Dead*, the "other" with which humans are most concerned is the "undead." Relations between other humans are only of passing interest.[23]

In a true apocalyptic novel, there are no zombies—because the threats are not from outside alien forces but rather from the environment and its inhabitants themselves, and because a true apocalyptic novel does not require that one suspend the laws of science and nature in order to create a story. Thus, a true apocalyptic novel might feature individuals who are changed as the result of science and technology gone mad, but would not include such impossible feats as, for example, people who arise from the dead as "the undead."

Although all of the novels chosen have the same end—the "death" of the United States (about which I will say more later)—they differ greatly in their time frames, their characterizations, and the events which are seen as leading up to that death. McCarthy's *The Road*, the most lyrical of all the novels, features only two main characters known only as The Man and The Boy. The novel takes place approximately eight years after most of America has been destroyed in a nuclear explosion. The climate is harsh, one can no longer grow food, and America's inhabitants have begun to prey upon one another. *A World Made by Hand*, in contrast, takes place approximately twenty years after America's government suffered a sort of internal collapse brought on by terrorist attacks, the end of globalization and interdependence, and the end of oil. Here the action takes place in a small town in upstate New York and is narrated by Robert Earle, a former computer executive turned carpenter. English writer Jim Crace's *The Pesthouse* takes place in a ruined America a thousand years from now. The main character, Margaret, doesn't conceptualize of herself as "American" at all. She is illiterate, believes in magic, and is seemingly unaware of America's history. Finally, Justin Cronin's *The Passage* jumps between three different time periods: America ten years from now (when another hurricane has hit New Orleans and Jenna Bush is president); America one hundred years from now (when genetically enhanced human-bat hybrids have killed all of America's population save 60,000 people); and the international system one thousand years from now, when America is apparently the subject of interest by ancient historians.

At an editor's suggestion, I have also included in this analysis two literary works—a novel and an essay—which deal directly with the events of September 11. I consider both Martin Amis' collection of essays titled *The Second Plane* and Dom DeLillo's novel *Falling Man*. In making the case that apocalyptic fiction is not merely a case of "September 11 anxiety," it seemed important to distinguish post-911 literature from post-apocalyptic literature. To my surprise, I find both vast differences in the two types of literary works, but also some surprising similarities—as I relate later in this work.

The method of analysis here is neither positivist nor is it quantitative. There is no explicit attempt to show how apocalyptic literature as the independent variable has led to a 3 percent increase or decrease in U.S. public support for an aggressive foreign policy as the dependent variable. Rather, the reader of the volume is asked to buy into certain assumptions which are spelled out later in this chapter—namely, that words matter, that popular culture matters, and that politics is a deeper and broader phenomenon than one can indicate in a chart or a bivariate correlation. Certainly there is room for quantitative analysis of the American public's literary tastes and purchasing patterns and their relation to IR theory, but that would be a project for someone else at some other time.[24] Instead, I aim to provide a "reading" of these novels within the tradition of critical discourse analysis, showing how the themes and language of the novels resonate within a particular time period, through language play and intertextuality. Furthermore, I do not claim to be making a generalizable argument about the political function of literature—in current U.S. society or in societies in general.

In a seminal international relations article in 1993, the analyst Roxanne Doty suggested that analysts of foreign policy were too wedded to an approach which asked "how" rather than asking "why?"[25] That is, she argued that we tended to be fixated on showing how a particular variable of series of events led the decision-making to end up at point A. However, she argued that seldom did we ask a larger question—namely, how was the original decision set formed? How did we end up with a decision set which included certain options but excluded others? In short, how did we decide which were possible in the first place? Why were some options thinkable while others were unthinkable? The approach which Doty takes assumes that there are more options available than those which can be captured using a purely positivist approach, focusing on identifying a correlation between two factors.

My work thus builds upon hers and that of others[26] who have adopted her approach in asking questions about why apocalypse is thinkable in some contexts but not others, and why it is that some queries about the future of a nation are considered reasonable while others are not. That is, I seek to ask not "how" but "why" and "why not"? As noted earlier in this introduction, it is my intent to show that empires in particular militate against the creation of alternate narratives of identity, and that for this reason, science fiction literature may be a particularly appealing vehicle for creating alternate narratives of identity. In making this point, I consider a number of cultural products from Victorian Britain, which are both compared and contrasted with the products of present-day imperial America. I consider five novels—two of which might be classified as apocalyptic, while the others are classified as utopian. First, I consider Jonathan Swift's *Gulliver's Travels*, which I argue is a vehicle for interrogating the narrative of England as uniquely cultured and special among the world's nations. I also consider Samuel Butler's *Erewhon*, which has been labeled by some as the first utopian novel. H. G. Wells' *The First Men in the Moon* is similarly considered as a vehicle for both voicing and interrogating the narrative of British exceptionalism. Finally, I consider the novels *News from Nowhere* and *The Machine Stops*, each of which looks at one future

INTRODUCTION   13

trajectory for England. In Morris' *News from Nowhere*, Britain voluntarily abandons its mission of global economic and political domination, while in E. M. Forster's *The Machine Stops*, a technical malfunction halts Britain's narrative of technological progress which—until that moment—had seemed to be unassailable.

Table I.2.   Five Victorian Novels to Be Considered

Novel	Author	Date	Subject Matter
Erewhon	Samuel Butler	1872	British subject goes in search of new land to colonize and visits a new society which causes him to reflect on his own.
Gulliver's Travels	Jonathan Swift	1726	British sailor is shipwrecked and lost and visits new societies which cause him to reflect on his own.
News from Nowhere	William Morris	1890	English industrialist finds himself travelling to an imagined future England in which the Industrial Revolution has been reversed.
The First Men in the Moon	H. G. Wells	1901	Two English gentlemen hope to colonize the moon and exploit its resources. In their journey they reexamine key assumptions about their own society.
The Machine Stops	E. M. Forster	1905	The writer and reader imagine themselves journeying to a future England where technology is very powerful, until it is erased.

Each of the works described here is not merely a novel which the citizens found entertaining. Rather, in each case, the work was significant because of the ways in which it provided a new lens or new stance for considering a number of old problems. Each novel allowed readers to ask the questions: Who are we and what is our place in the world? What is our history and how can we know that it will turn out as we have predicted? But this literature is not only of interest to readers and writers of literature. It is of interest to political scientists as well.

WHY SHOULD IR THEORISTS CARE ABOUT APOCALYPTIC LITERATURE?

In recent years, political scientists have increasingly acknowledged that we live both in a world of concrete objects and in a world of ideas.

Critical and constructivist international relations scholars have argued that words and the game of language are significant determinants of action and worthy of further study.[27] However, despite this acknowledgment, political analysts in the contemporary period have not been significantly concerned with the analysis of literature—preferring instead to focus on how language has been used in academic discourse, political speechmaking, and the media.

This lack of attention to the literary worlds which writers create and inhabit, as well as the impact that literary worlds may actually have on "real" worlds is easily justifiable. Few political scientists have much training in literary analysis. Furthermore, most international relations scholars are still preoccupied with questions of hard power and political realism. From the 1950s onward, international relations in particular were wedded to the positivist approach, in which true knowledge was defined as that which was measurable, calculable, and rational. As Goodwin and Taylor argue, policy analysts traditionally found little redeeming about literature, including utopian science fiction, since they regard it as "dealing with the unverifiable and the unreal."[28] Science fiction is not empirically provable, and defies many of the conventions of positivist social science. Even when one finds common ground between literary renderings of the political world and the political world itself, many would argue that the most one could hope to gain from reading such work is to be exposed to some form of morality play or normative argument.[29]

However, it is time that political scientists began to take literature more seriously. Fiction is not simply a "story" which is divorced from empirical reality. Literary analysts tell us that good stories are those which, while fictionalized, speak to us on some level about things which are real to us—our hopes, dreams, identities, and fears. Although they are "made up," they have a level of veracity which enables the reader to be drawn into the story and to imagine himself or herself in that story. Fiction frequently builds upon real-world events—in order to reflect political reality back through a new lens or to extend or distort political reality in some way through extending the realm of possible actions.

Science fiction in particular rests on the premise that is something more than made-up. The literary analyst Peter Swirsky argues that all writers are essentially in the business of creating alternate or virtual worlds.[30] In doing so, they use a similar methodology to that of social scientists. In constructing entire imagined worlds—as the science fiction writer may do—the author acts like a social scientist or political analyst, researching current issues in politics, demography, and economics, then building out from current developments to make and inhabit predictions about future developments. He then goes on to create a model.[31] Here the writer may utilize a number of variables in his analysis, controlling for some variables and leaving them constant throughout the story, while making a decision to alter certain variables and then testing for their effects. He may describe the effects of gender, race, and social class on the outcomes for his characters, or consider political or economic events which have the potential to alter the world his characters inhabit.

That is, to use the language of international relations, apocalyptic literature in particular can provide an alternate mode of discourse—which can be used to speak about two topics which are of particular interest to international relations theorists, the topics of identity and security. Language can thus create or reinforce inequities within groups, as well as reflect existing inequities which already exist.[32] That is, language reflects the existence of social structures in the world, as well as helps to create or undermine existing social structures. As Van Dijk argued, language often becomes a "tool"—used or wielded by powerful elites over those who are powerless. The subjects of governance find themselves and their problems labeled and defined by those in power. They are not consulted and often are not even aware of the ways in which they have been labeled and defined.[33]

In examining the ways in which the United States in particular loses its identity and its security in the post-apocalyptic space, one can better understand how it is that both identity and security are constructed in the present day. Stern speaks of a "security grammar," noting that an individual or a group's identity exists in relation to a story about who "we" are, and whether we are secure or insecure, and who we need to be protected and defended from.[34] Every culture has a narrative about safety and danger which can be interrogated and understood. Here I would argue that apocalyptic literature too allows us as international relations scholars to ponder how and why we have constructed U.S. identity and notions of U.S. security interests and security threats as we have.

This analysis rests on certain assumptions which not all international relations theorists will agree with. First, I assume that language matters and that language can be used to construct and to create identities and norms within the international system. Furthermore, I assume that our notions of U.S. national identity and notions of what threatens America are constructed not only by national leaders, the media, and the thoughts of analysts, but also by popular culture. Popular culture is thus both a reflection and a creator of U.S. citizens' and policymakers' thinking about what it is to be American and what it is that threatens America.

In his work, Thomas Ricento refers to "the discursive construction of Americanism," noting that American identity rests on a national narrative.[35] The narrative includes understandings that all Americans share certain ideals, as well as the notion of American exceptionalism—or the idea that America is preternaturally blessed with certain geographic and ideological advantages which predispose it towards internal success and a leading role in the world. Thus, American identity and American nationality is as much the product of language and imagining as they are the product of historical experience. What matters ultimately is the interpretation of that historical experience—which may occur through academic writing, but which may also occur through novels, movies, and plays about the American experience. In addition, the nation itself is an "imagined community"—in the words of Benedict Anderson. American national identity is invented and carried out through shared ideals—which are expressed in political discourse, the media and in popular culture. (Anderson argues, for example, that the Romantic Movement in music helped to shape ideas about what it meant to be German, for example.)[36]

America is thus a package of cultural understandings which are formed through movies, literature, and culture, at least in part. As Kareeman and Alvesson argued, our discourse works to form our sense of ourselves—including our feelings, thoughts, and orientations towards the world. Thus, as they argue, "discourse is a structuring principle of society."[37] Language and culture forms our sense of self, and our sense of who we are—as a people—in the world. Whether we describe the United States as shining city on a hill, as John Winthrop famously did—or whether we ask citizens to envision it one hundred years from now, vacant, emptied of its citizens, and as a sort of shell of its former self

INTRODUCTION 17

(as Cormac McCarthy does), in each case, we are creating—or taking in—a vision of America, which works to affect how citizens, policymakers, and analysts think about this nation and its place in the world. Thus, language can be used to shore up the U.S. position of hegemony in the world, and it can be used to undermine or query it, through asking readers to imagine a world in which the United States does not enjoy hegemony, and as a result, to imagine a new and different world, supported and upheld by different structures. In his novel *Falling Man*, the author Dom DeLillo has his American protagonist argue with a European acquaintance, noting that:

> If we occupy the center, it's because you put us there. This is your true dilemma. Despite everything, we're still America. You're still Europe. You go to our movies, read our books, listen to our music, and speak our language. How can you stop thinking about us? You see us and hear us all the time. Ask yourself. What comes after America?[38]

Culture thus allows citizens to voice and think new thoughts about the question "What comes after America?" It might also serve to create the notion that America should be worried about its lifespan and threats to its existence. Culture can thus help to shape threat.

In recent years, constructivists within international relations have argued that states cannot think about security or security threats in a neutral, academic manner.[39] Rather, they note that the analyst's thinking about security is constructed, largely through speech acts which seek to represent threats. Security threats thus exist within a specific cultural context—since they are a product of that context. In this view, threats themselves are not real—rather, it is the speech acts which make them so. According to this logic, it is talking—and thinking—about a threat which makes it significant—because merely voicing the notion (through policy speeches, media coverage, or proposed legislation, for example) that a threat exists to some degree makes the threat real or at least imaginable. Norms, beliefs, and ideas about threat are thus also the stuff of international relations. In this model, it is possible for a state to identify a threat, mobilize resources to preempt or defend against a threat, and justify the actions taken in the same way, whether or not the threat actually materializes. Thus, a nation might spend as much time and political energy marshaling against a threat which never occurs as one which does. Society and its institutions can be changed as deeply through the ways in which a threat is imagined or envisioned as it might be if the threat actually occurred.[40] (For example, even an airport which never experiences a terrorist event might still have all of its personnel hiring decisions, security decisions, and its budget altered. Those who visit the airport will still have a fundamentally different experience than they might have had ten years previously—even though nothing has specifically happened at the airport which they are visiting. Even a country which never experiences domestic terrorism may still find itself behaving differently as the result of events since September 11.) That is, preparing for a threat can have significant effects—even if the threat never occurs. And if this is true, then literature can also become a part of that conversation—since the threats which we fantasize about, think about, and scare ourselves with also serve to construct our understandings of what threatens America.

The notion that preparation for and envisioning of a threat alone has effects on society has already been demonstrated in one other area within the field of international relations. This is the area of disaster assistance. As Aradau and van Munster suggest, "catastrophe increasingly functions as a signifier of our future."[41] That is, they argue that there is a "politics of disaster" which involves envisioning the future of the system (alternatives to the present) on a local, national, OR international level. The politics of disaster involves understanding and modeling politics and political interactions in both current and changed political systems. Furthermore, politics of disaster involves going to the limits of our existing knowledge of a system as we begin to think about how it will change. This is because catastrophe is the ultimate place of insecurity in the international system.

Because of the ways in which the state reacts to threats (those which occur and those which are envisioned), security threats have the ability to affect the identity of participants, both individually, socially, and on a state level. As Michael Williams notes, "Societal security is threatened by 'whatever puts its . . . identity into jeopardy.'"[42] Thus, one can imagine the apocalypse as an existential event which jeopardizes our conceptions of ourselves as members of a family, society, state, and the international system. In imagining an apocalyptic event, individuals and IR theorists

INTRODUCTION 19

can thus begin to imagine a new world system in which neither the institutions nor the identities which they engender hold true anymore.

THE LITERATURE OF SECURITY AND INSECURITY

Literature has always served as a site for the reflection, discussion, and creation of narratives about politics and power—about security, about threat, and about the role and function of science and technology in society. As Neumann and Nexon suggest, for a constructivist in particular, international relations is often as much about the representation of events as it is about the events themselves. That is, events acquire their meaning within a particular context, and that meaning stems from how they are understood and interpreted—by politicians making policy speeches, by reporters writing articles and broadcasting film clips of an event, and even by novelists making sense of an event through literature. That is, political events may be represented or packaged in fiction, as well as in the arena of "real" politics.[43]

The overlap between the real threats which exist in the political world and the "imagined" threats which occur only in planning documents or in literature is ably demonstrated by the fact that citizens in particular may not clearly distinguish in their own minds between what they know about disaster based on empirical facts and what they know based on movies or television shows which they have seen. This overlap between fictionalized and real-world representations of political events or scientific theory has been referred to by Smith[44] as "blurring." Blurring can go in two directions—with the borders between the real and fiction being frayed either consciously by the producers of popular culture, or unconsciously by the consumers of popular culture.

Fictionalized representations of scientific issues can thus serve a variety of purposes: In some cases, fiction can serve as a public service announcement. Here, citizens might actually receive useful information about new developments in technology and science (though the danger, of course, is that such information might be either sensationalized or just plain wrong). The recent American popular movie "Contagion" contains numerous examples of this blurring—with actual members of the

Atlanta-based Centers for Disease Control serving as consultants to the movie-making staff, in order to ensure the verisimilitude of the finished product, and the well-known CNN science and medicine correspondent Sanjay Gupta appearing in a cameo role as himself, as he discourses at length about the fictional disease.[45] Although the events of the film were fictional, CDC officials were supportive of the endeavor, largely because they felt that citizens could actually learn real-world lessons about disease transmission as well disease prevention and precautions through this largely fictional device.

In some instances, fiction can serve as a rallying point—for example, when citizens are mobilized to act as a result of exposure to a fictionalized scientific scenario—perhaps organizing to change legislation or to prepare for eventualities. Here, one can point to Rachel Carson's *Silent Spring*, the academic work on environmentalism which launched a popular movement through asking citizens to imagine a world without nature or birds. Similarly, one can consider the spate of novels written in the post–World War II period which featured a nuclear attack on the United States which destroyed the world. Novels such as Pat Frank's *Alas, Babylon* and Walter Miller's *A Canticle for Leibowitz* did not merely tell a good story.[46] They also asked readers to consider the likelihood of nuclear war, the possibilities of living through or beyond it, and in some cases motivated citizens to political action against nuclear weapons.

Finally, scientific fiction can serve as a site for discussion, if, for example, citizens attempt to work out ethical issues which are raised by the advent of new types of genetic and reproductive technologies when they see them portrayed in a novel or onscreen.[47]

Given this blurring between the real and the fictional when speaking of security issues, it is not surprising that, as Quarantelli and Dynes point out, many citizens tend to overreact in actual disasters based on the images which they have assimilated through books, movies, and television shows.[48] Not surprisingly, citizens think they "know" about disasters based on the training and socialization they have received through popular culture. Decisions about whether or not to evacuate, what resources to bring, and what to expect are all thus filtered through the popular consciousness. That is, the "archive" which citizens draw upon to make sense of disaster may include both real and fictional elements.[49]

In addition, the language used to describe both "real" events and imagined events might overlap.[50] The media constructs heroic narratives about survivors of natural disasters which are later made into popular culture products, and even news reporters may borrow language from fictional events in describing real world events. (Here, one might recall a CNN reporter providing live coverage of the events on 9/11 who described the scene as being "just like Independence Day"—a reference to a Hollywood movie about an alien invasion.)[51]

Writing in 2001, Roland Bleiker first identified the term "the aesthetic turn in international theory" to describe the ways in which the aesthetic representation of political events has become increasingly important in both understanding and predicting political outcomes. He argues that we live in an increasingly visual world in which a camera angle or a photo may help to construct or reinforce a political narrative, thereby empowering the creator or the artist with a new voice in the representation of politics.[52] Here, we can think of the ways in which the iconic image of the collapsing World Trade Center became a physical representation for many of the ways in which history was cleaved in two—with the period post-9/11 bearing little resemblance to the period which preceded it.[53] There is little doubt that in our modern world today, images matter and words matter. They have the power to create a narrative and to tell a story. Indeed, increasingly we can see how politicians may invoke popular culture scenarios and may even work to create them—in order to marshal support for particular real-world policies.[54]

Thus, the insistence by some academics[55] that one draw a line between "real" and imagined security threats or between "serious politics" and the politics of popular culture seems to be more an internal battle within the academic field than a genuine criticism. Such criticisms are more about turf wars and differing opinions about what constitutes genuine academic analysis than a legitimate defense of the claim to the privileging of certain types of analysis over others. In fact, it seems almost a way by which the old guard seeks to consciously exclude events and ideas which defy easy slotting into the traditional categories within IR theory.

In Daniel Pick's work *Faces of Degeneration*, he notes the ways in which narratives about personal degeneration and decline were used both to reflect and construct a larger conversation about state degeneration and decline in England in the period from the 1840s to the 1920s.[56] That is, a discussion about individual pathologies was used both consciously and unconsciously by authors and their readers to underscore a larger conversation about pathologies within the state and the interstate system. And the question of whether human beings were becoming more degenerate with each successive generation was thus implicitly also a critique of the claim that the international system was evolving into a better system. Instead, literature of the time period helped to raise the question of whether it was perhaps not in some way going backward. In his work, Smith traces the Victorian preoccupation with such fictional "degenerate" creatures as Bram Stoker's *Dracula*, and *The Strange Case of Dr. Jekyll and Mr. Hyde*, as well as the preoccupation with real-life stories like that of John Merrick, the so-called Elephant Man or the London murderer known as Jack the Ripper. In each case, he suggests, the story creates a narrative which might cause the reader to ask: How did something go so wrong on the path to development? In each of these narratives one sees a convergence of real-life events and real-world scientific concepts with literary renderings. And in each case, there is a sort of blurring in which fact and fiction collide—each affecting the other.[57]

SPECULATIVE FICTION AND THE FUTURE OF SECURITY

In my own work, I do not dwell on degenerate human beings or the representation of particular individuals within society. Rather, I examine apocalyptic scenarios and the way in which they function as speculative fiction. The term "speculative fiction" in particular refers to a subset within the genre of science fiction in which the writer speculates in a realistic manner about future developments—including developments in the life sciences, in the realm of legal theory or in the realm of politics—based on an extension of facts which are currently accepted as true. Warren Wagar defines it as "any work of fiction, including drama and narrative poetry that specializes in plausible speculation about life under changed but rationally conceivable circumstances."[58] Thus, there are actually several different types of literary creations which go under the heading of speculative fiction—including utopian novels, dystopian novels, apocalyptic novels, catastrophe novels, and Biblical apocalyptics.

INTRODUCTION

This work is divided into three parts. The first section, "Apocalypse as Prediction" analyzes apocalyptic literature as a type of speculative fiction. In this section, I parse out the differences between the true apocalyptic novel, the mere catastrophe novel, and the utopian or dystopian novel. I provide grounds for identifying the type of speculative fiction one is reading, and suggest that each type of futuristic theorizing rests on a different set of ideological presuppositions. I also explain the particular social conditions which can lead to futuristic speculation in making an argument to explain the production of apocalyptic fiction in empires.

In Part 1, "Apocalypse as Prediction," I make three arguments about the utility of speculative fiction for today's political analysts. First, I argue that some types of speculative fiction actually replicate some of the same thought processes and analytical devices used by intelligence analysts. In the aftermath of the breakup of the Soviet Union and the recent terrorist attacks of September 11, analysts like Gregory Treverton[59] and Mark Lowenthal[60] faulted America's intelligence community for a failure of both creativity and imagination. They suggested that reliance on standard operating procedures for the prediction and analysis of evolving threats has rendered the intelligence community reactive rather than proactive, and that a field which should be characterized by risk taking has instead become characterized by caution. The policy fixes prescribed—encouraging the writing of better narratives including counterfactual thought experiments for the consideration of evolving threat, and encouraging analysts to engage in more long-range speculation with a timeline of ten to fifteen years—have, I argue, rewritten the job description for the average intelligence analyst, rendering him in some cases less of an analyst and more of a novelist. Both groups—intelligence analysts and fiction writers—aim to identify security threats, to offer an analysis of how identified deficits in national defenses may be remedied and ultimately, they aim to alter policy outcomes. The main goal of the catastrophe novel in particular is thus to predict. In chapter 2, I show how the groups share a methodology and I describe the constraints that both groups operate under—arguing that both catastrophe novels and intelligence scenarios tend to rely on Realist assumptions that serve to limit the scope of the inquiries conducted and the answers found.

In chapter 3, I move on from a consideration of the catastrophe novel to consider two other types of speculative fiction that are of interest to political scientists. I describe briefly the history of utopian and dystopian fiction, suggesting that—like the catastrophe novel—these novels rely on a methodology familiar to many political scientists. However, while the focus in the catastrophe novel is on the decision-making process leading to the event, the focus in the utopian or dystopian novel is more on the outcome of the event itself. The aim is thus not to predict but rather to forecast. The forecaster is thus interested in disclosing a problem and bringing it to the fore and in this way altering the policy discussion rather than the policy agenda per se. Thus, if a catastrophe novel relies on the sort of methodology used by a game theorist, a utopian or dystopian novel relies instead on the methodology used by a policy writer like Rachel Carson, who "forecast" the long-range effects of uncontrolled pesticide use in her 1962 classic nonfiction work, *Silent Spring*.

Both the utopian and dystopian novel are experiments in model-building as well as counterfactual experiments which theorize about social trends and social forces. But while catastrophe novelists engage in backward induction through identifying an end state and then working backwards to analyze the causes of a particular end state, the utopian and dystopian novelist engages in a process of projection—which involves casting an image forward into the future. The reader is then asked to reflect not on the consequences of choices not taken (as he is when he reads a catastrophe novel) but instead on the difference between the possible world which might develop if current trends continue and the world in which he presently lives. Here again, I describe the ways in which novelists and policymakers have overlapped, and the ways in which these types of fiction have been influential in establishing and setting policy agendas in both the United States and the British Empire. Then I ask questions regarding the propensity of certain types of societies and political systems to develop speculative fiction—while others do not, in suggesting that the building of utopian and dystopian fiction is a luxury which only certain types of states enjoy.

In chapter 4, I demonstrate that apocalyptic fiction has a political meaning which is different than these other types of speculative fiction. It is easy to conflate the different types of novels: catastrophe novels, dystopian novels, and apocalyptic novels—since all presumably deal with bad things that happen and the ways in which they affect the state and its inhabitants. All are scary, and frequently they seem real. We find all three of the types of stories upsetting. However, the apocalyptic novel in particular is a very different type of narrative—it deals less with the process by which the state is destroyed or nearly destroyed and less as well with the social, political and economic forces which lead to its destruction. Instead, the emphasis in the post-apocalyptic novel is explicitly on the aftermath of the events which led to the state's destruction. Analysts are thus drawn to perform a different type of thought experiment: Catastrophe novels allow us to experiment with notions of our state under threat and the possibility that there exist security flaws which need to be corrected. Dystopian novels allow us to experiment with the outcome of particular social, political, and economic trends which may lead to our state's destruction. But only apocalyptic novels allow us as analysts to actually inhabit (at least vicariously) the world of a state which is destroyed. Thus, the agenda of the catastrophe novel is realist and positivist—the goal of the writer is to identify and measure threat, theorize about its likelihood, and offer solutions to serve the goal of state survival. The agenda of a dystopian novel is usually liberal—in the sense that the creation of a dystopian world can be seen as a detour from the path of progressive liberalism including the growth of free market economies, the rise of secularism, and improvements in the overall standard of living.

After having established our theoretical understandings regarding the product called apocalyptic fiction, I delve into the ideology of apocalyptic prediction more deeply in the section entitled, "Apocalypse as Critique," arguing that apocalyptic fiction is the fleshing out an eschatological narrative which places the state in an eternal perspective. The apocalypse represents the "end of time" or (in the words of Stephen King) "the time that is no time. "Once the state has been "killed" in the apocalyptic narrative, we as readers are able to view the state as a corpse and take an out-of-body perspective in viewing the life of the state in its entirety, viewing it from its inception, through its life and placing its death in perspective. Like a pathologist, we are able to dissect the body politik. The eschatological perspective is significant because it implicitly provides a critique of the narrative of imperial exceptionalism, which rests on a teleological perspective. Both teleology and eschatology deal with the entirety of the object's life and both spell out the entirety of the narrative. However, the eschatological narrative of imperial apocalypse erases the notion that "my" state is somehow immune from destruction, which is one of the founding principles of the teleological narrative of the imperial state. In this way, the two stories are polar opposites.

In this section, I also argue that apocalyptic fiction allows the reader to view the state both from a new chronological lens and from a new geographic lens. To visit an apocalyptic scenario is to visit a new place as a stranger with a fresh eye, and to see anew the society which one has left through contrasting it with that which one now visits. Thus, we are able to look at our nation in the way a foreigner might—travelling to the region and approaching it anew without any imposed ideas or preconceptions. In this way, contemporary apocalyptic novels actually share much common ground with traditional Victorian colonial travel narratives—except that the "foreign country" being visited by us is our own. As a result of the disaster, we are able to view our nation thus not as a colonizer but rather as a site of colonization. In *Falling Man* and *The Second Plane*, the new America (post-9/11) is implicitly contrasted with the old America. In *World Made by Hand*, *The Road*, and the *Pesthouse*, America the superpower is contrasted with the America which is destroyed. In the Victorian novels *Erewhon* and *Gulliver's Travels*, the leading country of Great Britain is implicitly contrasted with a parallel universe where England is irrelevant. In *The Machine Stops* and *News from Nowhere*, industrial revolution England is compared with post–Industrial Revolution England. In chapter 6 I argue that post-apocalyptic novels are frequently post-colonialist. Their great achievement is to offer us a subaltern perspective on our own society. Each of these novels allows us to ask questions about power, situatedness, sovereignty, and agency.

In the third and final section, "Apocalypse as Ethics," I delve more deeply into specific instances in the apocalyptic fiction, introducing the notions of Self and Other. It is my contention here that apocalypse frequently serves to Other the imperial state, placing the imperial state in a new subservient position where it is now the object of Other's actions, rather than an independent actor. In viewing the state from this new perspective, readers can begin to develop a new ethics in which they (perhaps for the first time) view themselves as the Other. In asking "How should those in power treat me and my state?" the reader can

INTRODUCTION   27

begin to develop a new view of how the international system truly "is" through erasing his or her situated stance.

The apocalypse which destroys or nearly destroys a civilization can be understood as a sort of psychic wound (as well as a physical wound) inflicted upon a society. For those of us (American) analysts who are unable to theorize about politics except from a position of power by virtue of our class, education, and citizenship, the apocalyptic novel offers a unique opportunity to truly "see" the other—through at least imagining what it would feel like to switch places with that other. In his philosophical work, the theorist Emmanuel Levinas points out the problem of what he terms "metaphysical asymmetry."[61] He describes the ways in which "I" am unable to transcend my own situatedness in order to see myself from outside and on the same plane and in the same terms in which I see (and judge and claim to understand and thus to control and to own) the other. He refers to this lack as the impossibility of totalization. However, in reading apocalyptic literature, we as readers are able to undertake a very unusual stance. At least hypothetically, we can take on and carry the psychic wound inflicted upon our society. In doing so, we are able to dwell in a new position and to develop a new relationship to our own society. We occupy a different temporal stance (looking back at our society from a position in the future) and a different power position, in which we look up at our oppressors.

In Levinasian terms, we are granted a new 'optic' or viewpoint for viewing both our own society and our relations with our neighbors. Apocalyptic literature thus provides an "eternal" perspective which allows us to see the finiteness of the American (or British) experience in grand, totalizing terms. Just as we can now look back on the Roman Empire and see how it was both significant and insignificant, we can adopt a similar perspective for viewing and judging the American (and British) experience.

At its core, apocalyptic literature is about dispossession, powerlessness, being afraid or in fear for one's life and about being invisible through coming to occupy a space where one is not seen. Analyst Judith Butler meditated about the significance of September 11 and how it affected the American psyche in her groundbreaking work *Precarious Life: The Powers of Mourning and Violence*.[62] She claims that the injury of September 11 provides a site and opportunity for reimagining the world and rethinking our contemporary ethics including how we interact with the Other. In that work she wrote: "To be injured means that one has the chance to reflect upon injury, to find out the mechanics of its distribution, to find out who else suffers from permeable borders, unexpected violence, dispossession and fear and what it means."[63] She suggested that there might indeed be something emancipatory about the new position which America now found itself in as it offered "a dislocation from First World privilege, however temporary" and the opportunity to imagine a new world which might acknowledge the ways in which we are all interdependent.[64]

In this work I argue that apocalyptic fiction also carries out and allows for similar reimaginings and rethinking about American power and relations with neighbors. It offers us a way of thinking beyond our own situatedness—geographically, politically, and temporally. In a sense, the apocalyptic novel carries the September-eleventh grieving process and the adjustment to "the new normal" one step farther by allowing us to reflect, at least hypothetically, on the "death" of the United States (or Britain) as we know it. In imagining the death of our society, we are granted a third person stance in viewing the corpse of our state. Levinas states that "the imprisoned being, ignorant of its prison, is at home with itself."[65] However, through imagining the death of the state, we are freed from our bodily attachment to it. It is no longer the body in which we reside. Instead, we stand above it, we judge it, and we comment on the steps or the lack of steps which might have been taken to save it. The apocalyptic novel thus provides a sort of "out of body experience" or what Levinas describes as the ability to see and to conjecture "beyond history." We, the survivors, are able to look upon the state as a body and to see not only where it is now, but the sum total of its life.[66]

GOALS OF THIS WORK

In this work, I demonstrate how apocalyptic fiction provides a new discourse for talking about things we can't otherwise talk about—and offers a new way of asking and answering the question "Where is politics?" by showing how politics (as reflected through the lens of insecurity) can exist even in the absence of the state. It also allows American writers and those who observe America from elsewhere to put forth the questions: Why is America special? It is really invulnerable? The apocalyptic scenario—when read through this new lens—can provide a site of opportunity for academic theorizing about future political, social, and cultural formations. Apocalyptic fiction can serve a particular academic goal of forming a new stance for evaluating and interrogating contemporary political themes like progress, the spread of democracy, and what it means to be a "civilization." First, we can ask political questions about organizations and structures. Here, we can ask in what ways the apocalyptic lens allows us to reconceptualize of what it means to be a state, what it means to be a citizen, and what it means to be political. It is my contention that reading literature which forces us to see "beyond the state" can allow us to reconceptualize how we see political organization and what it means to be political. In his work on disasters, Lee Clarke somewhat optimistically notes that disasters are sometimes good for policy-makers because they lead them to stretch their imaginations, to consider new problems, and to break out of old ways of doing business.[67] Similarly, I make the claim that envisioning and imagining disaster and even the end of the state can allow political scientists to reformulate and reenvision stances towards international relations—by making us aware of our preexisting prejudices and assumptions which we might previously have taken for granted.

In addition, this fiction allows us to consider loss and in doing so, allows us to formulate a new stance towards our own position in the international system. Apocalyptic fiction in particular allows analysts to move beyond our own situatedness, by performing the somewhat strange trick of allowing the reader to look back on his own history—or rather, his own territory—from a hypothetical point in the future. In doing so, he gains a new perspective not only on that hypothetical future but also on his own present and the events from that time period which may lead to a particular outcome in the future. They provide an opportunity for "vision" in the words of Donna Harraway.[68]

It has been suggested that apocalyptic prophecy represents the end stage of all of our theorizing. Jacques Derrida has described the use of an apocalyptic tone as a way of reaching the extreme limit in our thinking about politics and philosophy. Writing in 1992, he suggested that all

Western discourse is eschatological, since it posits the end of history or the death of philosophy. Any system of analysis which posits that it exists within an historic framework in which there are various stages to be reached implicitly contains the seeds of that final stage.

Thus, any discussion of political science implicitly contains a statement about the death of politics or at least the possibility of moving beyond politics. The critical project of emancipation is one which comes about as we attempt to either free ourselves from politics or to widen the definition of politics to such a degree that everything is politics—or until nothing is politics. Thus our ability to posit an apocalypse points to our ability to envision a world without politics. If this is truly the case, then does the apocalypse not by definition raise the question of the absurdity of all politics and of the international relations project as it has traditionally been conceived? Really, if one can posit an American future in which it is theoretically possible that industrialization will die and your neighbors will harvest your organs for spare parts or your children for food, then does the fact that "democracies do not fight democracies" truly have any meaning? An apocalyptic perspective allows for a more critical viewing of the role of politics and the utility or futility of the political project. If the critical theorist project has thus been based upon recognizing that many of our organizing principles for understanding the world around us—including maps, labels, and schematics like time lines which are taken to denote stages of developments—are constructed, rather than real, and western, rather than universal,[69] then it is not surprising that the final stage of that project might involve envisioning what an environment absent those organizing schemes would look like. The apocalypse thus smashes the conceptual maps which we as analysts keep in our heads to organize the world into a center and a periphery, into an us and a them. It also smashes the conceptual schemes and timelines which we keep in our heads by forcing us to think of time as being a loop rather than a straight line, and to acknowledge that maps can be unmade and time can as easily move backward as forward. The question then becomes whether or not there is any international relations theory broad enough or complex enough to enable us to theorize about this invented space.

In conclusion, I would like to add one final note about methodology: In studying the language and language constructs used in post-apocalyptic fiction, my emphasis has been on the identification of particular structures which appear in all of the novels chosen here. As Cramer points out, one can see a great deal of how the world is constructed by looking merely at the pronouns used. In her analysis she shows how European Union representatives frequently create distance between themselves and the representatives of, for example, Turkey, through their use of the terms "us" and "you."[70] I rely on this methodology in the examples I provide from both *World Made by Hand*, and *The Passage*, when the narrator describes the "us" of post-apocalyptic Americans, comparing it to the "them" of those who came before, as well as the "us" who currently exist, as opposed to the "they" of the neighbors who have abandoned America. Here, my attempt is not to create the sort of quantitative analysis which Cramer does, coding the use of specific pronouns in transcripts of speeches given at the European Union meetings. Rather, it is simply to search for the existence of such pronouns in the literature itself—as an indicator that such distancing, comparing, and contrasting is occurring.

NOTES

1. Davinia Hamilton, March 2010, "Literature and the Apocalypse" "Text" literary blog, http://text.desa.org.mt/issues/march2010/davinia-hamilton-literature-and-the-apocalypse.
2. Justin Cronin. *The Passage* (New York: Ballantine Books, 2010), 572.
3. Penelope J. Corfield, "The End Is Nigh," *History Today* 57(2007).
4. Voltaire, *Candide* (New York: Create Space, 2011).
5. Simon Winchester, *Krakatoa* (New York: Harper Perennial, 2003).
6. Theodore Steinberg, *Acts of God: The Unnatural History of Natural Disaster in America* (Oxford, UK: Oxford University Press, 2000).
7. Scott C. Sagan, *The Limits of Safety: Organizations, Accidents and Nuclear Weapons* (Princeton, NJ: Princeton University Press, 1993), 27.
8. Richard Sylves, *Disaster Policy and Politics* (Washington, DC: CQ Press, 2008).

9. Lee Clarke, *Worst Cases: Terror and Catastrophe in the Popular Imagination* (Chicago, IL: University of Chicago Press, 2006).

10. For more on this point, see Arjen Boin and Paul t' hart, "Public Leadership in Times of Crisis: Mission Impossible?" *Public Administration Review* 63(2003): 544–47.

11. Edward Paice, *Wrath of God: The Great Lisbon Earthquake of 1755* (New York: Quercus, 2010); Nicholas Schrady, *The Last Day: Wrath, Ruin and Reason in the Great Lisbon Earthquake of 1755* (New York: Viking, 2008).

12. Paul Slovic, "Perception of Risk," *Science* 239(1987): 280–85.

13. Hugo Lindgren, "Pessimism Porn," *New York Magazine* (February 1, 2009). http://nymag.com/news/intelligencer/53858.

14. Clarke, *Worst Cases*, 121.

15. Frank Kermode, *The Sense of an Ending: Studies in the Theory of Fiction* (London: Oxford University Press, 1968), 42.

16. Charles Perrow, *Normal Accidents: Living with High Risk Technologies* (New York: Basic Books, 1984).

17. Keith Booker, *Monsters, Mushroom Clouds and the Cold War: American Science Fiction in Novel and Film, 1946–1964* (Santa Barbara, CA: Greenwood Press, 2001).

18. This is not to say that others have not read apocalyptic literature—in other contexts or in other times. As Mehdi Khalaji (*Apocalyptic Politics: On the Rationality of Iranian Policy*. Washington, DC: Washington Institute for Near East Policy, 2008) notes, many Muslim sects today are particular fascinated by tales of the Twelfth Imam, who is purported to arrive at the end of time in order to usher in a new era of history of faithful Muslims. However, I do not wish to provide a definitive history of apocalyptic thought in IR theory, nor do I intend to analyze every apocalyptic tale in every culture. I do not intend to engage with aspects of apocalyptic thought which are the province of political theory. Rather, I simply seek to establish why the subject is one of ongoing fascination for Americans in particular.

19. In addition, as I show in chapter 1, a Tom Clancy novel is not properly an apocalyptic novel. Rather it is merely a "catastrophe novel," which does not depart sharply from reality—but rather, alters only a few elements of the proposed scenario. Tom Clancy novels are thus interesting to those who aspire to examine whether literature can forecast events—but are less interesting to those interested in how novels can contribute to a reshaping of our worldview.

20. Quoted in Steve Benen, "American Exceptionalism," *Washington Monthly* (April 5, 2009). www.washingtonmonthly.com/archives/individual/2009_04/017614.php

21. Monica Crowley, "American exceptionalism . . ." *Washington Times* (July 1, 2009). www.washingtontimes.com/news/2009/jul/01/american-exceptionalism/?page=all

22. While the themes in those works are no doubt interesting, their limited readership does not make them exemplars of mainstream American thought. In addition, I am not primarily interested in the religious apocalyptic which is an interesting, but separate phenomenon—as I show in the following chapter. Those wishing to read more about religious apocalyptic thought and its relevance to IR theory are referred to the excellent volume *Mapping the End Times: American Evangelical Geopolitics and Apocalyptic Visions,* Jason Dittmer and Tristan Sturm, eds. (Surrey, UK: Ashgate, 2010).

23. Gayle R. Baldwin, "World War Z and the End of Religion as We Know It," *Crosscurrents* (2007): 413.

24. Although I originally considered performing this type of quantitative analysis, the data was not readily available regarding print runs of materials and purchasing patterns. This data is generally proprietary, and the costs of purchasing access to it are prohibitive for the average IR scholar. In addition, using this data presumes a level of knowledge about publishing which the average IR scholar does not possess.

25. Roxanne Doty, "Foreign Policy as a Social Construction," *International Studies Quarterly* 27(1993): 297–320.

26. Jack Holland, "Foreign Policy and Political Possibility," *European Journal of International Relations*. (2011). http://ejt.sagepub.com/content/early/2011/08/23/1354066111413310

27. Alexander Wendt, *Social Theory of International Politics* (Cambridge, UK: Cambridge University Press, 1999). Karen Fierke, *Critical Approaches to International Security* (New York: Polity Press, 2007).

28. Barbara Goodwin and Keith Taylor, *The Politics of Utopia: A Study in Theory and Practice* (New York: St. Martin's Press, 1982): 34.

29. Goodwin and Taylor, *Politics of Utopia*.

30. Peter Swirsky, *Of Literature and Knowledge: Explorations in Narrative Thought Experiments, Evolution and Game Theory* (London: Routledge, 2007).

31. Alex Argyros, "Narrative and Chaos," *New Literary History* 23 (1992): 659–73.

32. For more on this point, see Jan Blommaert and Chris Bulcaen, "Critical Discourse Analysis," *Annual Review of Anthropology* 29 (2009): 447–66.

33. Teun A. Van Dijk, "Principles of Critical Discourse Analysis," *Discourse Society* 4 (1993): 249–83.

34. Maria Stern, "'We' the Subject: The Power and Failure of (In)Security," *Security Dialogue* 37 (2006): 187–205.

35. Thomas Ricento, "The Discursive Construction of Americanism," *Discourse and Society* 14(2003): 611–37.

36. Benedict Anderson, *Imagined Communities: Reflections on the Origins and Spread of Nationalism* (London: Verso, 2006).

37. Mats Alvesson and Dan Kareeman, "Varieties of Discourse: On the Study of Organizations through Discourse Analysis," *Human Relations* 53 (2000): 1131.

38. Don DeLillo, *Falling Man* (New York: Scribner, 2007): 192.

39. Michael C. Williams, "Words, Images, Enemies: Securitization and International Politics," *International Studies Quarterly* 47, no. 4 (2003): 511–31.

40. For more on this point see Columba Peoples and Nick Vaughan-Williams, *Critical Security Studies: An Introduction* (New York: Routledge, 2010): 4–6.

41. Claudia Aradau and Rens Van Munster, *Politics of Catastrophe: Genealogies of the Unknown* (New York: Routledge, 2011).

42. Michael C. Williams, "Modernity, Identity and Security: A Comment on the Copenhagen Controversy," *Review of International Studies* 24 (1998): 435–39.

43. Iver B. Neumann and Daniel H. Nexon, "Introduction: Harry Potter and the Study of World Politics," in Nexon and Neumann, eds., *Harry Potter and International Relations* (Lanham, MD: Rowman and Littlefield, 2006): 7.

44. Andrew Smith, *Victorian Demons: Medicine, Masculinity and the Gothic at the Fin-de-Siècle* (Manchester, UK: Manchester University Press, 2004): 277.

45. See "How CDC Saves Lives by Controlling REAL Global Disease Outbreaks." www.cdcfoundation.org/content/how-cec-saves-lives-controlling-real-global-disease. October 6, 2011.

46. For more on this type of novel, see Paul Brians' *Nuclear Holocausts: Atomic War in Fiction* (Ohio: Kent State University Press, 2008).

47. Here, Michael Crichton's novels provide an example of this phenomenon. In his work *Frankenstein's Children* (Princeton, NJ: Princeton University Press, 1998) Iwan Morus makes the argument that readers were actually drawn to the novel as a way of exploring their own fear and fascination with the newly discovered science of electricity. More recently, it has been suggested that Dr. Steven Schlozman's novel *The Zombie Autopsy* is actually a canvas for readers to explore their worries and fears about global pandemics (See Elizabeth Landau, 2011, "Inside Zombie Brains: Sci-fi Teaches Science." http://edition.cnn.com/2011/HEALTH/04/25/zombie. virus. zombies. book/index. html.)

48. E. L. Quarantelli and Russell R. Dynes. "Images of Disaster Behavior: Myths and Consequences." University of Delaware Working Paper. http://dspace.udel.edu8080/dspace/bitstream/handle/197/6/375/PP5.pdf.txt?sequence=u.

49. Nexon and Neumann define the "archive," a concept drawn from the writings of French theorist Michel Foucault, as "the broad stock of social knowledge, forms, analogies, symbols and techniques through which actors are able to communicate and otherwise influence their environment." ("Introduction: Harry Potter and the Study of World Politics," 8.) Interestingly, in Spring 2011, a CDC Public Health official, Ali Khan, actually encouraged citizens to draw upon that archive of knowledge about danger which they might have derived from seeing disaster movies in an acclaimed blog post, where he prevailed upon citizens to use the knowledge acquired from "zombie attack movies" to prepare for and plan coping strategies for real-world disasters (See Ali Khan, 2011, "Social Media: Preparedness 101: Zombie Apocalypse." http://emergency.cdc.gov/socialmedia/zombies_blog.asp. See also Richard Allen Green, 2011, "Ready for a Zombie Apocalypse? CDC Has Advice." http: //edition.cnn.com/2011/HEALTH/05/19/zombie.warning/index.html.

50. Weldes refers to "intertextuality"—noting the ways in which politicians might borrow a phrase from popular culture to describe a threat, or the ways in which fictionalized versions of real-world politicians might appear in a popular culture production. See Jutta Weldes, "Popular Culture, Science Fiction and World Politics," in Jutta Weldes, ed., *To Seek out New Worlds: Exploring Links between Science Fiction and World Politics* (New York: Palgrave MacMillan, 2003): 53.

51. See Weldes: 2 for more on the overlap between real-world and fictional political discourse.

52. Roland Bleiker, "The Aesthetic Turn in International Political Theory." *Millennium: Journal of International Studies* 30 (2001): 509–33.

53. See, for example, Elleke Boehmer and Stephen Morton's discussion of media coverage of the 9/11 collapse of the World Trade Center in *Terror and the Post-Colonial* (London: Wiley-Blackwell, 2009): 11–12. They argue that the image of the tower's collapse took on a life of its own, becoming an actor in its own right in world politics. See also Arnold Berleant, "Art, Terrorism and the Negative Sublime." www.contempaesthetics.org/newvolume/pages/article.php?articleID=568.

54. Here one might want to consider what might have possessed the American conservative politician Newt Gingrich to author the foreword to a recent novel (*One Second After*, by William Forstchen) which features an electromagnetic pulse attack on the United States, ostensibly carried out by China.

Clearly, it was not simply his admiration for a good story which lay behind that decision. Rather, he saw the novel as a useful vehicle for raising awareness of a threat which concerned him as a political figure.

55. See, for example, D. S. Jarvis's essay "Identity Politics, Postmodern Feminisms and International Theory: Questioning the 'New' Diversity in International Relations," in Robert M. A. Crawford and Darryl S. L. Jarvis, eds., *International Relations—Still an American Social Science?* (Albany, NY: SUNY Press, 2001): 101–31.

56. His work is discussed by Andrew Smith, 14–23.

57. Smith, 177–78.

58. W. Warren Wagar, *Terminal Visions: The Literature of Last Things* (Bloomington: Indiana University Press, 1982): xiii.

59. Gregory F. Treverton, *Intelligence for an Age of Terror* (New York: Cambridge University Press, 2009).

60. Mark Lowenthal, *Intelligence: From Secrets to Policy* (Washington, DC: CQ Press, 2009).

61. Emmanuel Levinas, *Totality and Infinity: An Essay on Exteriority* (Pittsburg, PA: Duquesne University Press, 1961): 53.

62. Judith Butler, *Precarious Life: The Powers of Mourning and Violence* (London: Verso, 2004).

63. Butler, *Precarious Life*, xii.

64. Butler, *Precarious Life*, xii.

65. Levinas, *Totality and Infinity*, 55.

66. The analyst Farhang Erfani makes a similar claim in her consideration of utopian literature. She explains that the events of 9/11 actually increased the tendency of Americans in particular to "other" their opponents—due to increases in the fear and security risks now associated with the other. She argues that utopian literature is a way of imagining Levinas's infinity and that imagining utopia can thus provide a way past the dangers of increased othering associated with 9/11.

67. Clarke, *Worst Cases*, 144.

68. Donna Harraway, "Situated Knowledges: The Science Question in Feminism and the Privilege of Partial Perspective," in Alison M. Jaggar, ed., *Just Methods: An Interdisciplinary Feminist Reader* (London: Paradigm Publishers, 2008): 349.

69. See, for example, Simon Ryan, "Inscribing the Emptiness: Cartography, Exploration and the Construction of Australia," in *De-Scribing Empire*, ed. C. Tiffin and A. Lawson (London, UK: Routledge, 1994): 115–31. Daniel Rosenberg and Anthony Grafton explore the ideological and epistemological assump-

tions behind the time line in *Cartographies of Time: A History of the Timeline* (Princeton, NJ: Princeton University Press, 2010).

70. Jennifer Cramer, "'Do We Really Want to Be Like Them?' Indexing Europeanness through Pronominal Use," *Discourse and Society* 21 (2010): 619–37. John Oddo uses a similar technique in comparing the pronouns used by U.S. presidents in presidential addresses. See his "War Legitimation Discourse: Representing 'us' and 'them' in Four US Presidential Addresses," *Discourse and Society* 22 (2011): 287–314.

I

APOCALYPSE AS PREDICTION

1

APOCALYPSE AND NATIONAL SECURITY

In this chapter I define the specific meaning of apocalypse, describing the differences between secular and Biblical apocalypse. I describe the conditions which need to be fulfilled in order for an event to be considered apocalyptic, rather than merely catastrophic and the ways in which devastation is measured. Here I raise the notion that measures of catastrophe are inherently culturally specific, and that "one man's apocalypse may be merely another man's ordinary day in the developing world." As Steinberg suggests, every disaster can be interpreted in multiple ways and even within the same community different constituencies may disagree about the meanings to ascribe to a disaster both in the short term and historically.[1] Is the flooding which swallows one's town best understood as a story of how government officials have shirked their responsibilities and neglected their responsibilities towards the most vulnerable, poor members of society–or should it be seen as a call to renewal, or a sign of God's wrath? Perhaps it could be seen as all three.

For political scientists, apocalypse may be seen as a new way of talking about the possibility of state failure. Therefore, only one who *has* a functioning state can worry about its failure. The ability to worry about and imagine apocalypse is in many ways a particularly First World and imperial privilege.

WHAT IS AN APOCALYPSE?

In order to begin this analysis, it is important to first define several key terms. The first of these is the word "apocalypse" itself. In its original meaning, an apocalypse referred to a specific series of events which were believed to be described in both Jewish and Christian texts (including the Old Testament Book of Daniel and the New Testament Book of Revelation) which could be seen as leading to the end of the world. The term itself derives from the Greek word *"apokalupsis"* which means "to uncover" or "to reveal," since the events are described as being revealed in prophetic texts. Events described include famines, pestilence, plagues, fire, flooding—as well as a final sorting out of those who are good from those who are evil.[2] These apocalyptic events are said to lead to Armageddon, which is defined as the scene of a final battle between the forces of good and evil, prophesied to occur at the end of the world. That is, the apocalyptic narrative is, by definition, eschatological or concerned with the final events in the history of the world or mankind. The term is derived from the Greek word *"eschatos,"* which means last or farthest.

As Harding and Stewart point out, however, the term apocalypse was widened during the Middle Ages to refer to any vision of the end times put forth, whether by a secular or a religious authority, whether in written or in oral form.[3] Thus "apocalypse" also has a more general meaning of total devastation or doom, or a large act of destruction. In this secondary usage the terms "apocalypse" and "disaster" appear at first glance to be interchangeable. For example, the devastation which occurred in Lisbon in 1755, with an estimated 25,000 people either buried in the ruins of the disaster, burned in the fires which followed the earthquake, or washed away in the tsunami which washed over what remained of the city less than an hour later was described in reports at the time as "apocalyptic."[4] In the secular apocalyptic novel, the usual elements of the end times may include the breakdown of government and structures of authority within a region; the collapse of the state as a whole with a concomitant loss of its ability to provide for the security of citizens; and the abandonment or destruction of the intellectual constructs and norms which are taken to sustain the notion of civilization—including the absence of concepts of citizenship, rule of law, and the laws of war. It also usually involves the collapse of the nation's currency with a reversion either to a system of barter or the collapse of a market economy and the rise of practices such as hoarding and theft. Cultural materials which describe a secular apocalypse may focus either on the immediate aftermath of a devastating event which has led to state collapse in the short term (within a time frame of several months or a few short years), or they may focus on the long-term effects of state collapse. In this meaning, the events of 9/11 or of a nuclear explosion could rightfully be term, "apocalyptic."

But the secular apocalypse too uncovers and reveals that which has been hidden in the narrative from the beginning. While the religious apocalypse narrative claims that the ending of the story has somehow been hidden or revealed in the narrative since the beginning of creation, the secular apocalyptic may make an argument that the state which eventually collapsed was somehow "doomed" or "flawed" from the beginning. Thus, the final ending is less of a surprise than a logical outgrowth of a trend which was present in the state from its beginning. The ending can be traced back to the beginning or the founding of the state.[5]

Apocalypse and the Absence of Security

For international relations scholars, what is significant is the way in which "apocalypse" is used in mainstream cultural works as a shorthand phrase to describe an absence of security, broadly defined. In his work, *People, States and Fear*, Buzan notes that security can be described as affecting five sectors: military, environmental, economic, political, and societal elements are all invoked in evaluating the security of a region.[6]

Table 1.1 illustrates the effects of the loss of each type of security:

Table 1.1. Security Sectors and Their Effects

Security Sector	Absence of Security and Its effects
Political Security	Absence of the state, rule of law, political legitimacy, borders, territory
Economic Security	Shortages, unpredictability in economic sector, end of interdependence, end of markets, end of currency system
Societal Security	Lack of established notions of citizenship, reciprocity; high criminality; absence of rules, norms, mores
Environmental Security	Disease, lack of clean water, high infant mortality, lack of medicines
Military Security	Inability to practice territoriality; shrinking or irrelevance of territorial borders of the state; Absence of distinction between soldiers and civilians (end of professional Army)

In the recent secular apocalyptic novels which I consider, each of the effects in the right-hand side of the column appears as an element of the narrative. For example, in *World Made by Hand*, the state's ability to control its territory has vanished, and what now exists is merely a collection of localities rather than a state. The localities are not in contact with one another, nor do the citizens have any knowledge of or loyalty to any leader claiming to represent the United States as a whole. In contrast, in *The Pesthouse*, there are other states now asserting territorial claims on the land which used to be the United States. Here, too, as well, there is no national government, nor are the citizens aware of or loyal to a national leader. The citizens of the region are not organized or mobilized to fight off others who might lay claim to the territory of the former United States. In the novel, *One Second After*, the U.S. military and civilian population is thrown into disorganization through the launching of an electromagnetic pulse which destroys America's communications infrastructure. In this novel, China takes the opportunity to assert a territorial claim on the West coast of the United States. In each of these novels, the scenario is different, but in each the United States has lost its political security and ability to command its territory. Similarly, each novel features high casualty rates due to the lack of a functioning state infrastructure which can ration food, produce food, or ensure that individuals have an adequate supply of food. The narrative describes a trajectory of state failure, the ways in which citizens cope with this event and the significance of the events to the lives of the participants. The novelist Jim Crace describes the situation in the following sentences: "This used to be America, this river crossing in the ten-month stretch of land, this sea-to-sea. It used to be the safest place on earth."[7] Each story describes how America lost its ability to provide for its citizens, how citizens came to feel unsafe, and how people's understandings of what it meant to be American changed.

But the idea that apocalypse is about security threat is not a new idea—though the terminology used to describe it here may be. Indeed, even in the Biblical apocalypse, each of the Four Horseman of the Apocalypse who arrives signaling the end of the world essentially represents a new type of security threat. Table 1.2 illustrates this point:

Table 1.2. The Four Horsemen of the Apocalypse and Their Related Security Threats

HORSEMAN—Apocalyptic Threat	Related Security Threat
Famine	absence of economic, environmental, and societal security
Flood	absence of environmental security
Pestilence	lack of environmental and societal security
War	an absence of political and societal security

In addition, the events associated with the Biblical Tribulation (a period of time believed by many Evangelical Christians to follow the Rapture and to lead up to the Apocalypse) include a plague of darkness (as described in Revelation 8:12) and a situation in which the seas turn to blood and life cannot grow (Revelation 8:7–12). Each of these events could have biological or environmental causes (such as an oil spill which makes the seas uninhabitable, or oil well fires which turn the skies black and cause a "plague of darkness"). Thus, these Biblical apocalyptic events could also be understood as security threats with real-life causes.

What this suggests is that an apocalypse may be defined—in international relations terms—as a situation in which there is an absence of security for the long term, and in which the state and society's likelihood of recovering from this absence of security and rebuilding functioning institutions is low. Thus, the best historic example of a secular apocalypse is the collapse of Rome's Empire during the late 300s AD and the accompanying social, political, economic, and military breakdown—including the outbreak of the Plague of Justinian, the breakdown of traditional territorial formations, economic depressions including rapid inflation and currency devaluations, so-called barbarian invasions and shortages of goods, rising infant mortality, and declines in standards of living.

MEASURING DISASTER AND APOCALYPSE

However, the definitions above still do not fully convey the ways in which apocalypse represents something more than simply a series of bad or negative outcomes or events. Is an apocalypse merely "something bad that happens" or does it have a larger meaning? Emergency management personnel and government planners have used a positivist methodology to measure and classify different types of accidents based on the size and scope of the accident. Thus, a regular accident can become "disastrous" or even "apocalyptic" depending on how many are injured or killed and what other types of damage (such as property damage) occur. The Bradford Disaster Magnitude Scale thus arrays disasters along a scale from 1 to 10, with 10 most accurately corresponding to what we mean by the term "apocalypse" or "apocalyptic destruction." The positivist framework assumes that both risk and disaster are "real" and objectively observable and measurable conditions which remain constant regardless of any inherent qualities of the observer or his or her culture.[8] Thus, the International Disaster Database tracks the numbers and types of disasters as well as the magnitude of the disaster by considering the numbers of people affected; the amount of money it will cost to "fix" the disaster as well as the time frame before the area is restored to normal after the disaster.

However, this empirical definition of disaster neglects other types of costs associated with disaster—not all of which are measurable. Erickson notes that a disaster frequently destroys a community as well as injuring individuals. While some sufferers may lose family members to a disaster, others will lose the school their children attended, the church in which they were married, and may lose neighbors and friends if these individuals relocate after a disaster. Such losses, along with the psychic trauma which all witnesses to the event might undergo, are not usually incorporated into empirical measures of disaster.[9] These types of destruction are rarely counted or considered.

In contrast to the strict empiricist approach, sociologists argue that disaster is socially constructed.[10] For the sociologist, there is no clear empirical definition of what a disaster is, nor is the label necessarily defined evenly throughout the world.[11] Instead, what seems "disastrous" at one historical juncture or in one country might not seem so in another context. An event leading to a few deaths of prominent Westerners, for example, may receive as much media coverage as a similar event in a country far away—even though proportionally the loss of life was much higher in the event in the developed world.[12] "Why," sociologists ask, "do we consider both the Asian tsunami which killed an estimated 500,000 people and the events of 9/11 which killed 4,000 people to be disastrous?" Clearly, disaster is not merely a matter of scope—whether measured by mortality rates or economic losses.

One way to distinguish between disaster and apocalypse is to consider the notion of "dread"—which is a highly specific type of fear. Tversky and Johnson suggest that "dread" is a gut reaction which causes individuals to anticipate a negative outcome about which they are incapable of thinking either calmly or rationally. Thus, for example, one might experience dread if one anticipates a horrendous end—such as being eaten by a lion. This is a categorically different type of fear than, for example, the fear that one feels about the possibility of being killed in a car accident. That is, an event becomes dreadful not based on the likelihood that it would occur but rather on the sheer horribleness and unthinkableness of its occurrence. Thus, we know that it is extremely unlikely that someday within our lifetimes the United States will cease to exist, mass starvation will occur, and our fellow citizens will turn to cannibalism. Nonetheless, this scenario occurs in several of the post-apocalyptic novels considered in this manuscript—including Foerstchen's *One Second After* and McCarthy's *The Road*. Apocalypse fills us with dread because of the sheer magnitude of the loss—representing the end of civilization as we know it. Similarly, the nuclear apocalypse novels of the 1950s and 1960s like Neville Shute's *On the Beach* conjure up the emotion of dread, since nuclear annihilation is similarly unthinkable.

Dread can be also understood as a fear of something which is to come or shape of anticipated future suffering. It is a cloud which spreads out over our present decision-making as we consider the possibility of (and anticipate and prepare for) future loss. Dread both compels us or draws us to the apocalyptic novel and allows us to understand and make sense of the novel. But dread is a luxury emotion—since it is in essence the fear of something that may occur in the distant future. Dread is thus distinguished from terror, panic, or worry, which are emotions couched entirely in the present.[13] As Ian Savage suggests[14] individuals think differently about hazards they are likely to encounter depending on whether they are exposed to risk voluntarily or involuntarily, whether they have the ability to avoid death (through, for example, economic power or personal skill), and whether death is immediate or delayed. Individuals are most likely to feel "dread" when they think about a future risk which they cannot control or deflect and where they do not have the option of "opting out" in terms of their exposure to such a risk. That is, Savage and others distinguish between these special risks and more everyday risks. Here both disaster and apocalypse are special risks, which are viewed with dread. In thinking about these risks, individuals are able to picture future events which they cannot control and in which they will be compelled to participate. They are able to picture future events which are likely to reshape their identities, their behaviors, their sense of agency, and in a larger sense the identity and agency of their state. However, as noted above, dread—unlike terror—is predominantly an emotion of the wealthy and comfortable individual, and the wealthy and comfortable nation since it requires conditions which allow one to anticipate both the loss of one's present status and a "falling" into a lower status, where one has less agency and control.

That is, during and in the aftermath of disaster, all citizens can be said to occupy a lower rung on the ladder of human security, as they are now preoccupied with daily survival needs, rather than having the energy or resources to plan for long-run projects or accomplishments. Disaster thus represents (at least in the short term) an alteration in the status, security, and sovereignty of a geographic area and its accompanying political system in relation to its neighbors. At the moment when disaster is experienced, the area which may have formerly been autonomous and independent now instead becomes the subject of someone else's aid politics. And the donor nation performs a calculus which includes not only the interests of the affected area, but also its own interests. The disaster area thus takes on an instrumental status in which it is primarily of interest to its neighbors not because of its culture, its history, its power, or its contributions; instead, the object of aid policy is containing the disaster and preventing it from spreading outside the affected area. Donor nations are interested in containing the area's refugees, its diseases, and its environmental effects. The disaster-affected area thus experiences a loss of both identity and agency. It is no longer an independent area but instead a site for the practices of others. Other nations may seize control of its ports, its harbors, and its airspace. They may set up emergency headquarters in its government buildings and palaces, and they may appoint a spokesperson who now becomes the source of official news regarding the situation in the region. The region is, at least temporarily, voiceless and owned by others.

When considering the social construction of disaster, the sociologist Lee Clarke suggests that an event is considered to be disastrous or "worst case" by Western analysts and observers if two specific assumptions are violated: the assumption of safety and the assumption regarding what is seen as an "average bad outcome" versus a truly catastrophic one. That is, we are more likely to apply the label "disaster" when something is unexpected and when it occurs in a situation in which we had expected to feel safe. (For example, we expect to assume some risk when engaging in a risky activity such as riding in a car. If we are injured, this is not considered disastrous. On the other hand, a car which comes up on the sidewalk and kills pedestrians is viewed differently, since the pedestrians expected to feel safe.) Building on this logic, he suggests that only societies which regularly provide safety for their citizens tend to think in terms of either disaster or disaster planning. Thus, an epidemic is viewed differently in the United States than in a developing country, since Americans don't expect to see high rates of infant mortality associated with outbreaks of disease. One's shock is thus a function of one's viewpoint and the degree to which one expects to feel invulnerable in one's society.

Thus each citizen has determined what we think of as a "normal" level of danger or loss based on culture and historic experience. An American or a European citizen might expect that some small percentage of people who enter the hospital for treatment will not be cured but will rather succumb to their illnesses. However, in a developed nation, this number is likely around 4 or 5 percent. In such a situation, we would be shocked if half of all patients who entered the American hospital died of their illnesses, though this number would not be equally shocking, perhaps, in Afghanistan.[15] Similarly, there are still countries in the world in which 20 percent of children die before the age of five—a figure which might well be labeled "apocalyptic" if it happened in the United States or in England.

In addition, it appears that one's environment of human security alters one's individual perspectives. Those who do not enjoy high levels of human security have been described in Ronald Inglehart's literature on post-materialism as concerned primarily with day-to-day survival.[16] As

Jeffrey Sacks tells us, one-sixth of the world's population does not have food security, and must go to bed at night not knowing what they will feed their children the next day.[17] Olson and Gawronski explain that a society coping with disaster can be seen as "sliding down Maslow's hierarchy of needs."[18] But for those on the lowest rung of the socioeconomic and security ladder, there is no personal expectation of either short-term or long-term security—and in a sense, there is no lower place to which an individual can slide, since one is already at the bottom of the hierarchy of needs. One is already in survival model. In this situation, arguably, one does not have time to entertain the emotion of dread. In such a situation, both the terms disaster and apocalypse are already meaningless. In a society where the infant mortality rate is already the highest in the world or where the average life expectancy is already the lowest, how does one draw the line to conceptualize of unimaginable versus merely routine loss? If one expects to experience loss and hardship and is therefore less surprised and shocked when it occurs, and if one finds the experience of loss to be routine rather than extraordinary, is that same loss still labeled disastrous? or apocalyptic?

Similarly, it seems that the end of the world has come in *The Pesthouse* when we find that the citizens of this new United States territory in the year 3000 are illiterate, irrational creatures who believe in magic, do not know what money is, and are afraid of metal objects. Here, the reader understands that America has regressed since previously its citizens enjoyed a high literacy rate. However, for a nation where literacy is not currently the norm, would this description of the nation in the future carry the same weight? Would it be sufficient for the reader to understand that something terrible has happened to the population—since they are now illiterate and irrational? Calhoun argues that in the West, disaster is seen as a series of events which bring the state and society to a "state of emergency." However, this description leaves out the fact that at any given time, a large swathe of humanity lives in exactly such a state of emergency all the time. He notes that for the oppressed "the state of emergency is not the exception but the rule."[19]

In Western writing, an apocalyptic scenario is one in which society or state is "driven back" to an earlier historic time period or stage of development, due to a final and irreversible undoing of significant institutions—including a market economy, the institutions and ideology of the state, or the collapse of civilization. At the moment at which one is overtaken by disaster, the event is experienced as though even nature itself has agency over individuals. In an apocalyptic scenario, it may appear that man has lost his sense of agency permanently. Crace illustrates this point in *The Pesthouse*, when he describes a torrential rainstorm through the eyes of an apocalypse survivor: "The rain was unforgiving in its weight. It meant to stay and do some damage and some good in equal parts. It meant to be noticed. It meant to run downhill until it found a river and then downstream until it found a sea."[20] Here, apocalypse appears to have tilted the balance between rationalism and irrationality. In experiencing negative outcomes, the individuals, and groups affected have (at least temporarily) abandoned their long-held beliefs in man's ability to triumph over and transform the natural world. In a sense, they look at the world from the bottom-up, in a situation where nature is dominant rather than subservient to man.

However, the label "apocalyptic" may be applied not as the result of a particular casualty figure, or even based on a change to one's standard of living, but as the result of specific policy outcomes. That is, population loss may be labeled as disastrous when it affects the ability of a state to carry out other types of actions. Here, the United Nations Coordinating Committee for Disasters defines a disaster as "an event located in time and space, producing conditions under which the continuity of the structures and of the social processes becomes problematic."[21] For example, once a certain casualty figure is reached, it then becomes difficult for the remaining population to police its borders, to maintain its infrastructure, or to preserve its territorial integrity. In the apocalyptic novels the assumption is that no foreign aid will be forthcoming. However, in the real-life emergency management literature, the assumption is that a true disaster is one in which the population and the region is decimated to the point that it can no longer care for its citizens and its territory *on its own—without outside aid and assistance*. Thus, this literature defines disaster as "a serious disruption of the functioning of society, causing widespread human, material, or environmental losses which *exceed the ability of the affected society to cope using only its own resources*."[22] A disaster may be local, statewide, nationwide, or even larger—but what makes it a disaster is the inability of those affected to cope with it on their own, without foreign or outside assistance. Here, the analyst considers not merely what is destroyed but also at the likelihood that it can be reestablished.[23]

Rodriguez and Lee suggest that because the hazards associated with dread are particularly large-scale risks—such as nuclear annihilation—they are also hazards which necessarily require a collective rather than an individual response.[24] This is why one feels particularly helpless in confronting these risks, since there is little one can do individually to prepare for or divert them. Thus, to some degree, the emotion of dread is more relevant and meaningful for those individuals who live within a relatively stable working government, which would allow them to ask the question "Is my government prepared to deal with this risk?" Or "Why isn't my government doing a better job of confronting this risk?" Here, one can argue that those in developed nations with media access have been trained by the media to expect their government to take actions to protect them from negative outcomes. Henrike Viehrig, for example, explains how the media frequently covers a disaster in such a way that citizens are likely to conclude that their government was inadequately prepared, should have known about the disaster, or was insufficiently trained to respond.[25] Thus, it appears that the more access one has to the media, the more likely one is to consider it the state's responsibility to protect them from danger and the more likely one is to worry about the state's inability to do so. And the more likely one is to blame the government when it fails to do so.

Here, the world which we inhabit in the apocalyptic novel (or in real life after a disaster) is a failed version of the state we currently inhabit. Apocalypse reproduces the characteristics of the failed state—including mounting demographic pressures; the movement of refugees; a legacy of vengeance-seeking group grievances or group paranoia; uneven economic development along group lines; a sharp or severe economic decline; the criminalization or delegitimization of the state; a progressive deterioration of public services; the suspension or arbitrary application of the rule of law and a widespread violation of human rights; and frequently the rise of some new sort of security apparatus which acts as a "state within a state."[26] Readers are shocked to picture an America in which there is no reliable system of long-distance communications and a child who leaves town in search of a better life elsewhere might never be heard from again—as happens in Kunstler's *World Made by Hand*.

In *The Road*, the nameless main character, The Man, describes his son, The Child, as startlingly beautiful in his emaciated state—which the man then goes on to explain is the result of not having eaten for several days. In Justin Cronin's *The Passage*, one group of villagers believes themselves to be the last humans alive on earth and experiences their joy in meeting up with another group of villagers. Both groups believed that all of their kind had been violently slaughtered in the preceding years. In each case, what startles us is the descent from order into chaos—since we have wrongly assumed that our modern society was immune from this descent.

Furthermore, if we trace the discourse of apocalyptic disaster back to its application beginning in the mid-1700s to the Lisbon Earthquake, we find that an apocalyptic event appears to be one where "civilization" and its accompanying infrastructure are judged to have been destroyed or nearly destroyed. (A nation which was never judged as having a civilization cannot therefore suffer an apocalypse.) Bystanders and observers in eighteenth-century Portugal could not understand how a society which possessed great maritime wealth, treasures of art and culture, and a religious population could undergo such unparalleled destruction. It felt apocalyptic because of the unfathomable and immeasurable level of destruction as well as a sense that the citizens somehow did not deserve such a fate, as educated, rational members of society. Finally, it was apocalyptic because of the jarring contrast between the days before, when citizens dressed in their finery and ate imported foods—and the current situation, in which people came to blows over scraps of food and perhaps even practiced cannibalism.[27]

In contrast, those who presently live within the borders of a failed state do not have the luxury of considering that their government is unprepared for a future risk both because they do not have a working government to confront the future risk and because they are preoccupied with everyday hazards (like pestilence, drought, and lack of clean water) generated by the lack of that same working government. In addition, they may not have access to working media whose job it is to alert them to the ways in which their state has failed to protect them. As a result, they are less likely to worry about their government's capacity to do so, or to consider it the government's job to do so. In this context, application of the terms disaster and apocalypse might be judged to be meaningless.

In her work on the politics of mourning and violence, Butler describes the existence of a "hegemonic grammar" or a mode of discourse which is controlled by those in authority within the international system. Within that system, she argues, the word "slaughter," for example, is carefully applied to describe some types of killing, but not others. As she describes the situation, one is significantly more likely to read about Arabs "slaughtering" Israelis, than vice-versa.[28] Similarly, one might argue that the application of the word "apocalypse" or even "disaster" is not merely a neutral act. Rather, it appears that destruction is only described (by governments and the media) as apocalyptic if the target of the violence (either through an Act of God or an act of man) is judged to have somehow met preset standards of modernization which would create an extremely jarring disconnect between the world which existed before and that which exists after the violence.

In the present day, apocalyptic fiction derives its power from the way in which two competing narratives about American identity are juxtaposed. On the one hand, the narrative of American exceptionalism (explored in a later chapter) which undergirds American identity is a story of America as a uniquely blessed nation with a built-in trajectory of accomplishment. At the same time, empirical data tells us that the United States is particularly prone to natural disaster due to its large land mass, vast variations of weather which can occur within its borders, and the persistence of fault lines.[29] Thus, each apocalyptic novel brings together those two narratives—the expectation that America is somehow special and immune to the vicissitudes of both nature and history, and the reality that it is not. In addition to the narrative of American exceptionalism, Americans expect to feel safer because empirically great wealth has been seen to confer great power. Wealthy individuals—and wealthy nations—have historically been able to insulate themselves from the effects of both natural and manmade disasters. Individuals have more education which enables them to cope, better shelters, more money, and more resources. What is jarring in the apocalyptic novel is thus how far the citizens have fallen from their initial lofty perches, and the ways in which they have turned out not to be immune. They are, it turns out, just like everyone else.

An "apocalypse" thus only makes sense in a modern context, since the drama is only in the fall and the implications of loss. Defining an apocalypse rests thus upon locating what is known as an "apocalyptic moment." The apocalyptic moment is seen as a severing point, sharply delineating the events which preceded the moment from the events which followed. Once one's society has experienced an apocalypse, there is no going back to the former state, no matter how much disaster assistance might be brought to bear. As Keller et al. note in their work on modeling disasters,[30] disaster can be measured according to several different criteria—one can consider the geographic range of the incident, the number of individuals affected, as well as the time frame necessary to lead to a restoration of the society and state to its prior state. One's state or society may recover eventually from a natural event of great magnitude—even if recovery from that event takes years, as it did in the case of Hurricane Katrina, the Oklahoma dustbowls of the 1930s in America, or the breaching of the reactor at Chernobyl, Ukraine, in the mid-1980s. There is, however, no recovering from the actions of the Four Horsemen of the Apocalypse or from an event like the plagues of the Middle Ages that killed approximately 30 percent of the population and fundamentally altered the history, politics, and society of Europe as a result.

Similarly, within our own generation we may point to the example of the Former Soviet Union. In the past twenty years, we have seen this once mighty nation go from the status of donor nation to recipient nation. We have watched as Russia became the subject of other's foreign policies as individual nations and groups like the World Bank, International Monetary Fund, and United Nations moved into the region to restore Russia's shaky economy, assist in the establishment of democratic leadership, and distribute humanitarian and disaster assistance. In many instances, spokesman for these organizations spoke on behalf of Russia, and were involved in all aspects of Russia's governance, including the drawing up of legislation and budgets, the conduct of elections, and the hiring of city and state officials. It appears highly unlikely that Russia will regain its former status.

Thus, we begin to ask the question "Is cultural interest in apocalyptic scenarios a uniquely western or American phenomenon—because it is only from a position of great wealth and stability that one can then imagine falling so many degrees of magnitude?" Does one have to be a superpower or an empire to view this loss as catastrophic or apocalyptic?

We can ask whether what constitutes an apocalypse in America might merely constitute daily life in a society like Haiti or Rwanda. That is, the specter of contemporary "apocalypse" in America represents an entirely new reality for the average American who cannot conceptualize of living in an environment characterized by food insecurity, social instability, high unemployment, and spiraling prices. Rather, as R. B. J. Walker points out in his work, *After the Globe, Before the World*, the social processes of modernity have served to insulate citizens in modern countries from instability and chaos. He describes what he refers to as an inside/outside phenomenon in which those who live within the bounds of the so-called modern world occupy a sort of bubble in which they are insulated from many of the real problems which others in the world face.[31]

Apocalyptic narratives thus allow international relations scholars to move beyond the problem identified by critical theorists as "situatedness." Scholars note that for those who do their theorizing from the comfort of a university in the United States or the developed world, it is difficult to move beyond that ethnocentric view to theorize more generally about politics wrought large in a world where not all live in a secure, strong, and stable state. Here it is my contention that much current international relations theory rests on the assumption that the state is a permanent feature of international life and that the American state in particular is invulnerable. Apocalyptic literature thus provides a frame which IR theorists can use to imagine politics from the bottom-up, from a situation in which the United States is not the occupier but the occupied; where the United States represents the periphery and not the center; where the United States is no longer the guarantor of hegemonic stability within the international system. Thus, this new subaltern perspective allows us to identify assumptions which underlie our current understandings of American identity and its role in the international system and to find common ground with other states who operate from a position of weakness rather than strength in the international system.

"WE AMERICANS": MOVING BEYOND SITUATEDNESS

In the past ten years, analysts have begun to critique the "American-centric" feel of international relations theory. Critiques have focused on the ethnocentricity of the research agenda, the Americancentric assumptions behind much current research, a lack of reflexivity, the use of language which is far from neutral (often employing words such as "us" and "them"), and a hostility towards the use of certain methodologies. In 2001, Crawford suggested that there is a consensus or a "hegemony" among international relations scholars, arguing that this consensus is reflected in publication records, conference attendance, structure of the academy, and textbooks.[32] Nossal[33] suggests that young scholars are socialized into a variety of assumptions from the time they first encounter an international relations textbook—which is in all likelihood written by an American from an American perspective, with few attempts to specify or interrogate the assumptions which underlie this view of the international system as American-led with America at the center.

Joye echoes this sentiment in his analysis of media coverage of what he terms "distant suffering," arguing that the international media shows the world largely as Europecentric, with scant attention paid to suffering on the periphery of these boundaries.[34] He notes that "For most people living in the so-called developed world, disasters are a priori foreign news" as he goes on to describe the existence of a "regime of pity" to which the reader may or may not be called upon to respond. In such a frame, there is a clear distinction between what it is like to live in the developed world and what it is like to live in the developing world. Those in the developed world occupy a superior position in which their own security is seldom, if ever threatened, and where they have the power to decide whether or not to help the less fortunate.

Similarly, Etheridge refers to a type of "cognitive ethnocentrism," in which the analyst assumes that every other state's experience and perspective is merely some variant of one's own. The dominant nation or the hegemon thus writes the script through which the experiences of all other states—one's neighbors and one's foes—are understood and interpreted.[35] References to the "world out there" are limited, and as Nossal argues:

> More or less the story gets told like this—at different times in world history, there will be a country that, because of its superordinate powers and its desire for order, will selflessly apply its energies, its resources and its power to the creation and maintenance of a stable world order.[36]

America thus appears as a "rescuer," building institutions like Bretton Woods, NATO, and the UN in order to help other states who may seek to take advantage of U.S. largesse, acting as free-riders.[37] Leander refers to a "politics of protection" or the politics surrounding the definition of the threats and the protection needed to secure against them. In this rendering, the hegemon is seen as occupying a superior position as he alone contemplates how such problems are to be solved.[38] More recently, Chandler has suggested that the development-security nexus involves those at the center "experimenting" with development in the periphery "where there is apparently less to lose and costs of failure are lower."

Within the development-security nexus, the preservation of the international system in its present form (and preventing disruption) is portrayed as the ultimate goal of international relations theory, a situation which tends to serve the interests of the hegemon.[39] We do not see the assumptions which underlie this system: assumptions about the superiority of the hegemon, the power which he alone enjoys to label and define the situation, to experiment on other states, and to excuse himself from bearing the costs of failure in this arena. Rather, these assumptions are hidden in plain sight. We are so used to entertaining these assumptions that we tend not to notice them. And in such a story, there is no room for alternate voices—for an alternate retelling of the narrative, or the possibility that another narrative might be envisioned, in which the United States doesn't "rescue" anyone, and in which all states are active participants rather than the mere passive subjects of these activities.

In contrast, imagining the hegemon as also vulnerable allows for the development of what Rasmussen calls "reflexive security."[40] The creation of an alternate geography, in particular, can cause us to see the world anew, as Ivor Neumann points out in his analysis of muggle geography.[41] Thus, imagining apocalypse allows for a critique of certain propositions of contemporary realist IR theory. It is only when our assumptions and positions are reversed in a fictional scenario that we become aware of them and of the ways in which we have heretofore been conditioned to see the world.[42] Fiction thus allows the reader to engage in a process of "ontological displacement"—through adopting a different position on ongoing debates in international relations.[43] In the words of Reid-Henry, we need an "imaginary" in which the terms of the development security nexus (normally seen as fixed) are reversed. In this way, fiction and popular culture can allow for the envisioning of alternatives.[44]

Here, one can argue that this exercise in reimagining and reenvisioning the United States actually began on September 11. For the first time, Americans had an opportunity to ask not "What should we do?" in response to international catastrophe and tragedy, but rather to begin to ask "What if this happened to us?" or, as I suggest in this book, "What if We are really Them—and They are really Us?" In many ways, September 11 redrew the map and wrenched aside a curtain, allowing analysts and citizens alike to begin to view the international system through a new lens. The world became aware of several new facts (or facts which may have been true but which we were unable or unwilling to see).

The first "new fact" is this: International Public opinion does not favor American hegemony, and the backlash against hegemony actually threatens America. In his famous policy speech in the immediate aftermath of September 11, President George Bush noted in surprise and shock that "they hate us." In doing so, he publicly admitted to a situation which both surprised and confounded both U.S. policymakers and academics—since prior theorizing did not satisfactorily account for or predict this turn of events. Rather, U.S. foreign policy and IR theorizing had largely operated from the assumption and expectation that other nations would fall in line with end of the Soviet Union, both respecting and desiring American power. Here, the expectation was that U.S. power could serve to solve the problems of international relations.

Recently, analysts have increasingly begun to ask if America is losing its position of "strategic primacy" or if America is becoming irrelevant. Analysts have begun to engage seriously with the themes of American imperial or hegemonic decline, as well as to begin to question the assumptions of hegemonic stability theory.[45] Outside observers of the United States, such as the Chinese scholar Wang Jisi, asked if 9/11 might mean the end of the United States' privileged position as a hegemon within the international system.[46] And in 2011, Allan Noble suggested that a unipolar world is no more stable than any other type of international system.[47]

However, in the immediate aftermath of September 11, those who suggested that there might be understandable reasons why public opinion did not automatically favor American hegemony were pilloried in the press, accused of disloyalty and even treason. Novelists found it difficult to write about September 11, or about America, as there was a climate which militated against open discussion of these issues. In analyzing the crop of novels which dealt directly with the events of September 11, 2001, the English novelist Chris Cleave suggested—even in September 2010—that writing about such events involved "treading on hallowed ground." That is, the emotions surrounding the events were too raw and public feelings were too strong for a novelist to attempt to say anything controversial or provocative about the events themselves.[48]

The reclusive novelist Cormac McCarthy (who is said to have only given three interviews in his lifetime) did not speak directly about how his writing might have been influenced by world events. However, in 2005, after the publication of his novel *The Road*, he noted that many find his novels violent because Americans, as a culture, do not like to think about or witness death. He notes "to not be able to talk about it is very odd."[49]

As the British novelist Martin Amis noted, on some level, every novel written after September 11 became a "September 11" novel because it took place in a different world. He described the new climate, noting that "Everything is contingent. The verities that you depended on a few weeks ago are gone—and gone, I think for our lifetimes . . . after an hour, you suddenly realize you haven't been thinking about whether your kids are going to get anthrax, and there's a sort of weird, guilty feeling."[50] However, he also noted that in the aftermath of September 11, "because of the constrictions of correctness, there's less and less to joke about. More and more is unsayable."[51]

It was not until a full ten years after the events that the literary analyst Anis Shivani would suggest that a September 11 novel could be used to show that America is a "hypocritical whore"—which simultaneously welcomed new immigrants to its shore with the rhetoric of freedom and acceptance while at the same time subjecting them to search and seizure and accusing them of terrorism.[52] Prior to that, he notes, novelists tiptoed carefully around themes of terrorism and religious fundamentalism, as well as themes which questioned the morality of America or its hegemonic role in the world.

Apocalyptic novels thus allow the reader to turn his gaze back upon his own society, but in doing so to view America not through the lens of security but through the lens of insecurity. Increasingly, geographers like Joyce Davidson[53] have begun to explore the notion that places have not just a physical geography but an "emotional geography" as well. That is, places can be associated with emotions—of guilt, betrayal, fear, and safety. When analysts tell us that America "became a different place on September 11," it is this notion of emotional geography that is being referenced. Most of us did not move to a new residence after September 11, but many analysts, including Paul Pillar, would argue that we all moved to a new emotional place since in many ways to be American was to feel safe. And somehow living in an America which did not feel safe was akin to living somewhere else. Citizens asked if the place we lived now was now more like Jerusalem or Tel Aviv. Perhaps it was like Lebanon.[54]

That is, the same geographically fixed location can be experienced differently, depending on whether it is viewed through a lens of security or insecurity: When a region is viewed through the lens of security, the landscape seems fixed and incapable of changing. Individuals within the society enjoy food security, physical security, and a sense of safety and permanence. They are able to make long-range plans about the future and about their families. Power is rational and predictable in this society and operates according to the rule of law. As an inhabitant of the region, one understands why decisions are made, and is not merely subject to them arbitrarily.

In contrast, when viewed through the lens of insecurity, the landscape seems less fixed and more likely to change. The individuals inhabiting the region may be refugees, a minority group in the region, or the property of others. In any case, they are unable to make their own decisions about how long they will inhabit the land or how they will use it. From this perspective, it seems that power is exercised arbitrarily and capriciously, and one is subject to this power. The protagonists in this narrative operate and view the world from a position of alterity, where they are looking from the bottom up. The inhabitants do not have a sense of agency or control over their lives.

In recent times, we may look at an event such as Hurricane Katrina through both lenses. Those government decision makers in authority viewed the landscape of New Orleans from a position of comfort where they saw themselves as analysts making rational decisions about how to proceed. By contrast, those trapped in New Orleans when the levees broke saw only a chaotic landscape where they themselves had little control. The footage shown on CNN about the event showed individuals making statements such as: "I do not know where they are taking us" and "Why doesn't anybody help us?" Americans who were not in New Orleans claimed to be shocked to see such scenes of Third World devastation taking place on their own soil—but it is equally shocking to hear Americans speaking about themselves as victimized, weak, and at the mercy of outside rescuers. We do not normally associate this lens of insecurity with a superpower—unless something catastrophic takes place.

But apocalyptic novels go one-step further in applying the lens of insecurity—in positing that security may well be a thing of the past in America, and that prospects for reestablishing security are weak and nonexistent. Thus, the scenario created in the apocalyptic novel allows us to ask as Don DeLillo's characters ask in his novel about 9/11 *Falling Man* "What comes after America?"[55]

One can therefore view the apocalyptic novel as a peculiar form—which only works if that nation or writer is powerful, or representative of a superpower. Psychologically, the apocalyptic novel is about a loss of status and control. It represents a particular type of fear, coming from a particular place and a particular time. In addition, Olson and Gawronski have noted that disaster often represents a sort of "backsliding" to an area.[56] Disaster creates a situation in which the affected area swaps a more modern preoccupation with self-fulfillment and happiness at least temporarily with a more "primitive" set of concerns—namely those of food and shelter. In that way, disaster can represent not only a loss of status, sovereignty, and identity, but also a loss of modernity, and in a sense, a kind of time travelling. The state which was once at the forefront of human progress and so-called civilization is at one moment driven backwards, finding it behind or backward compared to the nations and organizations which now come to minister to it in its weakened state.

In the case of the apocalyptic novel, then, the unstated fear which underlies the story is the fear that a modern, developed nation can somehow be driven off course permanently, like a ship which becomes lost at sea. Somehow, the logic goes, if enough disasters occur and we do not anticipate them, or prepare for them, we risk losing everything. We will sustain catastrophic losses to our buildings, infrastructure, and people, but more importantly, we will sustain the loss of our identity in the international community, as well as our power, status, and autonomy. We will become the site of others' actions rather than the actor which causes events to occur. Rather than having our own foreign policy, we will become the subject of other's foreign policies.

It is a particularly twenty-first-century fear, founded upon the corpses of former nations like Yugoslavia and the Soviet Union, and bred in events like Hurricane Katrina and 9/11. And yet it is not wholly an American phenomenon. Rather, one can identify similar literary strains and experiments produced in Victorian Britain, as Britain itself wrestled with the ghostly specter of one day becoming powerless and irrelevant to the international system. At base, one can argue that all apocalyptic novels are thus *Left Behind* novels—except that the fear of being left behind does not refer to being left sitting in your seat on the bus while everyone else has been raptured up to heaven. Rather, being left behind refers to the phenomenon wherein a developed nation finds itself left out of the march of history as its neighbors move forward technologically and economically while one's own nation slides into anarchy and chaos before proceeding to eventual dismemberment.

9/11 and the Apocalyptic Moment

Literary theorists use the term "apocalyptic moment" to describe the singular event which results in the destruction of the old and the transition to the new.[57] Analysts have historically understood the apocalypse as occurring suddenly as the result of a single event which causes us to traverse that point of no return. After the moment, there is no possibility of returning to the previous place. This is what analysts mean when they state that the history was essentially cleaved in two on September 11, or on Pearl Harbor Day, or on the day a nuclear weapon was exploded in Hiroshima. The event itself created a point where our consciousness is now forced to grapple with two separate universes—a before and an after.[58] The French social theorist Rene Girard refers to 9/11 itself as an apocalyptic moment, since it represents a clear break between an old and a new America.[59] As a result of 9/11, he argues, the way in which Americans think about their nation and their world has been irrevocably altered, and social practices, language, and foreign policies have been reshaped as well. America's apocalyptic moment thus lasted less than an hour—the amount of time which elapsed between the attack by the first plane and the collapse of the towers after being hit by the second plane. Martin Amis tells us in his collection of essays titled *The Second Plane*:

> It was the advent of the second plane, sharking in low over the Statue of Liberty: that was the defining moment . . . The message of September 11 ran as follows: America, it is time you learned how implacably you are hated. United Airlines Flight 175 was an Intercontinental Ballistic Missile, launched in Afghanistan and aimed at her (America's) innocence. That innocence, it was here being claimed, was a luxurious and anachronistic delusion.[60]

In this description we see an expression of the ways in which it provides a dividing line between a pre- and a post-9/11 world. 9/11 is thus a real life apocalyptic event, due to the scale of the destruction as well as the way in which it represents a break with order in which the old order will never be fully restored. The "apocalyptic moment" thus represents a transition to a new space which can signal destruction but which can also signal emancipation.[61] Apocalypse is transgressive, since it involves going to the furthest edge of one world or one boundary and then moving beyond it to a different one. The apocalyptic event thus represents a sort of catharsis in which old institutions and understandings are smashed and new ones arise in their place. Depending on the character of the institutions which were destroyed, the new place may be either better or worse than the old one—and it may be better for some and worse for others. As Susan Bowers explains, the Civil War and the end of slavery represented an apocalyptic moment in U.S. history. A boundary was transgressed and once destroyed; the institution of slavery could never be reconstituted. The smashing of this institution was apocalyptic for both groups—both for African-Americans, for whom the moment was one of liberation, in contrast to how it was perceived by Southern landowners.[62] Similarly, the destruction of the Soviet Union or the assassination of Romania's president Nicolae Ceausescu in winter 1989 were both apocalyptic moments, though the majority of those experiencing the moment found it liberating.

Here it is important to note that post-apocalyptic literature is primarily concerned with the *consequences* of the apocalyptic moment, the ways in which society's norms and values and social practices will be changed as a result, rather than the moment itself. Nonetheless, the moment is important for two reasons: it is a distilling down of contemporary fears and ideas of threat into this one moment, as well as a necessary act within the script itself, which moves us onto the next event. In the novels to be considered in my analysis, the apocalyptic moment is sometimes imagined and sometimes a real-life event which actually occurred.

Imagining Apocalypse

In situations where the event is not real, it is important for the apocalyptic event to be real enough that the reader finds the story believable. As I argue later in this manuscript, science fiction novels and films play a particular role in a society because of the ways in which they represent a mixing of nonfiction and fiction. The best science fiction contains just enough reality to be plausible. Though the events described in the novel or film have not happened, to some degree they require the reader to buy into the story by admitting that at least on some level these events could happen. For this reason, the apocalyptic novel represents a uniquely American cultural product as it exists at present. Each novel is in some way a distillation of the fears of America's average citizen at a particular point in time—based, to some degree on reality.

If we think back over America's recent history, we can identify key events which may have led Americans to worry about or even to imagine a future loss of their economic, political, military, societal, and environmental security. In the 2000s, natural disasters like Hurricane Katrina and the Indonesian tsunami illustrated the precariousness of even our most basic territory, as the earth was literally reshaped by the force of water. In addition, the specter of anarchy and a battle for human survival in New Orleans raised questions about the strength of the state, the ability of the Army to provide order and to provide for its people in times of stress. The near collapse of America's banking system and the large-scale government bailout which it necessitated in spring 2007 has raised questions about America's ability to provide economic security—including a stable currency and the survival of a market economy. At the same time, political and military security have been called into question with the rise of terrorism even within the borders of America itself as well as the possibility of military defeat or withdrawal in Iraq. In the slightly more distant past, events such as the implosion of Yugoslavia and breakup of the Soviet Union show that state collapse is neither impossible nor improbable. In addition, new financial developments are perhaps leading to a resurgence of borders and the ending of globalization. Writing in the *New Republic* in 2009, Joshua Kurzlantzick noted that 70 percent of all worldwide trade measures enacted since November 2008 have restricted trade, and even the Obama stimulus package included a protectionist "Buy American" clause.[63] Given these events, it is not surprising that popular culture has begun to imagine and analyze a new Bogeyman—the collapse of the state and the undoing of globalization. Table 1.3 lays out these fears as a schematic.

Table 1.3. Real-World Security Threats

Security Threat	Real World Events
Political Security	Declining trust in government Illegal immigration crisis Inability of US to police its borders
Economic Security	US bank bailout (2007) Foreclosure crisis Rising unemployment External trade deficit Rise of protectionism
Military Security	Terrorist attacks on US soil Discussions of US withdrawal in Iraq
Environmental Security	Gulf oil spill Hurricane Katrina
Societal Security	Declining trust in government Increasing interest in conspiracy theories Bankruptcies in local government and cuts in social services, including schools

Several of the novels considered here use the fears to create an apocalyptic moment in which the old America—the superpower and the hegemon in the international system—has been erased entirely, leaving the physical geography of America untouched while its inhabitants float through the landscape, leaderless and lost. In these scenarios, a barrier has been traversed and there is a clear break between the former and the new world. In this new world, America's infrastructure has crumbled, globalization has failed, and there is no reliable communications system linking the fractured country together.

The Privilege of Imagining the End of the World

Regardless of the "flavor" of the apocalyptic created, it is nonetheless true that the apocalyptic novel is a specific cultural product since it is, in essence, a product of privilege, arrogance, and hubris. The ironic stance which it necessitates—in which it is possible to express one's own ambivalence for the products of Western, progressive liberalism—can only be attained by having experienced the products of Western cultural privilege and having found them wanting. To contemplate throwing away civilization, one must have civilization in the first place.

In the apocalyptic novel, this conceit reaches its highest stage since the reader is meant to equate his own society with the world itself. Thus, destroying Britain at the height of its power—or destroying America today—is seen as akin to destroying the world itself. This view is revealed in the opening paragraph of another novel which is more realistic—though it still shares certain qualities with apocalyptic literature. In the novel *Falling Man*, the American writer Don DeLillo describes America's own apocalyptic moment, September 11, with the following words:

> It was not a street anymore but a world, a time and space of falling ash and near night. He was walking north through rubble and mud and there were people running past holding towels to their faces or jackets over their heads. . . . They had shoes in their hands. . . . They ran and fell . . . with debris coming down around them and there were people taking shelter under cars. [64]

In this powerful paragraph, DeLillo gives voice to the panic and confusion that the participants in this event surely felt, but he almost manages to convey the sense that something is awry with the entire universe. Somehow, the world is upside down, and the order of civilization itself has been violated—because here we have people from the First World in the situation of people in the Third World. They are refugees. They are terrified. They are powerless. Surely, this is someone's reality, but it's not supposed to be ours.

This same understanding, that America somehow is the world and that there is nothing beyond it, appears as well in Justin Cronin's *The Passage*, when Wolgast—a citizen who has fled to the mountains after a plague of genetically modified humans has managed to kill most of the population of the United States—describes his own reality: "The world off the mountain had become a memory; remoter by the day. . . . If what was happening was what he thought was happening, he reasoned, they were better off not knowing. What could he have done with the information? Where else could they go?"[65]

The apocalyptic novel can therefore only be produced by a culture which views itself as both superior to other cultures, and as one which views itself as central to the international system—since its decline is equal to the world's decline. In addition, the ability to hypothesize and conjecture about the future at all is a luxury only available to those in modern societies. Only in the absence of immediately threatening events (like famine or extreme poverty) are we able to think about the future at all, and only in a society with rational rules and structures can we then go on to theorize about how these same rational patterns might play out in the future.[66] In other words, in a society characterized by personal, charismatic authority, a cult of personality, or the unrestrained actions of the secret policy in society, it might be pointless to theorize about the course of events in the future since one's immediate day-to-day existence is simply too precarious to think beyond it. The future danger is simply not significant in comparison to the present danger.

Apocalyptic novels also rely on a highly developed notion of autonomous personal fulfillment which is likely to be found only in developed societies, since it is simply a "luxury" that those living in poverty do not have. Susan Napier argues that many Japanese writers are preoccupied with the spiritual consequences of our present-day dependence on technology. These writers are exploring the topics of overdependence on technology and its dehumanizing, isolating effects, in many ways reproducing the work carried out by the British writer E. M. Forster in his 1905 dystopian novel, *The Machine Stops*.[67] The problem is that if Japanese post-apocalyptic fiction deals with the loss of spiritual identity, it rests on a claim that individuals deserve spiritual identity and that it is important to have it. In other words, those who worry about spiritual identity are post-materialists, to use Inglehart's phrase. In his work on world values, Inglehart argues that there is a hierarchy of development in which individuals and nations first worry about how they will provide for their survival-type needs (such as food and water), and then later proceed to a preoccupation with meeting their spiritual needs, including the longing for meaning and community.[68]

This means that only those at the highest levels of material comfort are able to have the luxury to contemplate destroying our present world in order to experience spiritual fulfillment. Only the most privileged are in a position where they can make a claim that we should destroy technology to save humanity. Most of the rest of the world would be only too happy to have the technology and might be completely unconcerned about its purported soul-destroying spiritual consequences.

Thus far, I have argued that the apocalyptic scenario is a cultural luxury in which those who live in wealth and stability entertain themselves by imagining what it might be like to lose their privileged position—both individually and at a state level. Individuals can thus speculate on the individual ramifications of that loss (including the spiritual implications) as well as the larger corporate and even historical implications of that loss. This might explain, for example, why the majority of those conducting Google searches for the term "apocalypse" live in the developed world, rather than the developing world.

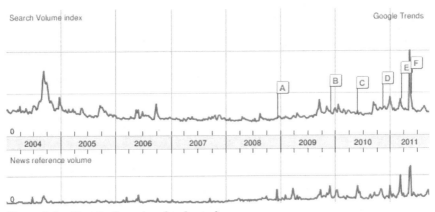

Figure 1.1. Google Searches for Apocalypse

As figure 1.1 shows, "googling" of the term apocalypse has increased sharply in the years since 2009. As Google Trends data indicates, the top ten "googlers" of the term are, by country, the Philippines, Canada, the United States, France, Australia, Belgium, the United Kingdom, Sweden,

Romania, and Finland. (Here, it has been suggested that the inclusion of the Philippines in this list may be related to the significant seismic activity levels in that country, as well as its place in the apocalyptic mythology of Asian citizens. Many believe that the end of the world will occur first in the Philippines). And lest one think that it is only fundamentalist Christians googling apocalypse within the United States, the breakdown by states lists the top ten states as: Kentucky, Indiana, Arkansas, Oklahoma, Oregon, Kansas, Washington, Nevada, Rhode Island, and Wisconsin. The inclusion of several Southern states in the Bible Belt suggests that some of this googling might be of the Biblical apocalyptic variety—but that not all of it is. Rather, it appears that those who read articles online about the apocalypse are from the developed world, rather than the developing world—and from states known for high education and literacy rates rather than those known for less education and literacy.

While search volume is perhaps lower due to lower computer access in the developing world, it also suggests that a preoccupation with the apocalyptic frame is both rising over time, and is rising predominantly in the developed world—both in terms of general interest in the phenomenon and in general interest in the pop-culture products associated with the phenomenon.

As entertaining as Google searching may be, speculating about the apocalypse is not merely a form of entertainment. As I suggest in the next chapter, speculating about scenarios involving the loss of one's position, the loss of stability, and the failure to anticipate and prepare for accidents which could create such a loss is an activity actually practiced by two seemingly diverse groups of individuals—speculative fiction writers and intelligence analysts. In many ways, the narratives being created at present (as well as those created in the past) which attempt to anticipate and prepare for the loss of security are quite similar—whether they are found on bookshelves or in the policy papers. The stories—and the reasons why they have been created—may in fact be quite similar. For that reason, they are of interest to theorists of international relations.

NOTES

1. Theodore Steinberg, *Acts of God: The Unnatural History of Natural Disaster in America* (Oxford: Oxford University Press, 2000).

2. For more on the Biblical apocalypse, which will not be considered in depth in this work, please see Jason Dittmer and Tristan Sturm, eds., *Mapping the End Times: American Evangelical Geopolitics ad Apocalyptic Visions* (Surrey, UK: Ashgate, 2010).

3. Kathleen Stewart and Susan Harding, "Bad Endings: American Apocalypse," *Annual Review of Anthropology* 28 (1999): 285.

4. Edward Paice, *Wrath of God: The Great Lisbon Earthquake of 1755* (New York: Quercus, 2010): 257.

5. This is the argument made by many Russian studies experiments that have attempted to explain the collapse of the Soviet Union. Celeste Wallender, for example, argues that the collapse of the Soviet Union was inevitable and built into the DNA of the institutions which comprised the Soviet Union—since institutions like the Communist Party and central planning were untenable in the long run. Celeste Wallender, "Western Policy and the Demise of the Soviet Union," *Journal of Cold War Studies* 5 (2007): 137–77.

6. Buzan is quoted in Columba Peoples and Nick Vaughan-Williams, *Critical Security Studies: An Introduction* (London: Routledge, 2010): 23.

7. Jim Crace, *The Pesthouse* (London: Nan A. Talese, 2007)

8. For more on this point, see Eugene A. Rosa, "Metatheoretical Foundations for Post-Normal Risk," *Journal of Risk Research* 1(1998): 15–44.

9. Kai Erikson, *Everything in Its Path: Destruction of Community in the Buffalo Creek Flood* (New York: Simon and Schuster, 1976).

10. Lee Clarke, *Worst Cases: Terror and Catastrophe in the Popular Imagination* (Chicago: The University of Chicago Press, 2006).

11. Rosa, "Metatheoretical Foundations," 21.

12. See William C. Adams, "Whose Lives Count? TV Coverage of Natural Disasters," *Journal of Communication* 36 (1986): 113–22.

13. Lulu Rodriguez and Lee Suman, "Factors Affecting the Amplification or Attenuation of Public Worry and Dread about Bioterrorist Attacks," *Homeland Security Affairs* 6 (2010): 1–16.

14. Ian Savage, "An Empirical Investigation into the Effect of Psychological Perceptions on the Willingness to Pay to Reduce Risk," *Journal of Risk and Uncertainty* 6 (1992): 75–90.

15. The question, however, is to what degree the assigning of normal levels of danger and the propensity to think in terms of norms is a function of Western types of analysis and rationality. Those who come from different academic traditions might not view the problem in quite the same way.

16. Ronald Inglehart, "Globalization and Postmodern Values," *Washington Quarterly* 23 (1999): 215–28.

17. Robert David Sack, *Human Territoriality: Its Theory and History* (Cambridge: Cambridge University Press, 1986).

18. Richard Stuart Olson and Vincent T. Gawronski, "From Disaster Event to Political Crisis: A '5C+A' Framework for Analysis," *International Studies Perspectives* 11 (2010): 208.

19. Craig Calhoun, "A World of Emergencies: Fear, Intervention, and the Limits of Cosmopolitan Order," *Canadian Review of Sociology and Anthropology* 41 (2004).

20. Jim Crace, *The Pesthouse* (London: Nan A. Talese, 2007): 25.

21. Juan Jose Lopez-Ibor, "What Is a Disaster," in Juan Jose Lopez-Ibor, Georgios Christodoulou, Mario Maj, Norman Sartorius, and Ahmed Okasha, eds., *Disasters and Mental Health* (New York: John Wiley and Sons, 2005): 4.

22. Ibrahim Mohamed Shaluf, "An Overview on Disasters," *Disaster Prevention and Management* 16 (2007): 687.

23. Shaluf, "An Overview," 688.

24. Rodriguez and Suman, "Factors Affecting," 1.

25. Henrike Viehrig, "Mass Media and Catastrophe Prevention: How to Avoid the Crisis after the Crisis," in I. Apostol, W. G. Coldewey, D. L. Barry, eds., *Risk Assessment as a Basis for the Forecast and Prevention of Catastrophes* (Brussels: IOS Press, 2008): 258–67.

26. Here my thinking has been shaped by my reading of Kai Erikson's powerful analysis of the Buffalo Creek disaster, *Everything in Its Path: Destruction of Community in the Buffalo Creek Flood* (New York: Simon and Schuster, 1978).

27. Paice, 257.

28. Judith Butler, *Precarious Life: The Powers of Mourning and Violence* (London: Verso, 2004): 13.

29. Steinberg, *Acts of God*.

30. A. Z. Keller, H. C. Wilson, and A. Al-Madhari, "A Proposed Disaster Scale and Associated Model for Calculating Return Period for Disasters of Given Magnitudes," *Disaster Prevention and Management* 1 (1992): 215–28.

31. R. B. J. Walker, *After the Globe, Before the World* (New York: Routledge, 2010).

32. Robert M. A. Crawford, "International Relations as an Academic Discipline: If It's Good for America, Is It Good for the World?" in Robert Crawford and Darryl S. Jarvis, eds., *International Relations—Still an American Social Science?* (New York: SUNY Press, 2001): 1–23.

33. Kim Nossal, "'Tales that Textbooks Tell': Ethnocentricity and Diversity in American Introductions to International Relations," in Robert Crawford and Darryl Jarvis, eds., *International Relations—Still an American Social Science?* (New York: SUNY Press, 2001): 168–87.

34. Stijn Joye, "News Discourses on Distant Suffering: A Critical Discourse Analysis of the 2003 SARS Outbreak," *Discourse and Society* 21 (2010): 586–601.

35. Lloyd Etheridge, "Is American Foreign Policy Ethnocentric?" (Conference Paper for Annual Meeting of American Political Science Association, 1988): 5–7.

36. Nossal, 192–93.

37. Simon Reid-Henry, "Spaces of Security and Development: An Alternative Mapping of the Security-Development Nexus." *Security Dialogue* 42 (2011): 97–104.

38. Anna Leander, "The Power to Construct International Security: On the Significance of the Emergence of Private Military Companies" (London: Conference Papers of London School of Economics "Facets of Power in International Relations," 2004).

39. A. J. Groome and Peter Mandaville, "Hegemony and Autonomy in International Relations: The Continental Experience," in Robert M. A. Crawford and Darryl S. J. Jarvis, eds., *International Relations—Still an American Social Science?* (New York: SUNY Press, 2010): 151–67.

40. Mikkel Rasmussen, "It Sounds like a Riddle": Security Studies, the War on Terror and Risk, *Millennium* 33, no. 2 (2004): 381–95.

41. Ivor Neumann, "Naturalizing Geography: Harry Potter and the Realms of Muggles, Magic Folks, and Giants," in Iver Neumann and Daniel Nexon, eds., *Harry Potter and International Relations* (New York: Rowman and Littlefield, 2006): 157.

42. Neumann and Nexon, "Introduction: Harry Potter and the Study of World Politics," in Nexon and Neumann, eds., *Harry Potter*, 18. See also Cynthia Enloe's comments on "silences" in international relations, quoted in Jutta Weldes, "Popular Culture, Science Fiction and World Politics," in Jutta Weldes, ed., *To Seek out New Worlds: Exploring Links between Popular Culture Science Fiction and Politics* (New York: Palgrave MacMillan: 2003): 5.

43. This term is taken from Neumann and Nexon, in "Introduction: Harry Potter and the Study of World Politics," in Nexon and Neumann, eds., *Harry Potter*, 12.

44. Neta Crawford makes this point in her essay, "Feminist Future: Science Fiction, Utopia and the Art of Possibilities in World Politics," quoted in Jutta Weldes, "Popular Culture, Science Fiction and World Politics," in Jutta Weldes, ed., *To Seek out New Worlds: Exploring Links between Popular Culture, Science Fiction and Politics* (New York: Palgrave MacMillan: 2003): 19.

45. John Lee, "Understanding and Preserving the Foundations of America's Advantage in Asia" (Washington, DC: Hudson Institute, 2009). www.hudson.org

46. Wang Jisi, "The Logic of American Hegemony" (December 10, 2003). www.ou.edu/uschina/harmony.pdf

47. Allan Noble, "US Hegemony, Global (In)Stability, and IR Theory." http://asrudiancenter.wordpress.com/2008/11/26/us-hegemony-global-instability-and-ir-theory-2/

48. Chris Cleave, "Too Soon to Write the Post-9/11 Novel?" *New York Times* (September 12, 2005). www.nytimes.com/2005/09/12/opinion/12iht-edcleave.html

49. "Reclusive novelist Cormac McCarthy gives first interview in 13 years." (July 8, 2005). www.seattlepi.com/ae/books/article/Reclusive-novelist-Cormac-McCarthy-gives-first

50. Martin Amis, "Interview with Jonathan Curiel," *San Francisco Chronicle Sunday Review* (November 4, 2001): 2. www.martinamisweb.com

51. Tishani Doshi, "Laughter in the Dark: Interview with Martin Amis," *Hindu Literary Review* (October 6, 2002). Retrieved from Martin Amisweb: www.martinamisweb.com/interviews-files/doshi_interview. pdf)

52. Anis Shivani, "Announcing the Death of the Post-9/11 Novel." *Huffington Post* (April 5, 2010). www.huffingtonpost.com/anis-shivani/announcing-the-death-of-t-b-525805.html

53. Joyce Davidson, Liz Bondi, and Mick Smith, *Emotional Geographies* (Hampshire, GB: Ashgate Publishing, Ltd., 2007).

54. For more on safety and threat perception see Paul Pillar, "American Perceptions of Terrorism in the post-9/11 Decade," *CTC Sentinel* (September 26, 2011). www.ctc.usa.edu/posts/

55. Don DeLillo, *Falling Man* (New York: Scribner, 2007): 189.

56. Olson and Gawronski, "From Disaster," 189.

57. Ibid.

58. It should be noted here that not all utopian literature requires an apocalyptic event. There are other ways for the narrator to take us to utopia—through stepping through a wardrobe to Narnia, for example, or off of Platform Nine and Three Quarters to Hogwarts. In the Victorian utopian novel, *News from Nowhere*, it is a dream sequence or a feat of time travel which places the narrator firmly in the new scene. However, in these instances, the utopia can exist side by side, simultaneously in time with the "real world." Only the post-apocalyptic scenario requires the destruction of the previous world.

59. Robert Doran and Rene Girard, "Apocalyptic Thinking after 9/11: An Interview with Rene Girard," *SubStance* 37, no. 1 (2005): 25.

60. Martin Amis, *The Second Plane: September 11: Terror and Boredom* (New York: Vintage International, 2009), 3.

61. Keller, "A Proposed Disaster," 223.

62. Susan Bowers, "Beloved and the New Apocalypse," in *Toni Morrison's Fiction: Contemporary Criticism*, ed. David Middleton (London: Routledge, 1996): 210.

63. Joshua Kurzlantzick, "The World Is Bumpy," *The New Republic* (December 9, 2009): 19.

64. DeLillo, *Falling Man*, 3.

65. Justin Cronin, *The Passage* (New York: Ballantine Books, 2010): 229.

66. Aaron Wildavsky and Mary Douglas, *Risk and Culture: An Essay on the Selection of Technological and Environmental Dangers* (Berkeley: University of California Press, 1983).

67. E. M. Forster, *The Machine Stops* (Amazon. com: Kindle Edition).

68. Inglehart, 1999.

❷

CATASTROPHE NOVELS AND PREDICTION

As noted in the previous chapter, certain time periods have produced an unusually large outpouring of speculative fiction—including scenarios in which disaster is narrowly diverted as well as those in which disaster prevails. Nations which produce this product have much in common—they are undergoing periods of rapid modernization and industrialization with accompanying rapid social changes. They are also undergoing periods of outward growth in which the nations are spilling beyond their own borders, exporting their products, their values, and their cultures. On the one hand, the process of growth and change appears to be inexorable and incapable of being stopped. On the other hand, states have always anticipated threats to themselves and their agendas. Thus, catastrophe novels in particular have focused on naming, identifying, and creating consensus regarding the potential hazards to that growth.

Indeed, the emphasis on identifying and naming threats to the state which provides the basis for catastrophe novels is the same emphasis that one finds in intelligence analysis. In this chapter, I take up the task of unpacking the relationship between intelligence analysis—aimed at identifying threats to the growing state—and speculative fiction analysis—which similarly imagines threats to the growing state. As we shall see, the two types of analysis share common grounds both methodologically and epistemologically.

INTELLIGENCE AND SPECULATION: SIMILARITIES IN SCOPE

In carrying out speculations regarding future political, economic, and social trends, today's science fiction writer shares much common epistemological and methodological ground with an intelligence analyst. Particularly in the years since the end of the Cold War, there has been a drawing together of the functions of the creative writer and the intelligence analyst—as intelligence analysts seek to widen the scope of their inquiry, in the process becoming more imaginative and creative. Military planners and intelligence analysts now admit that in making new knowledge including forecasts about the future, they find themselves engaging in conceptual stretching as they create new hypothetical scenarios which are nonetheless based on realistic, probabilistic equations about what could happen—although it hasn't happened yet.[1] The evolving field of so-called "futures intelligence" has been defined as "a subdiscipline in which analysts look ten or twenty years ahead and imagine what some aspect of the world will look like at that time and what the strategic environment is likely to be."[2]

Intelligence analysts and the authors of speculative fiction share a similar job description—since both consider matters of causality, prediction, and the organization of bias. Both hone in on so-called "rare events"—defined as "an extreme, deliberate act of violence, destruction or socioeconomic disruption, such as an attack of 9/11 scale or greater."[3] Both groups use similar sources—including demographic trends, environmental trends, and political-military trends to create narratives about possible future threats in the short or long term. Both groups start with a real-world concern and then forecast how that event might play out in the future—what its ramifications might be for individuals, a society, or the nation. Both catastrophe novels and intelligence scenarios aim to hew closely to existing reality, taking few speculative turns, since the overall emphasis is on the creation of a product which is highly probable. The theme is of disaster (as defined in the introduction to this work) diverted in the nick of time—rather than of apocalypse.[4] In addition, as the analyst Darko Suvin notes, the "audience" for speculative fiction consists of many of the same individuals who read other types of intelligence speculation products. It includes policy analysts, government bureaucrats, and high-level military planners and decision makers.[5]

In short, both intelligence analysts and catastrophe novelists identify hazards or dangers—where hazards are defined as "conditions, events or circumstances that could lead to or contribute to an unplanned or undesirable event." In short, the equation which catastrophe novelists are concerned with is:

$$\text{Hazard} \times \text{Probability of occurrence} \rightarrow \text{accident}.$$

Here both catastrophe novelists and intelligence planners aim to identify the hazards which might lead to accident, and to lower the probability that the outcome occurs. In this situation, an "accident" is defined merely as an unplanned event which may or may not result in injury or property damage.[6]

Both intelligence planners and catastrophe novelists thus agree that accidents are preventable, not inevitable, and that mitigating or preventing accidents is both a worthwhile and achievable goal. They also agree that accidents which occur are largely the result of organization or human error caused by either unsafe acts of commission or omission. In other words, it is worthwhile to identify the presence of hazard since hazard is a necessary but not sufficient condition in creating the accident. One cannot have an accident without a hazard, but the presence of hazard alone is insufficient to lead to accident.[7]

This is an important distinction because the recognition of hazard as a necessary but insufficient condition for creating accident places an analyst squarely within one of two competing paradigms regarding how one views the 'accident' in human history. Those who feel that accident is largely a result of human error combined with hazard, rather than a product of contingency, are said to subscribe to the "High Reliability Theory" school of disaster management.[8] Proponents of this approach do not, thus, use or recognize the validity of the phrase "An Act of God." Rather, HRT theorists believe that accidents have rational causes and that the goal of preventing accident is worthwhile.

In contrast, those who subscribe to the "normal accident" school of disaster management do *not* accept the premise that disaster is always and everywhere preventable and rational.[9] Rather, proponents of this school believe that certain types of highly complex, technological processes may almost have failure "built into" their models. To some degree, one thus regards the eventual failure of this technology as inevitable. In this situation, accident is neither preventable nor reversible. And in such a situation, the exercise of blame-seeking carried out after an accident seems almost pointless, since ultimately the list of causes may come to include: the technological equivalent of a "fog of war" which made decision-making while the accident was occurring chaotic and irrational; a cascade effect in which many interlinked small decisions ultimately led to system failure; or a rare and unanticipated event which had unexpected consequences. For that reason, the scenario which relies upon and considers the normal accident in its speculation is the apocalyptic novel, while the scenario based on high reliability theory is a catastrophe novel.[10]

Thus, for example, every apocalyptic novel written in the 1960s and 1970s which began from the premise that nuclear war had occurred rested on the assumption that nuclear war had either been deliberately instigated or that some form of "accidental nuclear war" had occurred. Here, both groups of novelists implicitly incur an intellectual debt to the analyst Scott Sagan, who examined nuclear weapons from the "normal accident" perspective in his work *The Limits of Safety*.[11] In the present day, one can see how Cormac McCarthy's work *The Road* relies on the idea of accidental and inevitable nuclear war as the starting point for his own novel. In this work, the reader is informed only that: "The clocks stopped at 1:17. A long shear of light and then a series of low concussions."[12]

Here the reader does not need to know how or why the weapons which eventually burned the countryside and rendered the world uninhabitable were launched. Rather, the reader is invited to embrace the understanding that weapons, once invented, will inevitably and always *be* launched. This understanding is perhaps best illustrated in what many regard as the ultimate apocalyptic novel, Walter Miller's *A Canticle for Leibowitz*, written in 1959. In this novel, where the action stretches over a period of several thousand years, the reader is invited to imagine that following an accidental launch of nuclear weapons in the 1950s, most of the population of America (and the world) is destroyed and civilization is set back thousands of years. However, mankind eventually prevails, reinventing automobiles and airplanes and even space travel. Alas, due to the inevitability of accidental nuclear war, mankind manages to achieve the pinnacle of technological superiority only to once again destroy itself two thousand years later with the same weapons.[13]

That is, only catastrophe novelists have as their goal the identification of hazard and the identification of risks likely to increase the probability that a hazard could become an accident. In short, the catastrophe novel is (like an intelligence scenario) in essence an exercise in the construction and manipulation of hazard perceptions. The catastrophe novel (or its author) seeks to construct a new hazard or to change how one is perceived. Here, the goal is to ask the question: Are we safe enough? and to answer the question with a "no."

Here, the catastrophe novel's emphasis on identifying purported hazards and mobilizing a consensus towards the addressing of hazard rests on a number of assumptions about disaster, to continue the themes of the previous chapter. First, the catastrophe novel implicitly rests on the assumption that it is the state's responsibility to both predict and prepare for hazard, as well as the assumption that the state at the time of writing is doing an inadequate job. Always and everywhere, the message of the catastrophe novel is: We are unprepared, but we can make a choice to be better prepared. Thus, the catastrophe novel does not address or consider the possibility that hazard can be constructed, created, or manipulated. Rather, like the intelligence scenario, the catastrophe novel is written from a positivist perspective which tells the reader that "this is a real, genuine, existing hazard that has been identified, measured, and found to be a significant threat."

Thus, like intelligence analysts, catastrophe novelists engage in imagining the consequences of choices taken and not taken by policy makers, as well as the consequences of information scarcity and perfect information. In doing so, novelists rely on the creation of conditional clauses—just as political analysts do in the creation of game theoretic scenarios. The catastrophe novelist thus follows a similar methodology to that of a counterfactual historian like Philip Tetlock[14] who seeks to identify critical junctures through identifying decisions which were path dependent and which set up chains of events. Once historians have identified these critical junctures, they then consider the possibility that decision makers could have taken a different path and as a result created a different future. That is, in thinking about the future—and the existence of multiple, possible futures—analysts and writers both create speculative chains of events.

As Jaeger, Renn, Rosa, and Webber point out, risky situations usually spark the creation of new and novel solutions to problems. They describe how when a decision or situation is framed as being risky (as in a catastrophe novel), it creates a new decision set. It raises some decision options while excluding others. A risky situation can thus be seen as presenting both threats and opportunities—because the possibility of danger therefore allows the decision-maker to consider some options that might not have been considered acceptable in other situations.[15] (Here, one only needs to consider how many more options were available to the U.S. military on September 12, 2001, than were available on September 10 of that same year.)

In writing counterfactual history, analysts aim to "hold everything else constant," while examining the effects of only one seemingly minor decision which nonetheless has the ability to change the course of history.[16] Thus, the emphasis is on agency over structure, with narratives which emphasize both characters making decisions regarding how to cope with adverse events and the state and its agencies responding to real-world events. In both cases, the writer's aim is to construct a tight narrative which can be followed easily and tested thoroughly. The aim is to create a narrative with the highest probability of actually occurring through creating a decision tree which branches off only once rather than a number of times. Here, both groups are interested in the ways in which the scenario can be used to predict the future—in order to prevent and prepare for unanticipated events.[17] The narrative is thus a way of anticipating and controlling for strategic surprise. This is the foundational agenda of both intelligence planners and catastrophe novelists. The catastrophe novel is thus a shared product produced by individuals in the literary, military, and intelligence communities—whose identities may frequently overlap.[18]

Speculative fiction in particular—as opposed to fantasy fiction—rests on the establishment of what Aumann terms "substantive conditional clauses."[19] A straightforward conditional clause rests on conditions which have the possibility of being true without remarking on whether they are or are not true. For example, "If I was a mechanic, I could fix my car" is a conditional clause. The person speaking is not either a mechanic or not a mechanic. Rather, he is simply laying out the conditions which could lead to his fixing his car—whether or not the conditions are met. They are theoretical in the sense that they have not occurred.

Conditional clauses, by definition, allow for the construction of multiple possible worlds. The statement "If I was a mechanic, I could fix my car" creates one possible world in which the subject is a mechanic and is able to fix his car, as well as an alternate possible world in which the subject is not a mechanic and is not able to fix his car. Both outcomes could conceivably happen, though they may have different probabilities of happening. But in either case—whether the writer is or is not a mechanic—the series of clauses leads to an end state which is possible. The reader is thus asked to behave as though the events being described have actually come about. Paul Alkon refers to the end state created in a science fiction novel thus as a state of "counterfeit verisimilitude"—since the endpoint of the story is not a mere fantasy, but is rather meant to be taken as a new reality which is treated as "real" since it rests on existing assumptions about science and society. Although it has not happened, it is not *merely* hypothetical because it *could* happen. It is not scientifically impossible.[20] Here, the illusion that the world being described is "real" is built throughout the novels by the author's making reference to such documents as fictionalized conference reports, newspaper reports, telegrams and correspondence, as well as e-mails. That is, in the matter of a scientific researcher, the author provides "empirical evidence" for the events which are said to have occurred in the novel, though the empirical evidence itself is fabricated or fictionalized.

A *substantive* conditional clause is seen as one which is logically or scientifically possible, and which has the potential to occur. Aumann offers the example: "If I push my pawn, the black queen will be trapped"—in a game of chess.[21] In contrast, if the writer was to say "If I were magic, I could cast a spell and fix my car"—then he would have moved away from the theoretical to the hypothetical or fictional, because he is describing a set of conditions which are scientifically and physically impossible. Thus an outcome in which the mechanic is magical and is thus able to fix his car could be described as an impossible or fantasy world—since embracing this ending involves violating the possible conditions associated with the game. In a fantasy novel, the army might thus fight off invaders by using magic—but in a catastrophe novel, this is not an option. There are limits to what may be imagined in a catastrophe novel.

Finally, substantive conditional clauses may be either regular or "subjunctive." Here, a subjunctive conditional clause is essentially a counterfactual statement—which describes something which could have happened (it had the potential to do so) but did not.[22] A subjunctive conditional clause might be: "If I had been a mechanic, I could have fixed my car" in which the action is possible but where it did not occur—either because the conditions were possible but not present, or because a choice was not made.

Both types of substantive conditional clauses—regular and subjunctive—rest on the assumption that the decisions being described are strategic interactions in which one player's choices will affect the reactions of another player. Thus, the catastrophe novel might set up a conditional clause such as "If the United States or Great Britain neglects the security of its harbors, then another player will respond by carrying out a particular type of strike."[23] The subjunctive conditional clause would thus read: "If the U.S. had not neglected the security of its harbors (or if it had been aware of the threat to the security of its harbors), then the terrorists would not have responded by destroying Norfolk, Virginia." Again, both outcomes have some probability of being true and both are theoretically possible—but only one can occur at a time.

As Kray et al. note, counterfactuals are most likely when potential mutations to a sequence of events are salient and potential alternative worlds are close in time and space. That is, they suggest that it is easier to think counterfactually about what might have happened had you not missed the plane by ten minutes—than it is to think counterfactually about what might have happened had you missed the plane by several hours.[24] Similarly, the catastrophe novel is more like a counterfactual experiment than its cousin the apocalyptic novel—which requires speculation in the long term as well as the short term. The intelligence planning window also does not extend beyond fifteen years—as this is seen as the time horizon beyond which analysts are unable to speculate.[25] The emphasis is thus on the events which transpire immediately after the threat materializes—rather than on how society or its government are changed in the long run as a result of these events.

Catastrophe and Reality

In advancing the claim that speculative fiction is of utility to those in the policy world who also think about the future, it is important to introduce three related but discrete ideas: possibility, probability, and plausibility.

The catastrophe novelist, in his work, makes the claim that the events he is describing are *possible*—in the sense that they are capable of occurring. That is, to imagine these events occurring does not require violating any known laws of science. (In other words, a scenario which envisioned a bomb in a stadium—like the British novelist Chris Cleave described in his novel *Incendiary* in 2004[26]—is possible, because it relies on technology which is already invented. In contrast, a novel which described an attack by aliens, vampires, or Godzilla is not possible, since such things are not known to exist (or are known to not exist).

Furthermore, the catastrophe novelist makes the claim that the events he is describing are *probable*. That is, he foresees that there is at least a reasonable likelihood that the events he describes will actually occur. It may only be a 5 percent probability—but the probability is not infinitesimally miniscule. That is, he is not predominantly concerned with what military planners call "rare events" or "extremely low probability catastrophic events." He is justified in worrying about another terrorist attack on the United States, for example, because the odds indicate that such things do happen. On the other hand, he is not likely to write about a meteor strike or a tsunami with a wall of water thousands of feet high swamping New York City, since this is improbable.

Finally, the catastrophe novelist makes the claim that the events he is described are *plausible*. Here, the philosopher of science Wesley Salmon has distinguished between two "types" of probabilities. He notes that when scientists (or intelligence planners) talk about whether something is "probable," they're actually referring to the relative frequency with which a similar event has happened in the past (1 in 10,000 times or 1 in 1,000,000 times) which has then been calculated to give the likelihood that such an event would occur in the future. Here, relative frequency as probability is assumed to be a "clean" or neutral measure of the likelihood that something will occur.[27]

The other type of probability, however, is more subjective. (This is the quality which I refer to as plausibility). Salmon describes subjective probability as resting on degrees of belief or strengths of conviction.[28] In other words, it refers to the ability of the planner or thinker to place what he knows about the perceived relative frequency of an event in a larger context and decide how it applies to him. Salmon notes that personal probabilities (or subjective probabilities) can change—either because one's beliefs about the subject are incoherent, as the result of a new idea, or in light of new evidence. Here, one can draw a parallel between Salmon's thinking and the political scientist Bruce Bueno de Mesquita's inclusion of the variable of "salience" in his decision-making models. Bueno de Mesquita speaks of salience as being the amount of personal investment that the analyst has in achieving a certain outcome (how much the outcome matters to him).[29] Similarly, we could argue that the decision maker's personal investment in achieving a particular outcome might affect his assessment of personal probabilities. In addition, one might suggest that recent changes in his environment might affect this assessment of probabilities (i.e., if he has recently read about genetic advances in curing disease, he might assess the plausibility of such a speculative fiction scenario higher than he would have one week ago.)

That is, personal probability or plausibility is a dynamic measure which is socially constructed. Our assessments of the plausibility of a particular political event (or our personal probabilities) may differ depending on our social world. Clearly the British in 1909 were willing to buy into the possibility that the Germans might be planning an attack against them—such a threat scenario was plausible. But other threat scenarios—like the idea that the Americans were going to come across the sea to seek revenge for having been colonized in the 1700s—might be less plausible. The grounds for deeming a scenario plausible might be found in newspaper editorials and political writings at the time, as well as past patterns of behavior by the actors in the story.

What is important to bear in mind, however, is that in comparison to other types of speculative fiction—utopian fiction, dystopian fiction, and apocalyptic fiction—catastrophe novels are the only ones that meet all three criteria: probability, possibility, and plausibility.

Methods of Prediction

The logic of the catastrophe novel rests on a process which economists refer to as "backward induction." In essence, the writer begins with a particular final outcome. He then goes back and in essence recreates or imagines the chain of decisions which led to this particular outcome. The reader is thus asked to consider both the choices by players which will lead to the undesired outcome, as well as the choices which the player would have had to make in order to avoid the undesirable outcome.[30] Similarly, Noel Henderson writes in a training manual for U.S. military officers learning how to write futures intelligence scenarios:

> The process of counterfactual reasoning has three stages. . . . First, one must establish the particular way in which the alternate possibility comes to life (i. e. develop its 'back story'). Second, one must evaluate the events that occur between the time of the alternate possibility and the time for which one is considering its consequences. And third, one must examine the possible consequences of the alternate possibility's back-story and the events that follow it.[31]

In other words, whether one is reading a catastrophe novel or an intelligence scenario, the process is the same. The reader is asked to consider a series of counterfactual suppositions having to do with choices which were not made but which might have been made. (That is, they were possible). The writer in essence goes back and reconstructs the subjunctive clauses and conditions which would have to have been fulfilled in order to avoid the possible negative outcome. The condition which writers rely on in using backward induction to set up these chains of strategic interactions is perfect information (or what Samet terms, "hypothetical knowledge," since the decision-maker essentially goes back and asks what he would have done, had he had all the information). The end state is thus seen as predetermined unless certain assumptions or conditions of the game are altered.

The purpose behind the writer's creation of the fiction is thus the idea that "If I see the end of the decision tree and all of the strategic actions that led to this outcome, then I can make different choices to prevent it." (In disaster planning, this is referred to as the "accident trajectory." If one plans backward from the not inevitable accident, one can then build into the model a series of safeguards which should ideally prevent the accident from ever happening. Reason describes this as a "Swiss cheese model"—in which there are a variety of security holes identified. Ideally, the accident would never happen unless all of the holes or weaknesses in the security lined up.[32] An accident thus results from either unsafe acts of commission or omission. It is not merely random.[33]) Here, what is altered is the amount of information available.

The first decision point in the game is thus seen as the mistake—where player A acted without having full information about his own weaknesses, the costs they would add, or about his opponent's intentions. He made the wrong choice and as a result unleashed a cascade of decisions which led to the undesired outcome. In doing so, the novel implicitly attributes blame for the specific catastrophe—labeling it the result of poor policy planning by an individual or a group due to imperfect information or an intelligence failure. This type of novel usually leads to straightforward policy prescriptions—including the possibility of hardening targets, spending more money for the military, or placing more emphasis on intelligence. Because the target or blame in a catastrophe novel is so obvious, there is little room for subtlety or deeper analysis on the part of either the author or the reader. For example, the recent novel by William Forstchen, *One Second After*,[34] allows the reader to think about whether the Pentagon is doing enough to prepare for an electromagnetic pulse attack—but it does not explicitly take on the larger issue of whether economic interdependence renders the modern state more vulnerable to collapse. It also does not ask why another state might want to attack the United States or what its reasons or agenda might be.

The game is thus seen as predetermined or leading towards a particular end—unless player A changes the chain of moves which he makes. The catastrophe—or final outcome—is thus interesting as an end state to be avoided rather than explored. The interesting part of the story, in contrast, is the actions of player A, the decisions made, and the quality of the strategic interactions.

The author's purposes in writing the catastrophe novel are thus: to add to the information available to player A (through enlightening him about his opponent's intentions and decision-making process, or through enlightening him about a weakness of his own which he has failed to perceive); to change the decisions made by player A as well as the interactions between player A and B that result and finally to change the conduct of the game (though not the game itself) to change the game so as to avoid the undesired outcome. The catastrophe novel thus lays out what Tetlock and Lebow would term a "close call counterfactual"— a situation in which history could have been different if one variable had been changed, even slightly.[35]

However, Wagar points out that the catastrophe novel can also err in the warnings which it gives. If the writer decides that a particular outcome is likely and focuses all of his energy on warning individuals and officials against actions which might lead to that outcome and the outcome does not occur, then the novel merely becomes a somewhat entertaining story about something which did not in fact occur. Here, Wagar points to fiction writers in the 1920s who were obsessed with the possibility of a poison gas attack. Despite their many warnings about its dangers, the scenario which they envisioned did not come to pass. Instead, Wagar points out that it was not the major weapon used in World War II, nor did it play any significant role. And despite the warnings which writers gave about the dangers of what we have come to call Mutually Assured Destruction, Wagar points out that it is impossible to trace the non-use of nuclear weapons to the writings of novelists.[36]

The problem here is methodological. While it is useful to consider the correlations between actions and their effects, it is less clear how we would go about considering the correlations between actions and their noneffects or between nonactions and their noneffects. This is particularly true when the subject of the query is an individual-level question such as: How might decision-making have been altered if a particular decision-maker had been made aware of the possible outcomes of choosing action A or action B? While one might claim that "had the decision maker made a different choice, a different outcome might have occurred," in point of fact the outcome did not occur and therefore it is difficult to "prove" that Action A would have led to that outcome, or that the decision maker in point of fact engaged in this calculus. One cannot actually create a counterfactual "proof" to show why something did not occur.[37]

If the writer thus benefits from writing a catastrophe novel through having the ability to anticipate strategic surprise, to imagine that he has full information, and to recommend changes in decision points as a result, the question still remains: how does the reader benefit from indulging in the occasional Saturday afternoon catastrophe novel? This particular form of story asks something more from the reader than merely that he follows the plot and keeps the characters straight in his mind. As the examples provided above indicate, the particular mental processes which individuals undertake in considering "what ifs" and "might have beens" are actually highly complex. Kray et al. argue that particular skill sets and practices within the brain are involved in "doing counterfactuals"—and that pondering such scenarios can often force the thinker to change the way he weights explanatory variables in his own mind, as well as to reconsider the ways in which variables are interrelated.[38] That is, the creation of alternate trajectories as well as the establishment of the preconditions which might lead to them is a way of forcing planners to break out of a mold in which they see only one possible future. David Muller, a government intelligence analyst, thus writes optimistically that the identification of multiple future scenarios and the existence of conflicting views about what the future might look like is the sign of a healthy intelligence community—since it suggests that each group that creates a scenario may start with slightly different assumptions and biases.[39] The creation of multiple future scenarios thus acts as a "check" against each group's biases by making them aware of the existence of multiple, conflicting future scenarios. Thus, both writers and intelligence analysts accept—to some degree—that the future is wide open. While it is possible to speculate about one future scenario, and to make an argument regarding path dependency factors that will bring it about, it is also necessary to accept that there are multiple other possible future scenarios that can be created. Here, having a counterfactual mind-set allows writers and readers to become aware of the underlying assumptions on which their reasoning is based which they might not have previously queried. In addition, according to Kray et al. using a counterfactual mind-set may cause participants to think more critically through causing them to be skeptical about the dominant hypothesis. In thinking about what might have happened or what could have happened, readers find themselves querying the chains of events which previously might have been seen as predetermined.

Much current international relations theory rests on the assumption that the state is a permanent feature of international life and that the American state in particular is invulnerable. Counterfactual scenarios help make us aware that this may not be true, and may thus cause analysts to initiate a search for security weaknesses—even though it may be hard to believe that a unipolar superpower has any. Indeed, some suggest that it was actually the scenarios regarding security weaknesses suggested in British catastrophe novels or "invasion literature" written in the late 1800s that were the impetus for the creation of Britain's intelligence services MI5 and MI6 in 1909. Thus, reading apocalyptic novels can serve to make readers more aware of relationships as well as more aware of the connections between variables—as we ponder the likelihood of events including global economic collapse, the likely course of pandemics, and the ways in which a state might erode.

Limits of Prediction

However, like those who use game theory in making political and economic predictions, catastrophe novels likewise operate in a tightly constrained decision space where they are both bound by clear rules in creating their scenarios. An economist who wants to theorize about how consumer home prices might affect consumer's spending of their disposable income cannot just create a free-form argument. Rather, he begins with assumptions about how consumers derive and measure utility and how they evaluate competing choices within those parameters. He operates within a positivist framework which assumes that it is possible to measure utility and attaches value to choices, as well as the assumption that the consumer is a rational actor who is capable of evaluating and assigning utility to his choices. Similarly, catastrophe novels implicitly use a positivist framework based on the assumption that citizens will behave in certain ways—hoarding food, fighting for survival, and attempting to take the belongings and territory of others.

The catastrophe novel—in addition to being positivist—is realist. In every case, the novel contains a thematic focus on the loss of territory in general and strategic territory in particular. Factors which are constants in the catastrophe novel include actor and state preferences: Each actor prizes survival and is willing to engage in conflict to guarantee that survival. On an individual level, survival may be defined as food and goods, and on a state level, the preference for survival may be exhibited as a preference for territorial expansion. Each actor is motivated to increase his likelihood of survival, even if doing so necessitates engaging in conflict with opponents. Each actor values the payoffs received that increase his likelihood of survival over the likelihood of being injured or killed. A state "wins" the conflict if it keeps or enlarges its territory, while it "loses" if it is invaded or toppled by another state. The constants of goals, motivations, and payoffs are what render state and individual behavior both predictable and constant. One's opponents are presumed to have the same preferences that you do. Thus, the options available in the game are limited to those solution sets which might appear in a traditional realist game theoretical model. Thus, for example, we cannot quite conceive of a Cold War catastrophe novel in which Kennedy makes a deal with Khrushchev and agrees to cooperate, or perhaps rethinks his own preferences as he gets to know his opponent better. No matter how many iterations of conflict may occur in a catastrophe novel, the game does not evolve, nor do player preferences or behaviors. No one "learns" in a catastrophe novel in the psychological sense of evolving preferences or strategies. One only "learns" that it's always a good idea to guard your harbors, mistrust your neighbors, and make sure you have a lot of ammunition.

Because of the explicitly realist emphasis on territory, this type of literature does not allow for a critical analysis of the state or of international relations. Here, early English stories aimed at pointing to the strategic vulnerability of England's ports and port cities, while American versions pointed out flaws in the nation's air and naval defenses. But in these tales, if the nation or empire can be said to be lost or destroyed, it is predominantly a matter of physical destruction—rather than a larger sort of cultural or ideological destruction. The author assumes that the invader wants to control the empire because there is something desirable or useful to be had in doing so. It is a utilitarian approach. It does, not, however go deeper (nor does it allow the reader to do so) in interrogating the meaning and utility of territorial expansion. These works also do not interrogate notions of patriotism or citizenship. Rather, they tend to be dichotomous—painting those who defend the state as good, while the invaders and those traitors who help them are bad. There is no room for ambiguity in these tales.

However, catastrophe novels today do tend to be of broader scope than those written in earlier time periods. Increasingly, they deal with what is known as the 'unstructured disaster,' rather than 'structured disaster.' In a structured disaster, certain classes or groups of people may be protected from harm. For example, survival statistics from the sinking of the Titanic point to the fact that the poor, along with adult males, died at much higher rates than other passengers. Thus, social status, gender, and age could serve to cushion one somewhat from the effects of the disaster. An unstructured disaster is one in which no clear pattern of destruction may be readily identified. Terrorist attacks on civilians, for example, are considered to be unstructured disasters, since they might affect all equally.[40] Here, a present-day example of a catastrophe novel is the American novel *One Second After*, written in 2009 by William Forstchen. The author, a former military officer with extensive Washington experience, is also a close friend of the conservative American politician Newt Gingrich. His policy agenda in writing the work was specifically to raise American awareness of the dangers presented from an electromagnetic pulse attack which, according to the author, has the potential to paralyze and potentially destroy America's communications infrastructure. The story details the effects of an EMP attack on one small town in North Carolina where the citizens bravely rally and endure under the leadership of a former U.S. Army colonel. At the story's end, U.S. military forces are reassembled and they arrive in the town with the words, "Welcome back to America."[41]

This work, while it deals with a devastating attack on the United States, is not an apocalyptic novel—despite the high casualty rates described in America as a result of the attack. (Approximately 80 to 90 percent of America's population succumbs to starvation or violence in the aftermath of the attack.) This is because of the arc of the story—in which order is restored and the state does not fail. The "hero" of the catastrophe novel is thus identified with the state and is seen as complicit rather than standing apart from the state. He is not drawn with a great deal of psychological depth, nor is he seen to interrogate his own role in the drama or the role of his nation more generally. This literature relies on the typical hero—usually a white male who represents not only himself but in many ways the alleged innate superiority and patriotism of his culture (whether British or American). Others in the story—including women, minorities, and those from other cultures—are presented in stereotypical ways, and characters may become more patriotic, but beyond that do not develop.[42]

The enemy in the story is a similar sort of one-dimensional figure. The typical "terrorist" or "Soviet" in a Tom Clancy novel is thus portrayed as in many ways interchangeable with others of this type. The writer does not seek to inhabit or to understand the enemy character's life or to justify his motivations. There is no place in these tales for one to examine the validity of any of the invader's claims, nor is there room for an alternate reading or interpretation of these stories. In other words, *The Battle of Dorking* tells us that the Germans wanted England's ports, but at no point in the story are we asked to consider whether Germany resents English power or the overwhelming role it plays in the global system, nor are we asked to seriously consider the validity of such claims. In this way, the catastrophe novel suffers from many of the same problems that those of the Critical Terrorism Studies School iterate in critiquing modern empirical studies of terrorism.

Arguably, all catastrophe novels come not only from the same methodological space, but from the same ideological stance as well. *One Second After* can be read as a reactionary sort of novel—due to the subtext which states that through the harrowing events which the participants undergo, they experience a sort of drawing together which leads to a rebirth of American nationalism and patriotism. The book concludes with the restoration of an America which seems in many ways strangely dated. At the end of the book, the women are barefoot and pregnant, and there are seemingly no minorities and people of color left in town. The good country folk who bravely fought through adversity have defeated those from the city who came to destroy them, and they are rewarded when the federal troops eventually arrive and congratulate them on a job well done. (Throughout, the "barbarians" are said to be those who come from the city to prey on or contaminate the peaceful country dwellers. This drawing of boundaries between Us and Them can be seen to have racial overtones, with the city dwellers representing recent immigrants and people of color.)

Catastrophe novels are overwhelming pro military and supportive of a strategy of strong military defense based on a strong state. (Particularly when the catastrophe is an unstructured disaster, there is no emphasis on any type of preparedness which individuals could have engaged in in advance of the destruction. Instead, all are seen as equally vulnerable, and the only valid response is one which is collective rather than individual.) The novel is not progressive in the sense that the participants and the government do not appear to "learn" from their experiences—other than adopting specific military policy changes. These novels lack an introspective or reflexive dimension. The characters do not reflect deeply or question their values during times of trauma, and the catastrophe novel therefore also fails to open up a space for readers to interrogate their own values of patriotism, their feelings about the military, or the feelings they might harbor for their close or distant neighbors during a time of trauma. As Echevarria points out, at no point do the participants seriously examine the notion that war is necessary or look for alternate ways of solving problems with their neighbors.[43]

Due to the shorter time frame and limited scope of the events portrayed in the catastrophe novel, they are best understood as a type of survival narrative—rather than an apocalyptic narrative. While some catastrophe novels (as noted here) have received mainstream attention, others have been explicitly created for a subset of readers—making them in this way similar to Biblical apocalyptic novels. Many of today's survivalist narratives are published by small, boutique publishing houses and count among their readers right wing, sometimes Evangelical Christian, survivalists—who support the end of gun control in America and may also be part of other racist or conspiratorial groups.[44]

Production of the Catastrophe Novel

The catastrophe novel can be understood as an exercise in apocalyptic discourse, or the use of the language of disaster, rather than an examination of apocalypse itself. In their groundbreaking work on apocalyptic discourse in the discussion of global warming, the authors Killingsworth and Palmer imply that apocalyptic discourse may be utilized as a rhetorical strategy.[45] It manipulates the listener, and it may be that the creator of the discourse himself does not fully believe or buy into the framework. Thus, for example, journalists, policy advocates, and those testifying before Congress about the dangers of global warming may use scenarios in which they describe how entire nations will be buried by the sea, thousands will die in seasonal floods, and the agricultural cycle will be disrupted to galvanize public support for the problem and to move it to the top of the policy agenda. The creator of the apocalyptic discourse is mostly interested in seeing "his" problem assume a primary place in politics—moving it from the esoteric concern of a small group of policy wonks to the mainstream of political life.

Apocalyptic discourse (including religious apocalyptic discourse) may also be used to mobilize the population, or to advance a policy position—such as the need for a more aggressive foreign policy. As Michael Pesenson suggests, this was the goal of apocalyptic discourse in early-nineteenth-century Russia, where materials appeared in literary journals such as *Vestnik Evropy* and *Syn Otechestva* which compared Napoleon Bonaparte to the Antichrist. Here, writers called upon the tsar as God's representative to stand up to the forces of evil which Napoleon represented.[46]

Echevarria takes this notion a bit further—arguing that when a new technology (such as dynamite, the tank, or a nuclear weapon) enters the scene, there may be a debate among experts and within society about this new technology's significance and utility in the conduct of warfare. He argues that speculative fiction might thus be used to persuade readers about the future uses of a particular technology through depicting its use.[47] A particularly captivating book might thus ideally close down debate regarding the significance of this new change and lead to the formation of an agreement among the epistemic community. This dynamic is apparent in the introductions to two recent catastrophe novels—Glenn Beck's *The Overton Window* (2010) and William Foerstchen's *One Second After* (2009). Forstchen, for example, wants the world to take seriously his concerns about the possibility of an electromagnetic pulse destroying American civilization, and thus he admits that to some degree he has "spun" this scenario to raise public awareness of the problem.

The catastrophe novel is thus a peculiar cultural product. It is likely to be produced only in a highly advanced nation which is an early adopter of technologies, and it is likely to be produced in a moment when the international system is in crisis or transition. It requires a certain degree of mistrust or concern related to the new technology, as well as a certain degree of mistrust of the international system. It is a product of instability but not of fear, since it is generally produced by a dominant power with the underlying premise that it is good for the dominant power to stay in power (or in Realist terms, with the goal of advancing state survival). It also rests on the premise that the state enjoys agency in the international system such that it is capable of identifying danger or threat and altering its policies in order to respond to it. (It is not, thus, a prisoner of the international system, perhaps aware of the threat or danger but unable to respond due to budgetary shortfalls, the inability to mobilize the population or superstition and irrationality.)

The catastrophe novel as literary product actually emerged in late Victorian or early Edwardian England and in some cases, tales were solicited by editors who were concerned about Britain's defenses. The first invasion novel in Britain was the short story, "The Battle of Dorking,"[48] which described a hypothetical invasion of Britain by unknown strangers (who nevertheless spoke German), described from a perspective of fifty years on. The story was written by Lieutenant-Colonel George Chesney, who had recently returned from a tour of duty in India. He was worried by Prussia's successful invasion of France in 1870 and worried that it could happen in Britain too. The story actually ran in *Blackwood's* magazine, which was read by many government and military officials. Chesney, a frequent contributor of military stories, suggested to the editor that the story might be useful in raising awareness of the threat to Britain. The story soon became a best seller, with more than one hundred thousand copies printed throughout the British Empire. It was also translated into the major European languages.

If one were to draw a parallel between late Victorian England and the present day, one could argue that potboiler thrillers like Tom Clancy's works belong to the category of catastrophe literature. But while such works are clearly "political"—in the sense that they take political events as the starting point for their narrative—as well as being "politicized"—in the sense that they advocate for particular policies and positions within their works—they are actually only of limited interest and utility to those drawn to critical international relations theory for a number of reasons. In holding everything constant except for the decision point, planners and authors must be very specific about the assumptions which they accept at the beginning of their writing, and which they agree not to violate. For the most part, these assumptions are those associated with the Realist view of international relations. In this way, analysts are constrained in terms of the outcomes which they may reasonably entertain. For example, neither the writer nor the planner is likely to violate the assumptions that: states exist; conflict is fought among states; and institutions are relatively stable.

Here, for example, we might consider the problems which Noel Hendrickson presents to policy planners as likely counterfactual scenarios which they might wish to consider:

> What if Iran had nuclear weapons? What if al-Qaida sympathizers staged a coup in Pakistan? What if the United States had not abolished the Iraqi army in 2003? What if the United States had taken al-Qaida's threats more seriously after the bombing of the USS Cole?[49]

What is noticeable here is the lack of imagination behind the proposed theoretical scenarios, despite his emphasis on encouraging planners to be more creative. The possible worlds which he proposes, as a result of choices made, are not so different from our current worlds, nor are they so very different from the scenarios proposed in catastrophe novels.

Given that the catastrophe novel is a positivist, realist, and possibly right wing phenomenon, it is logical to ask whether it is also an artifact of a particular time period or of a particular type of state. In order for a writer to create a scenario in which the state is threatened by an as yet unidentified security breach and then to advocate for its successful resolution, certain preconditions need to be met. First, the nation which is threatened needs to view itself as largely invulnerable—due to its size and overwhelming economic, political, and military strength.

The catastrophe novel is essentially a David-and-Goliath–type story where a large nation is taken by surprise by a smaller, less-well-funded and less-well-organized threat. All catastrophe novels are about asymmetric warfare.

In his work, *Imagining Future War*, the analyst Antulio Echevarria lists three such catastrophe novels which were written in the late 1800s and early 1990s in England.[50] George Griffith's *Angel of the Revolution*, written in 1893, depicts anarchists systematically toppling the government in Europe. Edward Fawcett's *The Doom of the Great City*, written in 1893, describes the destruction of London by aerial bombardment, while William LeQueux's *The Great War in England*, written in 1897, features a cross-channel invasion of England by the French and the Russians.

In each case, the story resonated with the public through identifying a potential series of historic events, then identifying the security breaches which might make them possible. But in order for the story to resonate with its audience, there also needed to be an understanding that the nation was viewed as somehow invulnerable and not threatened by its neighbors. Thus, it is not surprising that such a genre evolved in Victorian England at the height of its power—nor is it surprising that the same genre would have such resonance with American citizens today. In the following chapter, I describe how American and British thinking about risk and threat evolved and was specifically expressed in the literature of the time. The scenarios described in the catastrophe novel would not make much sense were they to take place in Canada, Australia, or another nation which was powerful but not yet a preponderant power. The drama is produced by the David-and-Goliath scenario contained in the catastrophe novel itself.

In addition, as Roese and Olson suggest in their work on the psychology of the counterfactual, not everyone (or every nation, presumably) is equally skilled in entertaining or parsing out the counterfactual supposition.[51] They suggest that "high self-esteem" individuals are better able to entertain and participate in scenarios in which they are asked to think through questions such as: What would have happened had you made a different decision at that time? They were better able, as well, to visualize how an alteration of their own actions could lead to a changed result. That is, in order for a counterfactual argument to "work," the writer or agent in the counterfactual argument needs to see himself occupying a position of control—in which he actually has the agency to change an outcome.

This ability to envision an alternate history—for one's own nation and for the world—can also be expressed in the creation of an alternate literary product, the utopian novel. In the next chapter, I describe how utopian theorizing is also both a form of literary writing and a form of speculation or forecasting—since both writers and analysts "play" with questions regarding which future scenarios are most likely to occur.

NOTES

1. One of the leading generators of counterfactual scenarios as well as other future scenarios in the U.S. intelligence community is the Proteus organization, an interagency initiative which originated in the U.S. National Reconnaissance Office (NRO) in 1999. The program is currently jointly administered by the National Intelligence University, Office of the Director of National Intelligence, and the Center for Strategic Leadership, U.S. Army War College. Its mission is described as "examining uncertainty, enhancing creativity, gaining foresight and developing critical analytical and decision making processes to effectively provide insight and knowledge to future complex national security, military and intelligence challenges."

2. David G. Muller, "Improving Futures Intelligence," *International Journal of Intelligence and Counterintelligence* 22 (2009): 382.

3. Mitre Corporation, "Rare Events" (McLean, VA: The Jason Project, Mitre Corporation, 2009): 5.

4. For a look at this approach, please see Barry B. Hughes, *International Futures: Choices in the Face of Uncertainty*, 3rd ed. (Boulder: Westview Press, 1999).

5. Darko Suvin, *Victorian Science Fiction in the UK: The Discourses of Knowledge and Power* (Boston: G. K. Hall and Company, 1983): 261–83.

6. Both of these definitions are drawn from Ian G. Wallace, *Developing Effective Safety Systems* (New York: Institute of Chemical Engineers, 1995): 87.

7. Here, however, it is important to distinguish between two different types of simulations which may be created by government planners. While intelligence planners may create so-called catastrophe scenarios aimed at identify-

ing hazards and weaknesses in defenses in order to plan for the prevention of disaster, homeland security planners are increasingly more interested in the creation of so-called apocalyptic scenarios in which the disasters actually come to pass—since the aim of these exercises is to plan for *responses* to worst-case outcomes, rather than their prevention. Thus, one might wish to consider the land called Dystopia—with its two cities, Cape Hazard and Grim City. Dystopia is the brainchild of security planners located at the United States Naval Postgraduate School and the U.S. Department of Homeland Security's Center for Homeland Defense and Security. The virtual environment is used to run simulations in which players plan for emergency responses to a "seemingly unending series of civic crises." As the planners tell us, "Mayor Jennison declared Dystopia the 'disaster capital of the world, maybe even the galaxy.'" Dystopia may be accessed at www.chds.us/?dystopia.history.

In addition, one can consider the series of exercises developed by the Washington, DC-based Center for Strategic and International Studies (CSIS) for government planners, which included Operation Dark Winter, which focused on a simulated terrorist release of smallpox in Oklahoma City, Oklahoma; Steadfast Resolve which focused on government responses to a terrorist attack; Silent Vector, which focused on an attack on American critical information infrastructures in the United States; and Black Dawn which focused on a simulated use of a weapon of mass destruction against the United States. More information about these scenarios can be found at http://csis.org/program/simulations-and-tabletop-exercises.

The dual emphasis by homeland security planners on both prevention and response is discussed in Sharon Caudel and Randall Yim, "Homeland Security's National Strategic Position: Goals, Objectives, Measures Assessment," in David G. Kamien, ed. *The McGraw-Hill Homeland Security Handbook* (New York: McGraw-Hill, 2006): 261.

  8. Charles Perrow spells out the high reliability theory in "The Limits of Safety: The Enhancement of a Theory of Accidents," *Journal of Contingencies and Crisis Management* 4 (1994): 212–20.

  9. The "normal accident" theory is spelled out in Andrew Hopkins, "Was Three Mile Island a 'Normal Accident'?," *Journal of Contingencies and Crisis Management* 9 (2001): 65–72.

  10. The novels which appeared in the 1950s and the 1960s in America which dealt with ramifications of nuclear war were thus "normal accident" novels, since most assumed that once invented, nuclear technology would seek its inevitable conclusion in a deterministic fashion. One could not prevent nuclear explosion. One could merely prepare for it. Similarly, novels which deal with pandemics in the early twenty-first century tend to treat

them as "normal accidents"—with the implication that once germ warfare is invented, it is somehow inevitable that it would escape from the laboratory and kill us all.

11. Scott Sagan, *The Limits of Safety* (Princeton: Princeton University Press, 1993).

12. Cormac McCarthy, *The Road* (New York: Vintage Press, 2006): 45.

13. Walter M. Miller, Jr., *A Canticle for Leibowitz* (New York: Harper Collins, 1959).

14. Philip Tetlock and Geoffrey Parker, "Counterfactual Thought Experiments: Why We Can't Live without Them and How We Must Learn to Live with Them," in Philip E. Tetlock, Richard Ned Lebow, and Geoffrey Parker, eds. *Unmaking the West: 'What if' Scenarios That Rewrite World History* (Ann Arbor: University of Michigan Press, 2009): 14–44.

15. Carlo C. Jaeger, Ortwin Renn; Eugene A. Rosa, and Thomas Webber, *Risk, Uncertainty and Rational Action* (London: Earthscan Publications, 2001).

16. Thus, in the collection of essays titled *Unmaking the West*, historians gathered at Ohio State University were encouraged to consider the ramifications of such scenarios as: What if Lincoln had not been shot? And what if the crowd had decided to release Jesus instead of Barabbas? How might such decisions have affected Western civilization?

17. Here, a parallel can be drawn with the biblical Apocalyptic novels alluded to in the introduction to this work. Like those who write intelligence scenarios, those who write biblical Apocalyptic novels operate within a very strict set of constraints. They must follow a script—in this case, the events set forth in the book of Revelations and elsewhere in the Bible. While authors may differ in terms of how the characters are described as responding to events, there is very little flexibility in terms of the choices which characters are seen as having to make—and for good measure everyone knows how the book will end before one even starts reading.

18. Here, we can point to the English novelist George Orwell, who got his start as a journalist, or William Morris, whose utopian paean to sustainability owed much to his background as an artist and architect. More recently, one can think of James Kunstler, who is described as a social critic, as well as a writer—with policy interests in geography and the politics of oil.

19. Robert Aumann, "Backward Induction and Common Knowledge of Rationality," *Games and Economic Behavior* 8 (1995): 6–19.

20. Paul Alkon, *Gulliver* and the Origins of Science Fiction, in Frederik N. Smith, ed., *The Genres of Gulliver's Travels* (Newark, DE: University of Delaware Press, 1990): 165.

21. Robert Aumann, 6–19.

22. Ibid, 14.

23. Here, it is important to note that a substantive conditional is one which leads directly to a result—rather than setting up a larger chain of follow-on events. Here, Aumann gives the example of the statement "If Hitler had crossed the channel after Dunkirk, he would have won the war" (15). This is not regarded as a substantive conditional because the hypothesis is not completely specified. There are intervening variables and conditions which are not specified and the number of contingencies which must occur between the first decision and the final outcome are too many for there to be a high probability that event A would necessarily lead to outcome B.

24. Laura J. Kray, Adam Galinsky, and Elaine Wong, "Thinking within the Box," *Journal of Personality and Social Psychology* 91 (2006): 33–48.

25. Mitre Corporation, "Rare Events."

26. Chris Cleave, *Incendiary* (New York: Simon and Schuster, 2004).

27. Wesley C. Salmon, "Dynamic Rationality: Propensity, Probability and Credence," in James H. Fetzer, ed., *Probability and Causality* (Dordrecht, NL: Springer, 1987).

28. Salmon, "Dynamic Rationality."

29. Bruce Bueno de Mesquita, *Predicting Politics* (Columbus: Ohio University Press, 2002).

30. In game theoretic modeling, backward induction occurs when the theorist starts with the outcome and then works backward to construct the chains of logic and decisions which must have been made to lead to the particular outcome. In literature, the closest equivalent might be the process of "cheating" and leaping ahead to read the end of a whodunit-type mystery novel first. Then, one can speculate backwards to figure out who must have been the murderer.

31. Noel Hendrickson, "Counterfactual Reasoning: A Basic Guide for Analysts, Strategists and Decision Makers," www.csl.army.mil/usacsl/publications/Hendrickson_Counterfactual_Reasoning. pdf.

32. Quoted in Hopkins, *Was Three Mile Island*, 67.

33. Ian G. Wallace, *Developing Effective Safety Systems* (New York: Institute of Chemical Engineers, 1995).

34. William Forstchen, *One Second After* (New York: Forge Books, 2009): 218.

35. Philip Tetlock and Richard Lebow, *Unmaking the West: "What-If" Scenarios That Rewrite World History* (Ann Arbor: University of Michigan Press, 2006).

36. Warren Wagar, *Terminal Visions: The Literature of Last Things* (Bloomington: Indiana University Press, 1982).

37. Paul Schroeder, in particular, queries the academic utility of the counterfactual model—concluding that it is of limited utility—in his article, "Embedded

Counterfactuals and World War I as an Unavoidable War." www.vlib.us/wwi/resources/archives/texts/.

38. Kray et al., "Thinking within the Box," 33.

39. Muller, "Improving Future Intelligence."

40. Theodore Steinberg, *Acts of God: The Unnatural History of Natural Disaster in America* (Oxford: Oxford University Press, 2000): 127.

41. Forstchen, 218.

42. Margery Hourihan describes the "typical" hero in her work, *Deconstructing the Hero: Literary Theory and Children's Literature* (London: Routledge, 1997).

43. Antulio Echevarria, *Imagining Future War: The West's Technological Revolution and Visions of Wars to Come, 1880–1914* (Westport, CT: Praeger, 2007): 196.

44. Statistics by groups like the Southern Poverty Law Center suggest that such right-wing survivalist groups have sharply increased in the past ten years—as the result of September 11, economic difficulties, a rise in domestic terrorism and the election of an African American president. Thus, this type of literature may be on the increase as well. However, this literature is not considered influential within the larger American mainstream, and for this reason is of limited utility in my inquiry.

45. Here, apocalyptic discourse may be understood as a separate phenomenon from the "apocalyptic tone" which Derrida refers to in his recent writings. The apocalyptic tone will be explored more in the section of this work dealing with apocalypse—rather than catastrophe.

46. Michael A. Pesenson, "Napoleon Bonaparte and Apocalyptic Discourse in Early Nineteenth Century Russia," *The Russian Review* 65 (2006): 374.

47. Echevarria, xv.

48. Tom Reiss, "Imagining the Worst," *New Yorker* (November 28, 2005). www.newyorker.com/archive/2005/11/28/051128fa_fact.reiss.

49. Noel Hendrickson, "Counterfactual Reasoning: A Basic Guide for Analysts, Strategists and Decision Makers." Available at: www.csl.army.mil/usacsl/publications/Hendrickson_Counterfactual_Reasoning.pdf.

50. Echevarria, 49.

51. Roese and Olson, "Preface," in Neal J. Roese and James M. Olson, eds., *What Might Have Been: The Social Psychology of Counterfactual Thinking* (Lawrence Erlbaum Associates, Inc., Mahwah, NJ, 1995).

3

UTOPIAN NOVELS AND FORECASTING

While the catastrophe novel thus aims to predict an outcome and to change it, the utopian or dystopian novel has a slightly different function—despite the fact that both attempt to say something about the future. Here, it is useful to stop and consider the difference in meaning between the terms "to predict" and "to forecast." The verb "to predict" is defined as: to state, tell about or make known in advance, especially on the basis of special knowledge or inference (as in, for example, calling the outcome of the game.) The word "predict" comes from the Latin *praedicere*, which literally means "to mention beforehand." Thus, prediction rests on the notion that the predictor has superior information or as shown in the previous analysis, perfect information. As a result of that superior information, the writer is thus able to foretell the outcome of a decision—or in the case of the catastrophe novelist, of a series of strategic decisions between two players.

In contrast, the term "forecast" is defined as "to estimate or calculate in advance, especially to predict (weather conditions) by analysis of meteorological data." That is, forecasting is also a form of telling about something that will happen in the future—but here the knowing rests not on perfect information, but rather on an analysis of past patterns and trends—thus reproducing the work a weather man does when he analyzes meteorological data.[1] He speculates about tomorrow's weather based on what he knows about today's weather and the patterns he can predict. He does not add other variables which are unpredictable—including typhoons, tidal waves or volcanic explosions.[2]

Thus, the emphasis in the catastrophe novel is on analyzing the decision path that led to a particular outcome. In contrast, the utopian or dystopian novel is concerned with the social forces which led to the outcome, as well as the analysis of the outcome—as a critique of the real world. The two works thus differ both in their goals and their methodology. However, both share common ground with the work done by intelligence workers—with the stipulation that a catastrophe novel resembles an intelligence scenario, while a utopian or dystopian novel resembles an intelligence forecast. As the introduction to the U.S. government report Global Trends 2025—a publication of the Office of the Director of National Intelligence and the National Intelligence Council—states:

> We prepared *Global Trends 2025: A Transformed World* to stimulate strategic thinking about the future by identifying key trends, the factors that drive them, where they seem to be headed, and how they might interact. It uses scenarios to illustrate some of the many ways in which the drivers examined in the study (e.g., globalization, demography, the rise of new powers, the decay of international institutions, climate change, and the geopolitics of energy) may interact to generate challenges and opportunities for future decision makers. The study as a whole is more a description of the factors likely to shape events than a prediction of what will actually happen.[3]

In his handbook for military modelers, the analyst Noel Hendrickson distinguishes between two types of models which intelligence analysts can create, which he labels Models for Prediction and Models for Insight. Among the goals he lists for a "model for insight" is the provision of non-obvious insights, as well as the ability to shed light on new data and problems.[4] The Model for Insight aims less at providing short-term insights into decision-making processes and more at allowing analysts to explore problems from new angles, as well as to explore the relationships between variables in both the medium and long term.

These novels are, arguably, more useful to political scientists than catastrophe novels because of the ways in which they carry out the functions of policy advocacy as well as the function of interrogating existing beliefs and opening up new models of discourse. That is, utopian and dystopian—are, arguably, speculative in the second sense as well as the first. The author speculates not only about the likelihood of a particular outcome, but about the meaning and significance of the outcome. For that reason, the utopian or dystopian writer's aim has traditionally been seen as didactic and heavily normative. If a parallel is traditionally drawn between the speculative fiction author and the work of the political scientist, the utopian or dystopian writer is more frequently described as acting like a political theorist—rather than acting like a political methodologist from the behavioralist school.

For as Little tells us, utopia was fundamentally a political notion—but it was one based on Aristotle and his depictions of the perfect society. The Greek term means a place of ideal happiness and excellent order, and a utopia thus represents a type of critical literature, in which the author takes a stance against the present through "comparing it to a visionary system of political and social excellence."[5]

The term was first coined by the English writer Samuel Butler in 1872, the author of *Erewhon*—which is widely described as the first utopian novel. Butler himself claimed that the term was a combination of the word "eutopos" which means a good place, and "outopos," the place which is nowhere. His novel *Erewhon*, considered the template for the genre, actually contains the word "nowhere" spelled backwards, with only a slight change in the spelling.[6] Thus, while authors may produce a prototypical perfect society which is derived from the author's analysis of contemporary society and his predictions about developments and decisions which are likely to occur within it, they are more likely to be concerned with normative implications of that new society's existence. Thus, rather than asking, "What is the likelihood that such a society could occur?" (as one might in a catastrophe novel or an intelligence estimate), they are likely to ask "In what ways is this new society more or less just, equitable, or fair?" or "How is the concept of citizenship expressed in this new society?"

Dystopia shares a similar set of normative and policy-related assumptions with utopia—but it has a somewhat shorter historic pedigree. It is said to have originated less than one hundred and fifty years ago, with many crediting the British philosopher John Stuart Mill for having invented the term.⁷ If utopia represents the good society and allows readers to speculate about the philosophical and ethical impulses which create it, dystopia is rather a representation of the "bad" society wrought large. The large scope of dystopian literature as we currently understand it encompasses both literary explorations of domestic threats coming from impulses within society, as well as literary explorations of external threats including the possibility of invasion or takeover by (human or extraterrestrial) alien forces. Whatever elements were viewed by the current society as being most threatening (politically, economically, spiritually, morally, and ethically) to its way of life are exaggerated and drawn out to their logical conclusion in the dystopian novel—whether it is the threat of over-reliance on science and technology and a resulting loss of personal autonomy, the threat of a surveillance-type state that would gradually shrink the sphere of action whereby people enjoyed individual rights, or the threat of an ideologically or perhaps religiously motivated state run amok, whereby all would gradually be assimilated into adopting the same values and diversity would disappear.

METHODOLOGY OF THE UTOPIAN NOVEL

The analytical methodology used by the utopian author is also different from that used by the author of a catastrophe novel. In the previous section, I described the process of backward induction or the creation of chains of decisions which can be reconstructed if one knows the final outcome—in the case of the catastrophe novel. In contrast, the utopian novel looks forward rather than backwards. As Bertrand de Jouvenal writes in his analysis of the ways in which "futurologists" attempt to predict future political and economic trends:

> My imagination . . . jumps to a time not yet accomplished and builds something there, a signum, and this "construct" beckons and exercises a present attraction on me. Thus actions coming before this imagined future are determined by it and prepare it rationally.⁸

De Jouvenal describes the work of the futurologist as engagement in the "discovery" of new knowledge about the future, rather than in analysis of the processes which lead to an outcome. That is, arguably, the catastrophe novelist accepts that there are multiple possible futures which can come to fruition (or be prevented). In contrast, the futurologist focuses on identifying the future possible world which does come to exist—since it is the only one which can be—because if there were other choices, they were not taken. He does not accept the possibility of contingency, nor does he describe the decision maker as an important agent or determiner of outcomes, for he believes that there are not several possible worlds. There is only the one which will actually come about. Thus, the creator of a utopian world needs to believe that it is the future. (This is where the utopian novelist and the intelligence officer part ways—since even those who attempt to make "forecasts" in the intelligence community still acknowledge that there are multiple possible future worlds.)

If the accomplishment of the catastrophe novel is to make us as readers and analysts more aware of the importance of strategic choice, arguably the accomplishment of the utopian or dystopian novel is that it makes us more aware of the inborn prejudices and certainties which we hold about our environment and international system and its dynamic or static nature—since our projection of the future rests largely on the preconceived notions we have about the structure of the world in its present state. As de Jouvenal explains, we are only able to project forward and make predictions about the outcome of next term's U.S. presidential election if we accept certain premises about the world as it exists now. He refers to these premises as structural certainties.[9]

Thus, in order to hypothesize about who might be a candidate or who might win an election, analysts implicitly accept the premises that there will not be a coup but an election; that elections will continue to proceed through regularized and orderly channels of succession; that the state holding the elections will continue to exist and to be an autonomous actor in the international system with the necessary political unity and political sovereignty to hold its own elections (it will not be invaded or annexed). Theories about future elections thus exhibit consensus regarding the structural certainties on which these projections rest, and which make such predictions possible. In short, this is why CIA analysts and others argue that it is difficult to make projections outside a framework of about fifteen or twenty years—and why the projections which do end up being made frequently seem so boring and mundane to us. Analysts aren't "allowed" to do anything terribly interesting to the variables because the range of assumed structural certainties is fairly narrow. The analyst must assume that the major states will continue to exist, that states will not go to war except for reasons of state survival, and that states are unlikely to concede power, territory, or resources voluntarily. Indeed, the continuing stability of the international system provides the basis upon which it is possible to theorize at all.

However, while catastrophe novels tend to look very similar—since all of the authors are in a sense reading from the same script and operating out of the same set of realist, positivist decision rules—utopian novels exhibit a wider range of outcomes due to the absence of consensus regarding what the present and future structural certainties are. Every individual utopian or dystopian novelist makes his own decisions regarding the variables which he feels will hold constant in our own world and into the future and those which he feels will change (either through evolution or devolution). Here, the "variables" which he must consider include norms and roles for individuals and groups, as well as preferences and identities. Thus, for example, one author (like Jonathan Swift) might describe a utopia in which the roles of the old and the young have been reversed, or even those of the human and animal kingdoms[10]—but where nonetheless class differences are still important and pronounced, regardless of how far into the future we might travel.

Here, for example, utopian and dystopian novels seem to exhibit a wide range of interpretations regarding the future evolution of technology. On the one hand, we have what Nicols Fox has referred to as neo-Luddites. That is, among novelists there are those who fear that technology will evolve in a way that threatens humanity. (Here one can consider a novelist like E. M. Forster who worried in 1905 that someday machines might evolve a form of artificial intelligence and seek to displace humans.) On the other hand, there are many novelists who describe technology as a boon which will solve humanity's problems and make life better for humans in the future (as E. M. Forster's contemporary William Morris argued in his own utopian novel, *News from Nowhere*).

In addition, the absence of consensus regarding the evolution of technology means that there may some debate regarding what constitutes realistic and what constitutes a fantastical utopia. The line between fantasy and reality might be seen as less than certain, and it might be seen as constantly moving as well. For example, a utopian novel written in the 1950s which described a future in which children were conceived in laboratories, in which shoppers routinely selected genetically modified produce and in which patients were screened preemptively to establish their likelihood of contracting a disease in the future would seem fantastical in the 1950s. However after the advent of such events as the birth of Louise Brown, the world's first test tube baby; and the 2003 adoption by the European Parliament of strict new regulations regarding the labeling and sale of genetically modified food, the novel above might thus be reclassified by readers—who would no longer consider it fantasy but rather realistic science fiction.

Utopian and dystopian theorists also fail to display a consensus regarding how they view the state as a variable in their analysis. Some writers describe the state as gaining in strength through history to the point that future societies are totalitarian, with every aspect of one's life controlled by the state (as in, for example, Orwell's dystopian novel *1984*). Other analysts, however, view the state as likely to either collapse involuntarily or wither away as the result of social forces or human decisions (as it does, for example, in William Morris's [1890] *News from Nowhere*, where England has become part of something larger which, arguably, resembles the European Union).

As noted, decisions regarding which variables are likely to evolve, which are likely to devolve and which are likely to remain constant can vary due to the writer's own ideology, as well as due to the dominant values and mores of a particular geographic location or temporal period. And when the reader is steeped in the same cultural and political milieu as the author himself, he or she may not even notice the subtle ways in which the author's own biases have affected his decisions regarding the likely or unlikely evolution of a particular variable into the future. This is particularly true if the author is advancing a consensus view regarding which variables are likely to evolve in the future, rather than introducing a radical new interpretation of history including future history. Thus, for example, I argue later in this manuscript that many of our current dystopian (and apocalyptic) novels implicitly reproduce American biases stemming from Great Power politics, our own privileged position in the international system, and the history and practice of colonialism. We are unlikely to notice these practices, however, because of the ways in which our whole society has not formally interrogated or considered these biases.

Here we might consider the fact that in the popular American *Star Trek* movies which have been a Hollywood staple from the 1970s until today, the Starship Enterprise prides itself on "boldly going where no one has gone before" in order to discover lands which are not empty but populated and which do not need to be "discovered" by earthlings in order for their existence to be validated and ratified since they already exist. And we might also pause to consider the ways in which the Enterprise's team of linguists and anthropologists continually engages in colonial practices of cataloguing, mapping, classifying, and labeling the "foreign others" whom they find and befriend, in essence reproducing the great adventurous voyages of her British colonial ancestors. Here, the series' creators seem to have concluded that while the technology enabling a voyage could advance in the future, the colonial mission or imperative is a goal and set of practices which are constant and incapable of evolving.

Similarly, one can remark on the ways in which these series construct a "future paradise" where technology has advanced or evolved to the fact where most social problems have been solved, including hunger, war, and ethnic strife—but where gender roles appeared to have stalled in their evolution, having been permanently paused somewhere around 1950 or so. That is, technological evolution appears as a structural certainty, while gender role evolution does not. This is why, for example, an episode of Star Trek from the 1970s still has a "retro" feel even though it's ostensibly about the future. From our current stance, it seems humorous that male writers in the 1970s assumed that we would have spaceships and the potential to "beam people up" but that gender roles would remain static. These episodes reflect a consensus that racial and gender roles are fixed—while technology evolves. Similarly, in watching these episodes, we encounter the notion that such mores and norms were regarded as geographically universal as well as temporally fixed. That is, even when our intrepid "explorers" visit a new planet, they still encounter societies characterized by rigid (stereotypical) gender roles as well as class differences.[11]

STRUCTURAL CERTAINTIES AND STRATEGIC INTERACTION

However, both catastrophe novelists and futurologists see the future as being the product of strategic interactions since the future which is created is ultimately the product of forces, events, and choices made not by one player but by several. Thus, in establishing structural certainties, the writer frequently must establish not only what constants he sees as remaining in his own society into the future but also what constants he envisions persisting within the international system as well—provided his novel includes the possibility that "his" characters will interact with others from other nations or other worlds.

That is, implicitly we assume that our state will not change and that policies and structures of other states will not change as well. Thus the whole model rests on an element of risk. De Jouvenal refers to the strategic part of the equation as "contractual certainty"[12]—since it essentially means that in drawing up our models, we base them on assumptions about how our nation will behave, but also about how our neighbors (friends and enemies) will behave towards us.

However, the Wharton School behavioral economist Michel-Kerjan[13] calls our attention to a newly identified problem which he refers to as "the new risk architecture." Essentially, he claims that every state is now much more likely to suffer ill effects due not to its own actions but due to the actions of other states on which it is forced to depend. As he notes, many of the problems faced by states today—including preparing for disasters or planning for unforeseen events (like a crop failure)—are not problems which states can solve themselves, no matter how well prepared they might be. The question thus becomes: Can I depend on my neighbors to fulfill their parts of the international obligation in the future? Will I continue to cooperate with them and will they continue to cooperate with me?

Here, utopian and dystopian novels seem to divide sharply in terms of how they view the contractual certainty on which interdependence rests. Arguably, the first utopian novelist to describe economic specialization and interdependence was William Morris, who described how England cooperated with its neighbors and outsources many of its production functions in the future—from a literary vantage point of 1890. Since then, however, dystopian novelists like Kunstler and Cronin have focused in their work on America's isolation or abandonment from the international system or the end of globalization as a major theme. As Justin Cronin describes the situation in his 2010 novel *The Passage*:

> In the last days of the war, the NATO alliance, our so-called friends, banded together and made one last effort to contain the infection. Heavy bombing along the coasts, and not just conventional explosive. They blasted just about anything in the water. You can still see the wreckage down in Corpus. Then they laid mines, just to slam the door.[14]

In this way, dystopian authors in particular explore whether globalization and interdependence are contractual certainties or uncertainties. In addition, many explore the notion of American hegemony as a contractual certainty or uncertainty, with the possibility that in the future America may face a rising hegemon.

The utopian or dystopian novelist thus must make three sets of decisions in examining his new model world: He must determine which variables he will present as structural certainties and which he will change; next, he must determine which variables he will present as contractual certainties and which he will change; and finally, he must consider the matter of dominating and masterable futures. DeJouvenal presents the dominating future as something which an individual participant cannot change, but can only prepare for. Thus, if one relaxes structural certainties regarding the continued financial stability of the international system, the American state may now find itself facing an economic Depression. The dominating future cannot be changed. However, the masterable future refers to the way in which an actor can alter his actions so as to determine how the future will affect him. Thus, America's lawmakers might enact legislation to lessen the effects of the recession, or individual Americans might stock up on goods before inflation hits. (In other words, I may believe that it is inevitable that technology will evolve to include nuclear weapons—but I can still decide to build a Strategic Defense Initiative in my country or to build a bomb shelter in my backyard.)[15]

Thus, many of today's dystopian novels present the unwinnability of a war against terrorism as the dominating future. The assumption is that a terrorist attack on the scale sufficient to transform the fabric of a Western state is inevitable and this reality cannot be changed. However, the content of the novel then goes on to consider the masterable future, or how individuals and groups might adapt in the face of massive terrorist attacks and perhaps even the collapse of the state's infrastructure and leadership as a result. The 2004 novel *Incendiary* by Chris Cleave, for example, describes a fictional Al-Qaeda–sponsored terrorist suicide bombing which takes place in a soccer stadium in London during a packed-to-capacity game.[16] As a result, a bureau similar to the American Homeland Security Agency is formed, and limits are placed on citizen's rights. The assumption here is that neither the event nor the policy changes which ensued could have been prevented. However, citizens can choose how they respond to these changes. The masterable future might thus be described as the ability of the government to predict where the terrorists will attack, or the ability of citizens to determine how they respond.

One might also argue that currently a dominating future facing America is that the United States has enemies which seek to harm it. That is, prior to 9/11, citizens and policy makers alike assumed that for the most part, other states in the world were comfortable with the notion of America's global dominance and hegemony, that soft power was working, and that generally speaking America was seen as a nation to be emulated rather than eliminated. Analysts like Francis Fukuyama[17] spoke of a phenomenon called "convergence"—in which ideologies would cease to matter and nations which embraced capitalism in particular would embrace similar values. Arguably, nationalism would become less of a force in the world and globalization would be not merely an economic phenomenon, but one which had long-lasting repercussions on the shape and values of the societies drawn into its web.

However, in the years since the devastating 2001 terrorist attack on the United States, a new dominating future has been constructed—one in which there are enemies who seek to destroy the United States, and arguably one in which at some point they will succeed. Increasingly, analysts acknowledge that merely adopting capitalism does not make a society capitalist or a friend of the United States, and they acknowledge as well that there are nations which are suspicious of globalization and who may choose to remain outside its orbit. Thus, the dominant future is one in which America has enemies (rather than one in which enmity has ceased) and the masterable future is thus the stance which America could take towards those who wish to harm her. The question thus becomes not *whether* an attack on a global hegemon can be prevented or *whether* hegemony will at some point decline, but rather what the shape of that decline might look like and what the repercussions might be.

REALISTIC VERSUS FANTASTICAL UTOPIAS

How "real" are utopias and dystopias compared to the catastrophe novels analyzed in the previous section of this chapter? Here, one must apply the three criteria of possibility, plausibility and probability. In the case of the utopian novel, there is significantly less consensus among both writers and readers as to how to apply all three of these criteria.

Utopian and dystopian fiction might to some degree be regarded as falling along a continuum. Some novels are utterly fantastic while others are much more realistic. Those which are the most fanciful may include voyages to invented places which do not exist as well as characters which are invented. Here, for example, one can think of the earliest utopian novels—Samuel Butler's *Erewhon* and Jonathan Swift's *Gulliver's Travels*. In each of these novels, the narrator takes a voyage to a place which is impossible and implausible—since neither the laws of science nor the social, economic, political, and cultural norms of present society apply there. In such places, animals can talk and people are impossibly small and large. In these scenarios, the writer consciously decides to violate the laws of geography and physics—arguably so that he may engage in satire and social criticism, all the while claiming that he could not possibly mean to be commenting on British or French foreign policy, since after all he has only written a children's story about animals and magical voyages.

However, what becomes difficult when categorizing utopian and dystopian novels is that some novels which may have seemed fantastical when they were written (H. G. Wells's description of space voyages in the late 1800s, and E. M. Forster's description of a machine which now sounds suspiciously like the Internet in 1907) may come to seem both possible and plausible in later years when technology "catches up" to the forward looking vision. However, what is clear is that tales which seem both impossible and implausible at the time always also seem improbable.

To some degree, the decision as to whether to treat a utopia or dystopia as fantastical or realistic depends on the reader. As noted previously, even those utopias and dystopias which appear to violate the laws of science leave open the door for a reader to argue that "just because the reality described is not scientifically or physically possible now, does not mean that it won't be in the future."

The same argument can be made when it comes to how the reader or writer might weight the political factors and trends that he or she sees as comprising the fabric of the dominating future—that is, how plausible he finds the scenario. Generally, when there is a social consensus regarding the logical path of a future trend, it will be treated as plausible—whereas in the absence of consensus, the future described may be dismissed as implausible or merely fantastical. And political realities which seemed implausible in, for example, the 1950s, may come to be accepted as fact in later years.

Here, we might consider a statement made by the Russian analyst Igor Panarin in an interview with the *Wall Street Journal* in December 2008. The article notes:

> Mr. Panarin posits, in brief, that mass immigration, economic decline, and moral degradation will trigger a civil war next fall and the collapse of the dollar. Around the end of June 2010, or early July, he says, the U.S. will break into six pieces—with Alaska reverting to Russian control.[18]

Despite Dr. Panarin's impressive credentials as a former KGB intelligence analyst and Dean of the Russian Foreign Ministry's Academy for Future Diplomats, his predictions are not treated by the *Wall Street Journal*'s analyst as either plausible or probable, though scientifically they are possible. However, one can point to the plethora of novels written in the United States currently which begin with a scenario of America as a failed state which has essentially broken apart and lost its territorial integrity as well as the notion of citizenship. Arguably, there are writers and readers who do regard this scenario as at least somewhat plausible, if not probable.

Similarly, Philip Tetlock and his colleagues begin the introduction to their work of counterfactual analysis titled *Unmaking the West* with the following paragraph which posits a future in which the only superpower is not the United States, but China. The narrative begins with a description of a counterfactual future noting:

> We Chinese take our primacy for granted. . . . Our language and culture has spread far beyond the river valley where they originated; currently almost two billion non-Han people speak or understand standard Chinese.[19]

Arguably there are those who would find such a scenario both possible and plausible in the future, though they might disagree about how probable it is.

As noted previously, scenarios might thus be weighted as more or less plausible depending on the degree of social consensus which exists regarding a particular issue or the likelihood of a particular dominating future coming to fruition. Thus, for example, there was a growing consensus following the advent of the Industrial Revolution that machines and technologization posed a valid and credible threat to humanity and its way of life. Scenarios which began from this premise were thus regarded as plausible. Beginning in the early twentieth century and up until the end of the Cold War, there was a fairly sizable contingent of thinkers and citizens who found the narrative of liberalism to be credible. As a result, utopian scenarios based on the premises that poverty will be solved; conflict will be solved; there will be gender equality; or that race will cease to matter as a category were regarded as possible and plausible—though analysts may have differently regarded the probability of these scenarios actually coming to fruition.

Currently, if one looks for a "consensus view" in contemporary utopian and dystopian scenarios, one might argue that writers and readers find the following scenarios to be socially and politically plausible or credible: First, that it is reasonable to expect that at some point in the future our allies will abandon us—or even turn on us. (This scenario appears in four of the contemporary works considered in my analysis including *The Pesthouse*; *The Passage*; *A World Made by Hand*; and *One Second After*. Arguably, the reluctance of America's allies to join in the Global War on Terror beginning in 2001 may have provided the impetus for readers and writers to find this sentiment plausible as well as increasing their estimates of its probability. In addition, arguably, the events of 9/11 itself served as a wakeup call to Americans, driving home the message that not everyone likes the United States, and that even some of America's friends may at times feel ambivalent about it.)

In addition, there appears to be a consensus regarding the plausibility of a scenario in which the United States encounters a disease deadly enough to change the ways in which we interact with others as individuals and groups. (Here, in the wake of such scientific discoveries as the Ebola virus and SARS, as well as the anthrax attacks on the U.S. Capitol shortly after September 11, citizens may have now realized that such attacks were scientifically possible as well as plausible. Now, they may only disagree about the probability of these attacks).

Thirdly, in the wake of the failed attempts of the Federal Emergency Management Agency to restore order after Hurricane Katrina in New Orleans in September 2005, citizens might be more likely to consider it both plausible and possible that America's infrastructure could collapse and it could become a failed state. In addition, there may also be a higher consensus around the notion that in the future the fragile web of American identity could fray, shattering our nation and causing us to turn on one another.

EPISTEMOLOGY OF THE UTOPIAN NOVEL

The utopian and dystopian novel is implicitly reflexivist—as opposed to the positivist catastrophe novel. Since the new world which is created in science fiction is seen as theoretically capable of existing—provided different choices had been made—it implicitly functions as a critique of the current world which does exist. (For example, if a utopian novel posits a world in which racial strife does not exist and there is true gender equality, then the reader is prompted to ask, "If this can be the case in the future, then why is it not the case now? What is preventing it from being so?")

Science fiction in general relies on a device called "cognitive estrangement," which is an extension of the Russian formalist concept of defamiliarization. Cognitive estrangement essentially explains why the reader at first feels a bit lost upon entering a science fiction world, until he finds his footing—by realizing that "this is just like my world except . . . (there is no racism or sexism, or people will only talk to you if you pay them, or children are bought and sold like merchandise.)" In each case, his adjustment to the fictional world (or utopia) which he visits through literature requires a new sort of engagement with his own "true" world, as he realizes that something he has thus far taken for granted about his own world is actually open to debate. Science fiction's "unusual settings" thus provide a fresh perspective on the author's (or readers) own time and place.[20] For this reason, science fiction is particularly well suited as a method of political commentary and, according to Carl Freeman, can serve as a methodology for practicing critical theory.

Science fiction is thus distinctive as a medium because of what it demands from the reader. The reader is first of all called upon to keep the invented world and the one to which it is being compared separate in his mind.[21] In a sense he is required to navigate between the "real" and the utopian world every time he reads a work of science fiction. In addition, he is required to understand the new culture being described, and to understand how it differs from his own. Next, he is expected to have the ability to keep the new society straight in his mind (though it may contain a new class structure, new norms, or new rituals). Arguably, the main characteristic of science fiction is thus this tension between our present world and the one which is invented. As readers, we need to account for and reconcile this tension.

Thus, it requires the reader to engage in certain ethical tasks. Utopian literature (and dystopian literature) is a manifestation of our desire to know the other, to be the other, and to know what it is to be the other.

The task of the reader is complicated because of the fact that many of the contemporary utopian and dystopian novels essentially begin *"in medias res"* or "in the middle of things." In each case, the America which the reader would recognize today has already vanished. The action picks up from there. To some degree, this is because fiction classes recommend the "in medias approach" to writers, describing it as more compelling and more likely to draw the reader in than a novel which builds slowly and works in from there. It is, to some degree, a twentieth century literary convention.[22] Other devices are used in Victorian literature, including a convention in which the reader goes to sleep in his usual environment and then wakes up (as he does in *News from Nowhere*) in a new environment which, we are told, exists somewhere in the future. Thus, the task of the reader is to orient himself in this new world—attempting to figure out where in the world he is and in what time period (a task complicated by situations where, for example, technology has vanished and the reader is unsure if the world being described is thus earlier or later than his present time period.)

PRODUCTION OF THE UTOPIAN NOVEL

Just as I have argued that both the apocalyptic novel and catastrophe novel only make sense in certain temporal contexts and can only be the product of certain societies, the same argument is true for utopian and dystopian fiction. As Deweese-Boyd points out[23] utopian novels all exhibit a preoccupation with the nation's national identity, and the ways in which that national identity might change over time—through either policy choices or social trends. That is, they are as much a reflection on one's own society as they are an exploration of a new type of society.

What sort of society might thus provide the grounds necessary for the creation of a utopian novel? First, the society is likely to be highly developed technologically and perhaps even at the cutting edge of that technology. It is unlikely that a society which is striving to modernize would enjoy the privilege of critiquing and interrogating the logic of technology in the same way that a state which has already arrived at the pinnacle might. In addition, the desire to build a utopia arises out of a societal desire to push against the constraints of the current society. Thus, the utopian novel in particular has often provided a venue for critiquing one's present society—even if one's society was seen as in some way beyond criticism because of the strength and significance of its accomplishments. In order to create a new place with a different ideology, one must thus come from a place that has a strongly developed ideology of its own—even if that ideology rests beneath the surface and has heretofore gone unquestioned.

The utopian writer thus seeks to query beliefs, norms, and agendas that thus far seemed unquestionable. As Jackson notes:

> A fantasy is a story based on and controlled by an overt violation of what is generally accepted as possibility; it is the narrative result of transforming the condition contrary to fact into 'fact' itself. Such violation of dominant assumptions threatens to subvert (overturn, upset, undermine) rules and conventions taken to be normative.[24]

Thus, as Nicols Fox points out, some dystopian novels create a venue where one's "inner Luddite" can come out to play. Through the creation of a utopia or dystopia, we (writers and readers) can thus express our fear and our resentment of technology, even if doing so might be considered unacceptable in real life. As he puts it, "We love our machines—as we would a spouse in an enduring bad marriage, whose flaws are so familiar, whose irritating voice is much a part of the background that it is impossible to conceive its not being there. Alternatives are not even imagined."[25] Daniels raises a similar idea—suggesting that the "truth" which everyone knew in nineteenth and twentieth century Britain was that despite its alleged moral superiority and wealth, it was a "deeply unpleasant society."[26] He suggests that the reason British writers have produced so many superior dystopian novels is because of some quality of British social and political life that allows for the imagination and expression of this unpleasantness.

Here, it appears that only highly ideological societies are likely to produce utopian and dystopian novels. Only those societies where it is accepted that change can come about through the sheer force of ideas are able to produce fiction which rests so heavily on ideology and which weights the role of ideology so heavily. As I argue later on in this manuscript, the utopian and dystopian—as well as apocalyptic novel—rests on the conceit that someone from the present time of the reader is travelling elsewhere to a new society or state which can only be understood through the narrator's own gaze or lens. The form thus only makes sense with the insertion of a narrator (the traveler) who acts as a guide to the reader—as he views the society he is visiting from the stance of someone who is more modern, more wise, more technologically advanced,[27] and more powerful. He views the new place as an anthropologist, a scientist and a judge. Only a highly ideologically mobilized society, like an empire, can produce that sort of narrator.

NOTES

1. Both definitions are taken from www.thefreedictionary.com.
2. A good example of this type of intelligence forecasting is found in Barry B. Hughes, *International Futures: Choices in the Face of Uncertainty* (Boulder, CO: Westview Press, 1999).
3. The complete report can be accessed at: www.dni.gov/nic/PDF_2025/2025_Global_Trends_Final_Report.pdf.
4. Noel Hendrickson, "Counterfactual Reasoning: A Basic Guide for Analysts, Strategists and Decision Makers," *Proteus Futures Digest* 2 (2008): 39.
5. Judith Little, ed., *Feminist Philosophy and Science Fiction: Utopias and Dystopias* (Amherst, NY: Prometheus Books, 2007): 13.
6. Sue Zemka, "Erewhon and the End of Utopian Humanism," *ELH* 69 (2002): 439.
7. Little, *Feminist Philosophy*, 13.
8. Bertrand de Jouvenal, "On the Nature of the Future," in Alvin Toffler, ed., *The Futurists* (New York: Random House, 1972): 278.
9. De Jouvenal, 282.
10. Here I am referring of course to Swift's description of the relations between Houhynms (who resemble horses) and Yahoos (who resemble humans) in his classic utopian novel *Gulliver's Travels*. Of course, some would argue that the Yahoos and the Houhynms were not really animals and humans at all, but were rather symbols of the relations between the colonizer and the colonized. I explore this further in subsequent chapters of the book.
11. Here, one might wish to consider the controversy surrounding the 2010 publication of a new and very popular dystopian novel in China called *The Prosperous Time: China 2013*. The Chinese government has attempted to ban this book—because the continued existence of the Communist Party is not presented as a structural certainty. Instead, citizens and readers are asked to envision a future without China's Big Brother. The novel has been criticized as being 'not in keeping with Chinese values.' Xujun Eberlein, "China 2013," *Foreign Policy* (July 30, 2010): www.foreignpolicy.com/articles/2010/07/30/China-2013.
12. Justin Cronin, the *Passage* (New York: Ballantine Books, 2010): 44.

13. Erwann Michel-Kerjan, "Toward a New Risk Architecture: The Question of Catastrophic Risk Calculus," *Social Research* 75(2008): 819–54.

14. Cronin, 534.

15. The catastrophe novel is thus based on the assumption that there IS no dominating future, since the apocalyptic event can be avoided through better information and proper information. Thus, I argue it offers the least subtle analysis of the international system and the one which is most simplified.

16. Here it is notable that the novel arrived in British bookstores on the same day as the London subway bombing—suggesting to many that the fictional event or one similar was truly inevitable. In this case, the novel is seen less as having predicted the event than acknowledging the reality of the dominating future.

17. Francis Fukuyama, *The End of History and the Last* Man (New York: Penguin Books, 1989).

18. Andrew Osborne, "As if Things Weren't Bad Enough, Russian Professor Predicts End of US," *Wall Street Journal* (December 29, 2008). http://online.wsj.com/article/NA_WSJ_PUB:SB123051100709638419.

19. Philip Tetlock and Geoffrey Parker, "Counterfactual Thought Experiments: Why We Can't Live without Them and How We Must Learn to Live with Them," in Philip E. Tetlock, Richard Ned Lebow, and Geoffrey Parker, eds. *Unmaking the West: 'What if' Scenarios That Rewrite World History* (Ann Arbor: University of Michigan Press, 2009): 14–44.

20. M. Keith Booker, *Monsters, Mushroom Clouds and the Cold War: American Science Fiction and the Roots of Postmodernism, 1946–1964* (Westport, CT: Greenwood Press, 2001): 27.

21. Paul Alkon, *Gulliver* and the Origins of Science Fiction, in *The Genres of Gulliver's Travels*, ed. Frederik N. Smith (Newark: University of Delaware Press, 1990): 63.

22. Stephen King, *On Writing* (New York: Pocket Books, 2002).

23. Ian and Margaret Deweese-Boyd, "Appropriating Borges: The Weary Man, Utopia and Globalism," *Utopian Studies* 19 (2008): 97.

24. Rosemary Jackson, *Fantasy: The Literature of Subversion* (London: Routledge, 1981): 14.

25. Nicols Fox, *Against the Machine: The Hidden Luddite Tradition in Literature, Art and Individual Lives* (Washington, DC: Island Press, 2002): xii.

26. Anthony Daniels, "Blood and Smashed Glass," *New Criterion* 25 (2007): 35.

27. Daniels, "Blood and Smashed Glass."

4

THE ROMANCE OF THE WORLD'S END

> This heaven and this earth shall cease, and a new world shall begin. ... Then shall the world's corruptible qualities be burnt away, and all those that held correspondence with our corruption shall be made fit for immortality, that the world, being so substantially renewed, may be fitly adopted unto the men whose substances are renewed also.
>
> —Augustine, *the City of God,* Book 20, Chapter 14

If the catastrophe novel is seen as the fictional equivalent of an intelligence scenario, and the utopian or dystopian novel as the fictional equivalent of a long-term intelligence forecast, the apocalyptic novel may be described as the fictionalized version of the disaster-assistance scenarios and exercises envisioned and created by the United States Federal Emergency Management Agency, the Department of Homeland Security, and the United States Armed Services. These scenarios start with the assumption that the disaster has already occurred. The emphasis is on mitigating the disaster and on attempting to forecast how individuals and groups will react and mobilize in its aftermath. The apocalyptic novel should thus tell us how people are likely to behave once the disaster occurs as well as the ways in which the disaster will alter the state's trajectory and lead to a new meaning for the state.

Thus, the apocalyptic novel differs in scope, in assumptions, and most importantly in epistemology. Here, however, the goal of the analysis is different. The apocalyptic scenario assumes the outcome cannot be avoided and does not aim to produce to avert the outcome. Instead, it aims to produce a new way of experiencing and making meaning of the outcome, which is regarded as inevitable.

Thus, in both an apocalyptic novel and a disaster-assistance manual, the actors are constrained by a dominating reality which is accepted as given. The question for both cultural products then becomes: given the dominating reality under which we must operate (because of an event which was unavoidable), how may we respond to this event and hopefully mitigate or lessen its effects? How can we affect our masterable reality?

The parallels between the two cultural products can be explored through considering one of these cultural products, a training manual given to new volunteers and employees of the Federal Emergency Management Agency which was written in 2002.[1] The course for new employees begins with a short description of an imaginary event known as the Centerville Flood. While there are no individual literary characters introduced, nonetheless one reads a description in general terms of how people reacted to the event in which some survived while others perished. The introduction to the "story" or narrative opens with information describing the likelihood and probability of such an event which serves to establish verisimilitude. Here, the reader is told that such an event is not imaginary, but is rather something that we may envision actually happening in the future. The first lines of the document in the section titled "A Disaster Strikes" tell us:

> The disaster story you are about to read describes an event that is common in many parts of the United States—a flood. Floods are the natural events that most frequently result in the loss of lives and property damage, claiming an average of 263 lives every year. Although this example deals with the flooding of a river, many of the consequences described could also result from a hurricane, earthquake, or tornado.[2]

The writer then goes on to describe the unavoidability of the event, to establish in the reader's mind that the event is both likely and probable

THE ROMANCE OF THE WORLD'S END

and—for the purposes of this scenario—must be accepted as given. The flood thus becomes the dominating future:

> Before the flood, rain fell steadily for several days. An unusually wet season had already left the ground saturated and unable to absorb much more rainwater.... When flood waters finally overflowed the river banks, many telephone and electricity lines came down in affected residential areas. A number of residential streets were so severely flooded that they looked like rivers.[3]

The reaction is then described, with an emphasis on the masterable future. Thus, we are told:

> In areas where power lines and phone lines were down, only people with battery-operated televisions or radios could receive the call to evacuate. Many residents could not make phone calls to obtain information; those who could, frequently received busy signals. Some who tried to drive to safety were unfamiliar with which routes could still be traveled and were injured on flooding highways.[4]

Later in the same document, in the section "Myths about Disaster Assistance," the nature of the dominating reality is again emphasized. The training material's authors describe the myth that "the objective of Federal Disaster Assistance is to fix everything."[5] Here they write: "As much as we may wish otherwise, once a disaster has seriously impaired our homes and our communities, they may never be exactly the same. Nor will disaster assistance ever be adequate to restore everything that was lost by all those affected."

This document is in many ways just as interesting for what it does not say as for what it does. In seeking to educate the reader and get him to accept that even the government is unable to fix everything, the manual's writer performs the same job as the apocalyptic novel—forcing the reader to accept a certain reality, and then to move past it to a new place where new patterns of behavior can be learned and new ways of thinking may be developed. Thus, accepting the premise of the apocalyptic novel means that both the writer and the reader buy into the possibility of abandoning the narrative of liberal progressivism, in which the spread of market economics and democratic ideology leads to a world in which people are safer, healthier and the future is optimistic. Table 4.1 compares and contrasts the conditions of the catastrophe novel and the apocalyptic novel more specifically:

Table 4.1. The Catastrophe Novel versus the Apocalyptic Novel

	Catastrophe Novel	Apocalyptic Novel
Authority of Writer	• Technical expertise: Military, medical • Close association with policymakers	Established cultural figure
Goal of Writing	Influence or change policy	• Raise questions • Provide new language • Agenda-setting • Expression of popular consciousness
Plausibility	High	Medium to High
Time Frame	One to five years	May extend to multiple generations
Policy/Political Effects	• Warning • Explicit changes in strategy, policy	Alternate means of discourse
Examples	• *Battle of Dorking* • *War of the Worlds*	• *The Road* • *World Made by Hand*
Geography	Conforms to Reality	Different from reality
International Relations Orientation	Realist	• Constructivist • Critical theorist
Intended Audience	Policymakers Elites	Mass audience 'entertainment function'

As noted previously, the apocalyptic novel shares methodological ground with a disaster-assistance scenario since both attempt to predict what sorts of "worst case scenarios" are likely and the circumstances under which they might occur. However, the two cultural products diverge sharply from one another in two ways: While both types of scenarios agree about the likelihood of disaster and its unavoidability, they differ in how they view the role of the state as well as how they expect individuals to behave in the aftermath of disaster. In figure 4.1, disaster can be seen as comprised of three overlapping elements:

THE ROMANCE OF THE WORLD'S END

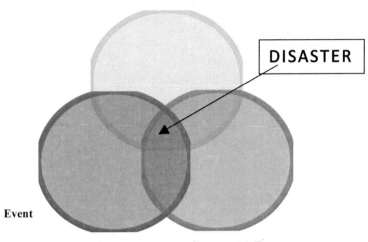

Figure 4.1. Facets of Disaster

Disaster-assistance management experts frequently speak of the first and then the second stage of disaster.[6] Here, the first stage, the manmade or natural event which causes the disaster itself, can only be endured. There is little that can be done to mitigate its effects once it has commenced (though steps can be taken prior to the disaster to mitigate its effects—such as building a levee or dike to prevent flooding, or not allowing people to settle in low-lying areas). However, the second stage of the disaster begins only once individuals and groups *respond* to the disaster. At this stage, many additional factors—including human nature and the social forces which existed in society prior to the disaster—can come into play, in some cases lessening the disaster through causing citizens to begin working together, and in some cases worsening disaster through introducing practices such as rioting, looting, and the creation of social unrest.

Social scientists have traditionally faulted novelists (and journalists) not for how they have portrayed the first stage of disaster, but rather for how they have portrayed the second stage. That is, the contemporary apocalyptic novel is initially seen as both possible and plausible in terms of its depiction of the events which occur (which may be drawn from current events). And as a result, it may also feel probable. However, the apocalyptic scenario departs from reality when novelists begin to speculate about how individuals and the state will behave in the *aftermath* of disaster. At that point, the novelist is no longer offering any sort of prediction of interest to planners. Instead, he is merely building a good story with highly stylized elements of behavior inserted in order to make the narrative more dramatic.

In particular, popular cultural renderings of the post-disaster time period have been criticized for their over-reliance on tropes of looting and shooting, as citizens are shown arming themselves and beginning to fight with their neighbors over scarce resources.[7] While this might make for good drama, disaster experts argue that while some disaster victims certainly panic and behave irrationally, not all do.[8] Analysts do concede that disaster (both real and imaginary) *is* socially disruptive—refugees are created, people move rapidly up and down the social hierarchy, villages and cities are depopulated, and possessions are sold, stolen, and looted. But some individuals may react to this disruption with shock, and they may simply stand around helplessly waiting for direction.[9] Still others pull together and display heroism as they seek to help their neighbors and family members.[10]

In addition, novelists have been criticized for their over-reliance on the assumption that in the aftermath of disaster, the state will wither— either immediately or gradually. The social critic Marvin Olasky in particular has criticized media portrayals of the second stage of the Hurricane Katrina disaster. He suggests that the depiction of citizens as out of control, dangerous to themselves and others, and ruthless and predatory is based largely in unspoken racialized assumptions made by the largely white reporting community. In addition, Stock suggests that writers who reported about Hurricane Katrina somehow became enamored of the new term "anarchic," which was applied indiscriminately and usually incorrectly (in the sense that most reporters had no actual grounding in the political theory of anarchy).

However, actual disaster planning simulation exercises created in recent years by the Department of Homeland Security, among others, *have* predicted both state breakdown and a breakdown in community values and commitment to the collective good. In 2001, the Johns Hopkins Center for Civilian Biodefense Studies, the Center for Strategic and International Studies (CSIS), the ANSWER Institute for Homeland Security, and the Oklahoma City National Memorial Institute for the Prevention of Terrorism developed an exercise in 2001 for a group of senior level elected and appointed officials in the Washington, DC, area. The exercise, known as Dark Winter, included three simulated role-playing exercises involving National Security Council Meetings.[11]

The fourteen-day exercise simulated an outbreak of a smallpox-like disease—perhaps caused by biological warfare—somewhere in Oklahoma. Participants experienced increased casualty rates and a vaccine shortage as the exercise wore on. The disease eventually spread to twenty-five states and fifteen foreign countries. As "news reports" discussed what plans might occur for the rationing of the vaccine, the participants took a number of actions including declaring martial law in the affected state. The acting "Governor of Texas" sealed his state's borders so that infected or exposed individuals could not escape into his territory, and Mexico was blamed for having transmitted the infection. Meanwhile, reports indicated that citizens had begun looting and shooting one another and eventually federal troops began firing on civilians.[12]

What is striking here is the fact that many of these "myths" appear in federal disaster simulations, either because they are written into the scripts or because participants act as if such actions and reactions are logical and expected. The same fears and myths that occur in apocalyptic novels also appear in disaster-assistance simulations. In particular, the theme that American citizenship is merely a myth and that when times get tough, neither municipalities nor individuals will be willing to sacrifice for the common good appears in both types of literature. While the Dark Winter scenario resulted in the closing of the Texas border to smallpox-infected citizens from Oklahoma, Justin Cronin speculates in *The Passage* that California would secede from the United States in order to keep its own people safe from the biological weapons threatening the rest of the United States. And while citizens in Oklahoma were quick to arm themselves and to take vaccine by force if necessary in the Dark Winter simulation, characters in many of the apocalyptic novels—including *The Road*—also quickly use weapons to defend themselves and their families. Finally, the idea that people do not behave rationally when confronting an "invisible enemy" like disease appears in both the Dark Winter simulation and the novel *The Pesthouse*.

However, apocalyptic fiction only offers two possible endings. In the first outcome, the state withers away—leaving only destruction in its wake, while in the second outcome, the state withers away and in doing so creates a site for personal and community renewal. The third possible ending is never explored. In this ending, the state is reconstituted as an even stronger state which seeks to maintain power through, for example, declaring martial law. Examples of "state strengthening" in the aftermath of disaster drawn from real life might include the declaration of martial law after the famed 1755 Lisbon earthquake, along with the implementation of executions, rationing, and forced labor. Both Shrady and Paice[13] describe the ways in which Portugal's King Joao V ceded unprecedented emergency powers to his Secretary of State Sebastiao Jose de Carvalho in the wake of the disaster. Carvalho quickly moved to institute a new type of martial law—in which surviving citizens were co-opted into a type of forced labor to clear land and bury the dead; food was rationed; controls were put on the freedom of movement of surviving citizens; and looters were publicly executed. Nonetheless, there were rumors of savage looting and even cannibalism. Some might argue that the passage of the USA Patriot Act in the United States in the aftermath of the 9/11 terrorist attacks is also an example of state strengthening as the result of unanticipated events, as is the use of federal troops to keep order in New Orleans after the 2005 hurricane and flood.

In cases of state strengthening, the phenomenon described is "decisionism," in which power is concentrated in the hands of the state during the state of exception. In such a situation, the state achieves the right to decide "over and above any existing law, constitution or elected body."[14] Here, one may make the argument that each apocalyptic novel actually contains elements of decisionism on a local level, though the overall central government has failed. This phenomenon is seen in *The Pesthouse*, where a theocratic government runs a sort of shelter which the main character Margaret stays in during the winter on her trip across a ruined America. Before Margaret can come into the shelter, she is required to give up any metal objects she might have since the believers argue that metal is dangerous and that it "kills." She is also required to participate in the care of the elderly men whom the community worships. In *World Made by Hand*, the reader is told of a gentleman in upstate New York who has in essence re-created the Southern plantation, complete with indentured servants who are provided with housing and food in return for their labor. Here, too, the overwhelming conditions of the emergency have allowed him to gather power in his own hands which far exceeds anything described in the laws of the land.

That is, both fiction and history suggest that disasters which cause threats to the state do not automatically lead to the withering of the state. Nonetheless, in the past ten or so years, there has been a heavy emphasis on the theme of the "threat of anarchy" both in fiction and in popular culture. Here, another interpretation would suggest that the threat of anarchy was somehow "in the air" prior to Hurricane Katrina itself and the 2005 events merely gave journalists and analysts the space to give voice to this sentiment, that the American state was perhaps not as strong or as permanent as its citizens had been led to think. Here, what is striking is the consensus of fiction writers about the likelihood of state collapse. Each of the stories considered in this work includes a type of state failure. In each instance, the American state, unable to cope with a confluence of international and domestic threats (manmade and natural) collapses inward. The state no longer exists as either the guarantor of personal security, the foundation of personal and corporate identity, and the creator of the infrastructure which sustains modern life. The state also fails to maintain territorial integrity, and America essentially fractures—though analysts differ as to whether the "fault lines" for the fracture will be geographic, economic, ethnic, or racial.

What fascinates here is the fact that the outcome which most frightens the reader (and our culture, perhaps) today is not the simple invasion narrative. It would be far simpler, perhaps, to write a story about a particular security flaw facing the United States, and the existence of an enemy who is witty enough to outsmart American security and exploit that flaw. Rather, what these novels suggest is that the bleakest future one can imagine is one in which modernity and civilization themselves come to unravel, not merely through the actions of outside invaders but perhaps in some way through the collusion of American citizens themselves. But how do we account for the unanimity surrounding this vision? Here, we might suggest that the average apocalyptic novelist is someone who feels that our present-day world is threatening and perhaps in a downward spiral. He or she may have experienced particular events that could be described as apocalyptic moments—either directly or vicariously as these events have infiltrated a culture. Thus, American novelists frequently mention the experience of watching or somehow participating in 9/11 and Hurricane Katrina as the impetus for their writing.

The author David Kushner explains how the reclusive American writer Cormac McCarthy decided to write the best-selling apocalyptic novel *The Road*:

> When the attacks of 9/11 unfolded . . . McCarthy began to wonder about the future facing his boy. "I think about John all the time and what the world's going to be like," he says. "It's going to be a very troubled place." One night . . . McCarthy imagined such a place . . . McCarthy gazed out the window of his room and pictured flames on the hill. He later decided to write a novel about it.[15]

Similarly, the writer Justin Cronin offers the following explanation for how he came to write *The Passage*:

> I was part of the evacuation for Hurricane Rita. . . . We managed to get all of fifty miles before jumping the median and heading home. . . . Nearly everyone was out of gas; all the mini-marts and service stations had been stripped bare; whole families were sleeping on the side of the road. It was like a scene out of the Old Testament.[16]

However, it may be argued that writers have grappled with the notion of totally destroying the state (at least fictionally) not only because it seems likely in some sense, in the aftermath of 9/11, but also because it seems desirable. That is, destroying the state can be compared to the dynamiting of a building to make way for urban renewal in a blighted downtown area. Architects like Bernie Jim have described the creative destruction involved in "wrecking the joint" or destroying a building. In their discourse, the destructive impulse is channeled or engineered. The destruction is both controlled and embraced, and its consequences are not punitive but redemptive. Here Jim tells us that "demolition was an aggressive, irresistible force that could realize, through brute strength and technological mastery, the ideology of creative destruction."[17]

Similarly, the disaster or the apocalypse provides a space where the ground is cleared and life (and its institutions) can begin anew. Institutions which seem entrenched, warped, mired in neglect, decay, and corruption can be blown apart, thus providing a new emancipatory space. The idea that disaster is a "world apart" from everyday politics, and that during disaster times individuals and institutions may discover a freedom to behave in new and different ways appears in both actual and imagined disaster narratives. Indeed, mainstream media coverage frequently includes the theme of "true life heroism"—in which narratives emphasize the behavior of individuals who acted in group- rather than individual-oriented ways at a time of great strife and suffering. In addition, articles may point out certain "positive" aspects of the disaster—including the greatly increased media coverage of a Third World region where suffering is commonplace but where it exists largely off the radar; the ability to rebuild in new and experimental ways or the outpouring of foreign aid which may eventually lead to better schools, more equitable gender roles, or a decrease in autocratic rule.

Thus, the writer H. G. Wells uttered words in support of this sentiment when he described the trend of "shattering and recasting of fundamental ideas" in the nineteenth century as giving way to a "period of ethical reconstruction" in the twentieth century.[18] The social critic William Morris made similar remarks upon reading the Victorian class apocalyptic novel *After London*. He noted: "I know now (civilization) is doomed to destruction. . . ; What a joy it is to think of! And how often it consoles me to think of barbarism once more flooding the world, and real feelings and passions, however rudimentary, taking the place of our wretched hypocrisies."[19]

The anarchist impulse in wrecking the state could be described in the following terms: Formerly, we were the captives of Western capitalism, industrialization, and the state. Now, after the apocalypse, we are free to engage in personal self-discovery, to grow closer to the land, to one another, and to overcome traditional "bourgeois" affectations such as class differences and racial differences. In essence what has been destroyed is the logic and practice of territoriality, where territoriality is defined as "an active strategy of controlling a geographic area."[20]

Apocalyptic destruction can be seen thus as freeing the characters within the narrative and allowing for a rewriting of the narrative. Suvin suggests that in Victorian times, apocalyptic destruction was a way of querying the "hegemonic consensus" regarding the utility and rightness of class differences and the good of the free market.[21] Similarly, apocalyptic destruction today is a way of querying the hegemonic consensus regarding America's leading role in the world, and the goodness and rightness of globalization.

But apocalyptic destruction narratives can be useful not only to novelists, but also for academics. Apocalyptic destruction can also be seen as freeing academics as analysts to begin to reenvision the international system in line with the new social formations put forth in the narratives themselves. The sociologist Lee Clarke suggests that real-life disasters can lead to progress on the part of the policy community. Those who react to and study disasters can learn more about who is most affected and why, and ideally, they can begin to reconceptualize and reorganize the institutions and structures used to study and respond to disaster.[22] Similarly, in positing the death of the imperial state and the destruction of the international system, apocalypse can allow political scientists to break out of what John Agnew has described as a "territorial trap" in which we are unable to conceptualize of land and territory without also making reference to the Westphalian state system.[23] In contrast, when the organizing framework of state power is imagined as finished or vanished, the reader is then forced to ask the questions "What does it mean to be American?" and "What are the aspects of our character that cause us to be American?" in the absence of that organizing framework. In some ways, this destruction is the equivalent of what occurs when a physical structure is destroyed and the individual items (like lumber) which made up the "house" are now understood outside of that context. One is forced to ask whether, in the absence of the house, the wood beams and posts are still part of some larger structure or whether they are now instead merely individual inputs.

In the anarchic apocalyptic novel then an emergency isn't something to be avoided but rather something to be accepted and embraced since in any case it is unavoidable. The changes brought about are simply too sweeping. And states cannot respond because the states too are destroyed by the actions of the emergency itself. Both Victorian and present-day utopian literature deals with two intertwined "wishes"—the wish to destroy the old structure and the wish to see history, politics, and culture take a new trajectory. While the accepted trajectory in each case is for more empire, more progress, more civilization, and more capitalist production, the "wish" is actually to see empire destroyed, and the wish to see industrialization destroyed.

In describing how one dynamites a building, Bernie Jim allows that destruction frequently allows the spectators to learn from the destruction. Once the building is destroyed, its architecture is more clearly visible and students can better understand how the building was put together from viewing its exposed beams, joints, and brick and masonry work. In taking the building down, students can better understand how it was built—including identifying where its weaknesses and its strengths were. That is, by looking at what is left after the smoke clears, one can see which features of the building were the most enduring. One can also see which parts of the underlying structure were the most rotten—which did not support their weight and which might have ceased to work and even helped to damage the structure further.

Similarly, one could argue that fictionally smashing the state (and the ideology which undergirds it) can both emancipate its participants and edify the spectators. Positing the end of the state and the international system can thus serve to expose its flaws and weaknesses, thereby teaching the reader. And as in the case of the decaying building, we can better understand which underlying state structures were rotten and dangerous, as well as which are likely to endure. In this light, we can understand Cormac McCarthy's description of the years immediately following apocalypse in *The Road:*

> In those first years the roads were peopled with refugees shrouded up in their clothing . . . their eyes bright in their skulls. Creedless shells of men tottering down the causeways like migrants in a fever land. The frailty of everything revealed at last. Old and troubling issues resolved into nothingness and night. The last instance of a thing takes the class with it. Turns out the light and is gone.[24]

Here, it appears that Cormac McCarthy has used the apocalyptic events to "burn away" many of our preconceptions about what America is and who we are as Americans. Here, Americans are "revealed" (in an apocalyptic sense) as "creedless shells of men." In this scene, McCarthy forces the reader to consider the possibility that Americans are not special creatures with a unique destiny or future. Implicitly, he critiques the narrative of American exceptionalism which would suggest that America (and Americans) is uniquely favored by providence or by God. Americans are not, it seems, immune to famine, pestilence, or fear. And when confronted with such threats, they are just as likely to become "creedless shells of men" as they are to triumph by rolling up their sleeves and displaying American ingenuity. When apocalyptic events smash the structure and leave Americans exposed, these Americans ultimately have neither a national nor a religious creed to fall back upon.

That is, what these apocalyptic novelists end up revealing through the events depicted is a "post-ideological" society. As early as 1982, the literary analyst Warren Wagar suggested that the increased production of cultural retellings of the story of "the end of time" signaled a sort of world weariness. He argued that what we were really witnessing was the end of 'history'—if history was defined as patterned forward movement in stages towards a better society. No one could figure out what came next, and so writers began to develop literary renderings of what this secular apocalypse or End of Time might look like. In his own words, "Great apocalyptic beasts . . . are easier to picture than metamorphoses of social orders."[25]

In this way, his own speculation was an early statement of the sentiments that the analyst Slavoj Zizek would later come to echo in speaking of "post-ideological society." To Zizek, post-ideological society rests on the wholesale abandonment of the myth that the state will somehow carry life forward in a progressive direction, solving problems and granting a vision or a narrative that allows one to make sense of one's past and one's future. Ideology thus provides a predictive model for how the world works—by fitting individual and corporate behavior into a web of belief systems. Zizek uses the term "post-ideological" to refer to situations where that overarching belief system has come to an end—as it did at the end of the Roman Empire or the former Soviet Union. A vision of a post-ideological society is thus an indicator of an underlying and profound crisis of belief.[26] The presence of apocalyptic envisioning is thus an indicator of that crisis.

The statement by Robert Earle at the beginning of Kunstler's *World Made by Hand* where he states "I don't know what kind of world we're living in anymore"[27] is in essence an agreement with the notion that he lives in a post-ideological world where the only meaning which life has is that which its citizens and inhabitants attribute to it. That is not to say that life or society is now meaningless. Rather, in typical post-modernist language, life and society now contain multiple meanings and multiple forms of organization—which are generated by and explained by the participants themselves.

Thus, today's anarchic apocalyptics are essentially a representation of a wish to undo what may be regarded as the worst excesses of capitalism and globalization. They are not, unlike, thus, the picture painted in *The Machine Stops*, written in 1909 by E. M. Forster, about a society which is dependent on machines which allow them to communicate throughout the world, but which somehow rob them of the relationships and real experiences which make life worthwhile. This wish to undo the capitalist (and imperialist) trajectory and to see one's nation shed the constraints of superpowerdom is thus neither new nor unique.

Three novels which embody the anarchist impulse in apocalyptic literature are the Victorian classic *News from Nowhere*, by William Morris; and the two modern classics *World Made by Hand* by William Kunstler and *The Passage* by Justin Cronin. In each of these novels, there is little ink devoted to the notion that the apocalyptic event could have (or should have) been prevented from occurring. Instead, the emphasis is on describing how and why we can move on after the unpreventable event—building anew on the corpse of the old state.

The ruined state thus provides a site for great powers to experiment with new building techniques and new modes of organization while those in greatest danger bear the risk of these experiments. Here we might pause to consider whether the anarchic impulse has been misstated thus far—I would venture to restate it as follows: it appears that *witnessing* destruction or *imagining* destruction may serve to launch the creative impulse involved in reimagining structures and society. However, when one is truly the subject of that destruction, the impulse is only to flee the building and to survive. The individual who stands across the street from the building being dynamited may benefit creatively, aesthetically, or spiritually from witnessing the destruction—but the person trapped in the building does not have that privilege.

NOTES

1. Federal Emergency Management Agency, Introduction to Disaster Assistance. (Washington, DC: Federal Emergency Management Agency, 2010).

This manual may be accessed at http://training.fema.gov/EMIWEB/downloads/IS7unit_1. pdf.

2. Federal Emergency Management Agency, 2.
3. Ibid, 3.
4. Ibid, 4.
5. Ibid, 10.
6. See, for example, Jose Juan Lopez-Ibor, "What Is a Disaster?" in J. J. Lopez-Ibor, G. Christodoulou, M. Maj, N. Sartorius, and A. Okasha, eds., *Disasters and Mental Health* (Chichester, UK: John Wiley and Sons, Ltd, 2005): 5.
7. See also Robert Stallings, *Promoting Risk: Constructing the Earthquake Threat* (New York: Aldine de Gruyter, 1995): 99–122.
8. Marvin Olasky, *The Politics of Disaster: Katrina, Big Government and a New Strategy for Future Crisis* (New York: Thomas Nelson, 2006). Also, C. C. W. Voorhees, John Vick, and Douglas Perkins, "'Came Hell and High Water': The Intersection of Hurricane Katrina, the News Media, Race and Poverty," *Journal of Community and Applied Social Psychology* 17(6): 415–29.
9. Lee Clarke, *Worst Cases: Terror and Catastrophe in the Popular Imagination* (Chicago: The University of Chicago Press, 2006): 57. In addition, Jaeger, Renn, Rosa, and Webler make the argument that individuals do not behave rationally in considering disaster before it occurs. This is why, for example, they resist buying flood insurance. See O. Renn, C. Jaeger, E. Rosa, T. Webler, "The Rational Actor Paradigm in Risk Theories: Analysis and Critique," (2000): 194. Available at: www.kent.ac.uk/scarr/events/finalpapers/renn.pdf.
10. Matthew Farish, "Disaster and Decentralization: American Cities and the Cold War," *Cultural Geographies* 10 (2003): 135.
11. All materials related to the exercise, including the script can be accessed at www.upmc-biosecurity.org/website/events/2001_darkwinter (as of November 8, 2010). See also Tara O'Toole, Michael Mair, and Thomas Iglesby, "Shining Light on Dark Winter," *Clinical Infectious Diseases* 34 (2002): 972–83.
12. www.upmc-biosecurity.org/website/events/2001_darkwinter/
13. Edward Paice, *Wrath of God: The Great Lisbon Earthquake of 1755* (New York: Quercus, 2010).
14. See Michael Dutton, "911: The Afterlife of Colonial Governmentality," *Post Colonial Studies* 12 (2009): 303–14.
15. David Kushner, "Cormac McCarthy's Apocalypse," *Rolling Stone* (December 27, 2007). http://74.22.215.94/~davidkus/index.php?option=com_content&view=article&id=61
16. Gasper Triangle, "Justin Cronin," *Texas Monthly* (July 2010). www.texasmonthly.com/2010-07-01/authorinterview.php

17. Bernard L. Jim, "'Wrecking the Joint': The Razing of City Hotels in the First Half of the Twentieth Century," *Journal of Decorative and Propaganda Arts* 25 (2006): 292.

18. Antulio J Echevarria, *Imagining Future War: The West's Technological Revolution and Visions of Wars to Come, 1880–1914* (Westport, CT: Praeger Security International, 2007): 25.

19. Quoted in Darko Suvin, "Victorian Science Fiction, 1871–85: The Rise of the Alternative History Sub-Genre," *Science Fiction Studies* 10 (1983): 147.

20. Hans Vollard, "The Logic of Political Territoriality," *Geopolitics* 14 (2009): 688.

21. Darko Suvin, "Victorian Science Fiction."

22. Clarke, *Worst Cases*, 143.

23. John Agnew, "The Territorial Trap: The Geographical Assumptions of International Relations Theory," *Review of International Political Economy* 1(1): 53–80.

24. Cormac McCarthy, *The Road* (New York: Knopf, 2006): 24.

25. Warren Wagar, *Terminal Visions: The Literature of Last Things* (Bloomington: Indiana University Press, 1982), xiii.

26. Slavoj Zizek, *The Sublime Object of Ideology* (London: Verso, 2009).

27. James Kunstler, *World Made by Hand* (New York: Grove Press, 2009): 142.

2
APOCALYPSE AS CRITIQUE

5

APOCALYPSE AND EPISTEMOLOGY

In this chapter, I argue that the apocalyptic scenario is perhaps the most politically subversive of all the cultural products explored here. By virtue of its very existence, the apocalyptic novel puts forth the claim that "it is possible that in the future my nation will not prevail. It is possible that instead we will fail—and that in the grand scheme of history, all of our accomplishments may come to mean very little, as we ourselves will." As Stewart and Harding argue, apocalyptic discourse is not just a narrative with a beginning, middle, and an end, but it is also a narrative *about* the beginning, the middle, and the end.[1] In a state which is highly ideologically mobilized towards the spread of its ideology and highly committed towards the notion of playing a leading role in the world, there are often pressures—both subtle and overt—which militate against querying the dominant ideology. For that reason, the apocalyptic novel becomes as a literary space in which writers (and readers) can indulge in speculation about their nation's death and the escape from empire which that death provides. This helps explain why some apocalyptics appear to be optimistic documents—in which citizens reforge bonds of community, rediscover their inner strength, and rebuild their cities and villages in new ways which are often seemingly preferable to the old.

In this chapter, I describe how apocalyptic literature utilizes the eschatological lens to view a state from an imagined vantage point in the future. In a catastrophe narrative, the events are viewed from the endpoint—the outcome which is to be avoided—and in a utopian or dystopian narrative the events are viewed from elsewhere, from one's own society which serves as a vantage point to look upon the idealized society. And in the apocalyptic narrative, the vantage point is that of an "out of body experience." That is, described in medical terms, the eschatological lens allows the reader and the writer to view the state as a dead subject and to carry out an autopsy on the state. For this reason, apocalyptic literature plays a particular role in critiquing the state whose identity rests on a narrative of exceptionality. The exceptionalism narrative is teleological, and prophesies what the state's future will look like. Bruce Feiler, the historian, describes the way in which John Adams wrote of the settlement of America as "the opening of a grand scene and design in Providence for the illumination of the ignorant, and the emancipation of the slavish part of mankind all over the earth."[2] In contrast, the eschatological lens queries this narrative through forcing the reader to imagine an ending in which the teleological endpoint was not reached. However, the eschatological narrative does not accept that the state had a number of different possible alternate trajectories which might have occurred during its "lifetime." The endpoint of state failure is thus not simply a case of a lost opportunity or the state taking a wrong turn. Instead, the assumption in the eschatological narrative is that the final end stage of the state was somehow coded in its DNA from its inception and that in that way, its destiny was fulfilled. Here there is a high degree of consensus among apocalyptic writers regarding what causes and circumstances might eventually lead to the end of the state. However, there are multiple interpretations of how life might develop in the post-apocalyptic world. In this chapter, I explore the notion of linear versus circular apocalyptics—which I refer to as Armageddon or Eden. In short, writers differ about whether the post-apocalyptic world is Kantian (Eden) or Hobbesian (Armageddon).

WRITING APOCALYPSE

In order to consider how the apocalyptic scenario differs from other types of predictive scenarios, it is necessary to pick up with the descriptions given in chapter 1 of the ways in which the secular apocalyptic parallels its more well-known cousin, the Biblical or religious apocalyptic. Here what draws the two types of apocalyptics—theological and secular—together is the notion of eschatology and the use of the eschatological lens. In *Unbuilding Jerusalem*, the analyst Steven Goldsmith suggests that the conceit of all apocalyptic writing is that we claim to know how the story ends although we ourselves are only somewhere in the middle of it. Thus, for example, he points to the fact that the final book of the Christian Bible, *The Book of Revelation*, is actually written in the past tense—though ostensibly the events in the book have not yet happened but rather are expected to happen somewhere in the future. Nonetheless, the perspective which the reader is expected to take is one of looking back and remembering future events.[3] Thus, for example, he is not told "and then, at the end of days, the seventh seal will be opened." Instead, he is asked to imagine a situation in which "Behold, the Lion of the tribe of Judah, the Root of David, hath prevailed to open the book and to loose the seven seals thereof" (Revelation 5:5). The reader thus holds himself at an historic distance from events. He is asked to behave as though he has already seen the future and is looking back on it, although it has not happened.

Korner[4] describes all Biblical apocalyptics (both Old and New Testament) as the sharing of a vision which the author has had, which he believes has been divinely granted to him. He points to the use of the phrase "And then I saw . . ." which appears in the narrations of visions found in the Old Testament books of Ezra and Daniel as well as in the New Testament *Book of Revelation*. Here, it is as though the narrator is overtaken by this glimpse of future history—and in his position as a bystander who watches it unfold, he cannot control its trajectory or its outcome. He can only watch as it is revealed to him. (He possesses no agency.) Similarly, in secular apocalyptic and utopian novels like William Morris's *News from Nowhere*, the scaffolding framework of a dream is used once again, with the narrator telling what he has seen of the future in his dream. The glimpses of the future and the present granted to Lemuel Gulliver in Swift's *Gulliver's Travels* have a similar feel. Gulliver is overtaken by a situation over which he has control—like a shipwreck—and in his weakened and helpless state, he then glimpses an alternate reality.

What is important here, however, is the fact that the use of this imagined future perspective—allows for a different kind of knowing. Here, if we posit that the state can be understood as a body, then we can consider the ways in which knowledge about the body is made. Annemarie Mol[5] argues that different medical specialties have different stances towards the body—in terms of how they understand its workings, the progress and meaning of disease, and how they propose to study the body. All claim to "know" the body, but the knowledge claims of the specialists rest on different epistemological and methodological grounds.

Mol describes the ways in which a present-oriented and a past-oriented lens towards the examination of the body differ. Here the physician who interacts with the living patient enjoys an advantage because he can interview the patient and benefit from the knowledge of lived experience of disease and health which the patient provides. His knowing is thus reflexivist, as it is not his alone but is rather created either in concert with or in reaction to the patient's knowing. Through interacting with a living patient, the physician ends up "knowing" more about some aspects of the patient's life but also risks losing his objectivity. In contrast, there is the pathologist. After the patient's death, this specialist can literally slice up the patient and place him under a microscope. He knows of the patient's pain not from the patient's narrative but from dissection and analysis of the patient's veins themselves. Thus, the pathologist "knows" the patient and his disease based upon the pathologist's own insights into the course of the patient's disease over his or her lifetime.

So how can these insights be applied to the study of apocalyptic fiction? Here, we can start from the assumption that the state, too, is a kind of body which the analyst can study from three different viewpoints. First, the analyst may focus on the story of the state's founding, honing in to examine the organism's DNA. Here, the analyst acts like a genetic counselor, utilizing a teleological approach to spin out projections about the state's future, its lifespan and the conditions of its eventual decline. This way of knowing elevates the creation narrative over other types of knowing—seeing within the creation narrative the end state of the organism, just as a theologian might talk about the future of mankind through an examination of the Biblical *Book of Genesis*. Next, the analyst can theorize from within the lifespan of the state (the state of which he is perhaps even a resident or citizen). Here, insights are of necessity reflexivist and situated. Finally, the analyst can theorize from beyond the lifespan of the state, using an eschatological approach in which the state and its "life" are understood within a much broader narrative. Here, he would begin his analysis not from the creation narrative but rather from the story of the state's demise. If he were a theologian, his analysis would start not with *Genesis* but with the *Book of Revelation*.

Traditionally, narratives about the state have rested on teleological claims regarding the future of the state. They have been creation narratives. Teleology says: based on what I know about an entity at present (about its essence, its character, and the trends occurring within it), I can extrapolate to describe the future disposition of that entity. In philosophical terms, the actuality of the object allows me to theorize about its potentiality.[6] Teleology is prophetic. That is, the analyst will tell you, because I understand the beginning of the story, I can therefore work out and predict how the story ends. The organism (or the state) is seen as having a natural trajectory within a larger history.[7] (Here, the analyst Jean Baudrillard reads even more deeply into the notion of a nation's teleology, suggesting that the prophetic vision of the final endpoint may actually serve as a basis for the state's feeling that they can *control* history. It is not just that the state can see its final triumphant end. The state may actually feel a sense of hurry, in wanting to move quickly to somehow bring about or "conjure up" that end. Interesting, he wrote presciently in 1994 that the only other group of political actors who had a sense of "how the story ends" and who felt empowered to move quickly to bring about that end—which they saw as the only possible, logical end—were terrorists. In that way, the teleological narrative of the terrorist can be seen as a sort of "Islamic exceptionalism" in which this group also feels that their god has his hand on their nation and that their group's travails and successes can make sense within this larger sweep of cosmological history.)[8] That is, the terrorists who finally acted in 9/11 after years of planning also had a vision of the end of history. It just wasn't the one which we are traditionally familiar with in the West or the one which we expected.

The narrative of American exceptionalism in particular is a teleological narrative which posits that the future of America can be understood with reference to two factors—the international system and America's "DNA." The story, in brief, explains that at present and in the past, the state (the United States or Great Britain) had always enjoyed a particularly favorable and blessed position within the international system. Blessed with a combination of skilled citizens, the "right" religion, and good geography, as well as matters of contingency such as being the first proponents of the Industrial Revolution or the first inventors of military technology, the state enjoyed a privileged position in contemporary times which would go on to allow the state to enjoy even greater rewards in the future.

The founding of the doctrine or ideology of American exceptionalism is most commonly traced back to a statement made by John Winthrop, the Governor of the Massachusetts Bay Colony in 1661. In referring to the colonies which would eventually become the United States of American, he stated:

> For we must consider that we shall be as a City upon a hill. The eyes of all people are upon us. So that if we shall deal falsely with our God in this work we have undertaken and so cause him to withdraw his present help from us, we shall be made a story and a byword throughout the world.[9]

Later on, American presidents including John F. Kennedy in the 1960s and Ronald Reagan in the 1980s have made reference to this same statement. And in the aftermath of September 11, then President George Bush used similar language in stating: "America was targeted for attack because we're the brightest beacon for freedom and opportunity in the world. And no one will keep that light from shining."[10]

This statement of the essence or the DNA of America's character is itself teleological in that it describes both the state of what America is as well as implicitly making reference to what America will be in the future. Here, teleology is necessarily solipsistic. The exceptionalist narrative is based on the following understanding: "I believe that the organism, which is me, has a particular trajectory within life and within history—regardless of what others do." That is, the exceptionality of the American (or British) state is such that the state does not have to adapt to its environment, the international system. Rather, the state itself both creates and builds its environment, the international system. Reinhold Niebuhr refers to this outlook as America's "dreams of managing history."[11] In this outlook, the international system is thus a byproduct of state action, rather than a catalyst which creates state action. (This distinction becomes important later, when the apocalyptic narrative is seen to stress how America "died" because it failed to adapt—a narrative strand which directly contradicts the exceptionalist narrative, which argues that American didn't "have to" adapt, since it made the international system. Or, as the analyst Robert Kagan put it, "American did not change on September 11. It only became more itself."[12] The system therefore would have to adapt to America, rather than vice-versa. In the apocalyptic narrative structure, one could argue that globalization killed America, or that America, in failing to adapt, killed itself.)

However, the emphasis in the original statement on the fact that God could "withdraw his help" implies that a contract or covenant *has* been created between God and his people, the citizens of the United States of America. That is, America seemingly does not have to answer to the international system, but it does have to answer to its God. In this case, God has not conferred complete immunity on his subjects but rather retains the right and responsibility to chastise and discipline his people as necessary, should they stray from this covenant. It is in this vein that the likelihood of America's citizens to see natural disasters as evidence of God's wrath and a need for moral correction can be understood.[13] Here, God is seen as using weather in particular as a way of "writing history" and altering outcomes of events. In his work on both American and British exceptionalism, the analyst Clifford Longley thus points to the importance of the story of the "Protestant Wind" in the narrative of England's own origins. According to this legend, it was God himself who decisively altered the outcome of the conflict between Protestant England and Catholic Spain in the year 1588 by causing a storm at sea to emerge which helped to turn back the mighty Spanish Armada and kept them from invading England.[14] The legend suggests that God commanded nature, hurting those who deserved punishment as well as rewarding those who pleased him. Here, God is seen as using nature to "shift the balance," during a confrontation, weighing in on one side or another. The English leaders struck a commemorative medal after the 1588 victory bearing the legend "he blew with his winds and they were scattered."

Thus, within the exceptionalist narrative, the experience of the Other is understood only within the context of one's own experience. This assumption is found in the statement by the poet James Lowell in 1870, when he stated that "next to the fugitives whom Moses led out of Egypt, the little ship-load of outcasts who landed at Plymouth . . . are destined to influence the rest of the world."[15] There is no similar assumption that others will influence the United States (nor presumably has America's geography been in any way shaped by its original inhabitants, the Native Americans). The relationship is seen rather as unidirectional. America seeks to make meaning from itself and from its relation to its God. But what is missing is a relation to the other. Here, the other may serve as the subject of America's narrative—he may be helped or led—but he does not participate in the naming or calling of America. He does not shape America. And America does not respond to the other's calling him (or calling him out). It only responds to itself.

Earlier in this work, I explained how there are actually two separate types of narratives having to do with imperial demise or near-demise: the catastrophe novel and the apocalyptic novel. Here, one can argue that the true apocalyptic novel retains this solipsistic stance, focusing largely on how it was that America came to its end, while the mere catastrophe novel adopts a stance in which it considers strategic interactions as well. Thus, the catastrophe novel would look at external security threats which America or Britain somehow failed to anticipate or prepare for—while the true apocalyptic novel would instead focus on the ways in which failure was written into the nation's DNA.

Using the unidirectional teleological lens means that, for example, an attack on America by Al Qaeda on September 11, 2001, can be understood only in relation to America itself. Here, Al Qaeda is described only as "the thing which threatens America." Beyond that, it has no independent identity or part to play in the narrative of what happened that day. The tendency of an imperial power to thus underestimate or ignore the advantages of its enemies and to explain its decline in retrospect with reference only to internal factors is thus widespread in any exceptionalist national narrative. Looking back to the decline of Rome, for example, we can note that until quite recently, there was a tendency for analysts to downplay the significance of the Hun threat which arose around Rome's borders. Instead, analysts interested in describing its end focused on internal factors such as the decline of Roman values, the lack of Roman military leadership, or changes to Rome's internal policies in the areas of taxation and citizenship policies.[16]

That is, exceptionalism is a lens which, when applied, overstates certain aspects of the narrative of America while downplaying others. Indeed, critics of the exceptionalist view have faulted it for the way in which its application allows American policymakers to overlook their own self-interest and its effect on guiding Americans in the decision to "share" democracy with others throughout the world.[17] Furthermore, the exceptionalist lens can, according to Bacevich, lead policymakers to overestimate their military capabilities—based on arrogance and hubris. It can cause policymakers to misread the intentions and interests of allies, and in the words of John Ruggie, can lead to "exemptionalism"—or the claim that international norms and laws which apply to other nations do not apply to the United States.

Thus, in the most extreme statement of the narrative of American exceptionalism, America is seen as both the creator of history and the international system and also, in many conditions (though not all), as the creator of the natural world and the mover of nature itself, through the wonders of science and technology.[18] The exceptional state is thus viewed both as "the master of the Universe" and "the master of its own fate." For this state to thus experience an apocalyptic end is both unthinkable and inexplicable, within the confines of this narrative. The narrative of mastery also helped to condition the citizens of the exceptional state to expect that their state will keep them safe and invulnerable—to threats of both the manmade and the natural kind. Citizens thus have a high expectation of safety, and little reason to believe that the state will ever fail to provide that safety.[19] When the state does fall down, the narrative of mastery is thus called into question.

EXCEPTIONALISM: A TYPE OF IMMUNITY

That is, the doctrine of exceptionalism implies a type of immunity. America (or Russia or Britain) is seen as having been promised a glorious future in which the dangers which threaten other nations will not threaten it by virtue of the special blessings and promises which it has been covenanted by its God. Instead, the exceptional nation is described as a sort of Promised Land, which citizens may enter as a reward for their virtue and deservingness.[20] To belabor the medical analogy, exceptionalism can be seen as a sort of "vaccine" which renders a nation invulnerable to the sorts of dangers which threaten other nations—the possibility of famine, natural disaster, or foreign invasion.

Exceptionalism also means that when disaster does threaten, Americans are much more likely to view it through a religious lens. Steinberg notes that as recently as 1993, a Gallup poll showed that almost one out of five people believed in the idea of Acts of God—that natural disasters like floods and earthquakes could be explained as occurring due to God's wrath and his judgment.[21] The exceptionalist lens thus does not imply that the trajectory of the state is without risk, or that the state will always prevail when entering into conflict. Rather, there is an understanding that at times God might withdraw his hand from the nation—in order to teach its inhabitants a lesson, to test them, or to correct them when they have gone astray. That is, as Rosa writes, "risk is coterminous with (society's) representations of it."[22]

In Darwinian terms, the exceptional nation may be viewed as more "fit" than other nations, and therefore more capable of surviving and reproducing. Here, the success of the exceptional state is described as resting success on a particular combination of exogenous factors (or the international environment) and endogenous factors (aspects of the state itself). Here, the analyst stresses first the conditions of the international system in which the story of America began—pointing to the advantages which America enjoys as the result of its unique geographic position—far away from the wars and chaos which engulfed Europe during the early and mid-twentieth century, for example. In addition, he might point to the divine favor provided by God himself. These are the exogenous factors which predict the success of an organism. Next, one might consider the endogenous factors. Here, analysts are likely to point to certain facets including perceived spiritual, moral, and economic fitness. Thus, the narrative goes, America triumphed over competitors to control and dominate an environment due to the advantages which it was born with.

The teleology of the exceptional state is described by the founder of the state of Rhodesia (now South Africa) Cecil Rhodes, who provided the following description of Britain's role in the world at Ruskin's Inaugural Address at Oxford in 1870.[23] Rhodes described England as having the duty:

> To found colonies as fast and as far as she is able . . . seizing every piece of fruitful waste ground she can set her foot on, and there teaching her colonists that their chief virtue is to be fidelity to their country and that their first aim is to advance the power of England by land and by sea.

In this brief turn of phrase, Rhodes has described the real meaning of what it is to "colonize"—Britain's ideology is seen as a sort of contagious virus which cannot be checked and which is destined to colonize and overtake the international system, which serves as a sort of host. The essential qualities of the state predict the end—and there is only one possible end. The teleologist thus explains why certain states become more successful or powerful and why they live longer in the international system based on two factors: preexisting conditions of the environment and certain essential characteristics of the organism (the state) itself. In scientific terms, the practitioner using a teleological approach might make the claim: I can tell you which individuals are likely to get sick or become cancerous.

Apocalyptic fiction writers, in contrast to the teleologists, are the pathologists of international relations, aiming to learn all they can about the state and its role in the international system by studying the process of its demise or perhaps even by dismembering or dissecting the dead body politic itself. The idea that disaster illuminates is not new. Sociologists in particular have argued that disaster allows us to "see" society.[24] Here, however, their unit of analysis is different. Sociologists argue that we can literally look at the corpses which emerge after a large-scale disaster (like a heat wave or a flood) to see whom the state has failed to rescue. In doing so, we can go beyond the "fiction" that the state is a healthy, functioning organism which provides for all of its citizens to see who, in fact, was left to die—frequently alone. In examining these corpses, we can then ask: Who is isolated in society? Whom does the state fail to serve?

However, the claim of the apocalyptic novel is even larger for it posits a type of state breakdown in which all are lost and abandoned. The state cannot serve anyone because it no longer exists. It fails. However, in positing this state failure, we can indeed "see the state," and we can see the state in relation to its citizens and in relation to the international system. From this state failure we can make a new type of knowledge claim. Here, the analyst says: I know how the story ends, and based on that knowledge, I can work backwards to tell you the story of who or what the entity is at present. Here, the analyst claims to "know" the organism based not on having been present at the creation but rather based on having been present at the organism's demise. The eschatological approach bases its knowledge claims on what is known about the organism's end. Here, the analyst tells us: I know who got cancer, and based on that knowledge, I can tell you which strategies aimed at staying healthy were actually successful and which were a waste of time.

The eschatological lens is utilized in the statement of Nash, the male protagonist in Jim Crace's *The Pesthouse* (2007), one of the post-apocalyptic novels to be examined in this work. Here Nash looks back from the perspective of approximately AD 3000 and provides the following description of the old America: "The far side of the river was an odd, perplexing place, he'd heard, haunted, wrecked and hard underfoot, with prairies of rubble where people had once lived in bastions and towers."[25]

In this brief sentence, Nash is able to sum up the very essence of twenty-first–century life and we, the readers, are able to see twenty-first–century life in an eternal perspective in which ultimately America's greatest accomplishments pale in significance to the breadth of history itself. [26]

Can Apocalypse Be Prevented?

Apocalyptic writing—whether secular or religious—thus utilizes an eschatological perspective, and in doing so achieves two ends: It is used both for predicting the course of future events and for formulating normative judgments about both the outcome and the events which preceded it. However, as noted earlier in this work, apocalyptic writing is *not* seen as having a sort of warning effect, and is not aimed at altering the final outcome of the events which are predicted. Rather, in the event that apocalyptic events which are prevented do not come to pass, their audience is likely to conclude that the prediction was either applied incorrectly and that the apocalypse is thus still to come, or that the warning was wrong. However, apocalyptic writing leaves no space for the possibility of altering the apocalyptic trajectory—since it is written not from beginning to end, but from end to beginning.

That is, if the catastrophe novel rests on a subjunctive clause which allows for the avoidance of disaster and a backing away from the undesirable end state, the apocalyptic novel does not recognize the existence of any possible alternative scenarios. The only possibility is that the prophecy which has existed from the beginning of time will be fulfilled at the end of time. In other words, a catastrophe novel might start with the substantive conditional clause: "If these germs escape from the lab, they will kill everyone." Then, it builds two subjunctive clauses: The positive subjunctive clause states "If the germs had been contained, everyone would have survived" and the negative subjunctive clause states: "If the germs weren't contained, then everyone would have died." Here, the catastrophe novel ends up with a situation where the undesirable outcome (a pandemic) is diverted—since the germs are contained.

In contrast an apocalyptic prophecy once written is seen as irreversible in all religious traditions—including Christian, Jewish, and Islamic. It cannot be diverted, its exact date cannot be predicted or known nor can its coming be hastened.[27] Teleology and eschatology thus remove the element of 'chance' which suggests that alternate ends are possible.[28] This does not, however, mean that one cannot alter one's own *individual* trajectory within the context of apocalyptic events. Thus, for example, in the Christian *Gospel of Matthew* (chapter 25, verses 32 and 33) readers are warned that on the last day "All the nations will be gathered before Him and He will separate them one from another, as a shepherd divides his sheep from the goats. And He will set the sheep on His right hand but the goats on the left." Readers are thus enjoined to reform their own lives in light of this new information about the last day, so that they can be counted among the sheep (Jesus's followers) and not among the goats (the sinners). In secular apocalyptic rhetoric, citizens may be warned about the long-term dangers to our earth from such damaging practices as refusing to recycle or an over-reliance on fossil fuels. However, true apocalyptic scenarios do not allow for the possibility that an event like global warming could be prevented or that the apocalyptic trajectory could be altered. Rather, the best that the individual can do is to go "off the grid" by installing solar panels or wind energy so that he himself can survive the apocalyptic events to come.

That is, apocalyptic theorizing makes the claim that the coming dreaded event cannot be stopped—though citizens may still alter their own personal fortunes in relation to that event. The apocalyptic narrative thus, by definition, forces man to view the coming situation with humility about both himself and his state. He acknowledges that there are situations which are beyond his control which he can prepare for and try to mitigate but which ultimately he cannot control.[29] Thus, meditating on the fact that there are certain types of events which are beyond the power of mankind to alter can be seen as an exercise in humility—or an antidote to imperial arrogance.

Here, in acknowledging that a state faces a crisis where it cannot control the outcome in literature, the writer may be in fact acknowledging a present reality in the international system. That is, we may be more likely to see apocalyptic theorizing in times of real-world cultural crisis.[30] Here, May suggests that apocalyptic language is more pronounced during periods when old structures and belief systems are being overturned. In the absence of organizing beliefs, events are more likely to seem mysterious. Similarly, Mercea Eliade suggests that apocalyptic language is a reference to the fact that we are "living in and through history."[31] Apocalyptic language and theorizing thus acknowledges the fact that change is messy and hard and that it doesn't occur without suffering. Thus, the apocalyptic way of making sense of history is fundamentally different than what May refers to as the "liberal progressive" narrative, which posits that change is predictable, logical, and perhaps even easy. Here, May describes liberal progressive ideology as couched in "transformation without suffering, progress without end"[32]—as opposed to progress through or beyond suffering. If there is a message then to contemporary apocalyptic narratives it might be summarized as follows: Change is messy. Change is hard. There are no guarantees.

Thus the apocalyptic novel represents a direct affront to the narrative of American exceptionalism. The apocalyptic novel is thus both a vehicle for creating new discourse and interrogating old myths. That is, it allows us as analysts to do "work"—in the sense of inventing and analyzing possible new futures and considering their ethical implications. Thus, the very existence of so much of this type of fiction is an indicator that something is afoot. Here, it is too simplistic to say merely that 9/11 made us aware of our own mortality and that of our nation. Arguably, 9/11 made us aware of something much greater than that since it forced us to interrogate the narrative of America's place in history, and to question

APOCALYPSE AND EPISTEMOLOGY

whether the trajectory which we had planned for America is as simple, as sure, and as easy as we had previously posited. That is, apocalyptic literature is simply the beginning point for this larger literary exploration of how the state can or cannot keep us "safe," what it means to be vulnerable, and what the outcome and meaning of suffering is.

As noted previously, however, the consideration of apocalyptic theorizing is not limited merely to the situation of the United States. Rather, what is striking beyond the *existence* of so many renderings of apocalypse at the height of imperial strength is the remarkable degree to which these visions *agree*. We can identify the construction of chains of causal reasoning in apocalyptic literature beginning with the Victorian era in Britain. In the mid-1880s, the British nature writer Richard Jeffries published an early apocalyptic novel called *After London*.[33] In that work, he described a future England in which some unspecific "accident" led to climate change, changes in vegetation and massive flooding in England. As a result of these events, Britain's government gradually lost its ability to govern, and the state eventually broke down into fiefdoms similar to those in medieval Europe.

In the twentieth century, a number of writers of speculative fiction have put forth descriptions of chains of events which alter the position of America in the world. Writing in 2008, the American writer James Kunstler offered the following picture of what America might look like ten years from now: As a result of a massive series of domestic terror attacks in the United States which resulted in the detonation of dirty bombs in Los Angeles and Washington, the American government makes the decision to implement strict new security measures in America's ports and harbors. This leads ultimately to a slowdown in trade and results in the uncoupling of America from the highly complex, evolved, and interdependent world. At the same time, America is struck by a disease known as "Mexican flu" which further disrupts travel and international trade, as well as causes massive casualties. As a result, America experiences a breakdown of communications, a failure of the U.S. government infrastructure as a shutdown in transportation, since oil can no longer be acquired from abroad. Consequently, famine and food shortages also come about.

Cormac McCarthy wrote in 2008 in *The Road* that in the future Americans might experience the detonation of a nuclear winter in which the climate changed and all forms of nonhuman life were extinguished. This led to the end of America's economic system, as well as its state infrastructure. Humanity turned to a savage state as a result.

In each case, the scenario produced rests on a number of shared assumptions: That resources are finite, the globalization is perhaps unworkable in the long run, and that the "dream of America" (with its open borders, minimal citizen surveillance and an ideology which suggests that everyone in America should bear responsibility for one another) in some ways contains the seeds of its own destruction. America, thus, was doomed from the start. Indeed, many of the secular apocalyptic tales analyzed here explicitly show that the events which transpired—the terrorist attack which ended "civilization" in *World Made by Hand*; the escape of plague-ridden half-humans in *The Passage* and the nuclear explosion which ended "civilization" in *The Road*—were only the final nail in a coffin which had been in process for some time. Thus, for example, readers are told that when the explosion lit up in the sky in *The Road*, The Man immediately ran to the bathroom and began filling the tub with water. While his wife asks in surprise if he plans to take a bath at four in the morning, readers know that The Man had somehow been expecting some form of large-scale event which would cause clean water to be scarce. Perhaps there had been other similar events in his recent past. And in *World Made by Hand*, readers are told that the final set of jihadist attacks which closed down ports in Los Angeles and Baltimore were merely the latest in an ongoing set of attacks.

Teleological and Eschatological Lenses

In religious apocalyptics, there is not a great deal of dissent between teleological and eschatological narratives.[34] This is largely because both narratives agree about the important question of how exactly the story does end. In other words, a teleological narrative notes that while on earth man will likely suffer and undergo trials and temptations, but that it will all be worth it because of the long-term story of salvation. An eschatological narrative points backwards from the moment of Final Judgment and assures those who lived morally and followed the rules that their sacrifice was not in vain since it ultimately led them to salvation. Here the two narratives almost appear to meet in the middle because both agree about who God is and who man is. They agree about the *essence* of the organism being studied. They agree as well about the *potentiality* of the objects being studied since teleologists view the narrative as one of striving towards this potentiality (salvation) while eschatologists view the narrative as one in which this potentiality has been fulfilled and has come to fruition.

A problem arises, however, with secular apocalyptic narratives, due to the fact that teleological narratives and apocalyptic narratives about the final disposition of the state do not match. In the teleological view, the state followed the Abrahamic narrative, in which God laid his hand on the individual or the state, spoke a covenant or an agreement into being, and promised that the individual would continue to grow and to prosper into the future. Within the teleological narrative of exceptionality, any setbacks which the state encountered or sacrifices which the state was asked to make were regarded as short term and inconsequential within the "grand scheme" of the state's infinite future (its potentiality).

Here, even if one does not believe in or accept the narrative of exceptionality, there are countless other teleological narratives for the modern analyst to choose from. He might choose Ronald Inglehart's narrative regarding the triumph of post-materialist values over survival-type values. Or he could choose Francis Fukuyama's Hegelian narrative about the end of history. He might even choose a Marxist narrative which posits the eventual end of the state. Nonetheless, as the analyst Slavoj Zizek notes, up until now, most of our knowledge of Western civilization has been situated within these teleological narratives which stress convergence, success of capitalism, and spread of democracy. However, with the advent of post-modernism and deconstructionism, these all encompassing narratives have increasingly been queried; however, there has been no new narrative to take its place. Rather, today, people are merely suspicious and distrustful of teleological narrative.

In contrast, the eschatological lens may offer multiple explanations for the final outcome. To belabor the analogy of the pathologist's report, an organism may be found to have expired from multiple causes—some of which were the immediate cause of death while others were secondary causes.[35] In either case, the cause of death is often found not to be explainable only by what the Other did, but also by what the body itself did. The outcome is seen as a strategic outcome which required an interaction with an environment and frequently with an Other as well. Not all eschatological pathologists, however, diagnose the exceptionalist state with the same ailment. Rather, there are a variety of different types of diagnoses which may be applied.

First, we have those who argue that somehow the DNA of the exceptionalist state was corrupt from the conception of the body politik. That is, the genetic code of the organism was flawed in such a way that it inherently carried instructions for its own self-destruction. Here, Paul Kennedy's "imperial overstretch" argument represents an eschatological revisiting of the history of the exceptionalist state since he examines a number of failed empires from the perspective in which their end has already taken place. Then, he works backwards to argue that every empire is ultimately its own worst enemy since it is preprogrammed to grow too fast (in essence, with a growth deficiency in its DNA). As it extends its territorial reach farther and farther, it eventually chokes itself, unable to feed and defend its existing extremely large body while simultaneously continuing to grow.[36] That is, America, unfortunately, belongs to a class of organisms (empires) which are inherently flawed and incapable of being cured. They all carry faulty DNA which causes them to grow too rapidly until ultimately they are unable to support themselves and they then expire, collapsing inwardly.

Amy Chua makes a similar argument about the "genetic code" of the empire—arguing that empires are inherently programmed to incorporate a diverse group of people which leads them to adopt ultimately self-defeating policies of tolerance. Thus, the empire is weakened from within because of the diversity within its membership. Here, too, she argues that the code of empire is flawed from its inception.[37] Within the apocalyptic literature, we can see a similar "flaw in the genetic code" argument in Justin Cronin's narrative from *The Passage*. Cronin describes the ways in which the imperial state contained elements of arrogance and hubris from its inception which allowed its authorities to mistakenly assume that they could control and steer technology and bioengineering, even when working with highly toxic substances. After the breach has been crossed and the bioweapons have escaped, Cronin allows his scientists to speak. What they tell the reader is, "We were extremely naïve and mistaken to think that we could control this outcome." America's defense industry officials apparently thought they could create weaponized human beings who could act with deadly force, that they could release these humans into 'the hills and caves' of somewhere like Afghanistan, where they could then be used to cleanse and clear areas of terrorists. Instead, the weapons proved to be uncontrollable; they escaped within the United States and proceeded to destroy civilization. Thus, the exceptionalist narrative which stated that man can control his environment and even technology proved to be the state's own fatal undoing.

Here, the notion that a state had a flaw in its genetic code from the start might be described as the state having a sort of chromosomal disorder. But we can also consider arguments which attribute the state's failure to a sort of autoimmune disorder (in the words of Jacques Derrida).[38] With an autoimmune disorder the state does not merely fail to thrive at some point. Instead, it turns inward and attacks itself since its security or "immune response" is actually too highly developed. In this scenario, the exceptionalist state's violent engine does not merely protect it from outside threats but instead, causes the state to begin to see threat everywhere. Thus, gradually the state strangles itself. This is the scenario described in *World Made by Hand*, where Robert Earle, the narrator describes how the United States "shut itself down" after losing a number of battles with jihadist attackers. He describes how bomb explosions in ports in New York and Los Angeles led the national leadership to make the decision to close the ports altogether. As a result of this policy of isolationism, the United States gradually becomes cut off from the international system and ultimately fails at being self-sustaining. (In this scenario, the exceptionalist state is not abandoned by its allies or by the international system. Instead, it appears that the state has committed suicide through voluntarily unplugging itself from the web of inputs which helped to sustain its life.)

A related diagnosis suggests not that the state killed itself, but that its "host"—the international system failed—and as a result, the state expired. Here, we can think of the exceptional state as both the architect of the international system and also as living in a symbiotic (or even parasitic) relationship with it. Thus, we have a variety of novels which blame the state's death on the end of globalization and interdependence. Here the claim is that the state knowingly and consciously put itself in a situation where it was dependent on a much larger international system without which it could not survive and which it could not control.

As a result of factors beyond the state's control, the international system broke apart, and as a result the organisms which depended on that system for their own support died—either quickly or slowly. These novels essentially make the claim that the state was again preprogrammed to continue to expand and to grow and to eventually create an international system. However, the state mistakenly assumed that it would always and forever continue to be the center of the international system and to exercise control over it. In a sense, it appears that the state at some point voluntarily put itself on life support—rendering it dependent on the actions of others to sustain its own life. When the others failed to comply, the state then died.

This diagnosis is described in the novel *One Second After*, in which the main character, Colonel John Matheson takes the reader through the succession of steps necessary to produce insulin, a medicine that his daughter depends upon every day. He describes how the production of this substance requires the cooperation of five different nations throughout the world. In the absence of interdependence, then, America is left in a situation where it can no longer feed itself, nor provide for its citizens' health and safety.

Thus, whether the state commits suicide, strangles itself, chokes, or fails to thrive in an environment which becomes toxic—the result is the same. The eschatological narrative helps us to understand how and why the patient died. Thus, in contrast to the teleological narrative of exceptionalism which paints any attack on the organism as merely a minor setback along the grand narrative of prosperity and eventual domination—the eschatological narrative of the apocalyptic novel posits that the state did not prosper, did not thrive into the future, and that at some point it and its people at best became irrelevant and at worst, became extinct. That is, the eschatological narrative queries the teleological narrative's claim about the potentiality of the organism.[39]

SMASHING THE STATE AND REIMAGINING THE END OF THE STORY

Earlier in this work, I raised the architectural analogy and suggested that "smashing the state" may serve the same purpose as "smashing" a building in that it exposes the interior architecture and the foundation of that structure. However, while the "smashing" of both objects occurs in the present, the smashing itself actually occupies three temporal dimensions—the past, the present, and the future. That is, when we confront a scenario in which America's government ends today, we also confront its end through two other lenses—that of the past and that of the future. If, in fact, the state ends today, then that would mean that the historic trajectory in which we had previously placed and understood the state was not actually, in point of fact, correct. To some degree, the state's current absence means that both our memories about the state and the "space" which it occupied in the past are now different as well. (To carry the architecture metaphor forward, if a famous building is destroyed, then what is destroyed is not merely the building but the place which the building occupied in history and in a sense the history itself which occurred there.) That is, the state which we thought we "knew"—the one which had an illustrious past, present, and future—also no longer exists, since its trajectory is now different. Furthermore, the knowledge which we believed we had about the state's future trajectory is also not correct since that too has been altered by virtue of its erasure in the present. Our future state no longer exists, nor do the other types of memories and events which hinge on its continued existence into the future.

Furthermore, the community which accompanied the state and which rested within it or even comprised it is now different as well. In his work on the politics of disaster, the sociologist Kai Erikson[40] explains how physical destruction is often accompanied by social disruption and social destruction as well. He describes the ways in which the Buffalo Creek Flood in 1972 destroyed not only hundreds of acres of land, several towns, and the livelihoods of the individuals from West Virginia who lived there. In addition, he notes that communities were destroyed—since people were uprooted and many fled the area, severing family and neighborhood ties. In the same way, the "smashing" of the state is not only the destruction of a means of governance. In destroying the institutions, one is also forced to contemplate the destruction of the American community and the American way of life, as well as the severing of the bonds which Americans see as binding themselves together. And again, temporally, one is forced to ask whether in point of fact these bonds were ever real, and if in fact, the "we" of America was in fact moving together towards some glorious end. What has been destroyed is not only the state at the present time but also the state which is to come, the *telos*. We can no longer live to see the end of the struggle to establish and "share" democracy throughout the world. What has been destroyed is a politics and a political theology. In Derrida's language, what has been destroyed is the "we" that we thought we knew, the brotherhood or fraternity shared amongst our members.[41] For "we" are no longer Us. We might even be Them. If that were true, it would necessitate rethinking our entire history.

The narrative of destruction then does not reassure those reading it in present times about the utility of their current work. Rather, it unsettles them since it forces them to ask the question: What if all of my (and my nation's) hard work, sacrifices, and trials are actually in vain? What if in the grand scheme of things they come to mean nothing? What if I am not, in fact, who I think I am? Here, the eschatological narrative negates the teleological narrative because they cannot both be true. They are contradictory and mutually falsifiable. America is either the savior of the world or they hate us. Both cannot be true. And given the differences between the two narratives, it is therefore not surprising that in times when the state is tested and doubts are being expressed about the future of the state, the eschatological narrative might make an appearance in popular culture. In modern times, the specter of 9/11 raised the possibility in many minds that perhaps the exceptionality narrative was not correct—and that the ultimate outcome might be different. What if, it asked, the United States is not Abraham but Job—destined to be tested and tried and treated not as an object of God's favor but rather as an object of God's wager? What if the sacrifices being called for at the moment (economic and military) are not ultimately worth it but are in vain? (Alternately, perhaps America is still Abraham, but we have fundamentally misunderstood who Abraham was and what he meant in history. In Derrida's reading of the Abraham narrative, we are asked to consider the possibility that Abraham was somehow caught between faith [defined as service and perhaps even blind obedience to God] and ethics [defined as love for one's fellow man]. For Derrida, Abraham represents the "costs of covenant" and the way in which politics calls for sacrifice, betrayal, and even cruelty.[42] In this case again, both the teleological and the eschatological narrative feature Abraham as the Father of American exceptionalism. However, his meaning is altered, depending on the stance one takes in telling the story—in short, whether one begins from the beginning or the end.) In the teleological narrative of American exceptionalism, the Abrahamic covenant which America makes with God is heroic and inevitable. In the eschatological narrative, reliance on the Abrahamic narrative may come to represent a peculiar type of American hubris which ultimately led to its downfall.

Apocalyptic narratives thus are more likely to appear in great power nations which are undergoing setbacks. This is because they are a way of querying two stories which do not appear to match—the teleological narrative which posits that greatness and potentiality reside in the genes of the state, and the present reality which suggests that the state may be flawed and even vulnerable. The eschatological lens is a way of testing the claims of exceptionality and of seeking to reconcile the competing models of the world. The eschatological narrative thus gives a readout from an imagined future perspective in which current events have a meaning which now seems "obvious." In retrospect, it is obvious that the state or body politic contained the wrong code or the seeds of its own destruction from the beginning.

Thus, both secular and religious apocalyptics speak of the end times and describe the logical conclusion of a series of events which trend towards a certain ending. From the perspective of one who knows how the story ends, it is now much easier to explain the trends which have occurred that led towards that end. However a religious apocalyptic writer imbues the events with theological or spiritual significance while the secular apocalyptic writer describes events as having political, ethical, or policy significance. Thus a story about a rebellious child in the popular religious apocalyptic series of *Left Behind* novels[43] would describe the child as participating in a trend of sinful rebellion which would lead to judgment being meted out on mankind on the last day. In contrast, a policy report presented to Congress might warn that citizens who keep wasting energy and oil will someday find themselves in a world without these resources.[44]

Both apocalyptic scenarios take an eschatological perspective in that they look back on contemporary events from the perspective of the last day and do so with a judgmental or normative ethic. Thus, Tim LaHaye would opine that the child should have known what the end result of his immoral behavior would be, and a representative of Earth First would argue that mankind should have known what the end result of refusing to recycle would be. That is, secular apocalypses also include a story of blame and guilt, though the target is less likely to be described as a sinful "whore of Babylon" whose citizens carried out morally questionable practices. Instead, the state and its citizens are likely to be described as having pursued greedy, short-sighted foreign and domestic policies.[45]

VARIETIES OF APOCALYPSE: ARMAGEDDON OR EDEN?

Although all apocalyptic stories seem to share similar circumstances—namely, the end of life as we know it—there is far less ideological and political consensus among the writers of these novels than there is among those who write catastrophe novels. Earlier in this section I suggested that the catastrophe novel is both right wing and reactionary since it aims to both identify an overt threat and then to spur readers to act to save the state through preempting the threat. In contrast, the apocalyptic novel actually comes in two different ideological and political varieties. One can argue that each apocalyptic novel in essence asks the same question: What comes after the state? And perhaps also: What comes after the international system? Here, the author's own political and moral convictions help him to answer that question.

Writing in 1972, May described two possible varieties of apocalyptic novel which were being produced.[46] In simplest terms, one can describe either a linear or a circular apocalypse. Here, the linear apocalypse is one in which history or ideology essentially stops. The best literary description for a linear apocalypse is that it is a metaphorical description of the last smoldering embers of a dying world. In linear apocalypse, the Last Man may valiantly (or not so valiantly) struggle on for a period of years in the face of tragic odds, occupying an environment inhospitable to human life, before succumbing to death—either at the hands of nature or at the hands of other remaining humans. In linear apocalypse, the state collapses, and the humans who are left in its ruins are Hobbesian. In this scenario, the author asks "What, if anything, really holds us together as a people?" and "What has become of our national mission now?" The linear apocalyptic thus makes pointed reference to the absence of many traditional markers of the state—the coins described in *The Pesthouse* and the "state roads" described in *The Road*.

In the linear apocalyptic the state is also smashed. However, while in the circular apocalyptic, the smashing of the state represents the creation of a new space of liberation, in the linear apocalyptic, the smashing of the state may represent the end of rationality. Here, the destruction is literal and symbolic. As Matthew Farish[47] argues, particularly in the modern era, cities were built, designed, and organized—and in creating spaces which were organized, the claim implicitly was the inhabitants would similarly act in an organized manner. A disaster which destroys the physical structures of the city is seen as having an effect on the social practices which exist in those cities as well. Thus, we see, for example, a scene in Cronin's *The Passage* in which the city officials in Philadelphia decide to dynamite the bridges into their town in a last-ditch attempt to keep the plague of vampires at bay. The young narrator describes hearing the noise of the bridges being blown at night, and knowing that it is unlikely anyone will survive since this is the last stand and it is unlikely to be successful. In this instance, the destruction of the bridges represents the final stages of civilization. While in the circular apocalyptic, the destroyed cities are replaced by agricultural fields and communal life with one's neighbors, the cities in the linear apocalyptic are replaced by either a fortress (as in *The Pesthouse*), what Marx refers to as "the idiocy of rural life," or quite simply nothing (as in *The Road*).

Bartter speaks of the symbolic importance of destroying the city as well, suggesting that the destruction of the city effectively disarms the state while simultaneously acknowledging that the state is responsible for its own destruction and the destruction of the international system. (At the height of the Cold War, the state was thus punished for having manufactured and launched the nuclear weapons which destroyed civilization. In modern times, the state may be seen as responsible for having invented a biological weapon or for having provoked terrorists into attacking the state.) Thus, the city (as proxy for the state) is punished by ceasing to exist. And the salvation of the international system comes about through being able to restart the world without the institutions of the state.[48]

The ways in which the city, and simultaneously the state, has been disarmed is illustrated by Kunstler in *World Made by Hand*. He presents the scenario in which Robert Earle and his friends have gone to Albany, New York, to bargain for some of the city's farmhands who have been taken captive by modern day "pirates." Robert Earle wanders into the capitol building in Albany and wonders what has become of the tens of thousands of civil servants who previously comprised the government. He encounters Eugene Furman, the Lieutenant Governor of New York State who describes the four or five people who still report to the capitol every day as "a skeleton crew . . . sailing a kind of Flying Dutchman of government."[49] Here, the ship of state has become a ghost ship, which exists largely in legend or in story, but which few can see or acknowledge.

However, where the circular apocalyptic suggests that in the absence of government, individuals are now free to reconstitute new and better forms of community, the linear apocalyptic suggests the opposite. In this narrative, the author portrays a new world in which the occupants of the former state and their neighbors are predatory and in which there no longer exists a notion of the common good. The emblematic figure in the emergency apocalyptic is thus the homegrown cannibal—one's former neighbor or acquaintance who no longer recognizes his neighbor's humanity. The new world is characterized by shortage and a drive for survival, and there are no norms and no checks upon the exercise of sheer human power. There is also no God to deliver his people—though America's presidents have traditionally ended their speeches with words such as "God Bless the United States" or "May God preserve the Union."

Here the author Cormac McCarthy describes the new post-apocalyptic environment as follows: "Night dark beyond darkness and the days more gray each one than what had gone before. Like the onset of some cold glaucoma dimming away the world."[50]

The journey which frames the narrative in *The Road*—in which The Man and The Boy attempt to travel to the Gulf Coast in the hope that the weather will be warmer, the climate less harsh and more survivable—can be seen as a retracing of the original voyage which their American ancestors took to arrive at America itself. Here, America itself does not represent Eden, nor does it represent the Promised Land. But the quest and the journey for the Promised Land still continue. However, when they arrive at the end of their journey, The Man and The Boy are disappointed to find that the place they have sought is no different than the place they have left. The weather is no warmer, food is just as scarce, there appear to be no friendly people, and The Man finally dies of the cold and his illness. He does not enter the Promised Land because there isn't one. (There are those, however, who find the final pages of *The Road* as ultimately redemptive. However, this is merely one interpretation.)

In addition, both *The Pesthouse* and *The Road* feature the reinstitution of the practice of slavery (the very institution which Moses and his tribe fled Egypt to escape.) The claim that America's DNA and its destiny somehow included a quest for the ultimate liberation of all mankind and that America is a promised land where all can be free is thus queried. Rather, from an eschatological perspective one might argue that the brief period of time in which America was a democracy was actually the anomaly and the America in which individuals are cold, frightened, and enslaved is the dominant reality.

In contrast, the circular apocalyptic posits a new world in which the state is destroyed but where humanity is still basically good with a concern for the surviving community. (Mankind is not Hobbesian but Kantian.) In this scenario, the state is viewed as problematic, and apocalypse is viewed as the solution. By erasing the vestiges of capitalism and militarism and withdrawing from the interdependent, globalized world, "Americans" are able to rediscover their innate goodness. In the circular apocalyptic, citizens do not ask *if* the state will ultimately come back, but when it will come back. In this scenario, patriotism is not dependent on the existence of the state but is an interior quality which allows Americans to recognize their neighbors as fellow humans deserving respect and caring. In the anarchic apocalyptic, the remaining resources are shared, and the death of the state is experienced as farce rather than as tragedy. Here, the emblematic figure is not the cannibal but rather Rousseau's noble savage who thrives in the beauty of the natural world, which takes over from the mechanistic world which is destroyed. In contrast, the impulse towards understanding disaster as a site for renewal is reflected in three of the apocalyptic novels considered here: First, Kunstler's *World Made by Hand* describes a new, pastoral future in which citizens know their neighbors better, struggle is collective rather than individual, and where the end of mechanization allows for an appreciation of wide open spaces and fresh air. Cronin's *The Passage* describes a new civilization which arises phoenix-like from the ashes of the destroyed world. In this place, people live in collectives according to an egalitarian code which includes elements of sacrifice and honor. Finally, Crace's *The Pesthouse* incorporates elements of the *bildungsroman* as the narrator, Margaret, matures spiritually and emotionally as she travels through the ruined land, acquiring a husband and a child and an identity in the harsh new world.

Arguably, this apocalyptic narrative more closely parallels the Biblical narrative—with life rising from the dead state. Here, the death of the state can be viewed as a necessary event for the rebirth of society. That is, the circular narrative rests on the assumption that in order for something new to be created (like a civilization), the old must be destroyed.[51] The narrative of destruction or chaos giving birth to something new appears throughout the Bible in, for example, the story of Jonah who is vomited out of the whale's belly after three days. Furthermore, we may see the story of Noah's ark (the first apocalyptic tale) as the archetype of the "circle" scenario. Each story features the following elements: A damaged people and a state which is drowned and finished. A promise is made for restoration and life begins anew. Here, Wagar describes the new civilization of the circular apocalyptic as a sort of post-holocaust Eden. He argues that this vision is implicitly romanticist—with overtones of a new type of nationalism. Thus, the circular apocalyptic could be seen not as a tale about the death of the state, but rather as a tale about the rebirth (or resurrection) of the nation in a sort of pure form.

In contrast, the linear scenario's archetype is the banishment of Adam and Eve from the Garden of Eden for their transgressions. As a result, they are doomed to live in a fallen, Hobbesian world. The themes of this apocalyptic novel are that what has been damaged cannot be made right, what has been done cannot be undone. Here, the apocalyptic scenario can be read as a warning rather than as a call to renewal.

Linear Apocalypse and Armageddon

The first understanding of apocalypse is one in which fictionalized or literary renderings conform most closely to the real life emergency or disaster assistance scenarios drawn earlier in the chapter. Here, an emergency is an event which is likely to overwhelm or significantly alter the workings of government and government's relationship to society. As the result of a catastrophe which the government either fails to identify in advance and prevent, or which the government is ill equipped to respond to, the government is forced to take measures outside its usual scope of activities. It may declare a formal "state of emergency," allowing it to reengage with the public in an unusual way or it may break down completely. The sociologist Craig Calhoun describes the "emergency" as a modernist social construct which rests on the assumptions that humanity (and states) are in control of the international system in all of its facets including the natural world. The events of an emergency are described as unpredictable and abnormal—and the state is likely to respond through the deployment of force. The emergency may be a nuclear explosion (as described in *The Road*), a pandemic or other event which undermines the state (as described in *The Pesthouse*), or some other confluence of natural and manmade events.

These novels first unmake the international system in general and the unipolar international system in specific through erasing both the hegemon and his leading role in that international system. In doing so, we are confronted with questions regarding the meaning of citizenship itself, and what it means to be American. By erasing America's leading role, readers are then able to ask if one can indeed be an American in the absence of an American 'mission' in the international system. or in the absence of American exceptionalism? or in the absence of capitalism or a democratic ideology? Here, one is reminded of the Yale historian Amy Chua's work on empires[52] where she raises questions regarding what exactly the "glue" is which holds an empire together. (She suggests that it is a broad and inclusive notion of citizenship.) In erasing America's democratic and capitalist identity as well as its leading economic role in the international community, one is then forced to ask what (if anything) holds America together. Many of these narratives thus include the theme of secession, as rural areas husband their agriculture resources, refusing to share with cities, while in Justin Cronin's *The Passage*, California itself secedes from the United States in a bid to protect itself from the encroaching plague of vampires.

In the apocalyptic scenario of the emergency, destruction is more likely to be described as punitive, with an accompanying narrative of unprecedented suffering and loss. Frequently, the narrative contains overtones of guilt and blame, with events perhaps being portrayed as existing through God's wrath. Here, destruction is unplanned and unwanted. It is unavoidable and often irreparable. The 2007 novel *The Pesthouse* by author Jim Crace conveys the sense of a state which has withered and is no longer meaningful to the inhabitants of the land still called America. He describes the main character Margaret fingering her "talismans," old coins which no longer have either cultural or monetary value since the state no longer exists.[53] He writes:

> Finally, she weighted the coins in her hands, the pennies and dimes and quarters that she had found among the pebbles on the river beach. . . . Was that the eagle she could feel? . . . Was that the one-cent palace with the twelve great columns at the front? She . . . tried to find the tiny seated floating man within, the floating man who, storytellers said, was Abraham and would come back to help America one day with his enormous promises.[54]

In the absence of the state, citizens no longer enjoy personal or collective security and are now vulnerable to both social and natural disaster. The book opens with a scene which describes the new America in which an avalanche has occurred. A hillside has slid down into a river which, destabilized, releases a bubble of poison gas, which silently kills six to seven hundred refugees sleeping near the lake. Crace writes:

> Everybody died at night. Most were sleeping at the time, the lucky ones who were too tired or drunk or deaf or wrapped too tightly in their spreads to hear the hillside, destabilized by rain, collapse and slip beneath the waters of the lake. So these sleepers . . . breathed their last in passive company, unwarned and unexpectedly, without any fear. Their final moments, dormant in America.[55]

Readers are told that the dead lay unclaimed and uncounted. In this novel, and others of the "emergency" variant, one of the most powerful themes is the change in the status of America's inhabitants. They have gone from being citizens to being subjects. They can no longer borrow the power of the state to describe their own lives. Instead they are powerless, rendered the same as all other subjects in the international system.

In this punitive scenario, the reader finds himself rethinking the relationship of the citizen not only to the state but to the natural world as well. (This is largely because the state no longer has the power to command either history or nature.) In this "new world," nature is the enemy of man, not his friend or his slave. Instead, the reader understands that science was often the agent which destroyed the world (through, for example, nuclear power or germ warfare). Therefore, man is no longer to think about harnessing the natural world, but should focus instead on how he might protect himself from this natural world.

Circular Apocalypse and Eden

The second variant is a tale of anarchy in which the author delights in describing the way in which the state, the international system, and its political and economic institutions are swept away or smashed. Here the writer is not entirely unhappy that the events have occurred—since in destroying the state the way has now been opened up for the creation of a new type of society. Here apocalypse allows for the creation of a post-industrial utopia in which small is beautiful, local communities are valued, and many of man's and the state's sins and guilt are forgiven. The anarchic apocalypse is thus a tale of redemption where the state's violent ending serves a progressive purpose.

We first encounter the anarchist impulse in Morris's *News from Nowhere*—which describes the end of industrial capitalism and the political and economic structures which derived from it in Victorian England. From the beginning of the novel, when William Guest wakes up in a London of the future, the reader is treated to a view of what the future of England and perhaps the international system might look like if only these structures could be smashed. The language is that of English pastoralism with lavish descriptions of a new, utopian place which features wide open blue skies (to replace the sooty, vile smog of Victorian England), a clean Thames River flowing through London, and plenty of trees. Family relationships have been restored, there is more leisure time for all, and England has moved towards an early type of sustainable development which appears to have replaced consumerism for its own sake. In his award-winning history of English industrial capitalism since the Victorian era, the English economist Martin Weiner argues that there has always been this tension in British society, ever since the advent of industrialization, whereby the political leadership voiced a firm state commitment to greater urbanization, and industrial production while other voices within society, including those of the nobility, called for a scaling back of the industrial project and a restoration of rural England, with its culture, history, and institutions. These ruralist sentiments, found within Marxism, posited that progress was only made through destruction, or through a smashing of these existing institutions—but that it was not, perhaps, too late to restore them and bring them back, even if the only way to do so was through smashing or undoing capitalism.

Thus, the activist William Morris was, in essence, building a world which was the expression of a sentiment he had expressed elsewhere, namely:

> I should be glad if we could do without coal and indeed without burrowing like worms and moles in the earth altogether; and I am not sure but we could do without it if we wish to live pleasant lives, and did not want to produce all manner of mere mechanism chiefly for multiplying our own servitude and misery, and spoiling half the beauty and art of the world to make merchants and manufacturers rich.[56]

This same ecological, pastoral impulse appears again in *World Made by Hand*, though the novel is written one hundred years later. The reader encounters descriptions of nature taking back space from industry, with weeds and grass poking through highways and overrunning the parking lots of shopping malls. Both the earlier circular apocalyptics written in Victorian Britain and those which followed in the United States can be seen as expressing what today would be known as the "new urbanism"—that is, the notion that cities are bad for one's soul and that nature is important for physical and societal well-being.

If the anarchist impulse can be described in ideological terms, it could be labeled leftist and Marxist. George Caffentzis somewhat jokingly calls the Peak Oil Movement (of which novelist James Kunstler is one of the architects) "the Left's answer to the Left Behind novels."[57] By this he means that in traditional Marxist ideological terms, oil can be seen as the commodity which fuels capitalism. Thus, envisioning the end of oil opens up space for envisioning a new political and economic system in which one can no longer take for granted a number of assumptions about how the world is "built." The new space no longer rests on (A) the existence of a small number of extremely wealthy commodity-producing individuals or organizations which have the ability to structure the marketplace in ways which serve their own interests; (B) the existence of a firmly entrenched class structure based on the political of ownership of commodities like oil; and (C) a situation in which other individuals, groups, classes, and sectors of society are dependent on those who control the commodity.

Here the cessation of oil production leads to the destruction or smashing of the class system, entrenched economic structures, and a system of commodity exchange which can be viewed as one which enriches the few at the expense of the many. In Justin Cronin's *The Passage*, one senses the theme of rebirth in the loving descriptions written of the First Families who escaped destruction to repopulate the earth after the biological weapons escaped and destroyed most of civilization. In the descriptions of new social institutions, the reader is told that race no longer matters in this new society since at some point "we got all mixed up." Christian apocalyptics thus posit the death of sinful industries and cultures, the clearing away of sinful individuals, and a new building of God's kingdom on earth. Left wing apocalyptics in contrast can be read as positing the death of industrial capitalism, misplaced and futile patriotism, and a clearing of the space for the reenvisioning and rebuilding of a sustainable, local, and perhaps classless society. Here, the apocalyptic impulse represents a sort of wish fulfillment.

Writing an apocalyptic novel allows the writer to admit that Western capitalism is broken, that it contains the seeds of its own destruction and that in sweeping it away it is possible to begin again. It parallels the utopian novel in embodying the theme that it is possible for humanity and the state to rescue itself from its own mistakes and to change the trajectory of its future. It allows for the envisioning of a world in which capitalism could be destroyed and replaced with a "better" socialist variant, for example, in the Victorian-era utopian fantasies by Morris and Bellamy. In both of these stories, the novel is a dream, with the subject of the novel awakening at the end to find—to his great disappointment—that he is not in the better place which he had imagined, but rather in his own time and land where the story started, though he returns enlightened with the tools (and the vision) necessary to get to work building a better tomorrow, as a result of all that he has seen. Thus, the anarchic apocalyptic novel contains a hero. There is something fundamental about the journey which has been undertaken. In these more optimistic scenarios—both the real-life and the fictional ones—disaster is seen as providing a site for building anew. The apocalypse opens up a moment for philosophical, political, and social reflection.

Apocalypse and the Ethical Vision

Thus, the eschatological perspective is not useful only for political theorizing, including counterfactual theorizing. It is useful for ethical theorizing as well. Levinas describes the way in which an eschatological vision or lens enables us to connect with the notion of infinity. In going beyond history or to the end of history, we are then able to look back on that which has occurred and to understand it in a different context. He tells us that "the eschatological vision . . . does not envisage the end of history within being understood as a totality, but institutes a relation with the infinity of being which exceeds the totality."[58] In doing so, Levinas tells us that we can confront the possibility of "signification without a context." Eschatology thus means considering and encountering the judgment of history.[59] That is, the apocalyptic tone in secular writing is a way of creating a secular notion of the theological concept of eternity—of a place beyond time as well as beyond space.

Thus, in a true apocalyptic, the end stage is *not* prevented but embraced and explored. We try on the end of the world and then we wallow in it and walk around in it—in a way that we do not in the catastrophe novel or the dystopian novel. This is because the writer of the apocalyptic does not accept the premise that there is an alternate trajectory. For this writer there is only one world, the world which came to pass, since its very end was coded into the DNA of the state itself from the moment it was created. As a result, different knowledge about the state is created, due to the use of the apocalyptic or eschatological perspective.

In this chapter, I suggest that writers may all have similar motives in writing the apocalyptic novel—fiction writers of all ideological stripes (and even many who may consider themselves to be nonideological or apolitical) are nonetheless interested in asking "What comes after the state?" or "What comes after America?" However, each writer's own understanding of human nature structures his response. He writes either a

Hobbesian or a Kantian post-apocalyptic. Both types of scenarios have different ethical and moral implications for how we understand the state in the future, and how we understand the state today.

In this way, both dystopian and apocalyptic novels present a hypothetical literary autopsy of both the state and the international system. As Gottlieb argues, every dystopian novel starts from the premise that society as we know it has died, thereby making the new world created a sort of corpse. Thus a novel written in the 1950s about nuclear war between the United States presents us with the actual incinerated bodies of the victims of the conflagration, but also with a "crippled global body" as well.[60] We cannot help but compare the present relatively healthy world with the corpse which may arise in the future.

The apocalyptic novel, thus, does not allow for travelling back to a position of safety since what brings the state to the brink is either a grand accident of unknown origin, the long range outcome of grand deterministic social forces, or the structure of the international system itself. The end can thus come about either through an apocalyptic moment, or a change in the dominating future. Here, the dominating future can be thought of as a broader phenomenon—encompassing a number of smaller events which unavoidably change the future one is facing. The change in the dominating future can come about through a particular significant event which constitutes a life-changing apocalyptic moment (e.g., the explosion of an atomic bomb); a long-range social, economic, or political trend (e.g., the decline of the Roman Empire); or a chain reaction series of events (as described above.) Thus, the apocalyptic moment can be viewed as a subset of the dominating future. The "apocalypse" of the apocalyptic novel may thus be the result of a change in the dominating future (as is the case in the utopian novel or dystopian novel) or the result of an apocalyptic moment.

While many of the novels which we consider thus depend on a specific, single apocalyptic moment, others posit rather a long, slow decline. But in either case, there is clearly no possibility of stepping back from the brink. Every state eventually goes over the brink—it is merely a question of when. In these novels, the state actually is destroyed. The bomb actually goes off, the aliens (or the Soviets) invade, or the technology on which we are dependent fails. In some instances, the machines actually do take over from the humans. The end becomes not unthinkable but rather expected.

NOTES

1. Kathleen Stewart and Susan Harding, "Bad Endings: American Apocalypse," *Annual Review of Anthropology* 28 (1999): 289.
2. Bruce Feiler, *America's Prophet: Moses and the American Story* (New York: William Morrow, 2009): 60.
3. Steven Goldsmith, *Unbuilding Jerusalem: Apocalypse and Romantic Representation* (Ithaca, NY: Cornell University Press, 1993).
4. Ralph Korner, "And I Saw. . ." An Apocalyptic Literary Convention for Structural Identification in the Apocalypse," *Novum Testamentum* 42 (2000): 160–83.
5. Annemarie Mol, *The Body Multiple: Ontology in Medical Practice* (Durham, NC: Duke University Press, 2002).
6. J. A. Simmons, "From Necessity to Hope: A Continental Perspective on Eschatology without Telos," *Heythrop Journal* 50 (2009): 955.
7. Simmons.
8. Baudrillard, 8.
9. John Winthrop, "A Model of Christian Charity" (1630). Available at www.mtholyoke.edu/acad/intrel/winthrop.htm.
10. George W. Bush, "9/11 Address to the Nation" (2001). Available at www.americanrhetoric.com/speeches/gwbush911addresstothenation.htm.
11. Described in Andrew J. Bacevich, *The Limits of Power: The End of American Exceptionalism* (New York: Henry Holt and Company, 2008): 8.
12. Quoted in Andrew Bacevich, 10.
13. Theodore Steinberg, *Acts of God: The Unnatural History of Natural Disaster in America* (Oxford: Oxford University Press, 2000): xxi.
14. Clifford Longley, *Chosen People: The Big Idea That Shapes England and America* (England: Hodder and Stoughton, 2002).
15. Bruce Feiler, *America's Prophet*, 19.
16. Mary Manjikian, *Rethinking Barbarism: Implications for the Roman Empire Analogy in International Relations* (Manuscript under review, 2010).
17. Bacevich, 10.
18. For more on this point, see Theodore Steinberg's discussion of the U.S. Army Corps of Engineers and their portfolio of engineering projects in the twenty-first century. He argues that their job description might be seen as one of "doing battle with nature" (Steinberg, *Acts of God*, 87). He argues that the Army Corps of Engineers has served the state through allowing policymakers to maintain the illusion that they are invulnerable and in control of their natural environment.
19. Steinberg, 129.

20. David Wrobel, *The End of American Exceptionalism: Frontier Anxiety from the Old West to the New Deal* (Lawrence: University Press of Kansas, 1996).

21. Steinberg, *Acts of God*.

22. Eugene Rosa, "Metatheoretical Foundations for Post-Normal Risk," *Journal of Risk Research* 1(1998): 21.

23. Alan Sandison, *The Wheel of Empire: A Study of the Imperial Idea in Some Late Nineteenth and Early Twentieth Century Fiction* (London: St. Martin's, 1967): 8.

24. Pitirim Sorokin and Irving Horowitz, *Man and Society in Calamity* (Westport, CT: Transaction Publishers, 2010).

25. Jim Crace, *The Pesthouse* (London: Nan A. Talese, 2007): 5.

26. Of course, any narrative or story which we are able to assemble as we view the corpse (here, the apocalyptic novel may be thought of as a sort of wake) is only one of many possible stories that might be told about the deceased individual. Depending on whom you ask, certain aspects of the corpses' life may be emphasized and others downplayed, and a particular narrative may be assembled.

27. Penelope J. Corfield, "The End Is Nigh," *History Today* 57 (2007).

28. Pheng Cheah and Suzanne Guerlac, "Introduction: Derrida and the Time of the Political," in Pheng Cheah and Suzanne Guerlac, ed., *Derrida and the Time of the Political* (Durham, NC: Duke University Press, 2009): 1–37.

29. Eugene Rosa, "The Sky Is Falling: The Sky Is Falling . . . It Really Is Falling!" *Contemporary Sociology* 35 (2006): 212–17.

30. John R. May, *Toward a New Earth: Apocalypse in the American Novel* (Notre Dame, IN: University of Notre Dame Press, 1972): 17, 19.

31. May, *Toward a New Earth*, 21.

32. Here, one can draw a parallel with David Bethea's work on Russian religious apocalyptic themes in fiction (David Bethea, *Shape of Apocalypse in Modern Russian Fiction* [Princeton, NJ: Princeton University Press, 1989]). Here he argues that the apocalyptic—with its emphasis on purging and suffering—is the "opposite" of the socialist realism variant of fiction which is always happy and optimistic, oriented towards describing the triumph of a political and economic and social system. Arguably, one could label the "myths" of the triumph of democracy and free market ideology, as well as Fukuyama's notion of ideological convergence as a type of "capitalist realism" for which apocalyptic fiction likewise provides the antidote.

33. Richard Jefferies, *After London; or, Wild England* (North Stratford, NH: Ayer Company, 1975)

34. Here I am generalizing only about Christian apocalypse because this is the narrative I am most familiar with. However, it is my understanding that Jewish apocalyptic writings also "match" with Jewish teleological writings.

35. Mol.

36. Paul Kennedy, *The Rise and Fall of the Great Powers* (New York: Vintage, 1989). See also Cullen Murphy, *Are We Rome? The Fall of an Empire and the Fate of America* (New York: First Mariner Books, 2008). The same arguments were made, in slightly different forms, by analysts of Soviet politics long before the empire actually collapsed. Writing shortly after World War Two, Ambassador George Kennan wrote in his "X telegram" which later became the template for America's strategy of containment that if containment was practiced and Soviet expansion disallowed, it would eventually collapse. Similarly, Helene Carrere D'Encause described an inherently conflictual relationship between nationalism and the Soviet state, which she saw as leading to its collapse. See Helene Carrere D'Encause, *The End of the Soviet Empire: The Triumph of the Republics* (New York: Basic Books, 1992). Finally, as early as 1970 the Soviet analyst Andrei Amalrik released a samizdat manuscript titled, "Will the Soviet Union Survive until 1984?" His pessimistic conclusion was that it would not since "any state forced to devote so much of its energies to physically and psychologically controlling millions of its own subjects could not survive indefinitely." Amalrik pointed to yet another inherent flaw in the Soviet Union's DNA (Andrei Amalrik, *Will the Soviet Union Survive until 1984?* (New York: Harper and Row, 1970).

37. Amy Chua, *Days of Empire: How Hyperpowers Rise to Global Dominance* (New York: Doubleday, 2007).

38. Giovanna Borradori, Jurgen Habermas, Jacques Derrida, *Philosophy in a Time of Terror: Dialogues with Jurgen Habermas and Jacques Derrida* (Chicago, IL: University of Chicago Press, 2003): 13.

39. Here, we might consider the curiously prescient writing of the analyst Brian Crozier who published an article in the *National Review* in May 1981 entitled "Apocalyptic Thoughts: The Protracted Conflict." In this article he speculated about the wake of Solidarity in Poland and its possible effects on the governability of the Soviet Union. He asked: "What would the Soviets do if first the European empire, then the USSR itself, becomes ungovernable?" Here, in the manner of an apocalyptic theorist, he embraced and inhabited the undesirable end state. He accepted the negative subjunctive and from this point began to speculate about it. In doing so, he became one of the only theorists to ever consider an event which many more conservative analysts simply dismissed as "unthinkable."

40. Kai Erikson, *Everything in Its Path: Destruction of Community in the Buffalo Creek Flood* (New York: Simon and Schuster, 1978): 114.

41. Etienne Balibar, "Eschatology versus Teleology: The Suspended Dialogue between Derrida and Althusser," in Pheng Cheah and Suzanne Guerlac, eds., *Derrida and the Time of the Political* (Durham, NC: Duke University Press, 2009): 76.

42. Jacques Derrida, *The Gift of Death* (Chicago, IL: University of Chicago Press, 1996).

43. Anne Norton, "Call Me Ishmael," in Pheng Cheah and Suzanne Guerlac, 61. Timothy LaHaye and Jerry Jenkins, *Left Behind: A Novel of Earth's Last Days* (Carol Stream, IL: Tyndale Publishing House, 1995).

44. C. R. Foust and W. O. Murphy, "Revealing and Reframing Apocalyptic Tragedy in Global Warming Discourse," *Environmental Communication* 3 (2009): 151–67.

45. However, as Kathleen Stewart and Susan Harding note, the distinction between secular and religious apocalypse is largely an academic one and many ideas have been trafficked between the two types of narratives (Stewart and Harding, 285). That is, the notion that "bad things happen because God is punishing us" can be found in both secular and apocalyptic discourse. Here, we might consider the remarks by fundamentalist preacher Pat Robertson in the aftermath of the 2010 earthquake in Haiti, in which he suggested that the event might be partially caused by God visiting his wrath upon a nation which had allegedly given up Christianity in favor of voodoo, in return for freedom from slavery.

46. Warren Wagar, *Terminal Visions: The Literature of Last Things* (Bloomington: Indiana University Press, 1982): 33–36.

47. Matthew Farish, "Disaster and Decentralization: American Cities and the Cold War," *Cultural Geographies* 10 (2003): 127.

48. M. A. Bartter, "Nuclear Holocaust as Urban Renewal," *Science Fiction Studies* 13 (1986): 153.

49. Kunstler, *World Made by Hand*, 169–70.

50. Cormac McCarthy, *The Road* (New York: Knopf, 2006): 3.

51. John May, *Toward a New Earth*, 7–8.

52. Amy Chua, *Days of Empire*.

53. Jim Crace, 23.

54. Crace, 23.

55. Crace, 1.

56. Martin J. Wiener, *English Culture and the Decline of the Industrial Spirit, 1850–1980* (Cambridge: Cambridge University Press, 1981): 119.

57. George Caffentzis. "The Peak Oil Complex, Commodity Fetishism, and Class Struggle," The Commoner.org (2008). Available at www.commoner.org.uk/wpcontent/uploads/2008/06/caffentzis_peakoil.pdf

58. Emanuel Levinas, *Totality and Infinity* (Pittsburgh, PA: Duquesne University Press, 1969): 23.

59. Michael Morgan, *Discovering Levinas* (Cambridge, UK: Cambridge University Press, 2007): 66.

60. Erika Gottlieb, *Dystopian Fiction East and West* (Montreal: McGill-Queen's University Press, 2001): 171.

6

EXCEPTIONALITY AND APOCALYPSE

Thus far we have considered the ways in which both utopian and apocalyptic novels serve a predictive function, allowing analysts to consider events likely to occur in the future, as well as to begin querying the grounds on which they base their future-oriented theorizing. In this chapter, I focus more closely on the interrogative function of both utopian and apocalyptic novels, describing the ways in which fiction can serve to widen the discourse about political issues including those which are controversial or difficult to talk about. I argue that both utopian and apocalyptic novels produced at the height of the British Empire and those being produced today in America share a preoccupation with three key themes: exceptionalism or the lack thereof, the trajectory of state progress or the lack thereof, and the contrast between the view from above and the view from beneath.

Previously, I noted that the apocalyptic novel is the product of privilege—offering those in a powerful nation a chance to imagine what it might feel like to live elsewhere. However, this still does not explain the timing of the production of these cultural products. Why is it that the United States is suddenly awash in apocalypse-themed movies, television shows, and novels? Cultural critics suggest that Americans are interested in the Aztec prophesies regarding the end of civilization in 2012, and many believe that somehow Americans are nervous—believing that they live in precarious times.

In this chapter, I put forth a more complex theory to explain the timing of apocalyptic production at the height of both British and American primacy. I contend that in both time periods, dystopian and apocalyptic literature provided a safe place for the public exploration and questioning of a number of imperial themes. Fox[1] notes that this type of literature was particularly well-received and of interest to readers in late Victorian England. Literature presented "visions of cataclysmic events and what might follow." In each case, what was being interrogated was a "global imaginary" of the dominant ideology writ large, essentially functioning as a language for the entire world. In each case, the novelist offered up an alternate "imaginary"—one in which the superpower had shrunk down to size. That is, cultural critics in both societies were examining the notion of exceptionalism—asking how and why it was that their nation achieved a particular position in the world, and querying the likelihood that such a position could continue indefinitely into the future. Writers interrogated the idea that one's nation was uniquely blessed or in possession of a unique destiny. Next, writers evaluated the themes of progress in history through reimagining the shape of the state's trajectory. Finally, writers took tentative steps towards retelling the imperial narrative from a new position of alterity—in this way setting and building the foundation of the postcolonial position.

IMPERIALISM AT A CROSSROADS

Kermode argues that apocalyptic thinking is more common than we might think. In short, one might make that argument that every powerful nation has the potential to think that they're having an apocalyptic moment and that they are poised on the edge of something. Here, every culture historically which has produced an apocalyptic mass culture (whether composed of religious or secular objects) has essentially thought that their apocalypse was unique or the most important. I suppose in that regard we are no different. Kermode notes that: "It seems to be a condition attached to the exercise of thinking about the future that one should assume one's own time to stand in an extraordinary relation to it . . . we think of our own crisis as pre-eminent, more worrying, more interesting than other crises."[2]

Thus, we might consider the use of the metaphors of Vietnam or Pearl Harbor in American news analysis today. In suggesting that what another nation is experiencing is "another Vietnam" or that what is occurring in another time period is "another Pearl Harbor," the analyst manages to downplay the significance of the event being described through suggesting that only the original Pearl Harbor or Vietnam events were real, and that any events being experienced today are merely an inauthentic imitation of someone else's "real" history.

Kermode asks the reader to consider whether our present situation is actually "uniquely terrible" or "a cardinal point in time." He suggests that in the grand scheme of things, neither the Americans nor the British will be the first or the only nations to consider their enemy to be the Antichrist or to consider that they are under a unique or deadly set of circumstances. He suggests that it is arrogant to regard our world as somehow more frightening than the worlds described by our ancestors or those to come.[3]

While it may be illogical to think of one's nation as both uniquely privileged and uniquely threatened, there is nonetheless a good deal of evidence that both the British and the Americans did and do so. In *The Lion's Share: A Short History of British Imperialism*, Porter describes ambivalence about empire which existed in Britain from the 1850s onward.[4] In his description, Britain is less a world leader which boldly went out and embraced empire. Rather, it was a cautious country essentially backed into accepting the mantle of empire as a result of political and economic processes which it did not fully control. Imperialism proceeded at a dizzying pace throughout the 1850s, with the end result being a public and a leadership left in the 1880s in a completely transformed world, one in which they looked around and asked quite honestly: how is it that we have arrived at this place?

One could argue that similar circumstances prevailed in the United States from the end of communism in 1989 to the present. In the intervening twenty years, the United States has become the world's only superpower, has adopted a leading role (again) in Western Europe, has played a commanding role in the drive to reintegrate Eastern Europe into the Western economy, and has attempted to restabilize and perhaps redraw the map of the Middle East. The terrifying near-collapse of America's economy in fall 2007 brought into sharp relief exactly how dependent everyone throughout the world is on the fate of America's economic and political decision-making. One single mistake, it seems, could lead not only to the collapse of America's civilization, but to an attendant collapse of the world economy. Thus, it appears, even if America wanted to relinquish its leading role in the world, it could not.[5] A sense of being trapped, of being a prisoner of history, rather than an engine of history, is therefore attendant in both the literature of late Victorian England and of the current United States.

In both cases there were cultural, political, and ideological pressures which militated against open discussion about the possibilities or dangers of relinquishing or losing an empire. In addition, intellectual constructs for thinking about empire—based on deterministic explanations about the inevitable growth of capitalism or the inevitable growth of democracy, as well as historicist explanations which described "developed" nations as the most advanced stage of history, with other nations eagerly leveling up to join them—left little room and no intellectual ability to even imagine an alternate view of history, in which the end of empire was certainly possible and maybe even probable. To imagine the end of empire was, to some degree, to imagine the end of "civilization" and the world itself, and we have no language or mode of discourse for considering what comes after civilization.[6] That is, while Kermode regards discussions of apocalypse as the logical outgrowth of imperial arrogance and hubris, I argue that discussions of apocalypse actually represented a way of interrogating imperial arrogance and hubris. Focusing on apocalyptic scenarios was less a way of accepting empire than it was a way of interrogating empire.

Judith Butler refers to a "hegemony" in the discourse of empire which tightened in the period following September 11. She refers to a uniformity and a consensus which prevailed in the application of certain terms like "terrorist" or "acts of terror," noting that any political or media analyst who might have questioned the application of these terms or the meaning behind them risked being labeled somehow disloyal or perhaps even un-American.[7] Thus, a space of discourse was created which allowed for little opposition to prevailing sentiments and did not allow for a fully encompassing discussion or interrogation of what it meant to be an empire experiencing danger or threat.

To continue the biological metaphor introduced earlier in this work, one can find expression of the sentiment that patriotism was somehow innate in citizens of empire. That is, empire was part of one's DNA and part of one's genetic heritage, a gift which could not be refused and which was destined to be passed down to one's children, like it or not. In *The Wheel of Empire*, Sandison quotes British Prime Minister William Gladstone who stated that: "The sentiment of empire may be called innate in every Briton . . . It is part of our patrimony: born with our birth, dying only with our death."[8] In such a situation, it might appear that the only way to divest oneself of empire was to create a scenario in which empire itself was erased.

In both the American and the British cases, it was thus both intellectually difficult and politically unpopular to seriously query the notion of empire's end—its likelihood, its meaning, and its significance. Yet both periods saw a vast outpouring of literary work which aimed to do exactly that. However, thus far, neither international relations nor literary analysts have attempted to read the Victorian works listed here through the lens of international relations and globalization. Political analyses of these works by Boos and Boos and others *have* focused on the ways in which British Liberals have laid out a critique of the then-existent global economic system, and the ways in which they have proposed an alternate economic system. However, few have noted that in each case, Britain has also lost its political role in the world—and thus, in addition to questions about morality, ethics, and poverty—questions about nationality, identity, and the global role of the imperial nation are also raised. Victorian political utopian and dystopian novels noted have been read as a critique of consumerism, a critique of capitalism, and a narrative about people's fear of technology. However, they haven't been read by international relations theorists, focusing on questions of power.

In this chapter, I argue that Victorian and American dystopian and apocalyptic novels have served and continue to serve three purposes: First, they interrogate the narrative of exceptionalism or specialness which often provides a foundation for empire. In each case, readers can see how the rise of empire was not inevitable, and how many elements which have been cited in explaining the rise of a superpower (including a unique geographic position, a unique founding myth, the favor of God or a unique mission in the world) are constructed rather than innate to the system. Next, they interrogate the narrative of progressivism, which likewise provides a foundation for empire.[9] Here, readers are led to consider the possibility that empires might fall as well as rise, and even that elements (like globalization) which have been cited as the engine behind a superpower's rise might be creating vulnerabilities, as well as strengthening that imperial quest. Finally, British and American literature interrogates the narrative of colonialism—which rests on the assumption that the spread of capitalism and democratic institutions is essentially a benevolent activity which benefits both the colonizer and the colonist and that the overwhelming reaction of the colonist to colonialism is one of gratitude and respect. (Here, I am not alone in calling attention to colonialist themes in British utopian literature in particular. Rather, analysts have increasingly noted the ways in which analysts like Swift and Butler play with the figure of the savage, the notion of "blank land" which is ripe for colonization and the subtle way in which racism and the language of development are both utilized and interrogated in this literature. However, I am the first to suggest that these three themes—exceptionalism, risk and fear, and colonialism—are linked and that these discourses are not unique to British writers but are instead a way in which many writers might choose to interrogate great power politics, whether the politics in question are British or American.)

Table 6.1 illustrates the three discourses which I begin to analyze in this chapter.

In each case, we can identify a particular theme prevalent in both British and American society which writers have attempted to both interrogate and undermine in fiction. In the following sections, I compare and contrast the ways in which these themes appear in both British and American dystopian and apocalyptic fiction.

EXCEPTIONALISM, INEVITABILITY, AND CONTINGENCY

In both of the cases to be explored here (late-nineteenth-century Britain and the late-twentieth-century and early-twenty-first-century

Table 6.1. Themes and Discourses in British and American Speculative Fiction

Theme	Interrogates or Undermines Narrative	Methodology	Examples from Literature
Discourse of Inevitability vs. Contingency	Exceptionality It is natural and right that our empire prevails. It could not have been any other way.	Historical Counterfactual Query the LIKELIHOOD of the assumption of uniqueness OR Subjunctive Counterfactual Imagine an alternate future for your country which "disproves" the assumption of specialness	VICTORIAN *Gulliver's Travels, Erewhon, Men in the Moon* CONTEMPORARY: *The Second Plane* VICTORIAN: *After London* CONTEMPORARY: *The Passage The Road World Made by Hand*
Discourse of Security and Risk	Progressivism Historicism Our empire will continue to rise to greatness. It will never BE any other way. Others will follow us.	Subjunctive Counterfactual Describe branching of decision tree, leading to alternate outcomes. Use backward induction to trace back.	VICTORIAN *Erewhon, The Machine Stops, News from Nowhere, After London* CONTEMPORARY *The Passage, World Made by Hand, The Pesthouse,*
Discourse of Modernism vs. Postmodernism	Colonialism Great Powers are benevolent in their actions with other nations. Their interference is welcomed.	Alterity Retelling of Story from a new viewpoint Reversal of colonist/colonized paradigm	VICTORIAN: *Erewhon, Gulliver's Travels* CONTEMPORARY: *Second Plane; The Pesthouse*

United States) each nation and its citizens viewed itself as largely immune or insulated from the pressures of the international system. Particularly in the case of Britain, which had experienced a position of political and economic preeminence for nearly four hundred years, the loss of that position was simply unthinkable. The citizens of both nations thought of their nation as a "leading nation" which was meant to enlighten and encourage other, less fortunate nations which might someday catch up to itself. Both Britain and the United States were thus "exemplars" in the words of Clifford Longley. These nations therefore occupied a unique cultural, moral, political, and even temporal location—as leading nations.

In both cases, the state produced or constructed a narrative of exceptionalism which rested on two assumptions. First, the state was described as unique in the entire world—better equipped technologically, with a unique ideology which held people together and moved them forward. The nation was described as larger than any other previous geographic empire and uniquely positioned to take advantage of historic and technological developments.[10] Uniqueness is thus a relative quality—both Britain and the United States regarded themselves as being somehow different or set apart from their neighbors. Both described themselves as having a uniquely favorable geographic location which conferred certain long-term military and economic advantages.[11] America is described as having a unique geographic position, with miles of coastline overlooking both the Atlantic and Pacific Oceans, which provide both opportunities for trade and protection from invasion by other nations. In addition, America is seen as endowed with many natural resources—fertile land, a variety of climates which have allowed for the cultivation of many types of food and other goods, vast forests which provided fuel and wood for development, and abundant wildlife, plant life, and sea life. These resources allowed America to take a leading role in trade and to increase in prosperity. The self-sufficiency of America's resources also made it possible to cast off the yoke of British imperialism since there was not a strong dependence on resources imported from Britain. In addition, it is suggested that America's unique distance from other countries (or relative isolation) made it less susceptible to disease which set back development, for example, in Western Europe.

Similarly, Britain as an island has always existed at the periphery of Europe. From the time of the Roman Empire, Britain is seen as having had greater autonomy and as less likely to be drawn into the wasteful and damaging territorial disputes which have plagued continental Europe. Europe has been envisioned as far from the center of the action, and therefore less likely to be invaded by others. In songs and culture, England is described as a green and verdant land which is said to resemble Eden.[12] In addition, it is suggested that both Britain and America's unique distance from other countries (or relative isolation) has made it less susceptible to the diseases which set back development, for example, in Western Europe.

This domestically produced explanation of America's (and Britain's) uniqueness has not traditionally been interrogated, nor have analysts like Longley considered the ways in which the discourse of uniqueness is produced. Rather, the quality of uniqueness appears to be derived from the environment—as a product not of agency but of contingency. In other words, one could simply state that these nations were both "lucky" to have been provided with the resources and positions which they enjoyed. This notion appears in the discourse of the United States and Britain with both claiming not to have sought empire, but rather to have somewhat reluctantly acquired it as the result of a number of factors beyond their control. In both cases, empire is thus seen as something which just "happened"—rather than being a product of planning. In this way, it is viewed both as deterministic (it could not have happened any other way because in retrospect it appears that all sorts of forces were driving towards this conclusion) and ethically neutral. If one views either the United States or Britain as having an empire because it was "lucky," then there is no place in the discourse for notions of blame or guilt. If the empire merely grew organically, then one cannot ask whether it was just or ethical to those who became part of it, nor can one ask about the motivations or sins of those who participated in it.

Longley quotes Walter Davis, who notes that "traumatic events confront the system of guarantees with the reality of radical, unendurable contingency."[13] However, if one is only leading because one is lucky, then is it possible that at some point one could become "unlucky"?

The manufactured notion that one's geographic space is somehow unique, irreplaceable, and special can, however, be viewed in Marxist terms as a brand of commodity fetishism. In his work on the aesthetics of architectural demolition, Bernie Jim describes the ways in which a particular architectural site can come to be viewed as singular and unique. He argues that sometimes a particular building—like the Empire State Building, the World Trade Center, or Carnegie Hall—comes to be endowed with a particular meaning (or a cultural biography) which gives it a value far beyond the replacement value of its actual bricks and mortar. Such a building might rightfully be described as "irreplaceable" or "priceless," and its destruction could be described as unthinkable. This building thus has a sort of privileged status amongst other buildings of its particular type. While other buildings might rightfully be described merely as a commodity called "real estate," Jim tells us that "an historic building is singular"[14] because there is only one architecturally and historically unique building like that, with that cultural history. However, an academic Marxist would recognize commodity fetishism as the construction of particular value or worth to be attributed to an object or rather than a reflection of anything "real." (It is the same instinct that causes one to covet designer jeans for their status value, rather than recognizing that there are other, cheaper jeans containing the same exact materials and workmanship.) Analysts disagree about whether the fetishistic value of an object is put into the product at the production stage or whether it can be attached to an object later by its users.

Here, one might argue that in positing (or carrying out) the destruction of the supposedly unique and special item, the manufactured nature of that uniqueness would then become obvious. In a sense, the attacks on the United States on 9/11 helped to break or at least to put into question the frame which constructed America as unique and irreplaceable.

In addition to being constructed as unique, the state has been constructed as special—with the sense of having been particularly chosen or anointed in its mission. Specialness is thus an absolute quality, rather than a relative one. Specialness is usually described as resulting from two factors: A special relationship with God (often described in a founding myth about the nation); and a particular mission in the world (which involves the spread and proliferation of one's religion or ideology) resting on a national identity founded on messianic nationalism. The exceptionalism argument states that Britain (and later America) as a Christian nation, has a special destiny or mission, that it is indeed favored or blessed by God, and that the history which has brought about Britain's (or America's) rise is actually being directed behind the scenes by that God. Longley notes that the British narrative includes the idea that God himself intervened and smashed the (Catholic) Spanish Armada before it could invade Anglican England in 1588. Later, Britain was described as a nation in which Nelson had avoided the risk of a Napoleonic invasion at Trafalgar in 1805 through beating the French fleet. (Here, the narrative describes the way in which God protected England because of what it still had to do.) As Longley notes, each exceptionalist narrative describes the nation—Britain or the United States—as a New Jerusalem, an engine of change in the world and a nation which will have an historic or eternal role.

Feiler[15] suggests that America in particular has always represented a sort of new Promised Land, with the pilgrims and later immigrants playing the part of Moses. The nation itself, like Moses, inherits an unlikely destiny—which is seemingly thrust upon it not by virtue of any inherent characteristics it possesses, but because it has been called into existence by God.

Previous authors have looked at the discourse of exceptionalism—noting that because of the way the narrative is constructed, certain themes (such as religious differences with one's enemies) may be overemphasized while other themes are deemphasized. (As long as one can claim that God frequently intervenes in one's history to alter the outcome of conflicts, one can perhaps devote less attention to the personal weaknesses of state leaders, as well as the mistakes or strengths of both tactics and strategy.) It is my contention here that the exceptionalism narrative might have been particularly troubling to citizens and analysts in late Victorian Britain (and to those in the United States today) because of three factors.

First, the discourse of exceptionalism routinely reframes defeat as merely a way station on the way to eventual victory. Situations such as the Sepoy Mutiny of 1857 and the bloody battles of the Boer Wars beginning in 1890 are reframed in the exceptionalism narrative as events which while personally and politically painful and troublesome in the short term—will have greater meaning in the long term and eventual history of Britain. Thus, the exceptionalism narrative routinely asks the hearer to adopt a stance of pretending to look back at the state from a point in the future in which the mission is achieved and victory is certain. In this backward glance, the trajectory of the nation is clear, and any defeats along the way can be minimized as having been in service to a greater goal. In a religious framework, they can be rewritten as the sort of suffering which purifies the people and the national mission. Longley in particular describes the relationship between nationalism and exceptionalism—noting that national myths allow unrelated people to die for the state.[16]

The backward glance thus erases any notion of imperial guilt, since any damage or sacrifice incurred by the imperial state is "excusable" in the grand scheme of things. As Caygill points out, the exceptionalism narrative does not leave any room for guilt—for two reasons. First, he notes that a chosen nation cannot be simultaneously anointed and guilty. If the chosen nation is seen to be acting within a larger story of history and as the result of divine guidance, then it becomes difficult to fault the nation ethically in terms of how, for example, it has behaved towards its neighbors. Rather, the narrative of the chosen nation allows the reader or the writer to focus again almost exclusively on the actions of the state itself—and the state's actions towards Others can be excused as a sort of byproduct of the imperial drive to fulfill its destiny. In addition, Caygill reads Levinas to state that guilt is an emotion or judgment which only makes sense within a relationship. (That is, a state can be guilty of either hurting another party or of violating a principle, but it cannot be simply "guilty in the abstract."[17]) Unfortunately, the imperial narrative does not historically acknowledge the existence of a party which can be aggrieved by the imperial state. Instead, the state is viewed as settling or clearing land which is "empty" rather than occupied, and as leading other states who follow through their own volition, rather than as the result of force.[18] The state is seen as responsible only to its own citizens and not to its "neighbors" who are not part of the covenanted agreement of the exceptionalist nation.[19]

However, if one does the reverse—and imagines the victory not as won but lost from that same distant point in the future—then one essentially has an apocalyptic scenario. From the apocalyptic stance, the events and hardships which one encountered earlier might easily be read not as small hurdles to be overcome on the way to victory—but rather as portents of the beginning of the end. They become not heroic moments but apocalyptic moments. Here we might take, for example, an event like the Siege of Leningrad during World War II. In the narrative of Soviet exceptionalism, these events were described as presenting both danger and opportunity. Through the events they underwent, the citizens of St. Petersburg were able to demonstrate their heroism and commitment to their nation, and the risks and dangers encountered and suffering endured were seen as moments within a larger narrative of the eventual triumph of Soviet communism. However, from a vantage point where one knows that communism has failed, the Siege of Leningrad might be read differently—as merely a scene of senseless and unconscionable suffering. In addition, while the exceptionalism narrative would thus emphasize the shared humanity and nationalism of the sufferers, an apocalyptic narrative would be more likely to emphasize the brutality, savagery, and cruelty of those who did not conform to norms in the situation of suffering.

In addition, the exceptionalism narrative can close down or censor any social discussion of the notions of blame and guilt. From a vantage point where the victory is seen as won, taking extraordinary measures to achieve this destiny can be seen as reasonable and excusable. In contrast, from an apocalyptic vantage point, taking risky gambles with people's lives might merely be seen as immoral if victory is not achieved. High human costs associated with technological achievement are thus often cited as evidence of the bravery, heroism, and commitment of the earliest colonists, while the costs borne by the colonized are rarely considered since they do not fit within the exceptionalism narrative. Thus, the exceptionalism narrative affects the framing of media stories recounting the deaths of British officers and their families in India, as well as in descriptions of casualty statistics sustained while building railroads in Kenya. We encounter it again in discussions of the removal of the Aborigines and the transport of British people to the Antipodes for resettlement. Similarly, one can point to Soviet-generated discourse about starvation in the Ukraine as part of the collectivization of the Soviet Union. In the United States, one can point to discussions regarding clearing Native Americans off of land in United Stataes. In each case, these measures are described as heroic—in the context of the exceptionalist narrative—and blame and guilt are not seen as relevant to the story.

The exceptionalist narrative thus reframes guilt and blame, suffering and defeat—by adopting a future stance in which the nation is said to have triumphed. From this imaginary vantage point, blame, suffering, and individual defeats are seen as unimportant—within the grand scheme of things. In contrast, from an apocalyptic vantage point the same events may look quite different. In retrospect, they may seem foolish, ill-timed, or meaningless. The two types of narratives thus reach vastly different conclusions regarding blame and guilt, the taking of risks by a hegemon, and the eventual historic perspective which will be shed on the hegemon's policies.

Countering the Narrative of Exceptionalism: Querying Uniqueness

Speculative literature, however, allows for the creation of a space where writers can begin to refute both the uniqueness of the state and the special destiny of the state. In doing so, the writer may also introduce notions of guilt and blame, suffering, and the significance of defeat.

First, the utopian/dystopian novel—by virtue of its very existence—calls into question the notion of uniqueness. By asking the reader to imagine a nation which is "just like my nation except for this one slight cultural or technological difference," the writer may introduce new characters, new species, or new lands which also feel themselves to be special—thereby suggesting that there is nothing unique about Britain or the United States. The utopian novel provides—not new evidence—but rather a set of tools for evaluating the likelihood and coherence of our belief in exceptionalism, given what we know about the world. That is, the utopian novel increases the reader's level of skepticism regarding the probability of the exceptionalism claim. It undermines not the claim itself—but the assumptions on which the claim rests, thereby causing us to view it more critically. In essence, the novel asks the reader to consider whether the claim to exceptionalism is rational and coherent.

Dannenberg notes that the act of reading fiction in general forces the reader to confront what she refers to as "possible worlds theory." She notes that in accepting the premise that the world—or series of choices which were enacted to bring about a particular event—about which we are reading is "true," we are implicitly agreeing with the premise that it is also only one of many other possible "worlds" (or the outcome of a series of choices) which the writer could have invented instead. Thus, in reading about "our world," we are forced to consider the existence of a plurality of other worlds—each of which may be both real and true to the participants within it.[20] Thus, reading about one's own world in a fictional context forces the reader to consider both the probability and the plausibility of the claim to uniqueness made by that world. Instead, the reader accepts that he is reading only about one outcome of choices which exists relative to other, different series of choices which could have been enacted.

The argument of exceptionalism states that there is a set of states that are uniquely endowed by God with resources, a history, and a belief system. There is only one state in this set. Thus, in geographic terms, one is asked to believe that all other nations radiate outward from the exceptional nation which possesses a set of unique advantages. Other states may differ in terms of how similar they are to the exemplar—with those nations which are nearly as developed as the exemplar (referred to as "near peers") occupying one ring which is closest to the exceptional nation[21] while other nations which are not at all like the exemplar being posited as quite a distance from the exemplar. Thus, the defining characteristic of the other states is how closely they mimic the exceptional nation. One sees this particular logic demonstrated in, for example, the writings of the current American analyst Thomas P. M. Barnett in his book *The Pentagon's New Map*.[22] Here, Barnett suggests that the world consists of a "functioning core" of stable, connected states which participate in globalization's ideologies and institutions, a group of "seam states" (including Mexico, Brazil, South Africa, Morocco, Algeria, Greece, Turkey, Pakistan, Thailand, Malaysia, the Philippines, and Indonesia) and a "disconnected or non-integrating gap" of states characterized by unstable, corrupt, bad governments; a lack of political norms and rules; and instability.[23] In his work on critical geography, Matthew Huber encourages us to interrogate the notion of entitlement which accompanies the exceptionalism myth, and how that sense of entitlement thus "constructs" a resource geography to support it. Huber[24] argues that those who see America as uniquely endowed with values and ethics which cause it to serve as an exemplar also implicitly set up the premise that it is the responsibility of other nations to supply America with the inputs—like oil and natural gas—which can enable America to continue to serve as a leading engine of production in the international system. Thus, in Marxist terms, Huber argues that an ideological system which posits that one nation plays a unique and special role automatically sets up a system of dependency in which other nations serve as merely a source of inputs for the more developed nation. America is seen somehow as having a "right" to claim the resources of others in service to its unique ideology.

Butler is more blunt in her critique, accusing the United States in particular of narcissism or the creation of a worldview in which the United States is the "center."[25] In her analysis, a blow like September 11 can serve to create a "narcissistic wound" which forces a recentering or a decentering, as the United States moves into the new and strange position of being the object rather than the inflictor of violence. Huber and Butler thus posit real-life situations in which the exceptional nation can become decentered through real-life events. However, it is my contention that the same work can be accomplished through the practice of fiction—either through the creation of the utopian or dystopian scenario in Victorian Britain or through the creation of the apocalyptic scenario in contemporary times.

This is the action which Don DeLillo carries out in his work *Falling Man*. He creates a conversation between the main character Keith's ex-wife Lianne, where she speaks with Martin, a Swiss friend of her mother's. Here, Martin states:

> There is a word in German. *Gedankenubertragung*. This is the broadcasting of thoughts. We are all beginning to have this thought, of American irrelevance. It's a little like telepathy. Soon the day is coming when nobody has to think about America except for the danger it brings. It is losing the center. It becomes the center of its own shit. This is the only center it occupies.[26]

The reader of the dystopian or utopian novel thus can ask himself: How likely is it really that there is only one nation in the world which is unique and special, which forms the center of the map, and which claims the resources of others in service to this ideology? Here, in order to undermine the argument that "Britain (or the US) is the only state in the set" or that "only Britain or the US is the center of the geographic map" it is only necessary to find one other state that might similarly claim to be uniquely endowed. (In the words of the philosopher Karl Popper, one only needs to find one black swan to disprove the claim that all swans are white.) In doing so, one necessarily "unmakes" the map which shows America or Britain at the center, with all other nations arranged around the core, distinguished in terms of how tightly they hew to or depart from the model of the exceptional state. One also, necessarily, erases or rewrites the ideological stance which upholds that claim.

As Richard Smith[27] argues, a map is not merely a rendering of physical geography. A map may tell us where the seas are, which ways the rivers flow, and where the mountains begin—but many of the "borders" which we construct on our maps and in our own renderings of the earth are based on cultural attitudes and understandings, including prejudices. He notes that late imperial Chinese maps seldom distinguish between China and "the world," since to many Chinese the two terms were synonymous. Similarly, one can point to maps produced in imperial Britain where the coloring of the maps represents the position of the other territory in relation to Britain. Territory is designated as belonging to the British Empire, belonging to another Empire, or "blank" in the sense that it does not currently belong to any empire but soon will. Joseph Conrad makes this point in his novel *Heart of Darkness*, which deals with the Belgian colonization of the Congo, when he writes:

> At that time there were many blank spaces on the earth, and when I saw one that looked particularly inviting on a map (but they all look that) I would put my finger on it and say, "When I grow up I will go there . . . True, by this time it was not a blank space any more. I had got filled in since my boyhood with rivers and lakes and names. It had ceased to be a blank space of delightful mystery—a white patch for a boy to dream gloriously over. It had become a place of darkness.[28]

The utopian novel, however, forces the reader to rethink his own cartography of the world. In entering the world of the novel, the reader is forced to consider the possibility that there exist other territorial formations—which are not colonized by Britain or waiting to be so absorbed. Instead, the reader is asked to posit an alternate world in which there is another nation similarly advancing a claim to uniqueness (that is, that there is more than one center). As the reader initially reflects upon the absurdity of the rival's claim to be that center around which everything else revolves, he or she also comes to see the absurdity of his or her own claim as the center of the world or the arbiter of civilization. It thus provides what the geographer Gillian Hart would term a new "critical conception of spatiality."[29] This new critical conception of spatiality thus causes us to rethink who or what is at the core or center of the international system; what the lines of relationship are between its members; how we conceptualize of distance between its members;

and how we conceptualize of the relations between the members in a temporal context through, for example, terming some nations as more or less "behind" other nations.

Thus, arguably, the utopian novel provides less a normative judgment on the rightness or wrongness of empire—than it does an examination of the logic of the underlying claim to exceptionality. As Salmon tells us:

> One aspect, at least, of rationality involves simply the management of one's body of opinion in terms of its inner structure. It has no concern with the objective correctness of opinions; it deals with the avoidance of blunders of various sorts within the body of opinion—for example, the kind of mistake that occurs when logical inconsistency or probabilistic incoherence is present.[30]

The critique of the imperial spatial vision thus might involve doing as Swift did in *Gulliver's Travels*, essentially creating a new invented land in which the inhabitants also think of themselves as being specially and uniquely gifted and favored by the Gods. In showing that all nations believe themselves to be exceptional, one might thus cause readers to evaluate the claim that their nation is also special.[31] Victorian writers who interrogated the uniqueness of Britain's achievements include Jonathan Swift in *Gulliver's Travels*; Samuel Butler in *Erewhon*; and H. G. Wells in the novel, *The First Men in the Moon*. In *Gulliver's Travels*, Gulliver points out the absurdity of the uniqueness claim in a number of different ways: In his voyage to Lilliput, the land of the impossibly small individuals, he acknowledges that they too are building an empire, and remarks upon the foolishness of their claim to empire. (Here, one might compare this to a similar small country like England attempting to take control of India or all of Asia.) He notes:

> So immeasurable is the ambition of princes that he seemed to think of nothing less than reducing the whole empire of Blefuscu into a province, and governing it by a viceroy; of destroying the Big-Endian exiles, and compelling that people to break the smaller end of their eggs; by which he would remain sole monarch of the whole world.[32]

Gulliver also directly raises the claim that there may be others besides the Lilliputians who have pretensions to empire and a sense of uniqueness in asking later:

Undoubtedly philosophers are in the right when they tell us, that nothing is great or little, otherwise than by comparison: it might have pleased fortune to let the Lilliputians find some nation, where the people were as diminutive with respect to them as they were to me. And who knows but that even this prodigious race of mortals might be equally overmatched in some distant part of the world, whereof we have yet no discovery?[33]

Finally, there is a scene in which Gulliver allows that he has gotten carried away in discoursing about his beloved England and describing its customs, history, its political parties, and its institutions to the Brobdingnagians. Their response is one of laughter, and the jesting question put to him as to whether he is a Whig or a Tory.[34] His larger companions regard his nation's customs as somehow a mimicry of their own, and find it funny that his nation too would try to have such things as courts, judges, legislatures, and laws—as sort of a small imitation of the Brobdingnagians own "real" institutions.

Swift thus does not present Gulliver as necessarily more advanced than the Others whom he encounters. They are neither primitive, nor is the territory which they occupy a mere blank space on the map. Rather, those whom Gulliver encounters are urbanized, capitalist (presumably), engaged in occupational specialization, and socially stratified. And as noted, the Others are educated, rational, and utilitarian—like the English themselves. They have universities, apparently in both Lilliput and Brobdingnag. Indeed, in Gulliver's voyage to the land of the Yahoos, the horse-like Houhynyms are presented as being *more* refined and *more* developed than the Englishmen themselves.

In Samuel Butler's *Erewhon*, likewise, the natives of the land he visited are presented as having had once been a great and rare civilization, though they have, it appears, voluntarily relinquished many of the strides which they have made technologically. Nonetheless, it is clear that the narrator's own ideas about what constitutes moral character, criminal behavior, and sin are regarded as strange by his interlocutors, who regard their own civilization as highly evolved and far superior to his.

Finally, in *The First Men in the Moon*[35] the narrator, Mr. Bedford, expects that his voyage to the moon will be essentially an expedition for gathering abundant resources from a blank land. Both he and his companion, Dr. Cavor, are surprised when instead they encounter an advanced race of people, known as the Selenites, who have technology, resources, and a civilization which rivals their own. The narrative ends with an unusual denouement—the Selenites choose to sever contact with the Earthlings, whom they come to regard as a brutal, savage race of people. Here, the "gifts" of British civilization are portrayed as neither desirable nor welcome.

Cantor and Hufnagel describe *The First Men in the Moon* as a tale which depicts the historic and geographic insignificance of the British Empire—when seen in a larger temporal and geographic context which is expanded to include the whole universe. Here, the claim by the British that they would somehow possess the moon and aspire to control the universe can be reenvisioned as the height of arrogance and hubris. These authors suggest that it is was not mere coincidence which inspired Hollywood's producers to make a movie based on the novel in 1964, the same year that U.S. president John F. Kennedy famously announced that "We shall go to the moon." Here, the movie's release can be seen as a restatement of Wells's original critique of British arrogance and hubris, though this time the target of the critique is not Britain but the United States.

Countering the Narrative of Exceptionalism: Querying Specialness

In contemporary literature, the writer likewise takes up the question of exceptionalism—using literature to explore the questions of whether one's nation is truly blessed, uniquely endowed, or possessed of a particular special mission in history. In the contemporary examples, however, writers are more likely to use apocalyptic literature than utopian literature to frame this query. Victorian writers took the reader to a new place and said to them in essence: "Here is another place that thinks of itself as exceptional. Do you see how exceptionalism is not a real idea but one which is constructed?" The contemporary analyst, in contrast, takes the reader back to his own land but erases many of the underlying assumptions which cause the reader to think of his land as exceptional. Then he says to the reader, "Here is what your land would look like if it was not exceptional, and here is how we might read contemporary events. Do you see how this is possible?"

Here, the device of the subjunctive counterfactual illustrates the subjectivity of the exceptionalism narrative. In a number of contemporary post-apocalyptics—including *World Made by Hand*, *The Road*, and *The Pesthouse*—the setting is that of a new world which occupies the same geographic space as the old world, but where the political, economic, social, and cultural understandings which were used to make sense of the old world have been destroyed or rewritten. Here, the British novel *After London* uses a similar methodology and reference will be made to that novel as well.

In interrogating or refuting specialness, the contemporary analyst may alter the geography of his or her own land, in essence reproducing it as being the same geographically but without the cultural and emotional landscape which renders it blessed, sacred, or holy—therefore suggesting that there is nothing "special" about Britain or the United States. In his work on the geography of Cambodia, the geographer James Tyner makes a distinction between the geography of a region (which he defines as physical) and the landscape of a region—which he regards as emotional, cultural, and temporal. Utilizing this distinction, we can describe America's (and Britain's) landscapes as having changed as a result of the erasure of social, economic, and cultural strides which occurred due to the apocalypse. Thus, while America remains in the same place, it no longer enjoys the same sense of itself as "the power center of the world." It feels farther away from the rest of the world, including Europe, since the end of technology and globalization has served to isolate it from the larger web of international relations.

As noted previously, the main literary device used in both utopian and dystopian literature is defamiliarization. Defamiliarization comes about by changing some elements of the setting of the story but leaving others alone, so that the setting seems almost like the reader's own world—but not quite. Part of the reason why one feels displaced at the beginning of the new American post-apocalyptics is that America is no longer blessed, special, out in front, or a "Christian" nation. It appears to be just another country and not a particularly successful one at that. As Richard Lebow tells us in his work on counterfactual scenarios, "stars, planets, mountains, rivers and lakes are 'brute' facts . . . because they do not require an institutional context to occur."[36] In contrast, social facts rest on a system of shared usage and understandings in which to place them. Daniel Cordle tells us that "the world is essentially a textual construct, read by each of us through a grid of cultural references."[37] When we remove those references, we can more clearly see the ways in which we have constructed not only the future world, but the world we live in now as well.

Frequently, the reader is "decentered" because the narrative he has used to make sense of the world has been rewritten, and as a result, his sense of place is different. The emotional landscape is no longer one of safety, but rather one of fear. Thus, in *The Pesthouse*, where most of civilization has been wiped out by plague, as well as *The Passage*, where a plague of vampire-like quasi-humans has achieved the same goal, the narrative of America's founding fathers as Moses and the United States as the new Promised Land has been turned on its head. What if, we might ask, the United States is not actually the Promised Land—but instead it is Egypt, the land from which the subjects flee (as they do in *The Pesthouse*) in hopes that a new civilization can be built elsewhere? In this case, the narrative is correct but Americans have misunderstood their part in the cosmic drama which is to unfold.

Each apocalyptic novel performs this "decentering" through the decision to alter some combination of brute facts and social facts. In our contemporary examples, only one author, Cormac McCarthy, has significantly altered the "brute facts" of the United States. He has rendered the land nearly uninhabitable, describing the earth as no longer able to grow food, and altering the climate, bringing on "nuclear winter." In other novels, the brute geographical facts of the setting are unaltered and to some degree, the new America retains some of the geographic advantages of the old America—including fertile soil, oceans, and rivers. In these instances, physical geography provides the link which tethers the new America to the old, just as the existence of London does in the Victorian novels *News from Nowhere* and *After London*. Although the post-apocalyptic landscape (by which I mean the emotional, cultural, and political rendering of space) appears almost completely divorced from the current landscape, the reader can still pick out physical features of the land including the Hudson River (in *World Made by Hand*), the mountains of Georgia (in *The Road*) and the Tidewater region of America's southeastern coast (in *The Pesthouse*). In many instances, physical remnants of the cities which dot our contemporary landscape remain: In *World Made by Hand*, Kunstler notes the destruction of the cities of Los Angeles and New York by "jihadist attacks" but also makes reference to Boston and the states of Maryland and Pennsylvania.

However, the economic landscape is different—since capitalism, interdependence, consumerism, and industrial production are erased.

In novels like *In a Perfect World*, *World Made by Hand*, and *The Road*, there is no longer any American industrial infrastructure, international trade or monetary economy. Instead, there is only barter and subsistence agriculture. The 'economic miracle' which gave America its unique position in the international system has been erased, both internationally and domestically.

In addition, the technological landscape is different. In the Victorian novel *After London* the writer creates a world in which man's ability to command technology has simply vanished. The fact that such technologies ever existed is regarded as nothing short of miraculous, and the technological exploits of past generations are remembered and recounted as part fact, part legend, and part quasi-religious utterance. Here, Jefferies tells us:

> They also sent intelligence to the utmost parts of the earth along wires which were not tubular, but solid, and therefore could not transmit sound, and yet the person who received the message could hear and recognize the voice of the sender a thousand miles away. With certain machines worked by fire, they traversed the land swift as the swallow glides through the sky. . . . Great holes were made through the very hills for the passage of the iron chariot. . . . Where are the wonderful structures with which the men of those days were lifted to the skies, rising above the clouds?[38]

Similarly, in *The Pesthouse*, America still has resources, but citizens no longer have the know-how or technology to exploit them. In addition, they might not have the desire to do so. And at one point in *World Made By Hand* the narrator's companion Britney notes, "We've lost our world," and Robert Earle responds, "No, just the part the machines lived in."[39] In this new landscape, machines can no longer be utilized to render geography itself irrelevant.

The political landscape is different as well—which has ramifications for how the physical geography is understood. In every instance the state itself has vanished—and with it, the ability of any organized government to command the territory which makes up England or the United States. The state's vanishing means that there is no mechanism for exploiting the resources of the land, or for providing for the orderly distribution of these resources. In every instance, the end of globalization has created a fuel shortage—and with it, an absence of all types of transportation. Without transportation, resources which exist in the interior of the nation are no longer exploitable by the nation's inhabitants. In this way, the geography of the United States begins to resemble the "wild interiors" of Africa which were described by the colonial writer Joseph Conrad. America is underdeveloped and travel through the interior of the country is neither safe nor wise. Manifest Destiny is replaced by the Heart of Darkness. The drive west is no longer seen as inevitable.

In Kunstler's *World Made by Hand*, the writer discourses at length about the notion of land and property—and its new meaning in the post-apocalyptic landscape. Readers are introduced to Jane Ann, a woman who was a realtor in her pre-apocalyptic life, a profession which may have previously been associated with the American Dream, but which now merely seems nonsensical. And while home and land ownership had ideological connotations of freedom and self-sufficiency in the pre-apocalyptic world, the new world features a character who bought up all the land in America's last days and now appears to be building a compound which is a cross between a medieval manor and an antebellum plantation, complete with serfs or indentured servants. America's own geography has changed as people leave suburban communities for the safety and companionship of the town. Vast open tracts of land thus no longer have the same ideological meaning in the post-apocalyptic world. In many post-apocalyptic novels, the worst devastation is routinely inflicted upon urban areas and their inhabitants. In an apocalyptic lens, cities are seen as having primarily cultural and social meaning and value—and have little to contribute in a survival situation.

Several novels also rely upon a device in which particular cultural objects which had great significance in the "old empire" are uncoupled from their social setting and ideology in the new setting. In the British utopian novel *Erewhon*, the narrator encounters natives who find his custom of smoking peculiar and who are repelled by his ownership of a watch, since they have abandoned such technology. In *The Road*, the man at one point finds a Coca-Cola which he gives to his child to drink. The child enjoys the drink but is completely unaware of the larger international significance of this item of American cultural production. In the new world, the construct of American soft power and the idea of other nations wishing to emulate the United States no longer exists. Later the child asks what a "state road" is after reading a sign along the destroyed highway. Finally, the man comes across a newspaper in an abandoned building. Here the newspaper represents not the state's support of press freedom or even the notion of technology and the transfer of information. Instead, it is regarded in terms of its utility for making fire or providing warmth. In *World Made by Hand*, the author depicts an old crazy man driving a car down the road before he crashes into a tree. The auto appears as a sort of fantasy or a mirage rather than an integral part of the social construct of a society—as it would have in an earlier era. Here, the authors use cultural objects from an earlier era to show how objects which represent the exceptional state can just as easily become trash or be thrown away or lose their meaning.

Similarly, the Victorian novel, *After London,* contains a poignant scene where London has somehow been submerged underwater, but is still visible from time to time by looking through the water.[40] Thus, it is possible for people one thousand years later to view the buildings, architecture, and vast intellectual and physical treasures of the City of London without regarding it is as either possible or desirable to somehow retrieve or exploit these treasures. The great works of civilization or literature contained in London's libraries, or the treasures of the British Museum, Buckingham Palace, and the Tower of London are merely physical things from the past which have no meaning in the present. London thus becomes merely an historic relic, which is desired by no one from the present-day—either native or foreign. However, it was once regarded as the pinnacle of civilization—just as Timbuktu or Ancient Rome might have been. It was once the most important spot in the world but is now irrelevant.

Jim Crace's *The Pesthouse* describes a place which is geographically America but which no longer is even aware of its own destiny or supposed "specialness." The end of American exceptionalism is perhaps most clearly displayed in a scene in *The Pesthouse* when Margaret, the main character, finds an old coin buried in a field. It appears to be a penny from the late twentieth century, and Margaret attempts to make sense of the figures on the coin—referring to "Father Abraham" in a way which suggests she has confused and conflated Abraham Lincoln, George Washington, and the original Abraham of the Old Testament. The scene allows the reader to consider America's history from a distant point a thousand years in the future when America seems as irrelevant and foreign as the Roman Empire seems today. The scene allows the writer to comment on how even a state which enjoys a position as a hegemon at the moment—setting the agenda in international relations; describing and enforcing norms and determining who may and who may not participate in that system—may someday see its greatest accomplishments rendered meaningless.

In Crace's novel, the advantages which feature so prominently in the narrative of American exceptionality—fertile land, hardworking citizens, and a variety of climates—are reinterpreted through the apocalyptic lens. In the new landscape, the land may still be fertile, but individuals no longer have the know-how or the technology to exploit them. Instead, Margaret, the main character comes up against some ruined farm equipment in a field. She describes it as "the metal animals which used to be used to plow the fields."[41] But they no longer have any utility, since America apparently destroyed its technology at some distant point in the past in a riot of Ludditism. (In this future world, Margaret knows only that metal is dangerous and that it can be used to kill people—apparently a reference to the guns and firearms which existed in the past.) In the apocalyptic lens, fertile land is not a resource to be exploited by the state's own citizens (if the state even existed anymore). Instead, that same farmland serves to draw others to the land so that they might exploit it and colonize it. Thus, America's strength becomes its weakness since it attracts the attention of other, stronger groups who may prey upon America in its weakened state. Here readers are forced to realize that America might just as easily have become a colony—since there is nothing inherent in the existence of resources themselves that forced development.

In two novels—*The Pesthouse* and *The Road*—America's greatest resource is actually the labor of the citizens, which can be "looted," taken elsewhere, and harnessed to the machine of economic development in service to someone else's nation or group. In this way, we are brought to see the fact that there is nothing unique about Americans that prevents them from entering into servitude elsewhere or being used in this way.

In both these novels, as well as in *After London*, the state occupies the same geographic place on the world map—but it has been somehow pushed to the periphery rather than the center. It has become part of the developing or underdeveloped world, and it thus marked as a source of inputs including labor (possibly slave labor, in the narrative of *The Pesthouse*) for another more distant point which is constituted as the center. In *The Pesthouse* in particular it becomes clear that the most important place in the new America is Tidewater (which is presumably Norfolk, Virginia) since it is an exit. That is where the boats come to take people away from America, leaving the periphery behind in order to travel to the center. The interior of America, in contrast, is presented as something dark and foreboding and not altogether safe. It requires bravery to enter the interior of the country or to travel towards it rather than away from it. In this way, the writing about America is reminiscent of Joseph Conrad's *Heart of Darkness*. I will take up this point in more detail when I describe colonial themes in the new apocalyptic—but here it is important to show that the exceptionalism narrative only works if the state is a colonizer. Thus, attempting to show that these same nations might just as easily be constructed as the colonized is a way of undermining the narrative of exceptionalism.

Both *The Pesthouse* and *The Road* thus illustrate the claim that the state's raw materials can be "constructed" in a variety of different ways—depending on whether one uses an exceptionalist or an apocalyptic lens. In James Kunstler's *World Made by Hand* the narrator Robert Earle attempts to describe the ways in which America has fallen apart, stating that "It seemed to me that the federal government was little more than a figment of our imaginations. Everything was local now,"[42] and in the darker novel *The Road* by Cormac McCarthy, the unnamed narrator describes a world no longer held together by a belief system. He states "The ashes of the late world were carried on the bleak and temporal winds to and fro in the void. Carried forth and scattered and carried forth again. Everything uncoupled from its shoring. Unsupported in the ashen air."[43] Later in the passage, a snowflake comes wafting down through the air, where it is described as being "like the last host of Christendom."[44] In this bleak novel, the reader is forced to think of an America which is no longer unique or special in its relationship to the rest of the world or to God. Instead, it is either world which has been abandoned or a world which never had that special relationship—since it was a construct rather than something that was real.

THE PROBLEM OF TIME AND THE TRAJECTORY OF PROGRESS

While the utopian novel undermines the notion of uniqueness, the apocalyptic novel undermines the notion of specialness. Obviously, describing a Britain or an America which has failed to achieve or to maintain a leading place in the world calls into question the idea that one's nation has or had a special destiny in the world and was therefore guaranteed success in its endeavors. Beginning with *After London*, tracing through E. M. Forster's *The Machine Stops*, through to *World Made by Hand*, *The Road*, and *The Passage*—we see that the state's promise has not been fulfilled. It has ended in ruins, just as other nations have in the past. Here again, the reader is forced to consider the ways in which specialness has been constructed socially, culturally, and politically—rather than residing in reality.

In addition, both British and American utopian and apocalyptic writings make reference to time and chronologies in a way which is arguably subversive. For exceptionalist nations have traditionally had a different relation to time and the exceptionalist narrative makes a claim to chronological significance. That is, the exceptional (or messianic) nation claims to have an eternal role in history in which it traces its roots back to its special or unusual inception or birth (for example, the creation of the Magna Carta, or the signing of the Declaration of Independence, or in the case of Israel, God's call to Abraham). The nation then goes on to make the claim that it is somehow part of a larger, ongoing history (that of civilization) which will culminate in the eventual triumph of the civilization.

The chronological role of the exceptional state thus established a power relationship between it and other nations in the international system. The exceptionalist nation claims to possess a wisdom and maturity which other younger, less mature nations do not—due to the way in which it is configured within a longer historic schema. This history is what gives the nation the ability to define the rules and norms of the international system and to label other, newer nations which attempt to utilize their power to query those norms as "upstarts."[45] Here, the solipsism that allows a nation like Britain to claim that a territory did not exist until it was discovered by a Western explorer also allows that same nation to make the claim that the territory's history essentially began with that discovery. Thus, in every encounter which Britain had up through the Industrial Revolution, there was an implicit claim that somehow what was occurring was that an older evolved and established Britain was meeting a new, immature, and underdeveloped territory.

Utopian literature in Britain, however, turns this claim upon its head. In every instance, from *Erewhon* to *Gulliver's Travels* to H. G. Wells's *The First Men in the Moon*, the traveler essentially lands in a foreign land where the foreigners have the advantage. The game is being played, in a sense, on their home territory. In each case, it is impossible for Swift's Gulliver, Erewhon's unnamed narrator, or H. G. Wells's Mr. Bedford to advance the claim that they represent an older civilization in comparison to the upstart civilizations which they are visiting when they are surrounded by the architecture, libraries, and other concrete evidence of an established history belonging to the alternate civilization. In each case, even the responsibility for naming the year is given to the foreign nation, and it is Britain itself which seems young, immature, and small in comparison to the mature nation being visited.

However, while the utopian or dystopian novel thus suggests that the imperial nation is neither as old, as special, nor as significant as it claims—apocalyptic novels actually go further in undermining this claim. They do not merely query underlying assumptions about the age and maturity of the state, but go on to query the notion of progress as well. Here, we see how the nation's destiny is not eternal but is rather capable of being undone and even reversed. In essence, what happens at the apocalyptic moment is a resetting of the clock. At that moment, the previous cultural achievements of the dominant culture are erased and time begins anew from the Year Zero. The apocalyptic event thus severs the two histories—the history of the established world and the brand-new history of the post-apocalyptic world. In this new world, the land and people have no history, no claim to maturity or to a special position in the world based on that history.

This new relationship with time is described in *The Road* when Cormac McCarthy's unnamed male narrator describes the post-apocalyptic landscape as follows: "Barren, silent, godless. He thought the month was October but he wasn't sure."[46] Similarly, Robert Earle notes in *World Made by Hand* that "it was obvious there would be no return to 'normality.' The economy wouldn't be coming back. Globalism was over. . . . The computer industry, in which so many hopes had been vested, was fading into history."[47] Finally, in Justin Cronin's *The Passage*, he utilizes a narrative device in which anthropologists and historians from the future are presenting papers at an academic conference about the history of post-apocalyptic America. The papers which the historians present are based on their analyses of hand-written journals and other artifacts rescued from the new post-apocalyptic civilization. These artifacts are described as the first evidence of the new civilization, implicitly making the claim that the group being studied has no prior history. In comparison to the established Australian society of the scholars who study the new world, the American post-apocalyptic world appears to be without significance, without civilization, and without history.

The resetting of the clock at the apocalyptic moment explains why the reader feels that he has gone both simultaneously backward and forward in time in reading an apocalyptic or dystopian novel. He knows that he is supposed to be in the future, and yet he feels that he is in the past. This phenomenon was first described by the anthropologist Alfred Gell, who wrote in 1983 about the ways in which analysts frequently othered their colonial subjects by describing them as separated not only spatially but also temporally from them. Gell labeled the phenomenon as allochronism. Allochronism describes a methodology in which the Western anthropologist frequently described his subject both as an exotic who came from a foreign place—but also as a primitive, who came from in a sense a different temporal dimension. Both the researcher and the subject thus exist at the same moment in time—and yet to the researcher, the subject somehow appears to be from an earlier era or to exist outside time altogether. The traditional Western researcher's gaze allowed him to describe his subject as being from an earlier era, where thought processes were different (perhaps less rational), the landscape was different (frequently untouched by technology and modernization), and social practices were different. Thus an analyst who journeyed to Bali might have the sense of simultaneously going both far away and also backward in time. And those who read anthropology have this same sense when they "meet" a group of people and they are told that "the Kung people are patrilineal." The sense is that the researchers themselves live in a dynamic world where social practices evolve, while their subjects—the

Kung—are static or frozen in time, existing only in that snapshot. We are not told that they were patrilineal, but rather that they are.

Similarly, one can identify the phenomenon of allochronism in contemporary American press writing in the immediate aftermath of September 11, 2001. The repeated references by President George W. Bush and other conservative politicians to "evil doers" and the "evil" of those who committed the terrorist attacks creates a sense of timelessness, placing the subjects in an eternal perspective. In addition, repeated references to Osama bin Laden's desire to reestablish an Arab caliphate such as the one which existed in the Middle Ages again creates this sense that he and his compatriots are from an earlier era. Finally press reports and academic analyses frequently put forth the argument that "they hate us because we are modern" again establishing a sense of Us versus Them which includes an element of temporal difference, as well as cultural and ideological difference.

The core of Gell's project was to query the sources of allochronism in the work of colonial and contemporary anthropologists as well as to examine the ways in which it served the imperial project. However, one can point out the ways in which utopian literature also plays with time and the notion of a trajectory of progress, and in doing so, perhaps suggest that the interrogation (if not the identification) of allochronism actually began as early as the 1700s. Then, one can trace the way in which this concept appears in the contemporary apocalyptic novel as well, perhaps as a reaction to the heavy usage of this concept in the post-September 11 era.

As noted in the previous section, utopian novels allowed readers to begin interrogating the claim that one's own nation is the only place that is special or unique—through asking the reader to imagine another similarly special and unique place. In addition, though, both utopian novels—through their preoccupation with the future—and apocalyptic novels—through their ability to both stop time and loop time—also force the reader to query the notion that every place which is foreign or exotic is also necessarily primitive or backward.

Here, the linear apocalyptic narrative creates a new space which is in some way "beyond time" since the narrative of history as progress has effectively ended. Within the linear apocalyptic narrative, thus, time is relevant only to itself. (That is, one can "tell time" in terms of noting that fourteen days have passed since the beginning of the action in *The Road*. One cannot, however, say definitely what month or year it is.) Although we as readers can view and consider the corpse of the state as it dies, we cannot write a traditional eulogy for that state in which we place it within history. Rather, it is assumed to be without meaning, without history. As Cormac McCarthy asks the question in *The Road*: "Do you think your fathers are watching? That they weigh you in your ledger book? Against what? There is no book and your fathers are dead in the ground."[48]

In contrast, the circular apocalyptic, with its emphasis on renewal, may literally restart the clock. Thus, in what some regard as the classic apocalyptic novel, *Earth Abides*, written in 1947, the characters who survive the pestilence which destroys most of mankind literally begin to renumber history over again, starting with the Year One.[49]

And in utopian and dystopian novels, the reader is asked to consider whether in fact he (or she) has incorrectly numbered the years as they exist at present. Thus, the two British novels *Erewhon* and *Gulliver's Travels*, in particular, ask the reader to imagine the possibility that there exists another society (coeval or in the same time as imperial Britain) which finds Britain itself to be primitive or backward. In such a place, the argument goes, it is possible that even the achievements which seem most magnificent and incomparable to Britain's own subjects (such as the creation of manufacturing plants or the availability of manufactured goods or the creation of the telegraph) might actually be regarded as primitive or backward relics by others who are more advanced. Thus, for example, in Samuel Butler's *Erewhon*, the narrator is taken to a museum full of technology. He asks:

> What was the meaning of that room full of old machinery which I had just seen and of the displeasure with which the magistrate had regarded my watch? . . . The people had very little machinery now. . . . How could it have happened that having been once so far in advance they were now as much behind us? It was evident that it was not from ignorance.[50]

Here, the utopian novel is used to other the British subject, painting him as a primitive in comparison to his more developed neighbors. The British subject thus appears as childlike with his magical faith in technology, which he sees as the answer to his present-day suffering and the solution to his problems. For those who have already experimented with technology, found it wanting, and cast it aside, the British subject's desire to embrace it (and perhaps even to serve it) appears as naïve and the product of a limited experience.

In the contemporary period, Americans are asked—like the British were—to imagine themselves as primitives. However, the device used to do so is slightly different. While British utopian fiction created a hypothetical place from which the British could gaze upon themselves as primitives, American apocalyptic fiction asks the reader to take his present self and then to gaze upon an invented future in which his society has actually become more primitive than it is at present. Thus, British fiction asks the reader to imagine himself as "backward" in comparison to other nations, while American fiction asks the reader to imagine himself as backward in comparison to where he is now. In each instance—the utopian novel and the apocalyptic novel—the powerful nation, its history, and its significance are redefined in reflexivist terms. The state is resituated, not as a dominant power with full control over the narrative which emerges, but rather as both the subject and object of inquiry. In British utopian fiction, Gulliver becomes an object of study by his Lilliputian, Brobdingnagian, and Laputan interlocutors, and his story is as much theirs as it is his. They define for themselves who he is and what his significance is within the confines of their world. Similarly, the narrator in *Erewhon* finds himself in a position where he must defend his belief system, his history, and his identity and in essence all that he believes to be true about himself from those who seek to reread and reanalyze his own history.

In contemporary literature, this reversal of the anthropologist and the subject is best described in Justin Cronin's *The Passage*, where much of the story of the post-apocalyptic world appears as a series of vignettes which the reader is told are from conference papers given at a social sciences conference taking place in Australia one thousand years in the future. At the conference, a more "advanced" researcher describes the lifestyle, belief system, and social structure of America in 2100—in the same way that a researcher today might describe the lifestyle and social structure of native Americans in the 1400s.

The Backward Loop of Progress

As noted previously, the apocalyptic novel thus posits a resetting of the clock as the result of particular events which are said to have undone the progress of civilization. Table 6.2 and Table 6.3 lay out the particular types of institutions which are undone in each of the apocalyptic novels.

As these figures indicate, in each novel the action of the story takes place in a place which is geographically reminiscent of either the United States or Britain. However, in each case the emotional and security landscape has changed—largely because institutions which citizens have taken for granted have been subtracted from the equation. In doing so, the reader feels as though he is in an unfamiliar scenario and is unable to place exactly where he is. In many instances, the reader concludes that the story must be taking place in an earlier time period or in a foreign country. As figure 6.1 shows, depending on which social elements have been subtracted from the landscape, the reader feels as though he has arrived at an earlier time period.

Thus, as figure 6.1 illustrates, in some situations authors posit an undoing of the social and economic gains of the American Revolution (causing America to thus assume its previous status as a colony or of land waiting to be colonized by others). In others, they posit an undoing of the Enlightenment with its attendant advances in philosophical and social thought, such that characters adopt pre-enlightenment values, including blaming individuals for somehow fostering or creating their own disease, or believing that it rains because the sky is angry.

Table 6.2. Victorian Apocalyptic Novels and Backward Motion

Novel	Political Institutions	Economic Institutions	Social Institutions
Erewhon		Technology	
The Machine Stops		Technology	
After London	The State The military	Capitalism Interdependence Production and manufacturing	Citizenship Rule of law
News from Nowhere	British Imperial mission	Mercantilism Capitalism The profit motive	Class structures

Table 6.3. Contemporary Apocalyptic Novels and Backward Motion

Novel	Political Institutions	Economic Institutions	Social Institutions
World Made by Hand	Political leadership (president, governor, etc.) Military (all levels) Territorial unity of the United States Infrastructure (fire department, courts, police, medical care, education, etc.)	Capitalist monetary economy (vs. barter) Fuel production and import Commercial farming	Feminism Globalization
The Road	Infrastructure Political leadership Territorial unity of the United States Buildings Environment	Fuel production and import Agriculture (all types) Capitalism	"humanity" Feminism Globalization Religion Rationalism
The Pesthouse	Infrastructure Environment Buildings Territorial unity of United States Political leadership	Fuel production Agriculture (except local) Capitalism	Empiricism Rationalism Religion Globalization Colonization Feminism
The Passage	The State Territorial unity of United States International Position Infrastructure Urbanization	Capitalism Interdependence Production	Class structures Racial divisions

In the most extreme circumstances, ecological, political, and physical events cause existing society to be "thrown back" to a period as remote as the Stone Age.

Here, the farther away from the end of the empire the novel takes place, the greater the erasing of empire which is likely to have occurred. Those post-apocalyptics which take place in a five- to ten-year period from the author's own time focus on the erasure of capitalism, imperialism, and globalization—while those which take place at a greater distance from the author's own time tend to also consider the erasure or undoing of the enlightenment, Western civilization, and the notion of scientific rationality. *The Pesthouse* erases both the legacy of

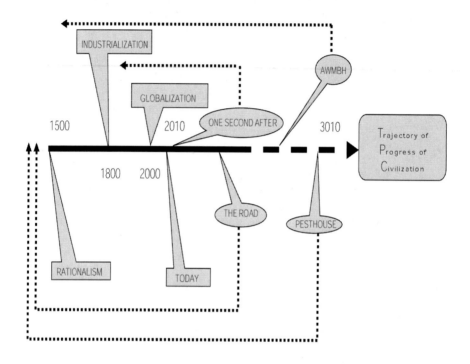

Figure 6.1. Counterfactual Trajectories

rationality and western colonialism. Table 6.4 illustrates the ways in which history is "undone."

In both instances, the net effect of this resituation is to cause the reader to query deeply held beliefs about his own nation's trajectory and the narrative of its future. In seeing how another outside analyst might reread his own history, he is forced to consider whether the history that he himself believes to be true is not simply constructed. In addition, the device used in the post-apocalyptic novel—in which a future point is identified and then contemporary events are reread as history by an omniscient narrator who already knows how the story turns out—can serve to create a sense of unease in the contemporary reader. He is "lost" in

EXCEPTIONALITY AND APOCALYPSE

Table 6.4. Chains of Events in Contemporary and Victorian Apocalyptics

Novel	Time Frame	Chain of Events
World Made by Hand	"The near future"	End of oil. Terrorist attacks and end of state
The Road	6–10 years from now	Nuclear war. Famine. End of state. Breakdown of social order (cannibalism)
The Pesthouse	1,000 years from now	Pestilence. End of United States. End of industrialization
After London	1,000 years from now	Natural disaster. Climate change. End of state. End of economy. End of citizenship

the narrative because it appears that thus far he has somehow misread his own history, mistaking events as, for example, progressive steps towards one future while in another narrative they are actually regressive steps towards a different, less positive end. Thus, American writing frequently turns on the notion that the apocalyptic moment might already somehow have occurred and been misidentified. Perhaps we are already on this downward trajectory and we are unaware of it.

Here again, *The Passage* is of particular interest since it suggests that America was headed on a backward trajectory long before the arrival of the vampires. Cronin writes of the 2005 Hurricane Katrina and then describes a fictive Category Five hurricane which occurred five years later, finishing New Orleans and much of the Gulf Coast off. Parts of America are abandoned, terrorist attacks have occurred, and America has a huge domestic security apparatus. America is still at war in Iraq, apparently, when the story occurs in 2015—and the decision to undertake a risky gamble in developing extremely dangerous biological warfare agents is understood against this backdrop. Thus, in a sense, America's trajectory backward is seen as predetermined—although the escape of the biological weapon is the "spark" which precipitates the wholesale slide into the past.

The accomplishment of the Victorian novels is to raise the subversive notion that perhaps Britain and the British imperial mission did *not* matter to many in the world. Rather, as Swift, Wells, and Butler suggested, perhaps there were somewhere other cultures with histories, political institutions, and belief structures which were neither derivative of Britain's nor imitative. Perhaps there were limits to Britain's imperial reach, and perhaps the machinations of empire building were *not* inexorable. And, in raising the notion that perhaps there are those who do not profit from inclusion in empire, the question thus surfaced as to whether Britain actually needed an empire and whether the world could survive intact without one.

In the American case, the query "Do we matter?" is less about how America is perceived by its neighbors (for here we already know the answer—they hate us); rather the question is whether America matters in a temporal context. Will it matter fifty years from now? one hundred years from now? one thousand years from now? For if the Boer War suggested to Britain the possibility that the empire could one day be dismantled, 9/11 suggested to the United States the possibility that we could one day be erased.

In this way, the apocalyptic novel actually comes to have much in common with colonial travel narratives. The post-apocalyptic United States or Britain is "othered" and described in terms similar to those used by colonial writers in travel narratives composed during the Victorian era and on into the twentieth centuries. Its land is described as blank and barren, and its people are described as savage. If the citizens of this new United States or Britain speak at all in these new narratives, they speak as subaltern peoples who are defenseless, powerless, and helpless to describe their own future. This literature can thus serve a powerful political function in causing America to develop a new perspective both on itself and upon its neighbors. The utopian, dystopian, and apocalyptic narrative can allow for a decentering of the imagined narrative and trajectory of a superpower by allowing us to both imagine and to speak from below.

NOTES

1. Nicols Fox, *Against the Machine: The Hidden Luddite Tradition in Literature, Art and Individual Lives* (Washington, DC: Island Press, 2002).
2. Frank Kermode, *The Sense of an Ending: Studies in the Theory of Fiction* (London: Oxford University Press, 1968): 94.
3. Kermode, 95.
4. Bernard Porter, *The Lion's Share, A Short History of British Imperialism*, 1850–1983 (London: Longman Publishing Group, 2nd edition, 1984).
5. Niall Ferguson makes this argument in his article, "The Reluctant Empire," *Hoover Digest* 3 (2004).

6. Here, it is interesting to note that post-modern historians of the Roman Empire have begun to move beyond the 'decline of civilization' construct to ask this very question—what comes after the decline of empire and how are we to understand it if we jettison long-held historicist notions which divide history into periods and assumed that there is a common trajectory to socio-political and cultural processes? In doing so, they have abandoned prior emphases on "the Dark Ages," instead invoking the term transformation in order to reconsider Roman rule, particularly in its final, weakened state as essentially being about a process of negotiation and adaptation—in which Roman ideas and civilization or the world didn't so much disappear as assimilate into a larger mix of world cultures which arose at that time. Unfortunately, international relations scholars have been slow to catch up with these developments in conceptualization and discourse. Mary Manjikian, *Rethinking Barbarism: Implications for the Roman Empire Analogy in International Relations* (Manuscript under review, 2010).

7. Judith Butler, *Precarious Life: The Powers of Mourning and Violence* (London: Verso, 2004), 4.

8. Alan Sandison, *The Wheel of Empire: A Study of the Imperial Idea in Some Late Nineteenth and Early Twentieth Century Fiction* (London: St. Martin's, 1967).

9. Here my reading is somewhat unique in that I suggest that one of the primary goals of this literature—in both the British imperial and American 'imperial' periods—was to critique foreign policy. Other analysts, including Darko Suvin, have suggested that science fiction in Victorian Britain was a critique but the emphasis has traditionally been on science fiction's critique of capitalism as an economic policy rather than imperialism as a foreign policy. Thus, if there was a 'hegemony' which was being interrogated, it was the overwhelmingly accepted notion that capitalism was good for everyone in Britain, that class differences were unimportant in the grand scheme of things, and that any economic suffering endured by Britain's citizens was worthwhile in the long-run. However, in focusing only on science fiction as an economic critique, I feel that analysts have not sufficiently explored the ways in which the somewhat broader political critique also raised questions regarding the ethics of empire and the personhood of those who were colonized. Suvin's critique appears in Darko Suvin, *Victorian Science Fiction in the UK: The Discourses of Knowledge and Power* (Boston: G. K. Hall and Co., 1983).

10. Here, it is important to note that other nations have also historically viewed themselves as both exceptional and unique. Leaders of the former Soviet Union frequently used exceptionalist language in describing the ways in which it was unique as the first communist nation. China's communist leaders,

as well, make reference to its uniqueness—pointing to its unusual resource endowments and its history.

11. Technology and ideology can also come together in creation of the exceptionalist narrative, as Huber (Matthew Huber, "The Use of Gasoline: Value, Oil and the American Way of Life," *Antipode* 41 no. 3 (2009): 465–86) points out in his work on America as a "car culture." He suggests that American automotive technology was frequently described in uniquely American ideological terms—with the creation of roads and automotive technology being described as increasing American's individual freedoms, as well as enabling them to follow Manifest Destiny in crossing America from one end to the other. Thus, I argue that an apocalyptic novel which erases the existing system of state roads can be seen as having both technological and ideological significance.

12. Clifford Longley, *Chosen People: The Big Idea That Shapes England and America* (London: Hodder and Stoughton, 2002).

13. Antoine Bousquet, "Time Zero: Hiroshima, September 11 and Apocalyptic Revelation in Historical Consciousness," *Millennium* 34 (2006): 742.

14. Bernard L. Jim, "Wrecking the Joint: The Razing of City Hotels in the First Half of the Twentieth Century," *The Journal of Decorative and Propaganda Arts* 25 (2004): 297.

15. Bruce Feiler, *America's Prophet: Moses and the American Story* (New York: William Morrow, 2009).

16. Longley, 5.

17. Wyschogrod, Edith. *Emmanuel Levinas: The Problem of Ethical Metaphysics* (New York: Fordham University Press, 2000): 105.

18. As noted earlier in this work, the state may be found guilty, or even punished, for violating its covenant with God or for having violated its own principles or values. However, in considering the state's relations with its neighbors, some other means must be developed for asking these questions—outside of the imperial narrative of exceptionalism.

19. For more on this point, see Kenneth Reinhard, *The Ethics of the Neighbor* (Charlottesville, VA: University of Virginia Press, 2005).

20. Hilary Dannenberg, *Coincidence and Counterfactuality: Plotting Time and Space in Narrative Fiction* (Omaha, NE: University of Nebraska, 2008): 10.

21. Gillian Hart, "Denaturalizing Dispossession: Critical Ethnography in the Age of Resurgent Imperialism," *Antipode* 38 (2006): 980.

22. Richard Peet, "From Eurocentrism to Americentrism," *Antipode* 37 (2005): 938.

23. Peet, 941; Hart, 978.

24. Huber, 465–86.

25. Judith Butler, 22.

26. Don DeLillo, *Falling Man* (New York: Scribner, 2007): 191.

27. Richard Smith, "Mapping China's World: Cultural Cartography in late Imperial Times." Available at www.kunstpedia.com/articles/mapping-chinas-world--cultural-cartography-in-late-imperial-times. html#axzz1Nm171klQ

28. Joseph Conrad, *Heart of Darkness* (Boston, MA: Hesperus Press, 2002).

29. Hart, 996.

30. Wesley C. Salmon, "Dynamic Rationality: Propensity, Probability and Credence," in James H. Fetzer, ed., *Probability and Causality* (Reidel: Dordrecht, 1987): 111.

31. One might also take the tactic which Samuel Butler did in *Erewhon*—producing a silly, pompous, unselfconscious narrator who spouts off at great length about the uniqueness and specialness of himself and his land. Thus, *Erewhon*'s unnamed narrator states: "But what I saw! It was such an expanse as was revealed to Moses when he stood upon the suit of Mount Sinai, and beheld that Promised Land which it was not to be his to enter" (37). Here Butler meant the passage not to signal a true level of support for the idea that lands were to be given to Britain through divine favor, but rather to force the reader to interrogate the assumption—since the narrator is in some ways both childish and unlikable.

32. Jonathan Swift, *Gulliver's Travels* (New York: Penguin Classics, 2003), 37.

33. Swift, 64.

34. Swift, 79.

35. H. G. Wells, *The First Men in the Moon* (New York: Echo Library, 2006).

36. Richard Ned Lebow, *Forbidden Fruit: Counterfactuals and International Relations* (Princeton, NJ: Princeton University Press, 2010), 35.

37. Daniel Cordle, *States of Suspense: The Nuclear Age, Postmodernism and US Fiction and Prose* (Manchester, UK: Manchester University Press, 2008): 71.

38. Richard Jefferies, *After London* (London: General Books, LLC, 2010): 26–27.

39. James Kunstler, *World Made by Hand* (New York: Grove Press, 2009): 223.

40. It thus comes to share an intertextual meaning with the lost city of Atlantis—being both somehow real and also legendary. It may also be compared to Pompeii—something which is excavated, but serves only as a tourist curiosity. Few tourists can ever really understand the economic position or importance of Pompeii.

41. Jim Crace, *The Pesthouse* (New York, Vintage, 2008).

42. James Kunstler, *World Made by Hand* (New York: Grove Press, 2009): 14.

43. Cormac McCarthy, *The Road* (New York: Vintage Press, 2006): 10.

44. McCarthy, 13.

45. Here, see for example Andrei S. Markovits, *Uncouth Nation: Why Europe Hates America* (Princeton, NJ: Princeton University Press, 2008). In this work, he analyzes British media coverage of U.S. foreign policy up to and including September 11 to make the claim that America is regarded as too young and immature to have the right to play a role on the international stage.

46. McCarthy, 4.

47. Kunstler, 24.

48. Cormac McCarthy, *The Road* (New York: Vintage Press, 2006).

49. George Stewart, *Earth Abides* (New York: Fawcett Press, 1986).

50. Butler, 43.

7

GOING NATIVE

Previously, I suggested that utopian and apocalyptic writing produced at the height of British and American empire served similar purposes. Both types of writing allowed for the creation of a literary space where writers and their readers could more closely interrogate the notion of exceptionalism. In this chapter, I suggest that these works can be read as a commentary not only on the nation itself but also on how the nation exists within the international system. By querying the narrative of exceptionality, the novels' authors have asked the reader to consider the possibility that his own nation was no different from other nations. Thus, these works performed a sort of "leveling"—in which the reader was encouraged to think of how his world might be different if his nation (Britain or America) was not actually the center of the world or the author of civilization but was instead merely one nation among many other similar nations. What if, he was asked to consider, exceptionality was merely a construct? These same novels also compel us to ask whether empire itself is merely a construct.

The analyst Homi Bhabha suggests that early modernist colonial literature—including works like Joseph Conrad's *Heart of Darkness*—performs "the work of empire slowly undone."[1] He argues that authors may actually only wish to represent the work of empire, but that frequently they nonetheless end up interrogating it. This is because colonial literature rests on a narrative about a meeting of two cultures which appear to be from two different time periods—the British in India or the British in Africa, or the Dutch in Indonesia, for example. The clash between the two cultures provides the basis for the story and for any learning which might take place as the colonizers find themselves surprised and shaped by what they find in their new environments. In many cases (though certainly not all), the travelers (and the readers of these travel narratives) are forced to see what sorts of prejudices and preconceived notions they have brought with them in their travels, and these prejudices are put under scrutiny as they proceed to meet the natives of the land themselves.

Similarly, both British utopian and American apocalyptic literature reproduce many of these same elements. For this reason, today's post-apocalyptic novels have a strangely British, post-colonial feel to them. In tone, they reproduce the same sort of nostalgia which has come to be the hallmark of British literature—in which the authors describe a longing for England's heroic past, and involve themselves with questions like "How do they remember us after we are gone? How should we remember ourselves? What does it mean to miss the British Empire? What does it mean to wish that it was gone or that it had never happened?" This same clashing appears in apocalyptic literature when the traveler confronts what he had in his "old life" and what he now must do without in his post-apocalyptic life. Can this clash of cultures similarly provide a site for learning and interrogation of the role of Britain or the role of America in the world? Can the traveler's view of the new land also highlight the prejudices and preconceived notions that he has brought with him from his "old world"—whether that world is imperial Britain or pre-apocalyptic America?

COLONIAL TROPES IN APOCALYPTIC WRITING

Earlier I suggested that all notions of history, the rise of civilization and progress are inherently colonialist, and that all of these organizing frameworks for understanding the world implicitly rest on a construct of time which equates modernization, industrialization, and urbanization with the future while the rural or the pastoral is associated with the past.

Here, the so-called primitive is seen to live in an earlier time in contrast to the more developed subject who is seen to occupy and represent the future. The land as well of the developed nation is seen as belonging to and representing modernity.

Thus, experiencing colonization and experiencing disaster are two very similar types of events. In each case, the one who is acted upon undergoes an event which causes him to lose status and to become disoriented as he struggles to understand his new place in the order of things. In addition, in each case, he loses agency as some larger, stronger force (a plantation owner or a hurricane) takes over his world, rearranging it in ways that no longer make sense. He wonders if his older, former world will ever return. He may feel that he has been banished from the center to the periphery. Thus, it is perhaps not surprising that the two types of narratives—disaster narratives and colonial narratives—and the two types of narrators (the colonial subject and the disaster survivor) would have so much in common, or that they would find themselves with such a large array of shared language, metaphors, and ideas.

In addition, the colonial period was characterized by the coming together of multiple cultures and shifting of boundaries as cultures came into contact with each other for the first time. Similarly, one can argue that today's globalization trends are performing a similar function. Thus, globalization may be seen to represent a fraying of the borders between the self and other. Both colonization and globalization presented certain risks to the one engaged in the process of discovering the larger world. In each case, the self is threatened with the risk of both encountering the same risks as the other and of literally "becoming" the other. That is, when the self encounters the other, there is a risk that the self will be overpowered by the other, which can lead to its letting go of the civilization myth, or watching that myth wash away through circumstances or simply the force of others in the world who threaten to overtake colonial power. Sewall describes the way in which colonization required not only that the colonist engage with the "barbarity" of the native, but also that the colonist become a bit barbaric himself. Colonial literature thus raises the notion of "going native"—in which the colonizer himself lets go of his civilized veneer and engages with his inner savage.[2]

Similarly, apocalyptic literature erases the boundaries between the so-called civilized world and the worlds which exist at its borders. In the apocalyptic novel, civilization is vanquished and the American inhabitants find themselves "going native." In Joseph Conrad's novel *Falk*, he describes a white colonizer who literally becomes a barbarian and a cannibal, as he deigns to try human flesh. Similarly, we encounter modern-day cannibals in *The Road* and *The Passage*. Thus, it appears that this new literature represents a way of interrogating the notion of globalization—both its virtue and its more sinister possibilities.

In addition, the act of imagining Americans engaged in these actions levels the playing field—by erasing again the rhetoric of specialness. In the scenarios described in apocalyptic literature, there is no reason to behave that Americans will behave any differently or any better than other humans—despite America's historic emphasis on its special ideology, belief system, or place in history. In point of fact, the reader may think, we do not really know how we might behave in a situation of radical human insecurity. We might argue that Americans would never sink to the level of cannibalism or genocidal warfare—but in point of fact we do not really know if that is true. In a sense, the very fact that it is conceivable suggests that it is on some level possible and perhaps even plausible. If mass slaughters could happen in Rwanda or in Bosnia, then it is perhaps possible that they could also happen in America—since Americans are, after all, not so very different from everyone else. In considering these possibilities, the reader is forced to consider and maybe even to answer some challenging ethical questions such as: Is my culture truly more moral or ethical? Are the citizens of my culture somehow immune from ever sinking to a level of barbarism—and if not, why have I historically thought that they are? Can those who do not experience disaster firsthand really judge those who do?

The Land Has Been Cleared

A brief survey of the apocalyptic literature indicates that many of the usual conventions of the colonial travelogue are present. These include first the trope which Spurr refers to as being "the master of all I survey." In this literary shorthand, the reader knows he is reading imperial literature because of the way the landscape itself is described through colonial eyes as being a site for future colonial land use patterns. (In other words, the narrator describes the landscape of an African village as "just

GOING NATIVE

perfect for building a plantation house—once those dirty mud huts are cleared away.") In looking at how this trope has appeared historically in colonial writing, Spurr describes the writing of Henry Morton Stanley, a British journalist. In this snippet from Stanley's journal, Stanley has entered Africa's interior in search of David Livingstone, the explorer who vanished while following the Nile to its source at Lake Victoria. In his own words, he describes the land called Anyamwezi. He writes:

> Hills of syenite are seen dotting the vast prospect, like islands in a sea, presenting in their external appearance, to an imaginative eye, rude imitations of castellated fortresses and embattled towers. Around these rocky hills the cultivated fields of the Unyamwezi—fields of tall maize, of holcus sorghum, of millet, of vetches, etc.—among which you may discern the patches devoted to the cultivation of sweet potatoes and manioc, and pasture lands where browse the hump shouldered cattle of Africa, flocks of goats and sheep.[3]

Spurr notes the manner in which Stanley inspects the land and in doing so, imposes order upon it. It appears that Stanley is actually sizing it up, like a surveyor, as though he's going to purchase it. Spurr refers to this viewpoint as "the doctrine of appropriation," noting that the surveyor's eye assumes that the empty, vacant land belongs to the surveyor or to "mankind," but not to any inhabitants who may already occupy the land. The 'master of all I survey' trope may also include language relating the notion that the land at present is waste land or blank land, since it has not yet come under imperial organization.

Victorian post-apocalyptic novels derive part of their subversive nature from the way in which they turn the traditional colonial travel narrative on its head. This "inversion" is obvious in the way which Swift's *Gulliver's Travels* utilizes the trope of "the master of all I survey." It is clear that Gulliver's meeting with the Lilliputian "natives" will not be your usual colonial encounter when Gulliver finds that the land he is visiting is certainly not blank or chaotic or in need of his colonial organizational services. Instead, Gulliver finds that the Lilliputians have carved up their land into neat, organized plots of their own accord. Here he describes the metropolis of Lilliput: "The city is an exact square, each side of which is 500 feet long; this square is in turn subdivided by two intersecting avenues into four quarters. At the center of the city, the emperor's palace is enclosed by a wall 'two foot high' and separated by three concentric courts and a distance of twenty feet."[4] And Gulliver becomes not a colonizer, surveying the land for his own use, but rather an employee of the indigenous people, helping them to survey the land (which is referred to by their own names, rather than names applied to the region by outside colonizers) for their own use.

In the contemporary novels considered here, America itself is viewed as having been cleared or made blank due to nuclear holocaust (in the case of *The Road*); the outbreak of some form of plague (in *The Pesthouse*); biological warfare gone terribly wrong (in *The Passage*), or as a result of terrorist attacks and the end of globalization (in *World Made by Hand*). As a result, Americans now occupy a new possession of alterity and powerlessness, and it is their own land—the new, ruined, dark America—which is now described as a blank space on the map. It is viewed by others largely in terms of the ways which it might increase their own utility—either as a place to resettle their own population surplus or as a source of resources which can be looted and brought back to their own homes. Here, Spurr describes how the Victorian explorer Stanley viewed the landscape near Lake Tanganyika through the eyes of the expropriator, in noting his words:

> What a settlement one could have in this valley! See, it is broad enough to support a large population! Fancy a church spire rising where that tamarind rears its dark crown of foliage, and think how well a score or so of pretty cottages would look instead of those thorn clumps and gum trees! Fancy this lovely valley teeming with herds of cattle and fields of corn, spreading the right and left of this stream! How much better would such a state become this valley, rather than its present wild and deserted aspect![5]

This same language of organization and appropriation appears in the apocalyptic work *World Made by Hand* when Robert Earle describes the plantation called Bullock's Farm. Here, in the wasteland that used to be America, Stephen Bullock, a former lawyer, has built a village which he hopes will one day be named after him. Earle describes the sense of order which has been created: "It really amounted to a village. . . . The cottages were deployed along a picturesque little main street with a few narrow lanes off it. There were thirty buildings in all. This

GOING NATIVE

main street lacked shops or places of business because the only business there was Bullock's business."[6]

Here the implication is that the rest of America is a wilderness which lacks order. However, Bullock has heroically imposed order upon this wilderness, even if the drive to do so has required the subjugation of the upstate New York natives, who are now indentured servants on Bullock's Farm. In international relations language, one can state that the "master of all I survey" rests on the notions of core and periphery, with representatives of the core nations describing how they might make use of the resources of the periphery. In suggesting that another might view American land through the lens of the surveyor, the authors of these works are also noting that America itself no longer belongs to the core, but instead has moved to the periphery. This new land is both removed and backward in compared to other nations.

The apocalyptic novel thus suggests that the land which geographically belongs to modernity can still slide backward into an earlier era as the result of a devastating apocalyptic event or series of events. In a sense, one can argue that the land has been "cleared"—of cities, complex forms of social organization, a large swathe of the population, and the complex transportation and communication infrastructure which allowed it to be perceived as organized, filled up, and owned. In the absence of these elements of modern life, the land has been rendered blank. If anyone "owns" the land, it is nature itself, which quickly moves in to take back the sidewalks, the roads, and the houses which are now abandoned and uncared for.

That is, the disasters which have ensued have effectively ended both the American state and the American empire. It has been "erased" from history, much the same way that the Roman Empire was. Bryan Ward Perkins describes the transition which occurred in Late Antiquity in the following terms:

> What we see at the end of the Roman world is not a 'recession' or an 'abatement'—with an essentially similar economy continuing to work at a reduced pace. Instead, what we see is a remarkable qualitative change, with the disappearance of entire industries and commercial networks. The economy of the post-Roman west is not that of the fourth century reduced in scale, but a very different and far less sophisticated entity. A

number of basic skills disappeared entirely during the fifth century, to be reintroduced only centuries later.[7]

Similarly, Earle describes America as having "shrunk back upon itself." In this new America, the scale is also different. Natives of upstate New York are no longer aware of the news about the country as a whole, and bulletins about what's going on in Washington or Chicago are only received if the news is conveyed orally by someone arriving from another region. Distances are described as "three days walk"; Earle's fondest wish is to own a horse; and surgery is practiced without electric power or anesthetic. People die from going to the dentist. Human security is a thing of the past, and entire industries and commercial networks no longer exist.

The erasing of the previous empire is described in similar terms in the Victorian apocalyptic novel *After London*. In this novel, it appears that British civilization has been erased and that Britain has been "thrown back" all the way to pre-Roman times. Both British political, social, and cultural practices and Roman practices have been erased. In this new land, the Roman achievements of urbanization, hygiene, and agriculture no longer exist. The new dwellers in this land are described in similar terms to those used by the Roman conquerors upon first encountering the Celts. The inhabitants are described as dirty, long-haired, and frequently naked. In this way, the description of "how far England has fallen," basically describes an undoing not only of British empire-building but of Roman empire-building as well—in essence, taking Britain back to the savage, undiscovered place it was *before* either British or Roman state-building efforts. As Jeffries describes the situation:

> The Bushmen often in fits of savage frenzy destroy thrice as much as they can devour, trapping deer in wickerwork hedges or pitfalls, and cutting the miserable animals in pieces, for mere thirst of blood. . . . Bushmen have no settled home, cultivate no kind of corn or vegetable, keep no animals, not even dogs, have no houses or huts, no boats or canoes, nothing that requires the least intelligence or energy to construct.[8]

To use the language of colonialism, in both these American and these British visions, the land (and the people) has been reenchanted, as they have abandoned modern beliefs and forms of social organization for the primitive. This destroyed environment is then visited by a colonizing foreigner from across the sea, or alternately is described by a narrator from an earlier time who looks back from a vantage point where America was at the pinnacle of success but now must gaze upon the ruins of its former self. In turning the colonialist lens upon itself, American writers thus allow us as readers to revisualize our own land through a new lens. Where once we saw order and organization, we now see chaos. Where once America appeared self-sufficient, autonomous, and developed, we now see a new ruined America which is underdeveloped and in need of saving by others. The story of America—when told by a post-apocalyptic American—thus becomes the story of Them, rather than the story of Us.

The trope of the surveyor's gaze, however, serves another additional purpose beyond simply that of surveying and appropriating the landscape. The analyst Sue Zemka notes that colonial travel narratives and indeed colonial social policy rested on the "myth of idyllic expansion." In this colonial understanding, colonialism was seen as an escape valve for domestic social pressures with plentiful land elsewhere serving as the solution to colonial problems of "surplus population." Travel and subsequent settlement rested on this "dream of new space, of liberation through geography from poverty or (especially in the nineteenth century) from the harsh conditions of life in recently industrialized economies."[9] That is, colonial language conveys both the notion that the land is blank and the notion that the language is available for the use and exploitation of others. In *Culture and Imperialism*, Edward Said illustrates this colonial worldview using a passage in Charles Dickens's *Dombey and Son* in which the entire world seems made for the British and for the privileged British man in particular. He writes:

> The earth was made for Dombey and Son to trade in, and the sun and the moon were made to give them light. Rivers and seas were formed to float their ships; rainbows gave them promise of fair weather; winds blew for or against their enterprise; stars and planets circled in their orbits.[10]

Said describes British cultural production as derived from the height of imperial hubris, where "all of culture—indeed all of life—could be seen as in service to the empire and its subjects."[11] Here, two British utopian novels—H. G. Wells's *First Men in the Moon* and Samuel Butler's *Erewhon*—also reproduce this way of speaking about land. The novel *Erewhon*, viewed by many as the first utopian novel, centers on an unnamed traveler who arrives in Erewhon in 1868. The narrative clearly has a colonial context—with the narrator arriving in a land which appears to be either Australia or New Zealand, with many sheep and mountain ranges. The reader is informed that he went looking for "waste crown land" in order to better his fortunes. He had been led to believe that the land was previously uninhabited "save for a few tribes of savages."[12] This traveler is clearly not wealthy, since he is interested in making money and profiting from his explorations. He hopes to make a discovery or a conquest which will allow him to enter the class of those who have power in English society. He notes, "I had no money, but if I could only find workable country, I might stock it with borrowed capital, and consider myself a made man."[13] The narrator embodies the colonial mind-set in the ways in which he looks to exploit the land where he has arrived for his own personal gain. He asks, "Even if I did not find country, might I not find gold, or diamonds or copper or silver? . . . These thoughts filled my head, and I could not banish them."[14] His gaze makes it clear that he is the "master of all I survey," with the land described in terms of its utility to settlers as well as the resources it contains. The narrator describes how "the part known to Europeans" contains timber and harbors and goes on to describe the "settlement of the region" with an air of inexorability.[15]

Later, in Wells's 1899 novel the reader is introduced to Mr. Bedford, the narrator, and his friend the scientist, Mr. Cavor. Bedford, an Englishman, is in exile, having been "banished" to southern Italy as a result of some financial problems he is experiencing. From the beginning, he acts like a typical imperialist, proposing to capitalize on a scientific discovery made by his acquaintance. Cavor discovers a substance (which Bedford names Cavorite). Bedford immediately attempts to expropriate Cavor's discovery (which he sees as having important military and commercial potential) and to harness it in service to the state. He waxes eloquently about the ways in which the substance will serve the trajectory of inevitable progress. The substance is used to facilitate space travel and exploration, which are described in purely monetary terms.[16] Bedford proposes an expedition to Mars to collect minerals which he feels rightfully belong to England due to the "right of preemption." He refers to his journey as "prospecting."[17] Bedford thus serves as the quintessential imperialist—proposing to colonize the universe itself. He regards all of the material objects, all of the territory, and all of the individuals he encounters in purely instrumental terms—looking at how he can press them into service towards his imperial ends. In this statist view, culture and technology are both meant to be harnessed for state ends. (Here analysts can argue about whether Bedford is to be viewed as a caricature of the imperialist explorer or whether the portrayal is without irony. The reader may choose, apparently, to be repulsed or impressed by the imperialist Bedford.)

Here, Bedford's journey to the moon is read as a journey to the periphery. When he goes into outer space he describes it as dead space, where nothing happens.[18] The space is viewed as empty and blank, and Bedford muses that it might someday make a fine home "for our surplus population" and proposes that it be annexed and named Bedfordecia. He then goes on to compare himself to Columbus, while comparing the moon's natives to insects. Clearly they are viewed as inferior.[19] No matter where Bedford travels, it is clear that only Europe is the center around which all else depends.

The colonial mentality is echoed in later works, including *World Made by Hand*. Here, however, the Americans are not the colonizers but the inhabitants of the land to be colonized. America itself is described as either savage and overrun or lush and primitive. The descriptions of the ways in which nature itself has taken ownership of the land and humans must wrest back control of this land (through establishing timber plantations, building cities, and so forth) are common in colonial writing. Here, references in *The Pesthouse*, *The Road*, and *World Made by Hand* to the way in which paved roads have been overtaken by dirt and shrubbery bring to mind a colonial mind-set.

In *World Made by Hand*, the narrator Robert Earle—a former Silicon Valley executive who has been forced to relocate to a small town in upstate New York—sees his land colonized when he is informed that his town's mayor has sold the town's schoolhouse to strangers who came to town seeking to settle there. When he questions his town leader's decision to give away his land, community, and identity to strangers, he is informed (in typical colonial fashion) that the schoolhouse was "vacant" and therefore subject to being claimed by others. As time passes, Robert Earle finds the settlers threatening as they begin to impose their culture on the native inhabitants, including himself. In the story, the fundamentalist Christian sect which settles in the town gradually imposes its style of clothing and clean-shaven look for men on the town's inhabitants. The novel even contains a scene where the Christian men forcefully grab hold of the townspeople and proceed to shave their faces against their will—claiming that the people in the town are "dirty" and need to be cleaned up. Robert Earle also watches in dismay as his fellow townspeople find themselves captivated by the foreign women in particular and seek to intermarry with them. While Earle is dismayed, both the mayor and the townspeople appear to both accept and welcome colonial rule or imperial authority. In essence, they adopt a colonial mentality, legitimizing the notion that rule by others is desirable, welcomed, and ultimately preferable. In Said's words, they "accept subordination—through a positive sense of common interest with the parent state."[20]

Post-apocalyptic novels (as well as British utopian novels) also include colonial themes of sea voyages and ships, as well as appearances by colonizers themselves. Colonial authorities appear in particular in *The Pesthouse*, where Margaret, a post-American native, is captivated by the shiny buttons on their uniforms. They moor their ships in the port at Tidewater—again, ironically, the scene of the First Landing and the establishment of the settler's colony in Jamestown in 1607—so that America's natives can be harvested and taken elsewhere to serve as slaves in the modernization of another country in the international system. Here the figure of the Lieutenant Governor of New York State in *World Made by Hand* shows him as a sort of useless colonial figure, who sits in an outpost surrounded by unruly natives while waiting to receive orders which never come. The exploitation-of-blank-land motif also appears in the catastrophe novel *One Second After* where chaos ensues in America after the detonation of an electromagnetic pulse which destroys all communications infrastructure. In this novel, the U.S. Army shows up many years later to restore order, but it is too late for California, which has already been colonized by the Chinese. (They required a home for their "surplus population" and chose the newly cleared West Coast of the United States).

NICE TO MEET YOU/NICE TO EAT YOU: THE CANNIBAL IN LITERATURE

> Cannibal: In 16th c. Pl. *Canibales*, a Sp. *Canibales*, originally one of the forms of the ethnic name *Carib* or *Caribes*, a fierce nation of the West Indies, who are recorded to have been anthropophagi, and from whom the name was subsequently extended as a descriptive term . . .
>
> —Oxford English Dictionary[21]

In addition, imperial literature employs particular ways of talking about people who are unlike the narrator. Here, the two classic ways of speaking of the Others whom the colonial explorer encounters are the idea of a noble savage, or the idea of a cannibal. Both are stereotypes which emphasize the absolute Otherness of one's new companions, either through emphasizing the ways in which they are pure and undefiled by the modern world (based on the ideas of Rousseau), or through emphasizing the fact that they are savages who can never be tamed and integrated into the colonial vision (which rests on a more Hobbesian vision of the world).

As Sewlall points out, the cannibal trope actually has a long pedigree in colonial discourse—not only in literary sources like Defoe's *Robinson Crusoe*, but also within genres of travel literature, as well as more scientific writing from the British Empire.[22] Scholars in general and anthropologists in particular are at odds regarding the veracity of any rumored instances of cannibalism within the territories which later became Britain's imperial possessions. Post-colonial analysts like Said and Homi Baba see the cannibal as a mythical figure which has traditionally stood in for the Other through centuries of literary writing.[23] Epics by Homer (*The Odyssey*) and Aeschylus speak of fierce one-eyed peoples who eat human flesh. In addition, Roman descriptions of the Huns frequently emphasized their nakedness, their illiteracy, and their tendency to eat raw flesh. Richard Jeffries employs a description of the gypsies in *After London* which emphasizes their blood lust, their love for feuding, and their tendency to eat raw meat.[24] Nonetheless, as Hulme shows us, the term was widely associated with the New World by European colonists, and the New World's inhabitants (specifically its Native American population) were repeatedly described as cannibalistic, or as a tribe of bloodthirsty savages. Clearly the cannibal is an image of alterity, as it represents a violation of even the most primal taboos—which include the eating of human flesh and the carrying out of acts of incest.

Within anthropology, a distinction has been made between two practices: *Anthropophagi* refers to the eating of members of one's own tribe or ethnic group. Here, the term is said to have originated with Ancient Greeks who used it to distinguish themselves from other tribes which were labeled as "barbarians."[25] *Cannibalism*, in contrast, refers more precisely to the eating of one's enemies or those unlike oneself. Cannibalism is not practiced merely because one is hungry. Instead, the eating of one's enemies is seen as having a sort of symbolic importance. As Dutheil describes the practice, "cannibalism radically abolishes the difference between inside and outside, the self and the other, through literal assimilation."[26] The native and the colonizer thus finally meet and mix when the native consumes his colonizer. The cannibal thus represents the degeneracy of human nature, or the crossing of the line between nature and culture. This term is said to have stemmed from Columbus's own voyages and is in many cases seen as having originated as a cultural and linguistic misunderstanding. It is unclear as to whether Columbus or any later colonial explorers actually found any cannibals.

In the colonial discourse, as the "natives" are civilized, they let go of cannibalism and adopt Western social mores, including Christianity and education. Cannibalism is thus a practice which people are converted away from, as they move towards a place of greater progress.[27] So what are we to make of narratives where the westernized, developed individuals actually become the cannibals? One possibility to consider is the ways in which historically people have turned to cannibalism in times of disaster—engaging in a sort of moral backsliding where the rules of civilization are suspended. Thus, Bryan Ward Perkins describes the incidence of cannibalism in August 410 when the Goths captured and sacked the city of Rome, an event which many describe as the beginning of the fall of the Roman Empire. He tells us:

> During one siege the inhabitants were forced progressively to reduce their rations and to eat only half the previously daily allowance and later, when the scarcity continued, a third. When there was no means of relief, and their food was exhausted, plague not unexpectedly succeeded famine.

Corpses lay everywhere. The eventual fall of the city ... occurred because a rich lady "felt pity for the Romans who were being killed off by starvation and who were already turning to cannibalism" and so opened the gates to the enemy.[28]

Similarly, Schrady suggests that earthquake victims in Lisbon in 1755 may have turned to cannibalism as the result of desperate circumstances. Furthermore, reports suggest that cannibalism may have occurred during World War II during the Siege of Leningrad, as well as in Ukraine as the result of the famine created by Stalin in the 1930s.

In each of these examples, disaster (whether natural or manmade) returns people to a state of nature in which they give way to their baser instincts in the absence of a strong state which is capable of restraining these instincts and maintaining order. The incidence of cannibalism is thus merely the strongest manifestation of the anarchic state into which society has fallen—whether temporarily or permanently. The underlying condition is that the state, which appears to be strong, is actually weak and vulnerable, and it appears that under the right circumstances (disaster or some form of internal unrest), its fragile hold on society could be lost, and mans' true nature would and could emerge. In each instance, disaster and internal unrest have tested the state and society—and they have failed.

Given this understanding and background, one can easily argue that contemporary post-apocalyptics describe an "unempiring" or a reversion of the land back to both wild nature and its original wild inhabitants. The cannibal bands which control the landscape in McCarthy's *The Road* are not thus a new civilization or life form which has "developed" in the aftermath of the Great Accident. Rather, the cannibals in both *The Road* and *One Second After* represent the reemergence of an earlier life form—which might have gone into hibernation but which really never left the landscape entirely. In that way, the cannibals perhaps represent the permanent life form which is meant to occupy and inhabit that landscape—while it is the contemporary Americans with their lust for oil, their urbanization, and their ideas about democracy who represent the anomaly. These "Americans" are the ones who are, in actuality, a "blip" on history's radar. Thus, the presence of the cannibals simultaneously undoes the historicist notion that history has a trajectory towards "progress" and furthermore reduces America's history in the years 1492 until the mid-twenty-first century to a sort of historic footnote (along the lines of "and then we took a detour"). One could argue that civilization was tried, but it didn't take.

Here, one might argue that the appearance of the cannibalism trope in contemporary literature is thus a manifestation of America's sense of state and social vulnerability in the post-9/11 era. Today, many conservatives make the argument that the greatest threat to Americans may be other disloyal Americans who embrace terrorism and foreign ideologies, who do not share traditional American values of patriotism, and who seek to harm and prey upon the nation which shelters and protects them.[29] The literary description of vampires or cannibals who lurk and hide among us is thus a symbolic rendering of the dangers of fourth generation warfare in which international conflict is no longer something practiced only far away and only by professional armies. Instead, conflict is now everywhere and on every level. Every American is implicated, whether they wish to be or not. In *Falling Man*, DeLillo describes the way in which the fictionalized 9/11 hijacker Amir (who is the leader, and may be Muhammad Atta) thinks about the others who will also become suicide bombers:

> What about the others? Amir said simply there are no others. The others exist only to the degree that they fill the role we have designed for them. This is their function as others. Those who will die have no claim to their lives outside the useful fact of their dying. Hammad was impressed by this. It sounded like philosophy.[30]

Here, Amir holds an instrumental view in which Americans are merely bodies to be counted or points to be tallied in a conflict which is larger than any individual. The American victims of acts of terrorism become similar to those individuals loss in mass catastrophes like a landslide—in which their individual lives and those individual meanings are lost in the newspaper tallies which simply state that "somewhere around 300,000 people are believed to have perished." In this way, the terrorists have succeeded in "othering" Americans, refusing to see them as human beings who are in any way like themselves. Western lives are seen as "inputs" into the terrorist machine in the same way that native African lives were viewed as "inputs" into the colonial machine or human beings were seen as "inputs" by the vampires and cannibals who appear in literature. The danger which comes from the barbarians residing among us emanates from this instrumentalist view—with which there is no possibility of finding compromise or common ground.[31]

Thus, the problem with the American cannibals—the vampires who appear in *The Passage*, the Posse which appears in the catastrophe novel *One Second After*, and the cannibals who appear in *The Road*—is that they cannot be "converted" away from cannibalism (as the cannibals encountered by imperial travelers and settlers were) and back to civilization since ostensibly they are already Americans. They ostensibly already belong, or belonged to civilization. The modern-day cannibal is not merely a savage around the cooking pot. Rather, the scenes of cannibalism in *The Road* actually arc back to Joseph Conrad's novel *Heart of Darkness* where an Englishman admits to having tried human flesh and thus crossed over from the land of the civilized to the land of the barbarian. (He has been turned.) Similarly, McCarthy's cannibals are sensate human beings who have consciously chosen to violate the norms of civilized society. McCarthy's cannibals do not simply consume other humans in a violent rage. Rather, they plan. They trap other human beings and store them in a larder or a pantry for later eating. And the cannibals of *One Second After* carve up their human meals, as if they were at a butcher's shop. McCarthy's descriptions of the larder and the process of storing human beings up (which we will come back to in our next chapter, on Levinasian ethics) actually parallel descriptions of the Nazi holocaust—with its descriptions of the ways in which humans were warehoused and used as a source of labor.

The American cannibals are thus *more* barbaric than the classical cannibal—and they are perhaps guiltier as well, since they should have known better. In post-apocalyptic literature, the presence of the cannibal thus suggests a failure of the modernization project or vision to achieve citizen socialization. Somehow, our modern social institutions and philosophy of liberal progressivism have still succeeded in producing Nazis (and the philosophy of eugenics), terrorists (who prey on the weak and the innocent), the sorts of torturers who appeared at Abu Ghraib, and in the final analysis, cannibals. In describing American cannibals preying on other Americans, the reader is forced to examine his own sense of Americans as both civilized and invulnerable.

And yet the very fact that Americans are conceived of as capable of performing such acts (though we know that historically these facts have occurred—for example in the incident of the Donner Party or more recently in the case of the serial killer Jeffrey Dahmer) suggests that the distinction between civilized and barbarian is an invention or a construct, with perhaps no basis in reality. If 9/11 extinguished our sense of Americans as invulnerable, one could argue that Abu Ghraib extinguished our sense of Americans as civilized.

Thus, the instances of cannibalism can be read in two ways: One reading suggests that the prevalence of flesh-eating in these imaginings of the future (in *The Road, The Passage, One Second After* and in such movies as *The Book of Eli*) represents merely an unwinding of the thread of civilization. In this narrative, history still has a shape and there is a trajectory of modernity, but the damaged nation has somehow fallen off that path and taken a step back to an earlier time period. Thus, it can be recivilized by a more modern outside power. The land and the people can be recolonized—as they are *One Second After*, for example. Thus, in a catastrophe novel, or in a circular apocalyptic, the cannibals can be slain, the land purged, and civilization can still begin again. However, the other reading, and the one which prevails in the linear narrative, suggests that the embrace of cannibalism—or more particularly the practice of anthropophagy, since those being killed are one's neighbors and they are being killed for food—is the final example that the world is Hobbesian and beyond redemption. In this narrative, the cannibals cannot be slain, slavery has overtaken freedom, and no one can be rehabilitated. Here, the cannibal is not Us or Them, but rather someone who has somehow passed over the border to the point that he no longer represents any type of human being. He is something else entirely. He is irredeemable and incapable of moving back over this border to the point that he can conceptualize of his food sources as humans, like he himself is. He is, in the words of Howard Caygill, the monstrous other.[32]

Martine Dutheil, however, offers a novel rereading of the cannibal trope in British colonial literature. She suggests that the eating which the cannibal engages in is actually an act of consuming vast quantities of resources and inputs. She states that British authors like Defoe were "aware of the cannibalistic aspects of an imperial economy trading in flesh and feeding upon its colonized bodies."[33] Thus, Britain becomes the great cannibal, and the problem of globalization becomes apparent. Thus, it is perhaps not surprising that the theme of cannibalism is once again prominent during a period of global expansion—and that this time America is the nation implicated as a cannibal. That is, American cannibalism may be a way of talking about colonial guilt. As Sewall points out, cannibalism and other similar "barbaric" practices of those who were conquered by colonizers—provided the justification for the colonizing act. Americans could justify taking the land of North America from the native people because of the narrative which suggested that what was going to be built after the land was "cleared" was something more holy, sacred, and noble than what had come before. (It was also what was destined if you believe the language of American exceptionalism.) The problem here, of course, is that if the Americans themselves are capable of becoming cannibals, then they no longer have any justification from having taken the land in the first place—since they are no better than the original owners, from whom the land was taken. If we can imagine that we know how the story ends and then look back upon that ending, the acts of settlement themselves no longer seem heroic—but instead seem futile and perhaps even pointless.

In colonial literature, the discourse of the savage may also include themes of purity and defilement, as travelers from "civilization" are seen as coming into contact with the natives and savages of the Other Place. Hinnant speaks of an "excremental vision" in which the developed world is seen as polluting a land which was perhaps a paradise or a place of innocence before the colonizers came.[34] (He may thus, for example, describe the rivers as teeming with fish, as Robert Earle does in describing upstate New York after the apocalypse.) This theme of purity and defilement also appears in the utopian novel *Gulliver's Travels* where Gulliver himself is viewed as the Other, and the natives whom he visits describe him as dirty and smelly.

The emphasis in apocalyptic literature on the theme of disease and pestilence can be seen as the reproduction of a colonial theme, as disease is seen as having the power to both shape and end a culture, in the process clearing the land. (Thus, it is perhaps ironic that American puritans were able to build their pristine New World due to the pestilence which killed its original inhabitants, and then almost three hundred years later, the land has once again been cleared by pestilence, erasing that civilization and making way for the new.)

Artifacts: Trinkets Which Represent Civilization

Finally, in colonial writing, the trope of the artifact or the trinket looms large. Both American and Victorian cultures can be said to be highly materialist—with a great deal of national energy devoted to the acquisition and curating of objects, the comparing of objects and a high degree of congruence between the objects one owns and one's national identity. As Pykett expresses it, "The Victorians, as we all know, were extremely interested in things—in making, acquiring, collecting and cataloguing things. As one famous Victorian, Karl Marx, put it—the discovery of the various uses of things is the work of history."[35]

The trinket helps to highlight the chasm which exists between the two groups—those who come from the modern world bearing trinkets and those supposedly primitive, superstitious, and backward individuals who receive the trinkets with a variety of emotions, ranging from suspicion and fear to puzzlement, bewilderment, and greed. Artifacts are seen to travel from one world to another, as they are carried by travelers who arrive to colonize a new place, or dug up as archeological finds from another era. In a sense, the trinket represents the so-called "gift of civilization" itself, which those cultures visited may reject, ignore, or grasp at greedily, hoping to possess it themselves. The trinket looms large in the narrative of America as well, which features three trinkets in particular:

First, we can consider the blankets given by European settlers which succeeded in wiping out Native Americas since they carried the pestilence of smallpox. (The facts about whether or not the carrying of pestilence was intentional vary, depending on who is telling the story. One narrative describes what happened as an accident, while another describes it as genocide.) Here the trinket is a disease vector which succeeds in altering a demographic landscape and the trajectory of a group of people. The trinket has a different meaning for their giver than for the one who receives it, and it is a symbol of exploitation, as well as the meeting of the two worlds—Modern Europe and the New World.

Next, we can consider the small coins given to the Native Americans of New York state in exchange for the island of Manhattan. Here, the coins represent a betrayal, since many argue that the land was essentially stolen from the Indians who were not cognizant of its true value.[36] The tendency to be taken in by shiny objects is thus seen as a sign of the primitiveness or inferiority of a group of people who do not understand the complex (capitalist) economic calculations which actually give an object its value. Thus, in Swift's *Gulliver's Travels*, the reader is informed that the human-like Yahoos are quite simple and simplistic in comparison to their overlords, the horse-like Houhynms. One of the "clues" that Yahoos are the more primitive race is the fact that they enjoy collecting shiny stones which they bring back to their kennels.[37]

The weapon is also a peculiarly American symbol. The narrative of America notes the way in which the settlers' superior firepower and advances in weapon's technology allowed them to overtake the Native Americans, colonizing the land and sweeping across America from one end to the other.[38] Weapons were also given to Native Americans by the settlers in certain circumstances, so that Native Americans were implicated in the betrayal of their own people. European analysts note the way in which American citizens are willing to defend the right to bear arms, which is written into the U.S. constitution, as well as citizen's ambivalence about allowing for government regulation of weapons.

Finally, the automobile has been described as the quintessential symbol of America. It was invented in America and figures in American mythology (along with roads) as the symbol of the freedom accorded by travel, the individuality which the personal automobile promoted (against the European ideal of public transportation), and the vastness of the American landscape which is best traversed by automobile.

As noted, those who are offered a trinket can react in a variety of ways. It is my contention that in those novels which attempt to query the utility or desirability of empire, the trinket is frequently regarded as undesirable by the natives. The trinket appears a bit ridiculous—and in this way, the reader is drawn to also contemplate the ridiculousness of empire itself. Alternately, it may simply appear as irrelevant—as a vestige of a long-ago time which no longer speaks to people today.

The trinket which no one wants thus appears in Samuel Butler's utopian novel *Erewhon*. Here, the colonial traveler assumes that he will encounter simple natives who will desire his brightly colored shiny objects, particularly if they are of sophisticated construction, like a watch. Instead, the unnamed narrator is astounded to find that in the land he visits, clocks are regarded as backward vestiges of a pre-enlightenment past. They exist in museums, where visitors gaze upon these primitive artifacts as "something which people used to use and venerate." The narrator is equally stunned to find that Erewhon's natives are not afraid of his watch. They simply do not want it, since they regard it as old-fashioned. Furthermore, he is shocked to find that they do not desire his tobacco nor seek to emulate him (in typical native fashion) when he engages in smoking. Rather than seeking to join his community of smokers, they view his desire to smoke as an individual eccentricity which they tolerate but do not desire. Similarly, the Lilliputians of *Gulliver's Travels* inventory Gulliver's pockets where they come upon such trinkets as a handkerchief and a box of snuff. These natives also do not desire tobacco. Instead, the Lilliputians simply find its existence baffling, describing it as "dust."[39]

In post-apocalyptic America, one frequently encounters the trope of the irrelevant trinket (or artifact). Here, the distance between the pre- and the post world is illustrated by the way in which some cultural items have become meaningless while others have become priceless. In DeLillo's *Falling Man*, the narrator, Keith, traverses two worlds (pre- and post-9/11 America), carrying artifacts with him as he travels. These artifacts then take on significance throughout the novel. In particular, Keith rescues a briefcase which a fellow office worker has left in the stairwell in her haste to flee the collapsing towers. In the weeks following the event, he seeks out the briefcase's owner and attempts to return it to her, while at the same time pondering the meaninglessness of the items in the briefcase in the context of the events which have occurred. DeLillo writes:

> The briefcase was smaller than normal and reddish brown with brass hardware, sitting on the closet floor. He'd seen it there before but understood for the first time that it wasn't his. Wasn't his wife's, wasn't his. He'd seen it, even half placed it in some long-lost distance as an object in his hand, the right hand, an object pale with ash, but it wasn't until now that he knew why it was here.[40]

He then describes how Keith "examined the items with detachment. It was somehow morbidly unright to be doing this but he was so remote from the things in the briefcase, from the occasion of the briefcase, that it probably didn't matter."[41]

And in *The Pesthouse* (which ostensibly takes place one thousand years in the future, when all memory of the mighty civilization which once prevailed has vanished), the new natives simply seem confused by goods like coins or farm equipment which they encounter in the abandoned landscape. Here, the objects are presented as decontextualized and robbed of meaning, like objects in a museum. They represent misunderstood clues about life in a world long vanished—in the manner of Roman ruins or Aztec coins. Here, the fact that they are meaningless to the subjects of the novels is less a commentary on the condition of the subjects than it is on the civilizations which they are meant to represent and on how quickly these civilizations have passed away into meaningless.

In *Falling Man*, DeLillo offers a description of Lianne's friend Martin's collection of historic passports which he has hung on a wall as decoration. The states represented in the collection (the Ottoman Empire, the Kingdom of Bulgaria) no longer exist, and the people in the photos are dead. The objects which once had value are now mere decorations hanging in a house halfway across the world. Once, the refugees who carried the passports were unmoored, but now it is the states themselves that are unmoored in the context of history. Lianne states:

> Pictures snapped anonymously, images rendered by machine. There was something in the premeditation of these photographs, the bureaucratic intent, and the straightforward poses that brought her paradoxically into the lives of the subjects. Maybe what she was human ordeal set against the rigor of the state. She saw people fleeing, there to here, with darkest hardship pressing the edges of the frame.[42]

However, the artifact can be used to query empire in two ways. In one narrative, the trinket itself appears as undesirable or irrelevant, while in the second narrative, the trinket appears as highly desirable. People may even be willing to kill for it. Here, the emphasis is on the way in which the desirers themselves have fallen from a place of power in the past where they themselves might have been the dispersers, rather than the collectors of tokens.

Thus, for example, in the post-apocalyptic *World Made by Hand*, the narrator Robert Earle describes the ways in which post-Americans are digging up the dump and salvaging the goods made in an earlier era. He describes how valuable items like plastic buckets are in this new world. Colonial trash is thus a treasure to the new natives of this harsh land. He states:

> In a world that had become a salvage operation, the general supply evolved into Union Grove's leading industry. When every last useful thing in town had been stripped from the Kmart and the United Auto, the CVS drugstore and other trading establishment of the bygone national chain-store economy, daily life became a perpetual flea market centered on the old town dump, which had been capped over in the 1990s.[43]

This theme of salvage appears as well in *The Passage*, where the new natives struggle frantically to keep the lights on and the vampires at bay, searching desperately for copper wire and batteries in the wreckage of the old world. In *The Road*, post-Americans engage in a quest for food, eating expired cans of peaches and pears which remain from the "world before."

The quintessential American artifact, the automobile, appears in post-apocalyptic literature in a variety of guises—alternately irrelevant, ridiculous, and highly desired. In *World Made by Hand*, the automobile seems to represent nostalgia for the American empire itself, with Robert Earle frequently dreaming about "experiencing a magical sort of flying sensation" which he comes to realize is a memory of driving a car. Later, however, in the same novel, Earle comes upon an elderly drunken man who is slowly piloting an automobile down the road until it winds up in a ditch. In this scene, the man's desire to drive a car appears as a sort of delusion, in which he is unable to accept the reality of what the world has become. In the same novel, Robert Earle also has a conversation with a young child who sees Frog and Toad riding in a car in the children's book *Frog and Toad*. She refers to it as a "motor car" and views it as something which might appear in a fairytale.

In McCarthy's *The Road*, cars and trucks are used primarily for shelter against the elements, and the complete irrelevance of the automobile and the likelihood that it will ever be resurrected as a form of transportation are illustrated in a powerful scene in which The Man cleans out his wallet, throwing away such quaint relics of "civilization" as credit cards, ATM cards, and his driver's license. In *The Road*, any functioning vehicles are driven by bands of dangerous criminals, and their appearance in the story symbolizes danger. They represent unrestrained power which can be used for evil.

Finally, the automobile appears in the narrative of *The Passage*, in a scene where the surviving humans attempt to travel across the country, following a radio signal which suggests there might be some survivors elsewhere. Here, the vehicles which are "resurrected" are U.S. military Humvees, which the survivors ride in while wearing old military uniforms. In this scenario, the vehicle seems to represent the state itself, and when the survivors are found by a remaining military detachment, it is the vehicle which helps the troops to recognize them as American.

Thus, discourses on trinkets and cultural objects, their meanings, and the ways in which they traverse geographic and temporal boundaries, are a sign that we are in the presence of a colonial narrative.

Enchanted People in an Enchanted Land

Colonial literature frequently included descriptions of the native's superstitious and naive beliefs in mythical creatures and events, which are described as evidence of their irrationality. This narrative device appears again in post-apocalyptic literature.

For example, the narrator of *World Made by Hand* describes the ranting which occasionally appears on the radio in upstate New York, as various types of millennial preachers attempt to explain the recent world events in Biblical terms. Similarly, the man who narrates *The Road* describes the various types of doomsday cults which flourished in the immediate aftermath of the explosion. *The Pesthouse* similarly includes a long description of a cult which flourishes in post-America, one thousand years later. The members of the cult live in community, observe a strict dress code and venerate a group of "distinguished gentlemen" who stand out from the common citizens by the fact that they do not use their hands to care for themselves or contribute to the community. (Thus, they represent, in a sense, a confused rendering of the notion that those who perform manual labor are inferior to those who do not and that those who are wealthy are simultaneously incapable of caring for themselves and worthy of the veneration of others.)

Even the landscape of the colonial voyage may seem in some way to be enchanted and less rational than the traveler's own land. The land may seem haunted or troubled and the narrator may make reference to inexplicable or unexplainable things that occur in the landscape, which the natives themselves explain in magical terms. This theme of the land as enchanted appears as well in *The Road*, where the reader is provided with few details about what exactly it was that caused civilization to end. In addition, the opening scene of *The Pesthouse* describes the way in which a landslide occurred which sent a large swathe of rubble tumbling down into an ancient lake. The rubble sank to the bottom of the lake and in the process, caused poisonous gases located on the lake's bottom to be released into the atmosphere. As a result of this poisonous gas, hundreds of people were killed, including all of the refugees sleeping on a hillside as well as the population of a small village. Here, the death of hundreds of people seems to come about almost entirely by chance, and it appears almost as though they were swallowed by an angry land or an angry god. This event signals to the reader that the new landscape they have just entered is unlike any they have ever known before. It is primitive, wild, unpredictable, irrational, and wholly Other.

In the next chapter, we will consider the character of the narrator himself, as he attempts to make meaning of the boundary crossings which take place in both utopian and apocalyptic literature, of which the trinkets are simply a small part of the story.

NOTES

1. Homi Bhabha. *The Location of Culture* (London: Routledge, 1995): 130.
2. Harry Sewlall,"Cannibalism in the Colonial Imagery: A Reading of Joseph Conrad's 'Falk,'" *Journal of Literary Studies* 22 (2006): 165.
3. David Spurr, *The Rhetoric of Empire: Colonial Discourse in Journalism, Travel Writing and Imperial Administration* (Durham, NC: Duke University Press, 1993): 17.
4. Charles H. Hinnant, *Purity and Defilement in Gulliver's Travels* (New York: St. Martin's Press, 1987): 4.
5. Spurr, 81.
6. James Kunstler, *World Made by Hand* (New York: Grove Press, 2009): 82.
7. Bryan Ward Perkins, *The Fall of Rome and the End of Civilization* (Oxford: Oxford University Press, 2005): 117.
8. Richard Jefferies, *After London* (London: General Books, LLC, 2010): 29.

9. Sue Zemka, "Erewhon and the End of Utopian Humanism," *ELH* 69 (2002): 440.

10. Edward Said, *Culture and Imperialism* (New York: Vintage Books, 1994): 13.

11. Said, 13.

12. Samuel Butler, *Erewhon or Over the Range* (New York: CreateSpace, 2009): 10.

13. Samuel Butler, 12.

14. Samuel Butler, 13.

15. Samuel Butler, 10.

16. H. G. Wells, *The First Men in the Moon* (New York: Echo Library, 2006): 17.

17. Wells, 17.

18. Wells, 24.

19. Wells, 44.

20. Said, 11.

21. Quoted in Peter Hulme, *Colonial Encounters: Europe and the Native Caribbean, 1492–1797* (London: Methuen, 1986): 16.

22. Martine Dutheil. "The Representation of the Cannibal in Ballantyne's 'The Coral Island': Colonial Anxieties in Victorian Popular Fiction." *College Literature* 28 (2001): 107.

23. Dutheil.

24. Jefferies, 31.

25. Hulme, 170.

26. Dutheil, 109.

27. Quoted in Dutheil.

28. Perkins, 17.

29. This is the thinking which lies beyond Samuel Huntington's Clash of Civilizations argument, Amy Chua's writing on the dangers of tolerance, and current policy statements by figures like Angela Merkel on the "failure of multiculturalism." The academic Will Kymlicka explores these themes in "Immigration, Citizenship, Multiculturalism: Exploring the Links," *Political Quarterly* 74 (2003): 195–208.

30. DeLillo, 176.

31. Arguably, the theme of "barbarians who hide among us" is very much an imperial one, going all the way back to descriptions of the ways in which Huns gradually overtook the institutions of the Roman Empire. The theme was one which President George Bush made reference to, particularly in the period after 9/11. In his speech of October 2001 on Afghanistan, then President George Bush noted: "The United States of America is an enemy of those

who aid terrorists and of the barbaric criminals who profane a great religion by committing murder in its name." Accessed at www.press.uchicago.edu/Misc/Chicago/481921texts.html.

32. Howard Caygill, *Levinas and the Political* (London: Routledge, 2002).

33. Dutheil, 107.

34. Hinnant, 2.

35. Lyn Pykett, "The Material Turn in Victorian Studies," *Literature Compass* 1 (2003): 17–41.

36. Here, arguably, the coins share a narrative background with those given to Judas by the Roman soldiers in exchange for his betrayal of Jesus Christ. The trope of "selling one's birthright for a few pieces of silver" may be one of the most ancient narrative devices.

37. Swift, 196.

38. See William Vizzard, *Shots in the Dark: The Policy, Politics and Symbolism of Gun Control* (Lanham, MD: Rowman and Littlefield, 2000).

39. DeLillo, 23.

40. DeLillo, 35.

41. DeLillo, 36.

42. DeLillo, 142.

43. Kunstler, 28.

8

THE TRAVELER

In the previous chapter, we examined the tropes and metaphors which appear in both utopian and apocalyptic literature. Here, we focus more specifically on the character of the narrator and the way in which the utopian and apocalyptic novel both represent a type of "travel narrative" and voyage. Both literary forms play with the form of a colonial travelogue, and in doing so, they highlight the assumptions of coloniality inherent in the writing and the mind-set of those who represent great imperial powers. In observing how the narrator functions in describing and explaining the new landscapes he encounters, we as readers become aware of how both British and American authors have occupied a privileged position which has affected the ways in which they make meaning of the international system. In considering the utopian and apocalyptic novel as a sort of travelogue, we can reconsider both how we claim to know about the international system and also how we claim to know the other. Thus, the utopian or apocalyptic novel allows us as reader to explore not only how we see the world, but how we claim to make knowledge about that world.

In traditional colonial travel narratives, the narrator functions as a sort of explorer, producing either a traditional colonial travelogue, or a "survival" narrative. In these stories, a representative of an imperial culture visits a foreign landscape populated by so-called primitive people with unusual cultural practices and histories. In the post-apocalyptic narrative, the modern traveler (a survivor of the apocalyptic events which have transpired) visits his own ruined landscape in order to remark upon the ways in which his own landscape has changed. Here, he gazes upon the remains of his ruined civilization in the same way as early colonial writers gazed upon the supposedly primitive lives and institutions of their neighbors.

In describing the British colonial experience, Bhabha noted the ways in which colonialism was not just about traversing physical and cultural spaces between, for example, Britain and India, but also about a sort of time travel which occurs. Here Bhabha describes the colonial land as falling between two time periods—ancient time and the time of modernity. He quotes Humphrey Ward, who describes the British rulers of India as people "bound to keep true time in two longitudes at once."[1] Thus, in a way, every colonial travel narrative is a sort of time travel story, except that in every case the forward thinking modern researcher is travelling *back* into the distant, primitive past which somehow exists simultaneously with the present. In traditional travel narratives, the traveler/narrator thus is in many ways a visitor from the future, looking back at what his own country "used to be" before modernization took hold and his nation leapt from the past to the future.

The literary theorist Charles Hinnant notes that British colonial narratives have a very specific formal structure. First, readers are informed as to the explorer's mechanism of arrival in the new place (whether it is part of a formal, planned expedition or as the result of an accident like a shipwreck). Next, they are given some form of commentary on the events which unfold and the individuals and institutions which are encountered in the new place. Finally, there is some form of resolution—either the narrator travels back home or he is rescued from the place where he has arrived unwillingly and accidentally.[2]

Similarly, in apocalyptic novels, the reader begins his narrative journey by feeling displaced or upended. He is not quite sure where he has ended up, or where the story will take him. He is confused because the world as he knows it has shifted. It is the same sort of feeling that one has when one travels abroad. The language is different, the customs are different, and however dominant or powerful one is within one's own culture, the power structures have now shifted now that one is no longer on one's own turf. Traveling lands one in a new situation where one is forced to play by someone else's rules, to consider someone else's norms, and in the process, where one may just wind up seeing a new situation through someone else's eyes.

The colonial travel narrative thus provides a site either for judging and labeling the Others whom one meets, or in rare cases for meeting the Others and coming to understand them and know them, in the process learning something about oneself. In simple terms, a traditional colonial narrative is positivist. The "researcher" aims to know and to possess the subject matter, mostly through taking in information according to one's own terms and then organizing information about the subject in terms which are in keeping with one's own stance towards the international system and one's own state. But we do not generally, however, have the ability to experience the other on his own terms or to get outside of ourselves to see him for who he truly is. We also do not have the ability to know ourselves or to get to know ourselves as we are seen by the Other, or to allow the Other to reveal us to ourselves.

However, it is my contention that post-apocalyptic novels represent a unique place for Us to meet Them (and for us to meet ourselves). This is because the post-apocalyptic novel in particular represents a daring new application of many of the ideas of the post-colonial critique in international relations. As the cultural critic Homi Bhabha has suggested, colonial culture represents a type of in-between, hybrid state or a drawing together of two cultures. Neither the British colonist nor the colonizer himself is either completely native or completely British. Rather, both exist in a sort of transient state in between full membership in both groups.[3] To borrow the language of R.B.J. Walker, both figures can be described as on the edge, poised between the inside and the outside boundaries of the international system.

Similarly, today, one can argue that the American identity straddles two time periods—if one views 9/11 as a sort of apocalyptic moment which broke history in two parts, then readers and writers today struggle to make sense of two different American identities—the pre- and the post-9/11 identity. This symbolism is evident in the apocalyptic novel itself, in which the current or present-day American narrator gazes upon the wreckage of what he imagines America will be some day in the future. Here perhaps the dominance of this type of language—with its references to hybrid populations and a fraying or blurring of the distinctions between Us and Them (or inside and outside)—is a particular symptom of our discomfort with the rapid march of globalization and the ambiguities which it creates. Thus, it is perhaps not surprising that both British utopian literature and contemporary American apocalyptic literature might embrace the language of colonization in attempting to make sense of the national position in the world.

In both Britain in the early 1900s and America today, there is a sense that the nation is somehow poised on the edge of history. One might argue, in apocalyptic fashion, that history has already come to an end and it is not entirely clear what comes next. There is no obvious next stage in terms of philosophical theorizing, current events or history. Thus, it is perhaps not surprising that in both time periods, writers have chosen colonial imagery to think about how one makes the transition from the current period to whatever comes next. And hence, it is not surprising that both British and American writers would choose to express some of that ambivalence about colonialism and empire through the creating of new literary forms which have to do with travelling or passing from one world to the next. In both British and American dystopian and apocalyptic novels, the narrator is both a disruptive and a transgressive figure—he forces the reader out of his own comfortable level of situatedness and into a new situation where he is forced to reflect not only on his new situation but also on his own self and the country which he represents.

It is the narrator or the traveler who thus gives the dystopian and the apocalyptic novel its subversive and emancipatory potential. That is, a colonial narrative *has* the power to be subversive—though it frequently is not. Many of the first colonial narratives which were described as satirical actually derived much of their humor from the ways in which role reversals took place. In *Gulliver's Travels*, for example, the colonial traveler is Othered. The tables are turned and he becomes the subject of other's quests for knowledge about him. He is known and judged by the others and in the process learns something about himself. In a sense, he comes to identify with the Others whom he visits—and brings back not only knowledge about the Other but about the self whom *he* represents. Charles Hinnant describes Gulliver's journey as having six phases: First, he transverses a boundary. Next, he appears a stranger, who enjoys an ambiguous and dangerous status. By the third stage of his journey, Gulliver begins to recognize his kinship with those he visits. In stage four, Gulliver enjoys the sort of power which a colonial leader might have—he is more prominent than he would be in England, and he engages in adventures, including conquering the Belfescudian navy, meeting the Brobdingnagian king, and becoming the point of a debate in the Houyhnhnm assembly.[4] Toward the end of his journey, he begins to break with the culture he visits and finally he leaves, engaging in the processes of tearing away and disillusionment.

Similarly, Zemka suggests that Samuel Butler's *Erewhon*, the first utopian novel, should be read as a parody of the traditional British travel narrative. It is what she terms "mock ethnography." She notes the way in which the narrator, an English adventurer (whose name we never find out), alternates between behaving like a missionary and a traveler. He muses that perhaps he has found a lost tribe from Israel while simultaneously plotting how to enrich himself at the expense of the natives, plotting to utilize the land to house Britain's "surplus population."[5] The greed and stupidity of *Erewhon*'s narrator are in many ways a comment on the greed and stupidity of other colonial travel voyages, and the narrator's expectations that the "natives" will embrace him, give him their land, and respect the learned ideas he brings from the "developed world" are quickly and harshly dampened. The narrator finds himself on the defensive as he is forced to defend his colonialist agenda and illusions of cultural superiority to a group of "natives" who are smarter and more developed than himself. The land he encounters is anything but blank and anything but empty. While he expects the natives to be without history of culture, he is surprised to find out that actually they are rational—in that their belief system is internally coherent and predictable—though different. They are utilitarians and are described at one point as having "high civilization." In comparing their belief systems to his own, the narrator—rather than serving as a pedantic tutor to primitive people—finds himself engaging with them in a critique of Enlightenment values and a critique of rationalism.

Subramanian argues that *Gulliver's Travels*, like *Erewhon*, was also a conscious attempt to engage with the model itself, effectively subverting many of its conventions.[6] While other analysts claim that Swift's primary goal in subverting the conventions of the colonial travel narrative was to create humor and satire through poking fun at present-day beliefs, Subramanian points to Swift's own colonial position as a member of a colonized minority (being Irish within the British Empire) and attributes political significance in his desire to subvert these structures. Thus, it can be seen as a commentary on colonialism itself, as well as on the genre of the colonial travel narrative—through pointing out its flaws, limitations, and biases.

Here, as well, H. G. Wells's *The First Men in the Moon* can be read as an attempt to subvert and question colonial ideas about the lands one visits and the people one encounters. In his voyage to the moon, the narrator, Mr. Cavor, is forced to admit that he is surprised to find the natives rational. He reproduces many of the British colonists' worst traits in, for example, speaking loudly to the inhabitants of the moon in broken English. He is surprised to find that the natives he meets are wholly uninterested in him and his world, do not desire to emulate him, and do not appear to "need" any of the knowledge or enlightenment which he had expected to bestow upon them (even as he harvested their resources and profited form their labor).[7] Cavor is changed by the experience of his voyage, and goes on to discourse about sovereignty asking, "What business have we in smashing their world?" He finds that the moon's inhabitants have "wisdom passing that of men," and finds that the men in the moon regard him as little more than a savage. In an anthropological aside, he notes that they have their own systems of organization in which individuals are sorted out by social position and rank. Thus, presumably, they do not need the British to come and overlay a system of organization upon them.

As these examples have shown, in the British utopian novel, frequently the narrator does not serve merely as a learned narrator who catalogues the lifestyle of those whom he observes. Rather, something curious happens—instead of the traveler arriving in a situation where the natives are Other, it is he himself who instead becomes Other. His customs, norms, and ways of observing the landscape are thus not taken as normative with his interlocutors forced to explain themselves and how they differ from these expectations. Instead, there is an opening for the possibility to norms, values, ways of life, and belief systems are open to inquiry. Neither side is assumed to be automatically right. Instead, both sides are forced to explain themselves. In this way, underlying assumptions which are not usually voiced are brought out into the open, and the possibility for change is presented. Such literary offerings interrogate many traditional understandings of what it means to be modern, what the significance of progress is, and both educate the reader through forcing him to reconsider the ways in which he is surprised when his colonial prejudices do not turn out to be correct.

The encounters which our narrators have with those from other countries—with the natives of Erewhon in Samuel Butler's *Erewhon* and with the Houhynyms in *Gulliver's Travels,* or with the European immigration officials in *The Pesthouse*—all allow the reader to consider the matter of imperial solecism and the possibility that the empire is somehow already moving towards irrelevance. The travel narrative thus has a particular importance to critical theory which other literary types, including the catastrophe novel, do not.

TRADITIONAL COLONIAL NARRATIVES

However, not all travel narratives which have existed have resulted in quite the same type of eye-opening experience. Rather, as Daniel Born has noted, colonial travelogues have frequently performed the opposite function. In the traditional travel narratives (both fictional and nonfictional) produced at the height of the British Empire, the narrator never really loses that sense that he is in control. He (or she)—as a privileged man—travels to a new environment but frequently does not take that next step in shifting perspective and viewing the scene through a new set of eyes. Instead, the narrator acts as a sort of anthropologist, cataloguing, labeling and measuring the natives, their landscape, their possessions and their customs according to his or her own cultural norms. Here, the reader is led to believe that the narrator is inventing order which is then imposed on something that is inherently chaotic and unordered. That is, the land which the narrator visits is seen as "blank" because it possesses no inherent organizational structure. The narrator or the explorer then goes on to survey the land or to classify the life forms, giving them Latin names and sorting them out by genus. Here, it appears as though the traveler himself is "making" the land, which is viewed as not even existing until it is visited and classified by a "neutral, objective" Western researcher.

The first type of narrative is the one we are perhaps most familiar with—it is a sort of travel diary, like we might see in for example, Charles Darwin's notebooks which he kept on the voyage of the Beagle, or perhaps the journal notes kept by Lewis and Clark as they explored America's Pacific Northwest in the early 1800s. Here, the narrator describes himself as a neutral, objective, "scientific" observer, and he is assumed to have no political or ideological agenda in compiling the facts of his travels. He may include sketches (both physical and verbal) of those he encounters, and may draw maps or landscapes as well. He frequently attempts to impose order on the landscapes he encounters which seem chaotic to him in comparison to his own ordered native surroundings. He may also construct typologies in order to better understand and organize his knowledge of the native peoples, flora, and fauna. Clearly, we can in retrospect read these narratives through a critical lens, noting the various tropes which appear frequently in these narratives—such as references to "savage" people, ways of describing the landscape as blank or empty, and the inclusion of racist and sexist frames of reference for classifying and identifying peoples and groups. However, at the time they were written, such narratives were produced using what passed for positivist language, with little introspection or reflexivity on the part of their authors. Such documents did not include, for the most part, the results of any exchanges with the natives or any attempt to insert their viewpoints into the document. They were not, thus, the product of dialogue but rather of observation. The ethnographic gaze means that the natives are viewed as different from oneself. They are viewed as primitive, attached to the land, and members of a primitive tribe. What is important in the text is the way in which we narrate their traditions and life forms, not anything they could conceivably contribute themselves to the dialogue.

The traditional colonial travel narrative, however, had two purposes. In addition to imposing order on chaos, the narrator simultaneously strove to impart a sense of exoticism to the western reader in comparing and contrasting the chaos of the primitive world with the order of the rational world. Thus, in traditional colonial narratives, the natives are alternately described as quaint and childlike or warlike and ferocious. Either way, they are seen as "not quite human" either by virtue of their childishness or their barbarity. That is, the narrator never relinquishes his sense that he is still Us, and the "natives" are Them. They are the Others.

That is, the traditional travel narrative appears to be merely a static cultural product which illustrates how a British (or American) native can travel and cross boundaries without being significantly shaped or changed by the experience.

REFLEXIVIST COLONIAL NARRATIVES

However, Bhabha and others have suggested that in the late 1800s and early 1900s, imperial culture took a reflexive turn, producing cultural products which no longer simply wholeheartedly supported the imperial presence in the colonial space but which rather sought to interrogate that form. Thus, in late imperial literature, the actions of the imperial agents on the colonial landscape and its people were no longer merely romanticized or described. Rather, they were evaluated from a variety of angles in, for example, *Heart of Darkness*. Bhabha argues that indeed, such literature may have signaled the beginning of imperial unraveling since it broke through prior simplistic, binary understandings of Us versus Them and began to interrogate notions like the heroism of the empire builder and the white man's burden. Thus, although these are "merely" literary works, clearly these are developments of economic, political, social, and cultural importance for they have served to alter and interrogate the terms of discourse. They helped to create a language for reconsidering the British presence abroad as well as the role of native. They may even have helped to dismantle the colonial project or to erode support for it. Similarly, Zemka describes the way in which late colonial relations were actually a sort of interactive game. Here she suggests that it is too simplistic to simply talk about how Britain imposed its values on India, for example. Rather, one needs to consider relations as a sort of complex dance which includes mimicry, modeling, borrowing, and syncretism. This "hybridity," she argues helped to deprive the colonizer of his authority.[8]

Here, it is important to consider how both British and American writers have used these colonialist narratives in their own times as the basis for a critique of imperialism. They have done so largely by creating a narrator or traveler who is *self-aware* as he crosses boundaries. The narrator recognizes that he is no longer situated within his own framework, and as he struggles to cope with the strangeness of his new situation, he forces the reader as well to reflect on what it means to be British or to be American. In each case, the narrator travels across a breach which is created—in several cases by an apocalyptic moment. That is, in the writing there is a space created between that which exists at present and that which will happen in the future. The traveler or the narrator is the person who then closes that space and becomes the translator between the two separate worlds—the one which existed prior to the break and the one which exists after the break. He is thus in some ways an immigrant—and as so he is frequently misunderstood or misinterpreted by those whom he encounters. In this way, the narrator serves as a representative of the American or British Empire itself, and he allows the reader to see how others view both himself and the empire which he sometimes represents. The self-aware narrator thus ends up changing himself—because he sees how he is viewed by others. In the process of serving as translator, he sees how what he took for granted is not necessarily true. Both the narrator and the reader can thus become aware of how we other those different from ourselves and of how we blame those different from ourselves. We become aware of how we impose norms on others, and we become aware of our expectations that others will be like ourselves.

THE SURVIVAL NARRATIVE: THE UTOPIAN VARIANT

Both utopian and apocalyptic travel narratives incorporate a second type of colonial narrative—the survival or "castaway" narrative. Like the traditional colonial travelogue, the survival narrative rests on the border between fact and fiction, with castaway narratives being produced in both genres. Examples of such narratives include the journals kept by Stanley as he explored the Nile in Africa, as well as the fictionalized accounts put forth in Daniel Defoe's *Robinson Crusoe* and Johan Wyss's *Swiss Family Robinson*. Here, the story rests on a situation where the protagonist enters an unfamiliar world where he confronts danger and struggles to survive. In this narrative, there is a lack of agency. The

THE TRAVELER

male traveler arrives alone, sometimes against his will (as the result of shipwreck, perhaps) and is in a weakened position vis à vis the "natives" whom he encounters. He arrives without either a scientific expedition or travelling party. He is alone among the natives, and frequently, he is not named—instead serving as a sort of everyman who takes the place of all readers who survey the new landscape. Here, he may still be a colonialist, but he is an accidental colonialist, rather than a planned one. In some instances, he is also a preemptive colonialist—seeking to establish a colonial foothold in a new land independently of the organized business and political interests which will come later.

Because the narrator arrives alone without the "baggage" of travelling companions, we might assume that he is therefore more open to introspection and self-reflection. However, this is not usually the case. Instead, the narrator of *Robinson Crusoe* reproduces racist assumptions about the inferiority and savagery of the natives whom he encounters, and embarks upon his imperial mission to civilize his companion (whom he renames, bestowing upon him a British name) and remake him in his own image. The brave adventurer is seen to display patriotism as he holds out and defends his colonial identity in a harsh new environment. The story frequently ends with rescue and the narrator being congratulated for his heroism.

However, because the traveler arrives in the new location alone in the stories which we consider here, he is by definition decontextualized, and his arrival does not carry with it the same force of culture and history. That is, while the traveler may be a sort of ambassador or representative of Britain, he is not *actually* Britain. Because he is unaccompanied by any sort of military force, usually carries no technology, and lacks compatriots, he does not project force over the new region, nor is it automatically assumed (either by himself or by those that he visits) that he is the dominant power in the region. One can thus read *Gulliver's Travels*, *Erewhon*, and *The First Men in the Moon* as types of survival narratives. In each of these stories, the traveler or travelers accidentally wind up visiting a strange place where they are outnumbered by the natives. In each instance, the traveler becomes the other and the object of attention from the natives who come to represent the dominant regime. His customs, norms, and ways of observing the landscape are not taken as normative with his interlocutors forced to explain themselves and how they differ from these expectations. Gone is the assumption that the visitor is the rational adult who visits childlike natives. History does not begin with the arrival of the colonizer. Instead, there is an opening for the possibility that norms, values, ways of life, and belief systems are open to inquiry—neither side is assumed to be automatically right. In addition, *both* sides are free to adopt an ethnographic gaze in whom they weigh and consider subjects like the clothing, food, habits, and quaint customs (like pipe smoking) of the other side. Here, the traveler is actually at a disadvantage since his own habits actually seem more quaint, old-fashioned, and nonsensical—divorced as they are from the habitat in which these activities make sense. In this way, underlying assumptions which are not usually voiced are brought out into the open, and the possibility for change is presented. Throughout the story, it is British imperial culture that is reflected back through native eyes that we are forced to reflect upon. When Gulliver visits the land of the Houhynyms, the ethnographic gaze is turned not towards his possessions but towards his physical characteristics, which his horse-like masters find to be all wrong—in proportions—and unattractive, in comparison to their own physical features.[9]

In the case of *Gulliver's Travels* in particular, the reader now sees many imperial qualities which have been portrayed unquestioningly in a positive light put up to a spotlight and reflected back. Gulliver's narrative makes clear that Lilliput had a history, a legal tradition (which is demonstrated in the drawing up of treaties with Gulliver for his release), and a history of both written and oral language prior to Gulliver's arrival. He is considered the interloper, and is considered to be less educated since he has no command of the native language and, being only one individual, is not in a position to require instead that the natives learn his language. Thus, in both *Erewhon* and *Gulliver's Travels*, the traveler is provided with a tutor who teaches him not only the language but also about the customs and history of the region which he is visiting.

In addition, Gulliver arrives in each land without agency. He is rather the subject of native rulings. Here, Gulliver states that on arriving in Lilliput "the emperor held very frequent councils to debate what course should be taken with me."[10] Furthermore, the traveler himself is viewed as a resource to be exploited (rather than the usual scenario, in which the colonizer figures out how he can harness the resources of his new surroundings). In response to the biddings of his new friends, Gulliver as a traveler is thus asked to survey the land, build walls, carry heavy items, and even engage in Lilliput's war with its longtime neighboring rivals. Gulliver *himself* becomes a military weapon, a force multiplier, a labor input, and a kind of technology.

In many of his travels, Gulliver is not regarded initially by those whom he encounters as either rational or fully human. When he visits Lilliput, he is labeled as the man Mountain, and described as a problem to be solved. The Lilliputians are incapable of understanding his true essence, but can only apprehend who he is in relation to themselves. Similarly, in the voyage to Brobdingnag, the farmer who first encounters Gulliver mistakes him for an animal, rather than an extremely small human (in comparison to the Brobdingnagians huge size), mistaking his coat for "some sort of covering which nature had given me."[11] Gulliver goes through a variety of motions, including offering gold to the farmer, before the farmer is convinced that he is both human and rational. However, Gulliver repeats as well the narrative which is told in Brobdingnag about how "my master had found a strange animal in the field, about the bigness of a splacknuck, but exactly shaped in every part like a human creature, which it likewise imitated in all its actions; seemed to speak in a little language of its own, had already learned several words of theirs, went erect upon two legs, was tame and gentle, would come when it was called, do whatever it is was bid."[12]

Here it is important to see that in Brobdingnag in particular, Gulliver is described as being "like a human" or having some human characteristics without ever being acknowledged as fully human himself. Rather, he is described as being domesticated—like an animal, or a slave, or a woman. He thus is described as a diminutive version of the Brobdingnagians—diminutive not only physically, but also in terms of being "less than." (Here, Said describes the ways in which the East is described as a "female" version of the west.) Here, Gulliver can be described as having been feminized, in contrast with the "big" Brobdingnagians—who represent size, sheer power, and maleness. The farmer's choice of his nine-year-old daughter as Gulliver's companion speaks to this discrepancy in size and power. Why would the king think that children, and female children at that, should be Gulliver's natural colleagues and interlocutors—though Gulliver himself is full grown and male? Later in the narrative, Gulliver is indeed sold by the farmer to the queen.[13] Here it appears that he is regarded as property and thus again not fully human.

Finally, in his voyage among the Houhynyms, Gulliver journeys to a land where the civilized inhabitants actually resemble horses and the individuals who resemble humans are used as workhorses for the Houhynyms. Here in particular, his horse-like masters find it remarkable that someone as inferior as himself would be capable of thinking rationally and learning their language. Here, again, though, Gulliver's masters view him as merely "imitating a rational creature" but do not acknowledge that he is in fact a rational creature.[14]

In the reflexivist travel narrative, disgust emanates from both sides of the encounter. While in the traditional travel narrative, the settler is disgusted by the natives, while they ideologize him, in the reflexivist narrative, disgust cuts both ways. Both sides are equally likely to regard the other as dirty or even disgusting and to worry about contamination through the foods one eats or one's habits. Thus, though Jonathan Swift was well-known for having a penchant for scatological humor, his discourse about the ways in which Gulliver's excrement was carried off by armies of Lilliputians who used shovels, horses, and carts for the task also serves another task. It serves to render the traveler himself as unclean and the object of disgust—reflecting back colonial assumptions about the indigenous peoples whom they encounter in colonization. Here, we are forced to acknowledge that indigenous people may be similarly disgusted by their colonizers, their colonizer's habits, and their physical persons. Indeed, Swift writes: "I would not have dwelt so long upon a circumstance, that perhaps at first might may appear not very momentous; if I had not thought it necessary to justify my character in point of cleanliness to the world; which I am told, some of my maligners have been pleased, upon this and other occasions, to call in question."[15] Later, again in the story of Lilliput, Swift describes how Gulliver assisted in putting out a fire through urinating on it, and in the process, befouling the empress's castle.[16]

Here the description of Gulliver as the producer of mounds of excrement also serves to make the reader aware that there is nothing inherently admirable about his bigness in relation to the others (the Lilliputians) whom he encounters. The fact that he is so much larger can perhaps be read as a comment on how Swift viewed the British Empire itself. Here, bigness can be read as grotesqueness, and as Gulliver's captors illustrate, being the largest individual does not necessarily provide one with immunity from capture nor is it inherently a source of strength. Rather, Gulliver is portrayed, to some extent as weak, since he seems to require constant new inputs of food and water, the construction of a suit of extremely large clothing, and is difficult to transport. (Thus, one could argue that Swift is commenting as well on the possibility that empire serves to weaken a state rather than strengthen it, due to its constant tendency to devour new inputs.) In a sense, Gulliver's war with the Lilliputians thus presents the first recorded instance of asymmetric warfare.

Here Swift reports the following conversation as having taken place in the King's Council in Lilliput, as the citizens debated whether they wanted to hang on to this very large person: "They apprehended my breaking loose; that my diet would be very expensive and might cause a famine."[17] Even shooting Gulliver to death didn't seem like a perfect solution, as there would still be the problem of what to do with the corpse. This passage can be read perhaps as a short discourse of the problems of empire—the possibility that a parasitical empire might leach resources from the state and that once an empire had been established, it was impossible for England to simply wash its hands of it—even if it desired to do so. Later in the same novel, Gulliver himself discourses against bigness—this time in relation to his dinner with the queen of Brobdingnag. He describes his nausea at watching her eat as much in a mouthful as twelve English farmers could eat at a meal.[18]

In Brobdingnag, Gulliver is in a real sense the "noble savage" himself, as a visitor among others who regard themselves as the rational and civilized ones. Thus, he describes how the farmer's wife on first encountering him runs away and screams, viewing him as something akin to a spider or an insect.[19] Later, he is taken on a tour and exhibited to other inhabitants for money, as a sort of "freak show." Here, Gulliver (and England, by proxy) represents the dark other—uncivilized, savage, and potentially dangerous—particularly, it appears, to women.

During Gulliver's sojourn in the land of the Houhynyms, the reader is introduced to the notion of hybridity or the ways in which the colonial native may come to identify simultaneously with his own people and his colonial oppressors. The hybrid subject is thus neither one nor the other—he is neither a native nor a colonizer but rather something in between. In the land of the Houhynyms, Gulliver's penchant for wearing clothing is regarded as novel and quaint, in comparison to the noble Houhynyms who are described as peaceful and at ease with their bodies without the need to rely on clothing.[20] It is here that Gulliver "goes native," in truly adopting the values of those he visits. After spending a period of several years with the sophisticated horse-like Houhynyms who look down on the humanlike Yahoos (which he himself resembles), Gulliver can scarcely bear to go back and live among humans. Instead, he has come to identify so closely with the horse-like Houhynyms that he is disgusted by his wife and children whom he describes as disgusting and possessing a terrible smell. Instead, he purchases horses and spends all day in the garage communing with them. Here it is clear that he thinks of himself and his family as lesser creatures compared with more noble beasts with which he has worked and lived.[21] Gulliver even puts forth the novel idea (for that time) that the British could learn from these natives whom he has visited. He concludes that instead of colonizing the Houhynyms, the British colonizers might come and spend time with them, becoming changed from the encounter.

In this way, both Gulliver and England (which he represents) are "constructed" through the eyes of the Other (the Lilliputian, the Brobdingnagian, or the Houhynym). This is perhaps the first example in Western writing about colonization which acknowledges the ways in which empire is constructed not only by the colonizer but also by the colonized. Paradoxically, the colonizer who thinks of himself as solving the native problem is at the same time constructed as a problem to be solved by those whom he assumes he is helping.

In Samuel Butler's *Erewhon*, the reader never even learns the name of the narrator. Here, emphasis is much less on the person of the narrator and rather on the fact that a completely separate, different culture has evolved within the world—which has completely different norms, values, and understandings of causal relationships than those which are accepted unquestioningly in England. In the world of Erewhon, both physical illness and luck are thought to be something one can control—and one receives no sympathy on, for example, a bad medical diagnosis or the death of a child or spouse. Instead, one is fined for allowing such a thing to happen. In contrast, what are regarded by Victorian society as vices and moral failings (like alcoholism or uncontrolled anger and rage) are treated with great sympathy, as one is regarded as unable to help himself. In a sense, it is the first constructivist reading of the idea of norms—with the attendant idea that behavioral expectations are not implicit but are rather a product of social projections.

The journey to Erewhon thus calls into question the "civilization" paradigm itself, with its implied notion that wherever one travels, the natives can be taught to adopt certain values and social norms. Rather, again the reader encounters the notion that the culture one visits is not blank or empty, and that the traveler's job is therefore not simply to paint new values onto a blank canvas.

Here again the author plays with the notion of the "gift of civilization" as well. Initially the narrator asks his traveling companion whether the people he is to meet are types of natives which one can Christianize or whether they are merely the type he can kill. In each case, his implied relationship to the Others is one of instrumentality. Whether they are seen as inputs into his civilizing project or nuisances to be cleared from the land, the implication initially is that they have no inherent value as fellow human beings. Certainly, the reader does not expect them to offer anything to the traveler—in terms of learning about culture, history, or values. The relationship is constructed initially as one of nonreciprocity (as it usually is with an exceptionalist nation). The narrator views himself as "immune" from learning or being changed by the encounter.

Many cherished ideas of British civilization are parodied in the Erewhon narrative. First, the notion that an older person is necessarily wiser than a younger person (and by implication, the notion that an older civilization has much to teach a younger civilization) is turned on its head in Erewhon, where the unborn are older than the born. The reader may find himself rethinking, as well, the idea that those who are colonized by Britain are recipients of both a privilege and a gift for which they should be grateful. In Erewhon, the reader is informed, those who are born into a family are a burden to the family. Therefore, they must apologize to the family for having saddled them with such hardships and come up with a plan for paying them back.

The Erewhonian citizens tell the narrator:

> Imagine what it must be to have an unborn quartered upon you, who is of an entirely different temperament and disposition to your own . . . who will not love you though you have stinted yourself a thousand ways to provide for their comfort and well-being—who will forget all your self-sacrifice, and

of whom you may never be sure that they are not bearing a grudge against you. . . . It is hard upon the duckling to have been hatched by a hen, but is it not also hard upon the hen to have hatched the duckling?[22]

Here, the reader is forced to see a parallel between the "ungrateful child" who is being blamed for having been born and the notion of a colony as a sort of dependent, clingy child who leaches resources from the parent. The parent in Erewhon is eager to divest himself of this burden, and here perhaps the implication is that Britain should consider divesting itself of similar burdens. Or perhaps Britain should stop blaming the colonies for "having been born."

Erewhon is seen as both the Other and as Britain itself, according to Zemka[23]—making it a sort of hybrid. In the narrative, Erewhon represents both a futuristic society, and also Britain's past. It is exotic and English at the same time. Zemka notes the way in which the Erewhonians simultaneously display "sophistication and primitivism, enlightenment and barbarism."[24] In this way, Erewhon alters the reader's worldview by forcing him to think beyond the simple, binary categories which he has previously used in his analysis.

In both the Erewhon and the Gulliver narrative (as well as in Cavor's voyage to the moon), the colonial explorer thus realizes the hubris which accompanied him on his journey and learns that he has vastly overestimated both his ability to conquer the Other, and the desirability of the gifts which he hopes to bestow upon the natives. Read through this lens, the travel narrative can be seen as both subversive and revolutionary, for there is no air of inexorability in either Gulliver's Travels or Erewhon. There is no assumption that the lands described will somehow inevitably be absorbed into Greater Britain, nor an understanding that economics drives the train of history. Rather, it appears that individuals and groups can alter their economic and political outcomes and that very little is written in stone.

THE LAST SURVIVING MAN

In apocalyptic novels, the narrator also serves a boundary crossing role. Frequently, he is a literary representative of the idea of the Last Man.[25]

That is, he is the sole survivor of whatever atrocities have led to the present situation in which his old world no longer exists. As the Last Man, he acts as translator or cultural ambassador between the two time periods. Like Lemuel Gulliver, the Last Man is weak. He arrives in this new place without status and without the backing of his history, culture, and its claim to power.

The apocalyptic Last Man is also self-aware. In each novel, the Last Man ruminates at length about such issues as guilt, privilege, and the ethics of power. Here, Zemka notes that in the Victorian survival narrative, the "accident" which causes the explorer to become castaway may have overtones of moralizing and guilt. The traveler may be an exile who has been banished from modernity and civilization to a barren place. For example, *Erewhon*'s narrator is banished first to the Antipodes. And in *The First Men in the Moon*, Cavor arrives at the new place as the result of business setbacks which can be seen as indicative of some sort of moral failing. In each case, the narrator may be judged as guilty for having wound up in an impoverished, backward land.

Similarly, the "last man" might be viewed as an exile who has come through the downfall of America to land in a newly backward land. Here, too, the new natives may be blamed for complicity in creating the circumstances of their new, backward life. In *The Pesthouse*, they are at least partly to blame for their rejection of technology which they display an irrational fear of. In *World Made by Hand*, the natives are judged as guilty, because they have been unappreciative of civilization's many advantages when they had them. And in *The Passage*, the survivors carry the burden of guilt for having exercised the arrogance and hubris which led to their own downfall.

In the linear apocalyptic in particular, the Last Man represents Adam—who has been cast out of paradise into a terrifying new fallen world. However, banishment can still represent an opportunity for taking responsibility for one's mistakes and thus growing in some way. The theme of banishment appears prominently in *World Made by Hand*, with the narrator, Robert Earle, frequently asking whether or not the world as he knew it is "coming back." Here, there is a sense that nature's balance has been unsettled and that if he can somehow figure out what crime has been committed, he will somehow be able to set it right, seek forgiveness, and reenter the paradise which is lost. In the circular apocalyptic tales considered earlier, however, the Last Man can be taken as a sort of figure of resurrection, as he himself is reborn in a new world.

In this new condition of exile, both Victorian and contemporary narrators express a certain amount of nostalgia for the world which they have lost. As Charnes explains, nostalgia is (again) a particularly colonial disease. The affliction only makes sense in an imperial context, since it rests on a number of assumptions—including the notion that what has been left behind at home is somehow better or preferable to that which one encounters and the idea that the past is somehow more desirable than the future. Goodman refers to it as "the disturbing disease of historicity." Nostalgia can thus be a reactionary sentiment grounded in an idealized form of nationalism with its longing for restoration, or it can be a more reflective sort of pining for a past which is fundamentally irretrievable. Walder refers to this second variant as "longing," and he notes that "longing is qualified and distanced by an awareness that the past cannot be restored; It is approachable through stories and secrets that lend it a precarious, transient air, while thriving on the hope of human understanding and survival."[26]

The problem with nostalgia, however, is that it is in many ways a reactionary pose—taken by those who are unable to accept the fact that the world has actually changed forever. It rests on the assumption that what has occurred is only a brief digression or detour from history's trajectory, and that in due time that trajectory will be restored. In addition, one needs to admit that nostalgia is both an "imperial disease" and a luxury which only those who are currently in a position of power are able to indulge in. Consider, for example, the following exchange which occurs in *World Made by Hand*. Robert Earle remarks fondly on the possibility that perhaps "today's world" is in some ways better than the old world. Here, it appears that he is nostalgic for a pre-industrial America, perhaps the America of the 1840s, and in some ways he is pleased to find himself back in that world which he has idealized. However, when he voices that sentiment, the middle-aged Earle is immediately taken to task by his younger neighbor who was only twenty when "the world was blown apart." As a younger man who never experienced the advantages of globalization and empire (including the chance to have a college education and a professional job), the neighbor is unable to experience the same amount of nostalgia for an earlier version of America. Rather, in his view, he has not been returned to a purer time, but rather to the position of a medieval peasant. His new position is experienced not as a gain, but as a loss.

Earlier the Victorian traveler was described as a privileged young man who is the "master of all he surveys," including even the weather patterns which he encounters. In contrast, the Last Man is a traveler who is both powerless and without agency. In the new world which he enters, he is far from a privileged young man and nothing on earth is subordinate to his rule. Instead, even the earth seems to conspire against him—as he is the subject of landslides and plague (in *The Pesthouse*), bitter cold and dangerous radiation (in *The Road*), and a constant, omnipresent threat of starvation as he ekes his existence from the land. The ethnographic gaze, which assumes that man in general and imperial man in particular is in control, has been reversed—and the sense of privilege has been erased. Thus, one can compare Dombey's description of the world with Franklin's description of the world—as presented in Crace's *The Pesthouse*. Here, he writes:

> Franklin had not expected so much rain. Anyone could tell from how brittle the landscape was that, in these parts at least, it had scarcely rained all season, and what clouds there'd been that day had been horizon clouds, passersby or overtakers, actually, for they were heading eastward, too—but hardly any time had gone before the last light of the day threw out its washing water, splashing it as heavily as grit on the brittle undergrowth and setting free its long-stored smells, part hope and part decay. The rain was unforgiving in its weight.[27]

Here, Franklin feels assaulted by the weather, as a hostile earth threatens to destroy him. Unlike the safe colonial explorer, Franklin lacks human security. The avalanches and downpours described can be read as assaults on the individual subject by inhuman but not benign forces. While the Dickens passage attributes agency to Dombey while the weather and the earth are presented as passive subjects, the lens is reversed in *The Pesthouse*. Here, Franklin the refugee lacks agency while the earth itself has power over him. In this passage, Franklin appears displaced within the larger world. While H. G. Wells's character Bedford was able to make the claim that the universe itself revolved around him from his position of technological mastery and control,

Franklin can make no such claim. He does not reside at the center from where he controls the world. Rather, somehow the world has shifted to the point that he himself (and his location) are peripheral. He has become Them, rather than Us.

REFLEXIVITY AND THE LAST MAN

That is, in Levinasian terms, the new ethical view of the apocalyptic novel is necessarily reflexivist. Levinas writes, "To recognize the Other is therefore to come to him across the world of possessed things, but at the same time to establish, by gift, community and universality."[28] In this new political, social, and ethical space which is created as a result of apocalypse, Americans now have the opportunity to encounter the Other by finding themselves in the position of the Other. In the apocalyptic novel in particular, the main character walks through the apocalyptic moment, and as he traverses the events, he shifts positions—going from the position of the powerful Us to that of the disempowered Them.

Thus, in *World Made by Hand*, the narrator Robert Earle, a former computer executive from the technology corridor outside Boston, traverses old and new worlds as he becomes a carpenter in a small town in upstate New York. And there is no question that The Man from McCarthy's *The Road* is a fictional "last man." Rather, at every turn we are reminded of the ways in which he represents both the dying of the old world and the blossoming of the terrifying new world which comes to replace it. For example, in his initial description of upstate New York's new geography and landscape—in which a distance of ten miles has become "a day's walk" in the absence of a car culture. The contrast with contemporary America is implied, since Robert Earle is in a position to understand and remember both places and locations and to mediate between them. The reader's own desire to know when, if, and how the contemporary America will be restored thus represents our desire to see our traveler return "home" at the end of his journey. In addition, the notion that Robert is not a "native" of this post-imperial America—but that others are—is reinforced by the way in which he relates to two demographics in the framework of the novel—

the very young and the very old. He acts as an ambassador or translator, explaining to the young child what a "motor car" is, for example, while at the same time feeling sympathy for the older dying woman who explains that she prefers the post-apocalyptic world which is actually more familiar to her, since it reminds her of her childhood. Here, she conveys the sense that she was actually an alien in the postwar world of high technology but that for her, the erasure of this technology allowed her to return "home."

In *Falling Man*, Keith Neudecker also becomes the mediator between two groups—those with direct experience of the tragedy and those who are at a remove from the events. He, as a "native" of these events, attempts to translate the occurrences in a way that is meaningful to his readers and his fellow characters in the novel—though he admits on several fronts that the task is simply too large and too impossible. Keith also serves to mediate between two different "worlds" or two different Americas—the America of before September 11 and the America that comes after. Each world has seemingly its own norms, belief structures that hold up the edifice, and ways of attaching meaning to and making sense of events. However, *Falling Man*, if it is a travel narrative, is very much a post-modern travel narrative, for it refuses to label or to frame the terrain which it surveys. Rather, there is sense that the terrain is unnamable and amorphous. It is constantly shifting. There is no one who has the authority to shape, define, and codify the new terrain—even if they want to, which perhaps they don't. This position is described by Keith himself in conversation with an older European gentleman when he states, "Ask yourself. What comes after America?"[29] DeLillo further describes the cutoff point between the two Americas and locates it at the moment the first tower came down. "By the time the second plane appears," Keith comments as he and Lianne watch the endlessly cycling video of the attacks, "we're all a little older and wiser."[30]

Here, what becomes obvious is the way in which the narrator is a time traveler—though he is brought to his new destination not through a time machine (as in H. G. Wells's *The Time Machine* or Twain's *A Connecticut Yankee in King Arthur's Court*) but rather through an unpredictable but not entirely improbable confluence of events which have altered the world as he knows it. The traveler keeps his identity as a citizen of the contemporary world with which the reader is familiar even as he ventures forward into a futuristic world of tomorrow. Thus he acts out a mediating or translating role which allows a way of moving beyond one's situatedness.

In explaining the uses of an object or the contours of a belief system to a stranger who may not share foundational assumptions or context, the traveler is thus forced to confront what he "knows"—although he does not know he knows it.[31] What he "knows" consists of normative assumptions, beliefs, and causal structures which are held implicitly but not usually voiced outright. Thus, in his conversation with Martin, Keith Neudecker of *Falling Man* is forced to acknowledge that he does and has considered America to be the center of the world. But beyond that, he is forced to acknowledge that he sees other nations as dependent upon the United States for their own identity, arguing that if America were to fall, the resulting identity crisis would affect not just America but the entire world. "What comes after America?" is thus a question not only for America but for the world.

In both the Victorian and the contemporary travel narratives, the narrator thus comes to know himself and his own culture by serving as an ambassador and a translator to another culture. In his new role, he is forced to articulate sentiments which he holds that he might be both unaware of and incapable of articulating. Thus, until the colonial travel is forced to convey these ideas to others, he may not actually realize that he "knows" that his society is superior, and that other races and cultures are inferior. He may not realize that he "knows" that other lands are a good home for his country's surplus population and that anything found when he goes exploring implicitly belongs to him and his countrymen.

Similarly, the American traveler may only realize what he "knows" in retrospect—that America is the center of the world, that America represents the future while other nations represent the past, and that other nations are required to view America is somehow special and immune from criticism or damage. He may not realize how he himself has viewed history—until the trajectory is changed.

Table 8.1 describes the ways in which each contemporary and each British novel can be read as a sort of colonial travelogue.

THE TRAVELER

Table 8.1. Elements of the Travel Narrative in Victorian and Contemporary Fiction

Novel	Genre	Narrator	Arrival Mechanism	Purpose of Journey
Erewhon	Survival/Travel Narrative	"Narrator"	Planned journey	Colonization
Gulliver's Travels	Survival/Travel Narrative	Gulliver	Shipwrecked	Accidental
First Men in the Moon	Scientific Expedition	Samuel Bedford	Planned journey	Colonization Business
News from Nowhere	Scientific/Cultural Expedition	William Guest	Dream sequence	Accidental
A World Made by Hand	Survival/Travel Narrative	Robert Earle	Terrorist attack	Apocalypse
The Pesthouse	Survival/travel Narrative	Margaret	Plague	Apocalypse
The Passage	Scientific Expedition	Conference Participants from Future	Vampire plague	Apocalypse
The Road	Survival/Travel Narrative	The Man	Nuclear accident	Apocalypse

The philosopher and ethicist Emmanuel Levinas has faulted Western academics and researchers for the ways in which they have traditionally conceptualized of knowledge as a type of possession. He points us to the expression "I've got it" and its implication that to know someone else or their culture is to subsume it, to make it part of yours and to understand it on your terms. The Victorian penchant for collecting souvenirs, labeling them, and documenting is thus seen as a type of colonial possession of the Other which enriches neither the colonial possessor nor the one who is possessed. The possessor might claim to know the Other, but in reality he has merely created a chasm between himself and the one which he claims to know through possession.

In the colonial narratives explored here, it is frequently the colonial explorer himself who comes to be the object of this type of possessive knowledge. This concept is most clearly expressed in the situation which Gulliver is literally possessed and made known by the large

Brobdingnagians. He is grasped in the fist of the farmer who takes him around the countryside, exhibiting him to farmers—all of whom seek to "know" him. Similarly, post-apocalyptic America becomes the subject of the other's gaze, when the cleared land that used to be America is now "known" and possessed by others who come, seeking to colonize the land and exploit its peoples.

However, we can also see in these narratives a second type of Levinasian knowing—which Levinas has described as not merely possessing but truly meeting and encountering the other. Levinas speaks of how one person can truly see another face to face. One feels the fear which the Other has, which is expressed as the command "Don't kill me." In this moment, the knower not only comes to know the Other, but also to take responsibility for him. Levinas refers to this encounter as optics, or a new way of seeing.

This type of seeing also appears in the subversive travelogue, when Gulliver literally asks the Lilliputians not to kill him. At that moment he is the Other, and he is able to truly see and not merely to classify and label the Other. The moment at which Gulliver "knows" the Lilliputians is when he says to them, "Don't kill me." It is only through becoming the Other that he is able to see the Lilliputians face to face, rather than gazing down upon them from a vast distance of cultural and historic superiority. This type of knowing is not about judging, but about responding to the other; about hearing the other and being heard. It is an "optics"—a way of seeing.

NOTES

1. Homi Bhabha, *The Location of Culture* (London: Routledge, 1995): 129.
2. Sue Zemka. "Erewhon and the End of Utopian Humanism." *ELH* 69 (2002): 439–72.
3. Bhabha, 195.
4. Here my reading is affected by Charles Hinnant, *Purity and Defilement in Gulliver's Travels* (New York: St. Martin's Press, 1987): 10.
5. Zemka, 450.
6. Shankar Subramanian, *Textual Traffic: Colonialism, Modernity and the Economy of the Text* (Albany, NY: SUNY Press, 2001).

7. H. G. Wells, *The First Men in the Moon* (New York: Echo Library, 2006): 91.
8. Zemka, 458.
9. Jonathan Swift, *Gulliver's Travels* (New York: Penguin Classics, 2007): 180.
10. Swift, 21.
11. Swift, 65.
12. Swift, 71.
13. Swift, 75.
14. Swift, 176–77.
15. Swift, 19.
16. Swift, 40.
17. Swift, 21.
18. Swift, 78.
19. Swift, 66.
20. Swift, 179.
21. Swift, 203.
22. Samuel Butler, *Erewhon* (New York: CreateSpace, 2009): 116.
23. Zemka, 441.
24. Zemka, 451–52.
25. Warren Wagar, *Terminal Visions: The Literature of Last Things* (Bloomington: Indiana University Press, 1982): 17
26. Dennis Walder, "Writing, Representation and Postcolonial Nostalgia," *Textual Practice* 23 (2009): 940.
27. Jim Crace, *The Pesthouse* (London: Nan A. Talese, 2007): 225.
28. Quoted in Lisa Guentner, *The Gift of the Other: Levinas and the Politics of Reproduction* (Albany, NY: SUNY Press, 2006): 76.
29. Don DeLillo, *Falling Man* (New York: Scribner, 2007): 192.
30. DeLillo, 21.
31. Slavoj Zizek, *The Sublime Object of Ideology* (London: Verso, 2009).

3

APOCALYPSE AS ETHICS

9

ENCOUNTERING THE OTHER

> Whatsoever therefore is consequent to a time of War, where every man is Enemy to every man; the same is consequent to the time wherein men live without other security than what their own strength and their own invention shall furnish them with all. In such condition, there is no place for Industry ... no Culture of the Earth ... no Knowledge of the face of the Earth; no account of Time; no Arts; no Letters; no Society ... continual fear, and danger of violent death.[1]
>
> —Thomas Hobbes, *Leviathan* (1651)

Earlier in this work I have suggested that the "privilege" of imagining the demise of the state is an exercise in arrogance and hubris available only to those in the developed world. However, despite the fact that the apocalyptic novel rests on arrogance, it can nonetheless become a vehicle for awareness and self-reflection by the writer and by his readers. For in imagining the end of our society and perhaps the world, the apocalyptic novel thus lets us move beyond our privileged stance as Western nations and to get beyond "situatedness" to begin to see our own state anew—as a sort of future failed state.[2] It allows us to consider notions of agency and the agent-structure problem. It allows us to consider notions of blame, guilt, and responsibility in the apocalyptic narrative, and it provides a new language or mode of discourse for raising issues which we do not typically consider in international relations.

In geographic terms, both utopian and dystopian fiction, as well as apocalyptic novels, essentially rewrite our understandings of the world's map, since they reverse the situation of the center and the periphery. In the apocalyptic novel, the first world essentially becomes the periphery—an object of charity and foreign aid in some situations, and a place to be conquered and exploited in others. Our citizens, likewise, become the barbarians, objects of pity, condescension, fear, and bewilderment by others who come into contact with them. Rather than conquerors, they become objects to be owned or fed upon. It as though we have traveled both geographically and also temporally—since the United States becomes simultaneously underdeveloped (in relation to its neighbors) and undeveloped (in relation to the narrative of history as progress).

In each case, the reader is only told later and perhaps only sketchily about the exact circumstances which led up to the demise of the empire or even of civilization. The political details are usually quite vague, since the narrator of the novel is not a political analyst nor is he often particularly interested in politics. If he is interested in the events which occurred at all, it is only because they have served to construct the situation in which he finds himself. That is, our narrator was not in Washington, nor was he a policymaker or member of Congress when the decision was made in *World Made by Hand* to close America's ports and harbors—a decision which later led to the end of globalization. In *The Road*, the narrator never even finds out which country dropped the nuclear weapon on the United States which destroyed the land, the climate, and agricultural sustainability. The implication here is that the stories to be told are going to be told not by those who made history but by those who were the subjects of history. Politics is something which was done to them, rather than something which they themselves did—willingly, knowingly, or consciously. The protagonist in the novel is usually not the planner of the events which occur, and he is presented as not knowing what is to happen on day one, day ten, or year ten of the novel. In this way, he is like a colonial subject who may react with surprise to the knowledge that someone else claims to own his land, that someone else has partitioned his land, or that he himself has been sold or deeded as a subject to another country. The novel thus allows us as readers to watch history (real or imagined) as it unfolds, without necessarily knowing *where* we are in the story. Our perspective is subaltern.

The post-apocalyptic novel allows us to imagine a future in which there is no heroic narrative informing the world's history, in which the notion of a forward trajectory of state-building towards progress is largely abandoned, in which physical geography and traditional understandings of power are inadequate to describe the relations between states and individuals in this new world, and in which the state is no longer a foundational unit for understanding international relations. Apocalyptic novels allow us to take away many of the constraints and rules which we rely upon to make sense of the international system. In the absence of these rules, we are able to think again about what it means to be political, about who holds power in the international system, and the trajectory which the international system is likely to achieve

The destructive impulse of the apocalyptic novel thus clearly serves to shake the reader up and as a result to see his own world differently. But, the political theorist Slavoj Zizek would likely read an even bigger meaning into the destructive impulse. For he suggests that a desire to "erase" certain facets of state power and the ideology which accompanies it rests at base on an implicit understanding that that state power and its manifestations within a culture are not actually real but are rather constructed. Thus, nullifying the existence of the state (or imagining it, as we do in the apocalyptic novel) is not about imagining anything. It is, rather, about allowing ourselves to acknowledge something which we already know (perhaps unconsciously) to be true—that "the state" and the actions which accompany its existence in fact do not exist at all, but are rather the true products of our imagination.

Susan Napier suggests that Japanese science fiction writers play with this idea of destroying their contemporary world to get at the "authentic world" which lies beneath it—in exactly this way. Napier suggests that Japanese anime fictions which begin with the destruction of an object or a city are in fact aimed less at destroying the real, but rather at problematizing the real. That is, it is not the destruction of Tokyo which is unfathomable but rather its mere existence—the unnaturally tall buildings and the spaces of concrete. It is a modern canvas which grew up so quickly and is so divorced from the countryside and the rest of Japan and the way that people live. Napier suggests that there is something inherently "phantasmagoric" about a city, and raises the idea that the growth of cities somehow "competes" with the real Japan or the real England, threatening to wipe it out. Thus, when it is destroyed, what breaks through is the original or restored "authentic Japan."

Here one can problematize American political and economic reality in the same way—and in its destruction, perhaps greater truths can be uncovered. Applying Zizek's ideas, one can suggest that perhaps the state is actually fiction while on some level the ruined state (the apocalypse) is a fact. In other words, the violence which reigns between individuals in the apocalyptic scenarios described in this work—the ways in which our fellow humans and American citizens can become the Other, the Barbarian, the Cannibal, destroying, savaging, and preying upon one another—is actually a depiction of the real, true nature of human relations. In the created fictional dystopia, we encounter scenes in which one's fellow citizens and human beings are treated as inputs, as commodities. In this fictional world, one might use one's neighbors in the way one uses farm animals—they can be hitched up to a cart or yoked together to plow a field (as they are in the novels *World Made by Hand* and *The Road*). They might be eaten when food is scarce (as they are in *The Road*). They can be used symbolically as objects in the conduct of human sacrifices to appease the gods or one's enemies in order to stave off danger (as they are in *The Pesthouse*, *World Made by Hand*, and *The Passage*). They could be used in the manner of inanimate objects like mechanical farm equipment, as they are when they are boxed up and shipped overseas to plow someone else's fields across the ocean where the soil is better (as they are in *The Pesthouse*). This notion, however, that there is nothing inherently sacred or dignified about human life, is a reality so savage and shocking to our Western sensibilities that we can only ultimately confront it through fiction.

But an analyst like Zizek might suggest that in erasing the veneer of civility and citizenship which appears to hold American society together, we as analysts are now able to see what is real beneath that veneer but which has existed all along. That is, perhaps what these novels show us is that ultimately there is nothing special or unique about being American, regardless of the patriotic rhetoric and heroic narratives which have frequently been applied to talk about America. In a bad situation, there is no particular reason to believe that Americans could not conduct genocide against their neighbors—like we have seen in Germany or Rwanda or Bosnia. After all, the human rights violations conducted at the prison in Abu Ghraib were carried out by American citizens who ostensibly represented the forces of liberation in the region. In that sense, one can argue that dystopian fiction's depiction of human relations is real, while the "fiction" of American exceptionalism represents the true lie.

Next, a common and enduring theme in the present-day American apocalyptic is of abandonment. In a variety of settings, American citizens and leaders experience a situation in which they are cut off from and abandoned by those other nations whom they regarded as allies and supporters. In *The Passage*, we experience a haunting sequence in which the next generation survivors of the pandemic visit their coastlines and harbors and become aware that they are not so much trapped within the continental United States as they are imprisoned by their neighbors, who have quarantined them so that the infection will not spread, sinking ships and mining harbors so that the coastline is impassable and no one can escape. In *One Second After*, survivors repeat the question: Why doesn't anyone come to help us? And again in *In a Perfect World*, citizens are turned away when they attempt to flee abroad to wait out a pandemic, and cordons are set up to keep Americans inside America. Here, the consensus is that NATO is a fiction and perhaps the United Nations is as well. In times of great difficulty, America may find itself without allies.

Finally, as noted previously in this work, many contemporary apocalyptics rest on the creation of chains of logic in which the apocalyptic moment itself takes us by surprise, but in which the long, downhill slide towards state failure has begun much earlier and this slide can usually be traced to actual current world events. Thus, the narrative has a basis in reality even if the apocalyptic moment is invented. In Justin Cronin's recent work, for example, the United States appears to have been headed for destruction long before the vampires showed up. The United States is presented as an increasingly embattled state within the world system with a leadership which has become increasingly detached from both American citizens and the larger international community. In their desperate attempt to maintain a hold on America's power, America's military leaders take an unacceptable risk in their drive to create a massive new biological weapon (which they envision unleashing in the caves of Tora Bora, so that the monstrous beings will destroy the terrorists forever) and this proves to be their undoing. However, here the implicit "truth" which can be uncovered in the passage is that even if the military didn't invent the vampires who ate up humankind, in their arrogance and hubris they would have invented something else. While the vampires provide the apocalypse, the unbalanced and unrestrained power of U.S. military might provides the impetus towards that apocalypse.

Apocalyptic narratives clear the way for new thinking about political spaces—through "erasing" certain facets of the international system, as well as notions of the state. In doing so, they make us aware of the unspoken assumptions which we have about our international system which prove not to be true. First, we unwittingly expect that over time political and economic structures will expand organizationally. Currently, our emphasis on the European Union and NATO involvement in Afghanistan and Iraq is an indicator of that expectation. Thus, we are surprised to find ourselves in a future world in which international structures, globalization, and even the state no longer appear to exist.

Secondly, it is not just structures, however, which we expect will become larger. We also expect that citizens' sense of personal identity will continue to expand and enlarge. Until quite recently, most analysts believed that over time, humanity was likely to become less nationalistic and less religious, and that people would identify with larger groups (for example, cultivating a European identity). Thirdly, we assume that once rationality and a drive towards progress take hold in a society, they are unlikely to be undone. Thus, people are expected to become more scientific and empirically minded over time, and the growth of superstitious or irrational ideas is viewed as unlikely.

Finally, we assume that there is a process called Westernization, which unfolds, creating a distinction between the modern world and the pre-modern or developing world. Myers speaks of historicism, or a tendency to divide human history into a series of stages. Here, Western nations like the United States are seen to be leading figures in the inexorable march of progress, with others merely "waiting in the wings" until they too can join in the process. We cannot imagine a situation in which the West becomes unwestern. We do not even have a word for such a development. Traditional political fictions assume that the state will prevail, that conflicts are between states, and that there is one central conflict which is deterministic. In contrast, these new apocalyptic visions are based on constructivist assumptions and methodologies. They assume that many structures (like NATO and the European Union) are not permanent, but are rather a product of our intersubjective understandings. It is only in literature that we give ourselves the freedom to redefine and even erase that intersubjective understanding. This has great relevance to geographers, because it assumes that geographic territory may remain fixed, but that territoriality and governance may shift.

Finally, these novels also force the reader to confront his own sense of historical inevitability and his assumptions about the trajectory or possible trajectories of history. This is the broadest critique because it indicts not merely empire but the whole enlightenment project. It forces us to think about whether history has a trajectory, whether it is moving toward "civilization" or "modernization" and whether in fact those of us in America have adopted a "privileged" vantage point from which to judge others who appear to be backward. (It is strange how when Americans react to disaster by acting similarly "nonrational," the terms are changed to reframe the same behaviors as extremely rational and not at all immoral.) Thus, this analysis engages the central ethical question of critical theory, which is, How might we think differently about these issues if we could view them from outside of our own situatedness? How might we view the world and practices of contemporary international relations if we too felt vulnerable and if we too were exposed to the same risks? What if Britain or the United States was not the dominant superpower and our culture did not provide the dominant template by which other's cultures were measured? What if we were the disenfranchised and the culturally unendowed? Would our culture, past, and history seem just as "quaint" to others as theirs does to us? What if others viewed us as a country without a past—and we existed only in the here and now? Would we seem just as irrational, primitive, and alien as others seem to us?

EXCEPTIONALITY AND THE VIOLENCE OF REPRESENTATION

However, if apocalypse opens up the way for imagining new social formations, it serves a second function which is even more important—opening up the way to imagine new forms of relations between citizens and subjects. It thus highlights and makes the case for a new type of ethics.

In her work *Precarious Life*, the analyst Judith Butler argues that the events of September 11 forced a shift in the consciousness of Western nations who became newly aware of "how easily human life is annulled."[3] She suggests that in becoming aware of the precariousness of their own human lives, privileged citizens might have an opportunity to become more aware of the precarious life of the Other within the international system. In her work, she asks how each nation and each individual's awareness of their place within the international system and the responsibilities and ethics which accompany that place might be altered if we could create a new narrative. She states that "the ability to narrate ourselves not from the first person alone, but from, say the position of the third, or to receive an account delivered in the second, can actually work to expand our understandings of the forms that global power has taken."[4]

Apocalyptic literature serves exactly this function. It takes citizens of a powerful nation outside of themselves and places them in the situation of another—someone who is powerless, dispossessed, and without agency. In imagining a future in which America is not strong but weak, the reader can begin to meet the Other on a more level playing field in which no one occupies a privileged stance. In each post-apocalyptic novel, the reader is initially displaced when he enters the story, unable to figure out the time frame in which it occurs, or who he is supposed to "be" or identify with in the story. To pick up the analogy of the pathologist introduced in the beginning of this analysis, one can argue that the reader finds to his surprise that he no longer inhabits a living body politik. Instead, he finds to his horror that instead, he has been deposited inside a dead body politik. (This, in short, is why we find the apocalyptic genre so frightening. It is in some ways a bit like being buried alive or imagining our own deaths. Many readers react to apocalyptic novels by asking the question: If this was actually me in that scenario, would I be one of the ones who survived? In this way, the reader seeks to reassure himself that he still has potentiality, that his own DNA is sound, and that he will not wind up dead at this future date. However, even if you conclude at the end of your own personal thought experiment that you yourself will have survived and furthermore, will have heroically managed to save your entire extended family, the fact remains that your state is still dead and therefore lacked potentiality.)

Earlier I showed how apocalyptic novels allow for a critique of the notion of exceptionality and specialness which undergirded the narratives of both Victorian England and our present-day United States. Both utopian and apocalyptic novels thus force the reader to interrogate the claim that "I am significantly and substantively different from my neighbor. My viewpoint is the one which dominates the international system and it is wholly unique." Here, Levinas also tackled the problem of exceptionality and "chosenness" in his work. In writing from his own perspective as an Israeli, he asked whether one could presume that his nation or group is special and bound by covenant (and immune from danger and suffering) and yet really approach the Other. For Levinas, the problem with exceptionality was not the implicit power politics which it created and sustained but rather the way in which it created boundaries—between a Them and an Us. Exceptionality, according to Levinas, created a situation in which We are inside and You are outside.[5] Our situations are incommensurable, and while we may feel an obligation towards You, we are not you. However, I feel that apocalyptic novels can actually come as close to reproducing what it might feel like to be You as we are able to come, and for that reason, they make a unique contribution to the creation of an ethical worldview.

The literary critic Keith Booker has argued that postmodernism is about the blurring of boundaries.[6] In apocalyptic literature, the boundary is blurred between the failed and the successful state. By taking the place of the person or state which is broken, we as readers are able to see the "face" of destruction within the failed state—by wearing it ourselves. In becoming the other, we are able to experience and see what it means to be radically other. Furthermore, we experience that moment of being "called" by the Other—through experiencing what it is like to be the caller.

In the science fiction of the 1950s and 1960s, we as readers were concerned with the blurring of the boundaries between man and machine. Now, however, it appears that we are concerned with the blurring of the boundaries between Inside and Outside the international system. In the 1950s, our literary works asked us to consider the following: What if, ultimately, we could not tell ourselves from the machines? Now, however, we are concerned with the question of "What if, ultimately, we are no different from those we seek to help in the

Third world? What if ultimately we have no special wisdom or unique historical destiny to pass on to those others? What if it turns out that we actually need rescuing ourselves?" Here, in imaging the possibility of welcoming and rescuing ourselves in the future, we also begin to entertain the notion of welcoming and rescuing the other. Thus, the switching of places which occurs in the post-apocalyptic offers us a way forward ethically—towards embracing and understanding the other and towards choosing to take responsibility for the other.

In her work, the geographer Victoria Lawson speaks of whether geography has an ethics, and whether it could be "an ethic of caring"—in which those who draw and use the maps might go beyond their place in the center to see what power looks like on the periphery. As we begin to hear what it sounds like when we are called from this place, we are better able to understand and respond. Lawson writes: "Care ethics begin from the deeply social character of our existence and the ways that caring relations of dependency, frailty, grief and love all shape the ways we reason and act in the world."[7]

UNMAKING THE STATE: APOCALYPSE AND CRITICAL THEORY

In contemporary international relations, the question of care and ethics is couched largely in the language of international structures and organizations. When a powerful nation discusses how and why it should give foreign aid or react to the suffering of another, the hierarchy still exists between the donor and the recipient. In this scenario, the water or the food or the medical aid provided by the rich nation is a type of largesse or excess. In giving these items away, the giver is not placed in a more precarious or dangerous position. He is not giving out of his meager supply, but is merely donating his excess.

In addition, for the most part any aid a citizen may wish to give is to some degree mediated through the actions of the state itself. That is, one acts morally and responds to others through one's participation in the state. One seldom (or never) encounters the Other in a more direct situation, nor does one do so in a way that one's own life is endangered or called into question. The morality of one's state and the morality of the individual are thus, to some degree, conflated. One can "feel" that one is moral because one is a citizen of a state which is usually regarded as acting morally. (One can also feel superior.) Beaver explains that Levinas referred to this as the establishment of a "side by side" rather than a "face to face" relationship. Globalization helped the citizen to feel simultaneously very close to those in other lands, while at the same time distancing people since they were to some degree reduced to categories ("The Africans," for example). He notes that "due to the ease of modern communications and transport, and the worldwide scale of its industrial economy, each person feels simultaneously that he is related to humanity as a whole, and equally that he is alone and lost."[8] Levinas's work also contains the notion of "proximity."[9] Here, Levinas describes the way in which we can care about our neighbor because he is close to us—but we can never fully cross the boundary which would enable us to experience substitution through putting ourselves in the other's place. "Proximity" thus is closeness—without ever really coming close enough.[10]

However, Levinas argues that each individual is most aware of himself when he is aware of the ways in which he is responsible for the other. Here, man transcends his animality and his Hobbesian nature. He is called out of the state of nature to recognize and care for the other.[11] Apocalyptic literature allows us to imagine being in this state of nature, and allows us to ask the question "How might I respond? What is the right thing to do?"

Levinas tells us that "the nakedness of the face is destituteness. To recognize the Other is to recognize a hunger. To Recognize the other is to give."[12] In Jim Crace's *The Pesthouse*, the author allows us to experience the moment of encountering the Other again. In this situation, the man who knocks on the door does not know if he will be welcomed or he will be endangered. Levinas speaks of this as the ultimate moment of infinity in which a myriad of possibilities await. The "I" has the ability to either reach across the divide towards the Other or to fail to do so—but in that moment, the possibility of healing and of caring exists. Levinas describes the Other's basic utterance at that moment as being one of powerlessness and of need. If he could speak, Levinas tells us that the face of the Other would say merely, "Don't kill me." The meeting of You and I, with the voiceless statement "Don't kill me" is reproduced in Crace's narrative in the following scene. Here, America is only an idea, and there is no shared national identity between its residents. They are fearful of one another and aware of the dangers which they represent to each other. A deadly plague (which still rages) has carried off much of America's population, and every encounter with a stranger is potentially deadly. Under such circumstances, how does one respond? Crace writes:

> Now (Franklin) made as much noise as he could, trying to sound large and capable. He called out, "Shelter from the rain?" and then when there was silence, "I'm joining you if you'll allow." And finally, "No cause of fear, I promise you," though he was more than a little fearful himself when there were no replies.[13]

Here Franklin recognizes the other as both deserving of protection and simultaneously frightening. Crace writes: "Franklin saw the bald, round head of someone very sick and beautiful. A shaven head was unambiguous. It meant the woman and the hut were dangerous."[14]

This same sentiment appears again in Stephen King's *Under the Dome*. Here the citizens of the United States have again become the Other. This time, American citizens are literally held hostage by the other as a clear but impenetrable dome has been placed over the small New England town of Chester's Mill. The citizens cannot escape the dome, even when the air quality becomes bad, a fire burns up most of the town, and the few remaining survivors are in danger of choking to death on the smoke residue. The following scene occurs when Julia, the heroine, grabs hold of a mysterious box which has appeared on the hillside of Chester's Mill at the same time the dome came down. As she holds onto the mysterious box, she finds herself communicating with the child alien who placed the dome above her—as a kind of game. The conversation—as told by Julia—is as follows:

> Please let us go. Please let us live our little lives.
> No answer. No answer. No answer. Then:
> You aren't real. You are—
> What? What does it say? You are toys from the toyshop?[15]

In this scene, Julia finds that the other has dismissed her and her kind as irrelevant. From its high position, the alien has dismissed the needs of her friends and her community as unimportant and incomprehensible.

ENCOUNTERING THE OTHER

Julia herself has been placed in the position of the subaltern, and is addressed by the larger and more powerful individual as childlike and not quite human. Later, during the same events, Julia expresses this notion in her own words:

> She is a cat with a burning tail, an ant under a microscope, a fly about to lose its wings . . . but mostly is a little girl who was punished for her innocent arrogance, a little girl who made the mistake of thinking she was big when she was small, that she mattered when she didn't, that the world cared when in reality the world is a huge dead locomotive with an engine but no headlight. And with all her heart and mind and soul she cries out: Please let us live! I beg you, please![16]

Here, one can notice the apocalyptic and Biblical language of the phrase "with all her heart and mind and soul," as well as what may well be allusions to the United States itself as "being punished for its innocent arrogance," and "thinking she was big when she was small." Note again the allusion to the world or the international system as a dead body rather than a living one (a huge dead locomotive). This is King's own apocalyptic moment, in which the Us and the Them meet in a place which he himself describes as "the time that is no time" and "the place that is no place."[17] In this moment, the playing field has been leveled, and Julia views the situation not from a place of arrogance and entitlement but from a place of weakness and fear—even though she is in America.

Such a feeling of displacement appears in Jim Crace's *The Pesthouse*, when the author describes a scene in which a primitive person watches from afar, both frightened and attracted by the foreign ship's personnel who have approached America's shore to loot and harvest its inhabitants. In the first moments in which the scene unfolds, the American reader is unsure whether to identify with the ship's personnel or the man or woman standing on shore watching. Who is he in the story? As an American, he knows that he is modern. Therefore, he should identify with the modern character in the story, the one in the suit with the shiny buttons. But wait! In this story the Americans are not the modern people—they are rather the frightened inhabitants of a devastated land. In order to continue reading the story, he is required to enter into the illusion that he is now dispossessed and powerless and that his land is gone.

This is the moment which Levinas describes in his writing—when the individual first becomes aware of and hears the call of the face. Each individual becomes aware that there are others who have a claim on him. Levinas describes the way in which the individual becomes aware of a knock at his door, and he has at that moment an infinite number of choices including the choice of whether to respond to the knock or not. In deciding to continue reading the story, the reader has decided to answer the door and to come to more closely identify with the dispossessed. He agrees to hear them. But Levinas also tells us of the absolute powerlessness of the face at that moment. He describes the other as articulating only a single sentiment: "Don't kill me."[18] At that moment, the other is completely powerless.

The reader of the utopian or apocalyptic novel also has the opportunity to experience that moment—in the scene where he first encounters someone more powerful than himself from his own position of submission. This is the moment which we encounter in Swift's *Gulliver's Travels* when Lemuel Gulliver is overtaken by the Lilliputians. At that moment, no one recognizes him as a representative of Great Britain, a country which is a superpower. He is owed no respect or dignity. No one cares who he is, beyond the fact that he is different, a foreigner, and a threat. Instead, Gulliver finds himself bound and tied and surrounded by hostile natives. Swift writes:

> When I awaked, it was just daylight. I attempted to rise, but was not able to stir, for as I happened to lie on my back, I found my arms and legs were strongly fastened on each side to the ground; and my hair, which was long and thick, tied down in the same manner. . . . I lay all this while, as the reader may believe, in great uneasiness.[19]

The sense of Americans (or former Americans) as powerless in their new, post-apocalyptic world is conveyed in Kunstler's novel *World Made by Hand* as well. In one scene, Robert Earle watches as a group of religious activists comes to his town and proceeds to change the norms of his society. He experiences an afternoon in which the religious officials force the townspeople to shave off their beards. In this scene, the reader feels what it must be like to live in Saudi Arabia and be the target of the religious police, or to live in Afghanistan and be the target of the Taliban.

The cry of the other is given a somewhat different twist in the work of the English writer Martin Amis. Here, his 2008 volume *The Second Plane* contains a fictional essay called "The Last Days of Muhammad Atta," which forces the reader to relive the events of September 11 through the eyes of one of the hijackers. The American writer Dominic DeLillo performs a similar feat in his 2007 novel *Falling Man*, describing the impact of the plane into the World Trade Center through the eyes of an invented hijacker named Hammad. In both cases, the writer is forced to consider the possibility that "if I were so desperate that I thought that terrorism was the answer to my alienation, this is what my experience might look like." Here, Amis does exactly what Butler speaks about, in producing the face. He allows us to see the face of Osama bin Laden or the face of the hijacker. The Other is personified—and also humanized. The reader thus comes to empathize with Hammad when the terrorist is lectured in Hamburg by another hijacker named Amir, who appears to be older, wiser, and more capable than himself. From the perspective of Hammad, DeLillo writes:

> But does a man have to kill himself in order to count for something, be someone, find the way? Hammad thought about this. He recalled what Amir had said. Amir thought clearly, in straight lines, direct and systematic. Amir spoke in his face. The end of our life is predetermined. . . . We are finding the way already chosen for us.[20]

Similarly, Martin Amis allows us to inhabit the life and the soul of Muhammad Atta, the chief hijacker and perhaps the ultimate Other, at the moment when he loses his life. Amis writes:

> How very gravely he had underestimated life. His own he had hated, and had wished away, but see how long it was taking to absent it—and with what helpless grief was he watching it go. Imperturbable in its beauty and its power. Even as his flesh fried and his blood boiled, there was life, kissing its fingertips. Then it echoed out, and ended.[21]

Here, in the words of Levinas, "the absolutely foreign alone can instruct us." He describes "the strangeness of the Other, his very freedom."[22] The stories recounted here force us to see the faces of the hijackers in a different light from the way we see the same faces on, for example, America's Most Wanted, where they are dehumanized. It is perhaps because the ability to reenvision the face in this new way is so powerful that the outcry against Amis' work in particular was so strong, and the point of his exercise was so misunderstood. In Britain's leading newspapers Amis was accused of empathizing with the hijackers and defending them. Here, Butler warns that "our fear of understanding a point of view belies a deeper fear that we shall be taken up by it, find it is contagious, become infected in a morally perilous way by the thinking of the presumed enemy."[23]

It appears that seeking to meet the Other is a dangerous position, since one risks losing one's own sense of arrogance, complacency, and the ability to judge. From this new vantage point, one might be driven to consider one's own guilt in encountering the other, or be made uncomfortable by the possibility that one has not done enough for the Other. We have failed to save him.

THE FRIEND AS BROTHER, FRIEND AS OTHER

The "work" of the apocalyptic novel is thus in part to cause us to query the two types of care ethics which we are presented with. Jacques Derrida has described what he refers to as "fraternal ethics," noting that "we love those who are our double."[24] In many of our post-apocalyptic novels, we see individuals drawing together in groups (as they are prone to do in the aftermath of disaster) and looking out for one another. Citizens of towns work together to preserve the lives of fellow townspeople in *One Second After* and *World Made by Hand* and *Falling Man* describes the ways in which New Yorkers pull together in the aftermath of September 11. Yet we also see evidence of division—the ways in which the citizens of a small North Carolina town police their borders after the EMP in *One Second After*, refusing to share their water with neighboring towns and refusing to accept refugees from elsewhere. And in Robert Earle's *World Made by Hand* his friends still look quite like himself. His "new world" is still gendered, socially stratified (with the poor and uneducated survivors taking up residence in the trailer park down the street) and segregated by race. In Robert Earle's new world old divisions still hold—the hillbillies are irrational and superstitious, a race of barbaric drug dealers who consummate their unions in public venues as part of a superstition that it will render them fertile. In contrast, the 'cultured' survivors have resurrected a Victrola on which they listen to Debussy.

In contrast to Derrida's version of fraternal love, Levinas presents an ethics in which we are called to love across boundaries, reaching out to those who are different. These were the surprising ethics which the so-called "Cajun Navy" displayed in the aftermath of Hurricane Katrina, in which racial and economic divisions were forgotten as all worked together to save those who were drowning inside New Orleans' broken levies. These are the ethics displayed in *The Passage* when Amy, the child who is immune to the vampires, allows that somehow she feels a connection to them, acknowledging the fact that despite their differences, she and the vampires are somehow joined. They are somehow the same. She cares even for those who seek to destroy her. These are the ethics of *The Dome* when the alien somehow exhibits and acts upon a feeling of sympathy towards the humans trapped in Chester's Mill. These are perhaps even the ethics on display in *Falling Man* when the young children who don't completely understand what exactly transpired on September 11 attempt to make sense of it. Throughout the novel, the main character, Keith Neudecker, struggles to find out what his young son is thinking, and who the mysterious man, Bill Lawton is. Here, the reader finds out that the children are hearing not "Bin Laden" but "Bill Lawton," a name which sounds Western and similar to their own. In their own way, they have put a human face on the tragedy. They have done the work of understanding, seeking to make rational that which previously was simply condemned. In her work, Butler quotes Mary Kaldor's statement that "in many of the areas where war takes place and where extreme networks pick up new recruits, becoming a criminal or joining a paramilitary group is literally the only opportunity for unemployed young men lacking formal education."[25]

Thus, the ethics of going beyond boundaries may require attempting to understand not only the hero of the apocalyptic novel, but also the barbarian—and to see that all are trapped in the world which is created. In each case, the reader is able to explore the question of how one can have a separate ethics in which one's responsibilities are to one's fellow citizens and to one's God—regardless of whether or not the state exists.

Here, Cormac McCarthy provides yet another reading of the encounter with the Other in *The Road*. In this encounter, the Americans are both Us and Them. At times, McCarthy's man and boy are in the subaltern position, chased and frightened by those who seek to kill them, while in other situations they still have more safety and security than the dying and destitute others whom they encounter. In this brief excerpt, McCarthy allows us to see how the child in the novel, who is representative of innocence itself, intuitively knows that he must help the Other, even at the cost of his own survival. The child asks:

> What if that little boy doesn't have anybody to take care of him? he said. What if he doesn't have a papa? . . . I'm afraid for that little boy.[26]

Finally, in *The Passage*, Cronin gives us a glimpse of two different post-apocalyptic societies. The group of survivors which forms around Las Vegas builds a fortress in the desert where it "breeds" children who will ultimately be fed to the vampires, in exchange for a peace treaty with the fearsome enemies. The Las Vegas community represents the rational society which has made a wager with death, agreeing to give up and sacrifice its weaker members in exchange for protection. They are contrasted, however, with the other, more egalitarian, fraternal society which welcomes the "walkers" who appear in the California desert. Here, the new members are not eaten or sacrificed, but are instead welcomed and fed themselves. In both cases, the weakest member presents his face to the community and asks: "Don't kill me."

The apocalyptic world thus presents both a politics and a moral choice. In the case of the group which accepts the walkers, they have decided to care for the other who presents himself even at greater danger to themselves. They have decided not to be immune to danger and to risk their safety for the other. Here, the "smashing" of the old international system thus provided a type of liberation which showed a way forward towards a new politics and a new ethics. If there is a lesson to apocalyptic literature, it is thus that it is necessary to break down the old world which presents barriers to our ever becoming the other or coming into contact with the other. In imagining our state's loss, we can thus gain a new purchase on our understanding of international ethics, as we envision a new world where we can truly see, understand, and embrace the other.

NOTES

1. Thomas Hobbes, *Leviathan* (Oxford, UK: Oxford University Press, 2009).
2. The failed states characteristics used here are taken from the Fund for Peace's website, which can be accessed at www.fundforpeace.org.
3. Judith Butler, *Precarious Life: The Powers of Mourning and Violence* (London: Verso, 2004): xvii.
4. Butler, 8.
5. Michael Bernard-Donals, *Forgetful Memory: Representation and Remembrance in the Wake of the Holocaust* (Albany, NY: SUNY Press, 2009).
6. Keith Booker, *Postmodern Hollywood: What's New in Film and Why It Makes Us Feel Strange* (Westport, CT: Greenwood Publishing, 2007): 33.
7. Victoria Lawson, "Instead of Radical Geography, How about Caring Geography?," *Antipode* 41 (2009): 210.
8. A. F. Beavers, "Emmanuel Levinas and the Prophetic Voice of Postmodernity." Andiron Lecture, University of Evansville, 1993.
9. Bernard-Donals.
10. Edith Wyschogrod, *Emmanuel Levinas: The Problem of Ethical Metaphysics* (New York: Fordham University Press, 2000): 104.
11. Lucy Sargisson, *Utopian Bodies and the Politics of Transgression* (London: Routledge, 2000).
12. Emmanuel Levinas, *Totality and Infinity: An Essay on Exteriority* (Pittsburgh, PA: Duquesne University Press, 1969): 33.
13. Jim Crace, *The Pesthouse* (New York, Vintage, 2008): 27.
14. Crace, 28.
15. Stephen King, *Under the Dome: A Novel* (New York: Pocket Books, 2010): 1,060.
16. King, 1,062.
17. King, 1,052.
18. Simon Critchley, *The Ethics of Deconstruction: Derrida and Levinas* (Oxford, UK: Blackwell, 1992).
19. Jonathan Swift, *Gulliver's Travels* (New York: Penguin Classics, 2003): 13.
20. Don DeLillo, *Falling Man* (New York: Scribner, 2007): 175.
21. Martin Amis, *The Second Plane: September 11: Terror and Boredom* (New York: Vintage, 2009): 120–21.
22. Levinas, 73.
23. Butler, 8.
24. Pheng Cheah and Suzanne Guerlac, *Derrida and the Time of the Political* (Durham, NC: Duke University Press, 2008): 11.
25. Butler, 12.
26. McCarthy, 72–73.

BIBLIOGRAPHY

Adams, William C. "Whose Lives Count? TV Coverage of Natural Disasters." *Journal of Communication* 36 (1986): 113–22.

Agnew, John. *Globalization and Sovereignty.* Lanham, MD: Rowman and Littlefield Publishers, Inc., 2009.

Alkon, Paul. "*Gulliver* and the Origins of Science Fiction." In *Genres of Gulliver's Travels*, ed. Frederik Smith. Newark, DE: University of Delaware Press, 1990.

Alvesson, Mats, and Dan Kareeman. "Varieties of Discourse: On the Study of Organizations through Discourse Analysis." *Human Relations* 53 (2000): 112–1149.

Amis, Martin. "Interview with Jonathan Curiel." *San Francisco Chronicle Sunday Review* (November 4, 2001).

———. *The Second Plane: September 11: Terror and Boredom.* New York: Vintage International, 2009.

Anderson, Benedict. *Imagined Communities: Reflections on the Origins and Spread of Nationalism.* London: Verso, 2006.

Appert, Lucille. "The Pen Is Mightier Than the Whore: Imperialism and Cultural Authority in Spenser and Swift." *South Central Review* 17 (2000): 47–60.

Aradau, Claudia, and Rens Van Munster. *Politics of Catastrophe: Genealogies of the Unknown.* New York: Routledge, 2011.

Argyros, Alex. "Narrative and Chaos." *New Literary History* 23 (1992): 659–73.

Atwood, Margaret. *The Handmaid's Tale*. New York: Anchor Books, 1986.
Bacevich, Andrew. *The Limits of Power: The End of American Exceptionalism*. New York: Henry Holt and Company, 2008.
Baldwin, Gayle R. "World War Z and the End of Religion as We Know It." *Crosscurrents* (2007): 412–25.
Balibar, Etienne. "Eschatology versus Teleology: The Suspended Dialogue between Derrida and Althusser." In Pheng Cheah and Suzanne Guerlac, eds., *Derrida and the Time of the Political*. Durham: Duke University Press, 2009.
Barkey, Karen. *Empire of Difference: The Ottomans in Comparative Perspective*. New York: Cambridge University Press, 2008.
Barnett, T.P.M. *The Pentagon's New Map: War and Peace in the Twenty-First Century*. New York: Putnam, 2004.
Bartter, J. A. "Nuclear Holocaust as Urban Renewal." *Science Fiction Studies* 13 (1986): 148–58.
Baudrillard, Jean. *The Spirit of Terrorism and Other Essays*. London: Verso, 2001.
Beck, Glenn. *The Overton Window*. New York: Simon and Schuster, 2010.
Benen, Steve. "American Exceptionalism." *Washington Monthly* (April 5, 2009).
Berleant, Arnold. "Art, Terrorism and the Negative Sublime." Available at www.contempaesthetics.org/newvolume/pages/article.php?articleID=568.
Bernard-Donals, Michael. *Forgetful Memory: Representation and Remembrance in the Wake of the Holocaust*. Albany, NY: SUNY Press, 2009.
Bethea, David. *The Shape of Apocalypse in Modern Russian Fiction*. Princeton, NJ: Princeton University Press, 1989.
Bhabha, Homi. *The Location of Culture*. London: Routledge, 1995.
Birth, Kevin. "The Creation of Coevalness and the Danger of Homochronism." *Journal of the Royal Anthropological Institute* 14 (2008): 3–20.
Bleiker, Roland. "The Aesthetic Turn in International Political Theory." *Millennium: Journal of International Studies* 30 (2001): 509–33.
Blommaert, Jan, and Chris Bulcaen. "Critical Discourse Analysis." *Annual Review of Anthropology* 29 (2009): 447–66.
Boehmer, Elleke, and Stephen Morton. *Terror and the Post-Colonial*. London: Wiley-Blackwell, 2009.
Boin, Arjen, and Paul t'hart. "Public Leadership in Times of Crisis: Mission Impossible?" *Public Administration Review* 63 (2003): 544–54.
Booker, M. Keith. *Monsters, Mushroom Clouds and the Cold War: American Science Fiction and the Roots of Postmodernism, 1946–1964*. Westport, CT: Greenwood Press, 2001.
Born, Daniel. *The Birth of Liberal Guilt in the English Novel*. Chapel Hill, NC: University of North Carolina Press, 1995.

BIBLIOGRAPHY

Bousquet, Antoine. "Time Zero: Hiroshima, September 11 and Apocalyptic Revelation in Historical Consciousness." *Millennium* 34 (2006): 739–52.

Bowers, Susan. "Beloved and the New Apocalypse." Pp. 209–31 in *Toni Morrison's Fiction: Contemporary Criticism*, edited by David Middleton. London: Routledge, 1996.

Brians, Paul. *Nuclear Holocausts: Atomic War in Fiction*. Kent, OH: Kent State University Press, 2008.

Butler, Judith. *Precarious Life: The Powers of Mourning and Violence*. London: Verso, 2004.

Butler, Samuel. *Erewhon*. New York: CreateSpace, 2009.

Caffentzis, George. "The Peak Oil Complex, Commodity Fetishism, and Class Struggle." *The Commoner*, 2008. Retrieved from www.commoner.org.uk/?p=49.

Calhoun, Craig. "A World of Emergencies: Fear, Intervention and the Limits of Cosmopolitan Order." *Canadian Review of Sociology and Anthropology* 41, no. 4 (2004): 373–95.

Cantor, Paul, and Hufnagel, Peter. "Empire of the Future: Imperialism and Modernism in H. G. Wells." *Studies in the Novel* 38 (2006): 36–57.

Caporaletti, Silvana. "Science as Nightmare: *The Machine Stops* by E. M. Forster." *Utopian Studies* 8 (1997): 32–47.

Caudel, Sharon, and Randall Yim. "Homeland Security's National Strategic Position: Goals, Objectives, Measures Assessment." P. 261 in *The McGraw-Hill Homeland Security Handbook*, edited by David G. Kamien. New York: McGraw-Hill, 2006.

Caygill, Howard. *Levinas and the Political*. London: Routledge, 2002.

Charnes, Linda. "Anticipating Nostalgia: Finding Temporal Logic in a Textual Anomaly." *Textual Cultures* 4 (2009): 72–83.

Chilton, Paul. "The Meaning of Security." Pp. 193–216 in *Post-Realism: The Rhetorical Turn in International Relations*, edited by Francis Beer and Robert Hariman. East Lansing: Michigan State University Press, 1996.

Chua, Amy. *Days of Empire: How Hyperpowers Rise to Global Dominance*. New York: Doubleday, 2007.

Clarke, Lee. "Using Disaster to See Society." *Contemporary Sociology* 33 (2010): 137–39.

———. *Worst Cases: Terror and Catastrophe in the Popular Imagination*. Chicago: The University of Chicago Press, 2006.

Cleave, Chris. "Too Soon to Write the Post-9/11 Novel?" *New York Times* (September 12, 2005).

Code, Lorraine. "Incredulity, Experientialism and the Politics of Knowledge." Pp. 290–303 in *Just Methods: An Interdisciplinary Feminist Reader*, edited by Allison M. Jaggar. London: Paradigm Publishers, 2008.

Corfield, Penelope J. "The End Is nigh." *History Today* 57 (2007): 11–16.

Council on Foreign Relations. "Public Opinion on Global Issues." 2009. Available at www.cfr.org/public_opinion.

Crace, Jim. *The Pesthouse*. London: Nan A. Talese, 2007.

Cramer, Jennifer. "Do We Really Want to Be Like Them?: Indexing Europeanness through Pronominal Use," *Discourse and Society* 21 (2010): 619–37.

Crawford, Neta. "Feminist Futures: Science Fiction, Utopia and the Art of Possibilities in World Politics." Pp. 202–42 in Jutta Weldes, ed., *To Seek Out New Worlds: Exploring Links between Popular Culture, Science Fiction and Politics* New York: Palgrave MacMillan, 2003.

Crawford, Robert M. A. "International Relations as an Academic Discipline: If It's Good for America, Is It Good for the World?" 1023 in Robert Crawford and Darryl S. Jarvis, eds. *International Relations—Still an American Social Science?* New York: SUNY Press, 2001.

Critchley, Simon. "Five Problems in Levinas' View of Politics and a Sketch of a Solution to Them." *Political Theory* 32, no. 2 (2004): 172–85.

Cronin, Justin. *The Passage*. New York: Ballantine Books, 2010.

Crowley, Monica. "American Exceptionalism . . ." *Washington Times* (July 1, 2009).

Crozier, Brian. "Apocalyptic Thoughts: The Protracted Conflict." *National Review*, May 29, 1981, 604–7.

Daniels, Anthony. "Blood and Smashed Glass." *New Criterion* 25, no. 9 (2007): 33–37.

Dannenberg, Hilary. *Coincidence and Counterfactuality: Plotting Time and Space in Narrative Fiction*. Omaha: University of Nebraska, 2008.

Davidson, Joyce, Liz Bondi, and Mick Smith. *Emotional Geographies*. Hampshire, GB: Ashgate Publishing, Ltd., 2007.

DeJouvenal, Bernard. *The Art of Conjecture*. New York: Basic Books, 1967.

Delaney, David. *Territory: A Short Introduction*. Malden, MA: Blackwell Publishing, 2005.

DeLillo, Don. *Falling Man*. New York: Scribner, 2007.

de Mesquita, Bruce Bueno. *Predicting Politics*. Columbus: Ohio University Press, 2002.

Derrida, Jacques, Harold Coward, and Toby Foshay, eds. *Derrida and Negative Theology*. Buffalo, NY: State University of New York Press, 1992.

Deweese-Boyd, Ian and Margaret. "Appropriating Borges: The Weary Man, Utopia and Globalism." *Utopian Studies* 19, no. 1 (2008): 97–111.

Dittmer, Jason, and Tristan Sturm, eds. *Mapping the End Times: American Evangelical Geopolitics and Apocalyptic Visions*. Surrey, UK: Ashgate Publishing, 2010.

Doran, Robert, and Rene Girard. "Apocalyptic Thinking after 9/11: An Interview with Rene Girard." *Substance* 37, no. 1 (2005): 20–32.

Dutheil, Martine. "The Representation of the Cannibal in Ballantyne's 'The Coral Island': Colonial Anxieties in Victorian Popular Fiction." *College Literature* 28, no. 1 (2001): 105–22.

Dutton, Michael. "911: The Afterlife of Colonial Governmentality." *Post Colonial Studies* 12, no. 3 (2009): 303–14.

Eberlein, Xujun. "China 2013." *Foreign Policy* (July 30, 2010). Retrieved from www.foreignpolicy.com/articles/2010/07/30/China-2013.

Echevarria, Antulio J. *Imagining Future War: The West's Technological Revolution and Visions of Wars to Come, 1880–1914*. Westport, CT: Praeger Security International, 2007.

Erikson, Kai. *Everything in Its Path: Destruction of Community in the Buffalo Creek Flood*. New York: Simon and Schuster, 1978.

Etheridge, Lloyd. "Is American Foreign Policy Ethnocentric?" Conference Paper for the Annual Meeting of American Political Science Association, 1988.

Farish, Matthew. "Disaster and Decentralization: American Cities and the Cold War." *Cultural Geographies* 10 (2003): 125–48.

Feiler, Bruce. *America's Prophet: Moses and the American Story*. New York: William Morrow, 2009.

Ferguson, Niall. "The Reluctant Empire." *Hoover Digest* 3 (2004). Retrieved from www.hoover.org/publications/hoover-digest/article/8070.

Fierke, Karen. *Critical Approaches to International Security*. New York: Polity Press, 2007.

Forstchen, William. *One Second After*. New York: Forge Books, 2009.

Forster, E. M. *The Machine Stops*. New York: Kessinger Publishing, 2004.

Foust, C. R., and W. O. Murphy. "Revealing and Reframing Apocalyptic Tragedy in Global Warming Discourse." *Environmental Communication* 3, no. 2 (2009): 151–67.

Fox, Nicols. *Against the Machine: The Hidden Luddite Tradition in Literature, Art and Individual Lives*. Washington, DC: Island Press, 2002.

Frank Kermode. *The Sense of an Ending: Studies in the Theory of Fiction*. London: Oxford University Press, 1968.

Freeden, Michael. "Confronting the Chimera of a Post-Ideological Age." *Critical Review of International Social and Political Philosophy* 8, no. 2 (2005): 247–62.

Fukuyama, Francis. *Blindside: How to Anticipate Forcing Events and Wild Cards in Global Politics*. Washington, DC: Brookings Institute Press, 2007.

Gannon, Charles E. *Rumors of War and Infernal Machines: Technomilitary Agenda-Setting in American and British Speculative Fiction*. New York: Rowman and Littlefield, 2003.

Geertsema, Johan. "Inventing Innocence." *Journal of Literary Studies* 13, no. 1–2 (1997): 38–61.

Gell, Alfred. *The Anthropology of Time: Cultural Constructions of Temporal Maps and Images*. New York: Berg Publishers, 2001.

Goldsmith, Steven. *Unbuilding Jerusalem: Apocalypse and Romantic Representation*. Ithaca, NY: Cornell University Press, 1993.

Goodwin, Barbara, and Keith Taylor. *The Politics of Utopia: A Study in Theory and Practice*. New York: St. Martin's Press, 1982.

Gottlieb, Erik. *Dystopian Fiction East and West: Universe of Terror and Trial*. Montreal: McGill-Queen's University Press, 2001.

Green, Richard Allen. "Ready for a Zombie Apocalypse? CDC Has Advice." Available at http://edition.cnn.com/2011/HEALTH/05/19/zombiae.warning/index/html.

Groome, A. J. and Peter Mandaville. "Hegemony and Autonomy in International Relations: The Continental Experience." Pp. 151–167 in Robert M.A. Crawford and Darryl S.J. Jarvis, eds., *International Relations—Still an American Social Science?* New York: SUNY Press, 2010.

Hamilton, Davinia. "Literature and the Apocalypse," Text (March 2010). Available at http://text.desa.org.mt/issues/march2010/davinia-hamilton-literature-and-the-apocalypse.

Hammon, Andrew. *Cold War Literature: Writing the Global Conflict*. New York: Routledge, 2006.

Harraway, Donna. "Situated Knowledges: The Science Question in Feminism and the Privilege of Partial Perspective." Pp. 346–51 in *Just Methods: An Interdisciplinary Feminist Reader*, Alison M. Jaggar, ed. London: Paradigm Publishers, 2008.

Hart, Gillian. "Denaturalizing Dispossession: Critical Ethnography in the Age of Resurgent Imperialism." *Antipode* 38 (2006): 972–1004.

Hendrickson, Noel. "Counterfactual Reasoning: A Basic Guide for Analysts, Strategists and Decision Makers." Available at www.csl.army.mil/usacsl/publications/Hendrickson_Counterfactual_Reasoning.pdf.

Hinnant, Charles H. *Purity and Defilement in Gulliver's Travels*. New York: St. Martin's Press, 1987.

Hobbes, Thomas, and J.C. A. Gaskin. 2009. *Leviathan* (Oxford World's Classics). Oxford, UK: Oxford University Press.

Hourihan, Margery. *Deconstructing the Hero: Literary Theory and Children's Literature*. London: Routledge, 1997.
Hoyois, P., R. Below, J. M. Sceuren, and D. Guha-Sapir. *Annual Disaster Statistical Review 2006: The Numbers and Trends*. Brussels, Belgium: Center for Research on the Epidemiology of Disasters, 2007.
"How CDC Saves Lives by Controlling Real Global Disease Outbreaks." Available at www.cdcfoundation.og/content/how-cec-saves-lives-controlling-real-global-disease.
Huber, Matthew. "The Use of Gasoline: Value, Oil and the American Way of Life." *Antipode* 41, no. 3 (2009): 465–86.
Hughes, Barry. *International Futures: Choices in the Face of Uncertainty*. Boulder, CO: Westview Press, 1999.
Inglehart, Ronald. "Globalization and Postmodern Values." *Washington Quarterly* 23 (1999): 215–28.
Jarvis, D. S. "Identity Politics, Postmodern Feminisms and International Theory: Questioning the 'New' Diversity in International Relations." Pp. 101–31 in Robert M.A. Crawford and Darryl S. L. Jarvis, eds., *International Relations— Still an American Social Science?* Albany, NY: SUNY Press, 2001.
Jefferies, Richard. *After London; or, Wild England*. London: General Books, LLC, 2010.
Jim, Bernard L. "'Wrecking the Joint': The Razing of City Hotels in the First Half of the Twentieth Century." *The Journal of Decorative and Propaganda Arts* 25 (2006): 288–315.
Jisi, Wang. 2003. "The Logic of American Hegemony." Available at www.ou.edu/uschina/harmony.pdf.
Joye, Stijn. "New Discourses on Distant Suffering: A Critical Discourse Analysis of the 2003 SARS Outbreak." *Discourse and Society* 21, no. 5 (2010): 586–601.
Keller, A. Z., H. C. Wilson, and Al Al-Madhari. "A Proposed Disaster Scale and Associated Model for Calculating Return Periods for Disasters of Given Magnitudes." *Disaster Prevention and Management* 1, no. 1 (1992): 43–64.
Keller, Catherine. *Apocalypse Then and Now: A Feminist Guide to the End of the World*. Minneapolis, MN: Augsburg Fortress Publishers, 2004.
Kermode, Frank. *The Sense of an Ending: Studies in the Theory of Fiction*. London: Oxford University Press, 1968.
Khan, Ali. "Social Media: Preparedness 101: Zombie Apocalypse." Available at http://emergency.cdc.gov/socialmedia/zombies_blog.asp.
Killingsworth, M. Jimmie, and Jacqueline S. Palmer. "Millennial Ecology: The Apocalyptic Narrative from Silent Spring to Global Warming." Pp. 21–46 in *Green Culture: Environmental Rhetoric in Contemporary America*, Carl

Herndl and Stuart C. Brown, eds. Madison: The University of Wisconsin Press, 1996.

King, Stephen. *On Writing*. New York: Pocket Books, 2002.

———. *Under the Dome*. New York: Scribner, 2010.

Korner, Ralph J. "And I Saw . . . An Apocalyptic Literary Convention for Structural Identification in the Apocalypse." *Novum Testamentum* 42, no. 2 (2000): 160–85.

Kray, Laura J., Adam Galinsky, and Elaine Wong. "Thinking within the Box." *Journal of Personality and Social Psychology* 91, no. 1 (2006): 33–48.

Kunstler, James. *World Made by Hand*. New York: Grove Press, 2009.

Kushner, David. "Cormac McCarthy's Apocalypse." *Rolling Stone* (December 27, 2007). Retrieved from http://74.22.215.94/~davidkus/index.php?option=com_content&view=article&id=61.

Landau, Elizabeth. "Inside Zombie Brains: Sci-Fi Teaches Science." Available at http://edition.cnn.com/2011/HEALTH/04/25/zombie.virus.zombies.book/index.html.

Lawson, Victoria. "Instead of Radical Geography, How about Caring Geography?" *Antipode* 41, no. 1 (2009): 210–13.

Leander, Anna. "The Power to Construct International Security: On the Significance of the Emergence of Private Military Companies." London: Conference Papers of London School of Economics "Facets of Power in International Relations," 2004.

Lee, John. "Understanding and Preserving the Foundations of America's Advantage in Asia." Washington, DC: Hudson Institute, 2009.

Levinas, Emmanuel. *Totality and Infinity: An Essay on Exteriority*. Pittsburgh, PA: Duquesne University Press, 1969.

Levy, J. "Globalization as a Political Invention: Geographical Lenses." *Political Geography* 26 (2007): 13–19.

Lindgren, Hugo. "Pessimism Porn." *New York Magazine* (February 1, 2009). Accessed at http://nymag.com/news/intelligencer/53858 on August 2, 2011.

Little, Judith, ed. *Feminist Philosophy and Science Fiction: Utopias and Dystopias*. Amherst, NY: Prometheus Books, 2007.

Longley, Clifford. *Chosen People: The Big Idea That Shapes England and America*. London: Hodder and Stoughton, 2002.

Lopez-Ibor, Juan Jose. "What Is a Disaster." In Juan Jose Lopez-Ibor, Georgios Christodoulou, Mario Maj, Norman Sartorius, and Ahmed Okasha, eds. *Disasters and Mental Health*. New York: John Wiley and Sons, Ltd., 2005.

Lowenthal, Mark. *Intelligence: From Secrets to Policy*. Washington, DC: CQ Press, 2009.

Manjikian, Mary. *Rethinking Barbarism: Implications for the Roman Empire Analogy in International Relations*. Manuscript under review, 2010.

May, John R. *Toward a New Earth: Apocalypse in the American Novel*. Notre Dame, IN: University of Notre Dame Press, 1972.

Michel-Kerjan, Erwann. "View from Dalian, China: The New Risk Architecture and Our Growing Interdependence." November 15, 2007. Available at http://knowledge.wharton.upenn.edu/india/article.cfm?articleid=4243.

Michel-Kerjan, Erwann, and P. Slovic, eds. *The Irrational Economist: Future Directions in Behavioral Economics and Risk Management*. Pittsburgh, PA: Public Affairs Press, 2009.

Miller, Walter M., Jr. *A Canticle for Leibowitz*. New York: Harper Collins, 1959.

Mitre Corporation. "Rare Events." McLean, VA: The Jason Project, Mitre Corporation, 2009.

Morgan, Michael. *Discovering Levinas*. Cambridge, UK: Cambridge University Press, 2007.

Morris, William. *News from Nowhere and Other Writings*. New York: Penguin Classics, 1994.

Morus, Iwan. *Frankenstein's Children*. Princeton, NJ: Princeton University Press, 1998.

Muller, David G. "Improving Futures Intelligence." *International Journal of Intelligence and Counterintelligence* 22 (2009): 382–95.

———. "Intelligence Analysis in Red and Blue." *International Journal of Intelligence and Counterintelligence* 21(2008): 1–12.

Murphy, Cullen. *Are We Rome? The Fall of an Empire and the Fate of America*. Boston: Houghton Mifflin, 2008.

Myers, D. G. "The New Historicism in Literary Study." *Academic Questions* 2 (1989): 27–36.

Napier, Susan J. "When the Machines Stop: Fantasy, Reality and Terminal Identity in Neon Genesis Evangelion and Serial Experiments Lain." *Science Fiction Studies* 29 (2002): 418–35.

Neumann, Iver. "Naturalizing Geography: Harry Potter and the Realms of Muggles, Magic Folks and Giants." Pp. 157–62 in Daniel Nexon and Iver Neumann, eds., *Harry Potter and International Relations*. New York: Rowman and Littlefield, 2006.

Neumann, Iver, and Nexon, Daniel. "Introduction: Harry Potter and the Study of World Politics," i–ix in Nexon and Neumann, eds., *Harry Potter and International Relations*. Lanham, MD: Rowman and Littlefield, 2006.

Noble, Allan. "US Hegemony, Global (In)Stability, and IR Theory." Available at http://asrudiancenter.wordpress.com/2008/11/26/us-hegemony-global-instability-and-ir-theory-2/.

Norton, Anne. "Call Me Ishmael." Pp. 57–77 in Pheng Cheah and Suzanne Guerlac, eds., *Derrida and the Time of the Political*. Durham, NC: Duke University Press, 2009.

Nossal, Kim. "Tales that Textbooks Tell: Ethnocentricity and Diversity in American Introductions to International Relations." Pp. 168–87 in Robert Crawford and Darryl Jarvis, eds. *International Relations—Still an American Social Science?* Albany, NY: SUNY Press, 2001.

Oates, Joyce Carol. "Rack and Ruin: Jim Crace Configures a Post-Apocalyptic America." *The New Yorker* (April 30, 2007): 11–12.

Oddo, John. "War Legitimation Discourse: Representing 'us' and 'them' in Four US Presidential Addresses," *Discourse and Society* 22, no. 3 (2011): 287–314.

Olasky, Marvin. *The Politics of Disaster: Katrina, Big Government and a New Strategy for Future Crisis*. New York: Thomas Nelson, 2006.

O'Leary, S. D. "Apocalyptic Argument and the Anticipation of Catastrophe." *Argumentation* 11 (1997): 293–313.

Olson, Richard Stuart, and Vincent T. Gawronski. "From Disaster Event to Political Crisis: A '5C+A' Framework for Analysis." *International Studies Perspectives* 11, no. 3 (2010): 205–22.

Osborne, Andrew. "As If Things Weren't Bad Enough, Russian Professor Predicts End of US." *Wall Street Journal.* December 29, 2008. Retrieved from http://online.wsj.com/article/NA_WSJ_PUB:SB123051100709638419.

Paice, Edward. *Wrath of God: The Great Lisbon Earthquake of 1755*. New York: Quercus, 2010.

Peet, Richard. "From Eurocentrism to Americentrism." *Antipode* 37 (2005): 936–43.

Peoples, Columba, and Nick Vaughan-Williams. *Critical Security Studies: An Introduction*. New York: Routledge, 2010.

Perrow, Charles. *Normal Accidents: Living with High Risk Technologies*. New York: Basic Books, 1984.

Pesenson, Michael A. "Napoleon Bonaparte and Apocalyptic Discourse in Early Nineteenth Century Russia." *The Russian Review* 65 (2006): 373–92.

Porter, Bernard. *The Lion's Share: A Short History of British Imperialism*. London: Longman Publishing, 1984.

Pykett, Lyn. "The Material Turn in Victorian Studies." *Literature Compass* 1 (2003): 1–5.

Quarantelli, E. L., and Russel R. Dynes. "Images of Disaster Behavior: Myths and Consequences." University of Delaware Working Paper. Available at http://dspace.udel.edu8080/dspace/bitstream/handle/197/6/375/PP5.pdf.txt?sequences=u

Rasmussen, Mikkel. "It Sounds like a Riddle: Security Studies, the War on Terror and Risk." *Millennium* 33, no. 2 (2004): 381–95.

Reid-Henry, Simon. "Spaces of Security and Development: An Alternative Mapping of the Security-Development Nexus." *Security Dialogue* 42, no. 1 (2011): 97–104.

BIBLIOGRAPHY

Ricento, Thomas. "The Discursive Construction of Americanism." *Discourse and Society* 14, no. 5 (2003): 611–37.

Rodriguez, Jose, Femke Vos, Regina Below, D. Guha-Sapir. *Annual Disaster Statistical Review 2008: The Numbers and Trends*. Brussels, Belgium: Center for Research on the Epidemiology of Disasters, 2009.

Rodriguez, Lulu, and Lee Suman. "Factors Affecting the Amplification or Attenuation of Public Worry and Dread about Bioterrorist Attacks." *Homeland Security Affairs* 6 (2010): 1–16.

Roese, Neal J., and James M. Olson. "Self-Esteem and Counterfactual Thinking." *Journal of Personality and Social Psychology* 65, no. 7 (1993): 199–206.

Rosa, Eugene A. "Metatheoretical Foundations for Post-Normal Risk," *Journal of Risk Research* 1, no. 1 (1998): 15–44.

Rosa, Eugene. "The Sky Is Falling: The Sky Is Falling . . . It Really Is Falling!" *Contemporary Sociology* 35, no. 3 (2006): 212–17.

Rosenberg, Daniel, and Anthony Grafton. *Cartographies of Time: A History of the Timeline*. Princeton, NJ: Princeton University Press, 2010.

Ruggie, John Gerard. "American Exceptionalism, Exemptionalism and Global Governance" (February 6, 2004). KSG Working Paper No. RWP04-006. Available at doi:10.2139/ssrn.517642. 2004.

Ryan, Simon. "Inscribing the Emptiness: Cartography, Exploration and the Construction of Australia." Pp. 115–31 in C. Tiffin and A. Lawson, eds., *De-Scribing Empire*. London, UK: Routledge, 1994.

Sachs, Jeffrey D. *The End of Poverty*. New York: Allen Lane, 2005.

Sack, Robert David. *Human Territoriality: Its Theory and History*. Cambridge: Cambridge University Press, 1986.

Sagan, Scott. *The Limits of Safety: Organizations, Accidents and Nuclear Weapons*. Princeton, NJ: Princeton University Press, 1993.

Said, Edward. *Orientalism*. New York: Vintage, 1979.

Saint Augustine of Hippo and Marcus Dods. *The City of God*. Peabody, MA: Hendrickson, 2009.

Salmon, Wesley C. "Dynamic Rationality: Propensity, Probability and Credence." Pp. 132–56 in *Probability and Causality,* edited by James H. Fetzer. New York: Springer, 1987.

Samet, D. "Hypothetical Knowledge." *Games and Economic Behavior* 17 (1996): 230–51.

Sandison, Alan. *The Wheel of Empire*. London: St. Martin's, 1967.

Santner, Eric, Keith Reinhard, and Slavoj Zizek. *The Neighbor: Three Inquiries in Political Theology*. Chicago: University of Chicago Press, 2006.

Sargisson, Lucy. *Utopian Bodies and the Politics of Transgression*. E-book, 2000.

Savage, Ian. "An Empirical Investigation into the Effect of Psychological Perceptions on the Willingness to Pay to Reduce Risk." *Journal of Risk and Uncertainty* 6, no. 1 (1992): 75–90.

Schrady, Nicholas. *The Last Day: Wrath, Ruin and Reason in the Great Lisbon Earthquake of 1755*. New York: Viking, 2008.

Schwartzmantel, John. "Hegemony and Contestation in Post-ideological Society." ECPR Joint Sessions of Workshops. Uppsala, Sweden, 2004. Retrieved from www.essex.ac.uk/ecpr/events/jointsessions/paperarchive/uppsale/ws3/Schwartzmantel.pdf.

Seabright, Paul. *The Company of Strangers: A Natural History of Economic Life*. Princeton, NJ: Princeton University Press, 2010.

Sewlall, Harry. "Cannibalism in the Colonial Imagery: A Reading of Joseph Conrad's 'Falk.'" *Journal of Literary Studies* 22, no. 1/2 (2006): 158–74.

Shaluf, Ibrahim Mohamed. "An Overview on Disasters." *Disaster Prevention and Management* 16, no. 5 (2007): 687–704.

Smith, Andrew. *Victorian Demons: Medicine, Masculinity and the Gothic at the Fin-de-Siècle*. Manchester, UK: Manchester University Press, 2004.

Smith, Dorothy E. "Women's Perspective as a Radical Critique of Sociology." Pp. 39–43 in *Just Methods: An Interdisciplinary Feminist Reader*, Alison M. Jaggar, ed. London: Paradigm Publishers, 2008.

Smith, Linda Tuhiwai. "Research through Imperial Eyes." Pp. 58–67 in *Just Methods: An Interdisciplinary Feminist Reader*, Alison M. Jaggar, ed. London: Paradigm Publishers, 2008.

Smith, Richard. "Mapping China's World: Cultural Cartography in Late Imperial Times." www.kunstpedia.com/articles 9/18/2009.

Sontag, Susan. "The Imagination of Disaster." Pp. 209–25 in *Against Interpretation and Other Essays*, edited by Susan Sontag. New York: Farrar, Straus and Giroux, 1966.

Spurr, David. *The Rhetoric of Empire: Colonial Discourse in Journalism, Travel Writing and Imperial Administration*. Durham, NC: Duke University Press, 1993.

Stein, Howard F. "Days of Awe: September, 2001 and Its Cultural Psychodynamics." *Journal for the Psychoanalysis of Culture and Society* 8, no. 2 (2003): 187–99.

Steinberg, Theodore. *Acts of God: The Unnatural History of Natural Disaster in America*. Oxford, UK: Oxford University Press, 2000.

Stewart, Kathleen, and Susan Harding. "Bad Endings: American Apocalypse." *Annual Review of Anthropology* 28 (1999): 285–310.

Stock, Paul V. "Katrina and Anarchy: A Content Analysis of a New Disaster Myth." *Sociological Spectrum* 27 (2007): 705–26.

BIBLIOGRAPHY

Subramanian, Shankar. *Textual Traffic: Colonialism, Modernity and the Economy of the Text*. Albany, NY: SUNY Press, 2001.

Suvin, Darko. *Victorian Science Friction in the UK: The Discourses of Knowledge and Power*. Boston: G. K. Hall and Co., 1983.

Swift, Jonathan. *Gulliver's Travels*. New York: Penguin Classics, 2007.

Swirsky, Peter. *Of Literature and Knowledge: Explorations in Narrative Thought Experiments, Evolution and Game Theory*. London: Routledge, 2007.

Sylves, Richard. *Disaster Policy and Politics*. Washington, DC: CQ Press, 2009.

Tetlock, Philip E., and Richard Ned Lebow. "Poking Counterfactual Holes in Covering Laws: Cognitive Styles and Historical Reasoning." *The American Political Science Review* 95, no. 4 (2001): 829–43.

Tetlock, Philip E., and Geoffrey Parker. "Counterfactual Thought Experiments: Why We Can't Live without Them and How We Must Learn to Live with Them." Pp. 14–44 in *Unmaking the West: 'What If Scenarios That Rewrite World History*, Philip E. Tetlock, Richard Ned Lebow, and Geoffrey Parker, eds. Ann Arbor: University of Michigan Press, 2009.

Treverton, Gregory F. *Intelligence for an Age of Terror*. New York: Cambridge University Press, 2009.

Triangle, Gasper. "Justin Cronin." *Texas Monthly* (July 2010). Retrieved from www.texasmonthly.com/2010-07-01/authorinterview.php.

Urstadt, Bryant. "Imagine There's No Oil: Scenes for a Liberal Apocalypse." *Harper's Magazine* 313, no. 1875 (2006): 31–40.

Van Dijk, Teun. "Principles of Critical Discourse Analysis." *Discourse Society* 4, no. 2 (1993): 249–83.

Viehrig, Henrike. "Mass Media and Catastrophe Prevention: How to Avoid the Crisis after the Crisis." Pp. 258–67 in *Risk Assessment as a Basis for the Forecast and Prevention of Catastrophes*, I. Apostol, W. G. Coldewey, and D. L. Barry, eds. Brussels: IOS Press, 2008.

Virilio, Paul. *The Original Accident*. Cambridge: Polity Books, 2007.

Vollard, Hans. "The Logic of Political Territoriality." *Geopolitics* 14, no. 4 (2009): 687–709.

Voltaire. *Candide*. New York: Create Space, 2011.

Voorhees, Courte C. W., John Vick, and Douglas D. Perkins. "'Came Hell and High Water': The Intersection of Hurricane Katrina, the News Media, Race and Poverty." *Journal of Community and Applied Social Psychology* 17 (2007): 415–27.

Wagar, W. Warren. *Terminal Visions: The Literature of Last Things*. Bloomington: Indiana University Press, 1982.

Walder, Dennis. "Writing, Representation and Postcolonial Nostalgia." *Textual Practice* 23, no. 6 (2009): 935–46.

Walker, R. B. J. *After the Globe, Before the World*. New York: Routledge, 2010.

Wallace, Ian G. *Developing Effective Safety Systems*. New York: Institute of Chemical Engineers, 1995.

Wallender, Celeste. "Western Policy and the Demise of the Soviet Union." *Journal of Cold War Studies* 5, no. 4 (2007): 137–77.

Weldes, Jutta. "Popular Culture, Science Fiction and World Politics," Pp. 51–72 in Jutta Weldes, ed., *To Seek Out New Worlds: Exploring Links between Popular Culture, Science Fiction and Politics*. New York: Palgrave MacMillan, 2003.

Wells, H. G. *The First Men in the Moon*. New York: Echo Library, 2006.

Wendt, Alexander. *Social Theory of International Politics*. Cambridge, UK: Cambridge University Press, 1999.

Wiener, Martin J. *English Culture and the Decline of the Industrial Spirit, 1850–1980*. Cambridge: Cambridge University Press, 1981.

Wildavsky, Aaron, and Mary Douglas. *Risk and Culture: An Essay on the Selection of Technological and Environmental Dangers*. Berkeley: University of California Press, 1983.

Williams, Michael C. "Modernity, Identity and Security: A Comment on the Copenhagen Controversy." *Review of International Studies* 24 (1998): 435–39.

———. "Words, Images, Enemies: Securitization and International Politics." *International Studies Quarterly* 47, no. 4 (2003): 511–31.

Winchester, Simon. *Krakatoa*. New York: Harper Perennial, 2003.

Wyschogrod, Edith. *Emmanuel Levinas: The Problem of Ethical Metaphysics*. New York: Fordham University Press, 2000.

Zemka, Sue. "Erewhon and the End of Utopian Humanism." *ELH* 69 (2002): 439–72.

Zizek, Slavoj. *The Sublime Object of Ideology*. London: Verso, 2009.

INDEX

abandonment, 289
accident: hazard and, 79; normal accident novels and, 101n10; normal accident theory, 80
Acts of God, 154
adaptation, 151
After London (Jefferies): backward loop of progress in, *218, 221*; cultural objects and, 209; empire erased in, 234; technological landscape in, 207
agency: dread and, 52; loss of, 48–49; nature and, 50–51
Agnew, John, 136
allochronism: apocalyptic literature and, 217; circular apocalypse and, 216, 217; contemporary media and, 215; *Erewhon* and, 216, 217; explained, 214–15; linear apocalypse and, 215–16; *The Passage* and, 214, 217; utopian fiction and, 215–17

Amalrik, Andrei, 182n36
Amis, Martin, 299; on September 11 attack, 60, 64. See also *The Second Plane*
anarchy: circular apocalypse and, 171, 175–78; Hurricane Katrina and, 130; impulse of, 133–35, 139; Morris on, 135
Angel of the Revolution (Griffith), 99
anime fiction, 287–88
anthropophagi, 239, 240
apocalypse: apocalyptic moment, 55; backward glance and, 196–97; defined, 42, 45, 55; dread and, 47–48; empirical methodology and, 46; ethical vision and, 178–79; failed state and, 52–53; Google searches regarding, 69, 69–70; hegemonic grammar of, 54; identity and agency loss from, 48–49; imagining, 65–67; mainstream interest in,

6; measuring, 45–56; nature as dominant in, 50–51; prevention, 156–60; secular, 42–43, 147–49; security absence and, *43*, 43–45, *45*; sociological methodology and, 46–47; theological, 147–49; theorizing about, 2–6; western/American situatedness and, 55–56; writing, 146–53. *See also* Biblical apocalypse; circular apocalypse; linear apocalypse

apocalyptic discourse, 95–96, 104n45

apocalyptic literature: academics and, 136; allochronism and, 217; alternative discourse and, 15; anarchy impulse and, 133–35, 139; architecture metaphor and, 137, 164–65; autoimmune disorder and, 163; body analogy and, 148–49, 155–56, 181n26; boundary blurring by, 293–94; cannibal trope in, 239–45; catastrophe fiction *vs.*, *128*, 152; chains of events in, 159–60, *221*, 289–90; change and, 158; circular apocalypse in, 171–72, 175–78; citizenship and, 173–75; critical discourse analysis and, 11–12; cultural conceit and, 67–68; cultural objects and, 208–10; decisionism and, 132–33; dominating future and, 126–27; economic landscape in, 206–7; economic structures and, 290; emotional geography and, 61; emphasis of, 25; empire and, 7–8; endings, 131–32; end times elements in, 42–43; eschatological lens in, 156, 161–64; ethics and, 178–79, 293; exceptionalism and, 8, 149–56, 158–59; failed state and, 52–53; foreign policy regarding, 223n9; genetic code flaw and, 162–63; geographic landscape in, 206; geography rewritten in, 286; goals regarding, 28–31, 127–28, *128*; going native in, 229–30; ground cleared in, 134–35; hegemonic consensus and, 135–36; horror fiction and, 10; host failure and, 163–64; human relations in, 288–89; identity shifting in, 257–58; individual trajectory and, 157–58; insecurity lens and, 60–62; interrogative function of, 185–86; IR theorists and, 13–19; liberal progressive ideology and, 158, 181n32; linear apocalypse in, 168–71; loss and, 62–63; luxury to hypothesize and, 68–70; masterable future and, 127; method of analysis, 11–13, 31; Muslim sects and, 32n18; myths contained in, 130–31; normal accident and, 80; overview about, 24–28, 125–26, 285–86; overview of books analyzed, 8–11; pathologist lens in, 155–56; plausible events and, 65–66, *66*; political details in, 286–87; political landscape in, 207–8; post-ideological society and, 138–39; power relations and, 27–28; prediction and, 25–26; production timing of, 185–86; pronouns and, 31; prophecy irreversibility in, 157; punitive destruction in, 173–75; purposes served by, 189–90, 223n9; questions surrounding,

7, 12; reflexive security and, 58–59; religious, 9, 33n22, 167–68, 183n45; Russian themes in, 181n32; scenario assumptions, 125–26; secular, 167–68, 183n45; Self and Other and, 26–27; shared assumptions of, 159–60; smashing state in, 164–68; state as imaginary and, 287–88; state strengthening and, 132–33; story structure of, 256–57; subaltern perspective and, 26; as subversive, 145, 258; technology and, 207; teleological approach of, 148–53, 161; themes and discourses in, *191*; travel narrative elements in, 279; U.S. and Victorian Britain and, 7–8; vantage point of, 146; Westernization process and, 290–91. See also *specific work*

apocalyptic moment, 55; clock reset at, 213–14; defined, 63; *The Second Plane* and, 64; September 11 and, 63–65; utopian fiction and, 74n58

apocalyptic scenarios, 100n7; media examples of, 1

apocalyptic tone, 104n45

architecture metaphor, 137, 164–65

archive, 35n49

Armageddon, linear apocalypse and, 172–75

artifacts: automobiles, 247, 250–51; blankets, 246; coins, 246–47; as desirable, 249–51; as irrelevant, 247–49; weapons, 247

assumptions, 81, 159–60, 290–91

asymmetric warfare, 99

Atlantis, 225n40

Augustine, 125

autoimmune disorder, 163
automobile, 247, 250–51

backward glance: apocalyptic stance and, 196–97; exceptionalism stance and, 195–96
backward induction, 87, 103n30
backward loop, of progress, *218*, 218–22, *219*, *220*, *221*
banishment, 273–74
Barnett, Thomas P. M., 199
bathtub, 160
"The Battle of Dorking" (Chesney), 97
Baudrillard, Jean, 149
Beck, Glenn, 96
Bethea, David, 181n32
betrayal, 246, 254n35
Bhabha, Homi, 227–28, 256, 257, 263
bias, 112
Biblical apocalypse: body analogy and, 148–49; circular apocalypse and, 172; creation narratives and, 149; defined, 42, 43; eschatological lens on, 147–49; future vision and, 147–48; novels of, 102n17; prophecy irreversibility in, 157; security and, 44–45, *45*; teleological and eschatological narratives and, 160–61, 166–67, 182n34; teleological approach and, 148–49
bigness, 268–69
bin Laden, Osama, 215
Black Dawn, 100n7
blankets, 246
blurring, 19–22, 293–94
body analogy, 148–49, 155–56, 181n26

Booker, Keith, 293
boundary blurring, 293–94
Bowers, Susan, 64
Bueno de Mesquita, Bruce, 86
Buffalo Creek Flood, 165
Bush, George W., 59, 150, 215
Butler, Judith, 188–89, 200; ethics and, 292; hegemonic grammar and, 54; *Precarious Life* by, 27–28, 292; on September 11 disaster, 27–28
Butler, Samuel, 107. See also *Erewhon*

Caffentzis, George, 176
Calhoun, Craig, 173
cannibal, 170
cannibalism: in apocalyptic literature, 239–45; civilization and, 243–44; consuming resources/globalization and, 244–45; etymology and, 240; historical examples of, 240–41; instrumentalist view and, 242–43; monstrous other and, 244; *One Second After* and, 241, 243; *The Passage* regarding, 243; reversion to, 241–42; *The Road* regarding, 241, 243; world literature and, 239–40
A Canticle for Leibowitz (Miller), 80–81
care ethics, 294
Carrere D'Encause, Helene, 182n36
Carson, Rachel, 20, 24
Carvalho, Sebastiao Jose de, 132
catastrophe: individuals reactions to, 130, 140n9; reality and, 85–87; scenarios, 100n7
catastrophe fiction: apocalyptic discourse and, 95–96; apocalyptic literature *vs.*, *128*, 152; assumptions of, 81; asymmetric warfare and, 99; *A Canticle for Leibowitz*, 80–81; Tom Clancy and, 32n19, 98; conditional clauses and, 81–84, 103n23; counterfactual model and, 81–82, 84–85, 87, 90–91, 103n37; decision point mistake and, 88; dominating future and, 124n15; enemy in, 94; goal of writing, *128*; hero in, 93–94; HRT and, 80; ideological stance and, 94–95; intelligence analysts and, 78–85; invasion fiction and, 97–98; other fiction compared with, 23–24; overview about, 23; plausibility and, 85–87; positivist framework and, 91; possibility and, 85, 87; prevention and, 157; probability and, 85–87; production of, 95–100; purposes in writing, 89; realist approach of, 92–93; technology and, 96–97; unstructured disaster and, 93; utopian fiction compared with, 106; vantage point of, 146. See also *specific work*
Centerville Flood, 126–27
centrality, 199–200
certainty, contractual, 113–14
chains of events, 159–60, *221*, 289–90
Chen Guanzhong, 123n11
Chesney, George, 97
children, as burden, 271–72
circular apocalypse: allochronism and, 216, 217; anarchy and, 171, 175–78; in apocalyptic literature, 171–72, 175–78; Biblical

apocalypse and, 172; cities and, 169; Eden and, 175–78; Leftist ideals and, 176–77; *News from Nowhere* and, 175; noble savage and, 171–72; *The Passage* and, 171–72, 177; *The Pesthouse* and, 172; rebirth and, 172; *World Made by Hand* and, 171, 176
cities, 169–70
citizenship, 173–75
civilization, 188, 213, 223n6, 243–44
Clancy, Tom: catastrophe novel and, 32n19, 98; jihadist scenarios and, 7
Clarke, Lee, 4, 49, 136
Cleave, Chris, 115, 124n16
clock reset, 213–14
close call counterfactual, 89
cognitive estrangement, 119–20
cognitive ethnocentrism, 57
coins, 246–47
colonialism: cannibal trope and, 239–45; children as burden and, 271–72; *Erewhon* as parody of, 259; *The First Men in the Moon* and, 260; globalization and, 229–30; *Gulliver's Travels* as satire of, 259–60; "master of all I survey" trope and, 231–33, 236; myth of idyllic expansion in, 235–36; sea voyages and ships and, 238; *World Made by Hand* and, 237–38
colonial literature, 227–28, 244–45, 251; identity shifting in, 257–58; narrator function in, 255–56; Others in, 257; structure of, 256; as time travel, 256. See also *Heart of Darkness*; narrator, colonial travel; narrator, survival
commodity fetishism, 193–94

community, 165–66
conditional clauses, 81; subjunctive, 84; substantive, 82–84, 103n23
Conrad, Joseph, 201. See also *Falk*; *Heart of Darkness*
Contagion (film), 19–20
contractual certainty, 113–14
counterfactual model: backward induction and, 87; close call counterfactual and, 89; intelligence gathering and, 81–82, 84–85, 87–91, 103n37; mindset, 90–91; trajectories in, *220*
Crace, Jim, 6, 11; on security loss, 44. See also *The Pesthouse*
creation narratives, 149
Cronin, Justin, 2, 114. See also *The Passage*
Crowley, Monica, 8
Crozier, Brain, 182n39
cultural conceit, 67–68
cultural objects, 208–10

Daniels, Anthony, 122
Dannenberg, Hilary, 198
Dark Winter, 131
Darwinian perspective, of exceptionalism, 154
decentering, 206
decisionism, 132–33
decision point mistake, 88
decontextualization, 265–66
defamiliarization, 205
Defoe, Daniel, 264
DeLillo, Don: on September 11 attack, 67. See also *Falling Man*
Derrida, Jacques, 29–30, 166, 300
disaster assistance scenarios: assumptions of, 125–26; Centerville Flood, 126–27; Dark

Winter, 131; myths contained in, 130–31
disasters: Acts of God and, 154; apocalyptic moment and, 55; defined, 51; disaster assistance and, 18; dread and, 47–48; economics and, 4; education and, 2; empirical methodology and, 46; as entertainment, 3; eschatological anxiety and, 5–6; facets of, *129*; hegemonic grammar of, 54; history and, 2; identity and agency loss from, 48–49; individuals reactions to, 130, 140n9; Krakatoa, 3; Lisbon earthquake, 2–3, 42, 53, 241; loss and, 62–63; magnitude of, 5; mainstream interest in, 6; measuring, 45–56; nature as dominant in, 50–51; normal danger level and, 49, 71n15; as pessimism porn, 5; safety and, 3–5, 49; security norms and, 49–50; sociological methodology and, 46–47; stages of, 129; theorizing about, 2–6; unlikeliness of, 4; unstructured *vs.* structured, 93. See also apocalyptic moment
displacement, 297–98
distant suffering, 57
dominating future: apocalyptic literature and, 126–27; catastrophe fiction and, 124n15; dystopian fiction and, 114–15, 124n16; U.S. and, 115
The Doom of the Great City (Fawcett), 99
Doty, Roxanne, 12
dread: agency and, 52; apocalypse and, 47–48
Dutheil, Martine, 244

Dystopia (fictional land), 100n7
dystopian fiction: author bias and, 112; cognitive estrangement and, 119–20; consensus view and, 118–19; contractual certainty/uncertainty and, 113–14; decentering and, 206; defamiliarization and, 205; dominating future and, 114–15, 124n16; epistemology of, 119–21; ethical vision and, 178–79; foreign policy regarding, 223n9; as forward looking, 108–9; gender roles and, 112; geography rewritten in, 286; human relations in, 288–89; maps related to, 200–201; masterable future and, 115; maturity of civilization in, 213; *in medias res* and, 119–20; origins of, 107–8; overview about, 24; political details in, 286–87; political scientists and, 106–7; production of, 121–23; purposes served by, 189–90, 223n9; realistic *vs.* fantastical, 116–19; as reflexivist, 119; society and, 121–23; state and, 111, 287–88; strategic interaction and, 113–16; structural certainties and, 109–10, 113–16; as subversive, 258; technology and, 110–11; themes and discourses in, *191*; vantage point of, 146; variables influencing, 111–12. See also *specific work*

Echevarria, Antulio, 99
economic landscape, 206–7
economics, disasters and, 4
economic security: effects of loss of, 43, *43*, 45; real world threats to, 66

INDEX

economic structures, 290
Eden, circular apocalypse and, 175–78
Eliade, Mercea, 158
emergency: defined, 172–73; Federal Emergency Management Agency training manual, 126–27; modernist social construct of, 173
emotional geography, 61
empire: apocalyptic literature and, 7–8; bigness regarding, 269; critique of, 263–64; discourse of, 188–89; erased, 233–34; hybridity and, 269–70; as innate, 189. *See also* imperialism; Roman Empire; Soviet Union; United States
enchantment, 251–52
endings, 131–32
end times elements, 42–43
enemy, 94
entertainment, 3
environmental security: effects of loss of, 43, *43*, 45; real world threats to, 66
Epic of Gilgamesh (Sumerian epic), 2
Erewhon (Butler, Samuel): allochronism and, 216, 217; artifacts as irrelevant in, 247–48; backward loop of progress in, *218*; children as burden in, 271–72; cultural norms in, 270–71; cultural objects and, 208; decontextualization and, 265–66; etymology regarding, 107; exceptionalism in, 271; as fantastical, 116; hybridity in, 272; "master of all I survey" trope in, 236; maturity of civilization in, 213; mock ethnography and, 259; overview about, 12, 13, *13*, 26; as parody, 259; survival narrator and, 270–72; travel narrative elements in, 279; uniqueness claim and, 203, 225n31

Erfani, Farhang, 36n66
Erikson, Kai, 165
eschatological anxiety, 5–6
eschatological lens: in apocalyptic literature, 156, 161–64; on Biblical apocalypse, 147–49; community and, 165–66; final outcome explanations through, 161–64; in *The Pesthouse*, 156; religious apocalyptics and, 160–61, 182n34; teleological lens negated by, 166–67
eschatological narratives, 160–61, 166–67, 182n34
eschatology, defined, 42
ethical vision, 178–79
ethics: boundary blurring and, 293–94; care, 294; fraternal, 300–302; globalization and, 294–95; Levinas and, 293; Other and, 292
ethnocentrism: cognitive, 57; IR and, 56–58
ethnography, mock, 259
exceptionalism: Acts of God and, 154; adaptation and, 151; apocalyptic literature and, 8, 149–56, 158–59; autoimmune disorder and, 163; backward glance regarding, 195–96; centrality and, 199–200; colonization and, 154–55; contemporary analyst and, 204–5; countering specialness and, 204–11; countering uniqueness and, 198–204; critique of, 8; Darwinian perspective of, 154; doctrine founding, 150; *Under the Dome*

and, 296–97; in *Erewhon*, 271; essence of, 150; ethics and, 293; genetic code flaw and, 162–63; God's covenant and, 151; guilt and, 196, 224n18; hegemonic grammar and, 54; host failure and, 163–64; as immunity, 153–56; imperialism and, 186–87; Islamic, 149; maps related to, 200–201; nations displaying, 191–92, 223n10; Obama on, 8; Other and, 151–52; possible worlds theory and, 198–99; Al Qaeda and, 152; results of, 153; *The Road* and, 137–38; self-centeredness of, 186–87; social discussion and, 197; spatiality conception and, 201–2; specialness regarding, 194–95, 204–11; technology and ideology and, 192, 224n11; teleology and, 149–50, 154–55; time and, 212–13; uniqueness and, 192–94, 198–204

excremental vision, 245

exemptionalism, 153; nature and, 153, 180n18

Falk (Conrad), 230

Falling Man (DeLillo): artifacts as irrelevant in, 248, 249; centeredness and, 200; fraternal ethics and, 301; insecurity lens and, 62; instrumentalist view in, 242; last man and, 277, 278; Other's perspective and, 299; overview about, 9, 11, 26; on September 11 attack, 67

Fawcett, Edward, 99

Federal Emergency Management Agency training manual (2002), 126–27

The First Men in the Moon (Wells): as colonialism commentary, 260; decontextualization and, 265–66; "master of all I survey" trope in, 236–37; maturity of civilization in, 213; overview about, 12, 13, *13*; travel narrative elements in, 279; uniqueness claim and, 203–4

forecast, defined, 105–6

foreign policy, 223n9

Forstchen, William R., 44; background of, 93. See also *One Second After*

Forster, E. M., 12. See also *The Machine Stops*

Four Horsemen, 44–45, *45*

Fox, Nicols, 122

Frankenstein's Children (Morus), 34n47

fraternal ethics: *Falling Man* and, 301; *One Second After* and, 300; *The Passage* and, 301, 302; *The Road* and, 302; *World Made by Hand* and, 300–301

Fukuyama, Francis, 161

futures intelligence, 78

game theoretic modeling, 103n30

Gell, Alfred, 214–15

gender roles, 112

genetic code flaw, 162–63

geographic landscape, 206, 286

Gingrich, Newt, 35n54

Gladstone, William, 189

globalization: cannibalism and, 244–45; colonialism and, 229–30; ethics and, 294–95; Victorian novels and, 189

Global Trends 2025 (U.S. government report), 106

INDEX

God, Acts of, 154
God's covenant, 151
going native, 229–30
Google searches, 69, 69–70
Great Britain: luck and, 193; specialness regarding, 194–95; uniqueness regarding, 192–94; U.S. and Victorian, 7–8. *See also* Victorian novels
The Great War in England (LeQueux), 99
Griffith, George, 99
ground clearing, 134–35
guilt, 196, 224n18
Gulliver's Travels (Swift): artifacts as irrelevant in, 248; as colonialism satire, 259–60; decontextualization and, 265–66; as fantastical, 116; future vision and, 147; Houhynms and Yahoos and, 123n10; hybridity and, 269–70; knowledge as optics in, 280; knowledge as possession in, 279–80; "master of all I survey" trope and, 231–32; maturity of civilization in, 213; narrator as less than human in, 267–68; narrator as noble savage in, 269; narrator as resource in, 266–67; narrator's bigness in, 268–69; narrator's journey in, 258–59; overview about, 12, 13, *13*, 26; powerless moment in, 298; as satire, 259–60; scatological humor in, 268; as survival narrative, 265–70; travel narrative elements in, 279; uniqueness claim and, 202–3

hazard, 79
Heart of Darkness (Conrad), 201, 227; as reflexivist, 263

hegemonic consensus, 135–36
hegemonic grammar, 54
hegemony backlash, 59–60
Hendrickson, Noel, 87, 98, 106
hero, 93–94
High Reliability Theory (HRT), 79; catastrophe fiction and, 80
Hinnant, Charles, 256, 258–59
Hobbes, Thomas, 285
homeland security planners, 100n7
horror fiction, 10
host failure, 163–64
Houhynms, 123n10
HRT. *See* High Reliability Theory
Huber, Matthew, 199
human relations: dystopian fiction and, 288–89; side by side, 295
Hurricane Katrina, 61–62; anarchy and, 130
hybridity: in *Erewhon*, 272; in *Gulliver's Travels*, 269–70

identity: IR theory and, 15–19; loss of, 48–49; shifting, 257–58
ideological stance, catastrophe fiction and, 94–95
idyllic expansion, myth of, 235–36
illiteracy, 50
immunity, exceptionalism as, 153–56
imperialism: civilization and, 188, 223n6; at crossroads, 186–90; exceptionalist perspective of, 186–87; as trap, 187–88
In a Perfect World (Kasischke), 207, 289
Incendiary (Cleave), 115, 124n16
Inglehart, Ronald, 161
in medias res (in the middle of things), 120–21
insecurity lens, 60–62

instrumentalist view, 242–43
intelligence gathering: catastrophe and reality and, 85–87; catastrophe fiction and, 78–85; conditional clauses and, 81–84, 103n23; counterfactual model and, 81–82, 84–85, 87–91, 103n37; futures intelligence and, 78; prevention and, 100n7; Proteus organization and, 100n1; response and, 100n7; speculative fiction and, 78–79
international relations (IR), 11, 33n24; apocalyptic literature and, 13–19; blurring and, 19–22; catastrophe vs. apocalyptic fiction and, *128*; disaster assistance and, 18; ethnocentrism and, 56–58; identity and, 15–19; language and, 13–14, 15–17; positivism and, 14; reflexive security and, 58–59; security regarding, 15–19, 58–59; subaltern perspective and, 56; Victorian novels and, 189
intertextuality, 21, 35n50
invasion fiction, 97–98
IR. *See* international relations
Islamic exceptionalism, 149

Jackson, Rosemary, 122
Jefferies, Richard, 207
Jenkins, Jerry, 167–68
jihadist scenarios, 7
Jim, Bernie, 134, 193–94
Joao V, King, 132
journey, 170–71, 258–59
Jouvenal, Bertrand de, 108–9, 113

Kagan, Robert, 151
Kaldor, Mary, 301

Kasischke, Laura, 207, 289
Kennan, George, 182n36
Kennedy, Paul, 162
Kermode, Frank, 5, 186–87, 188
Khan, Ali, 35n49
King, Stephen, 296–97
knowledge: as optics, 280; as possession, 279–80
Krakatoa, 3
Kunstler, James Howard, 6, 102n18, 114. See also *World Made by Hand*
Kushner, David, 134
Kymlicka, Will, 253n28

LaHaye, Timothy, 167–68
language, IR theory and, 13–17
"The Last Days of Muhammed Atta" (Amis), 299
last man. *See under* narrator
Lawson, Victoria, 294
Left Behind (LaHaye and Jenkins), 167–68
Leftist ideals, 176–77
LeQueux, William, 99
Leviathan (Hobbes), 285
Levinas, Emmanuel, 27, 28, 178, 276, 298; ethics and, 293; knowledge as optics and, 280; knowledge as possession and, 279–80; Other recognition and, 295; Other's perspective and, 293, 299–300; proximity and, 295
liberal progressive ideology, 158, 181n32
linear apocalypse: allochronism and, 215–16; in apocalyptic literature, 168–71; Armageddon and, 172–75; cannibal and, 170; cities and, 169–70; explained, 168–69;

INDEX

journey and, 170–71; *The Road* and, 170–71; slavery, 171; *World Made by Hand* and, 169–70

The Lion's Share: A Short History of British Imperialism (Porter), 187

Lisbon earthquake, 2–3, 42, 53, 241

literature: blurring and, 19–22; intertextuality and, 21, 35n50; as rallying point, 20; of security and insecurity, 19–22. See also *specific genre or work*

Longley, Clifford, 151

Lowell, James, 151–52

luck, 193

luxury to hypothesize, 68–70

The Machine Stops (Forster): backward loop of progress in, *218*; overview about, 12–13, *13*, 26

maps, 199–201

Markovits, Andrei S., 226n45

masterable future: apocalyptic literature and, 127; defined, 114; dystopian fiction and, 115

"master of all I survey" trope, 235; colonialism and, 231–33, 236; in *Erewhon*, 236; in *The First Men in the Moon*, 236–37; in *Gulliver's Travels*, 231–32; in *World Made by Hand*, 232–33

McCarthy, Cormac, 60. See also *The Road*

mediator, 276–78

metaphysical asymmetry, 27

Michel-Kerjan, Erwann, 113

military security: effects of loss of, 43, *43*; real world threats to, 66

Mill, John Stuart, 107–8

Miller, Walter, 80–81

mock ethnography, 259

Models for Insight, 106

Mol, Annemarie, 148

monstrous other, 244

Morris, William, 102n18, 113; on anarchy, 135; pastoral vision of, 176. See also *News from Nowhere*

Morus, Iwan, 34n47

Muller, David, 90

Muslim sects, 32n18

myth: apocalyptic literature and, 130–31; of idyllic expansion, 235–36

Napier, Susan, 287–88

narrator: function of, 255–56; *Gulliver's Travels* and, 258–59; identity shifting and, 257–58; as observer, 262; as Other, 260–61; overview regarding, 255; as reflexivist, 263–64; as self-aware, 263–64; story structure regarding, 256–57; traditional, 261–63; last man, as banished, 273–74; *Falling Man* and, 277, 278; as mediator, 276–78; nostalgia and, 274–75; overview about, 272–73; *The Pesthouse* and, 273, 275–76; as powerless, 275–76; as self-aware, 273; as time traveler, 277–78; *World Made by Hand* and, 273, 274–75; survival, as banished, 273; bigness regarding, 268–69; decontextualization and, 265–66; *Erewhon* and, 270–72; *Gulliver's Travels* and, 265–70; hybridity of, 269–70; as less than human, 267–68; as noble savage, 269; overview about, 264–65; as pupil, 266; as resource, 266–67

nature: agency and, 50–51; exemptionalism and, 153, 180n18

News from Nowhere (Morris): anarchy impulse and, 139; backward loop of progress in, *218*; circular apocalypse and, 175; future vision and, 147; overview about, 12–13, *13*, 26; travel narrative elements in, 279
Niebuhr, Reinhold, 150
9/11. *See* September 11, 2001
noble savage, 171–72, 269
normal accident: novels, 101n10; theory, 80
Nossal, Kim, 57
nostalgia, 274–75
nuclear anxiety, 6

Obama, Barack, 8
Olasky, Marvin, 130
One Second After (Forstchen): abandonment theme in, 289; backward loop of progress in, 220; cannibalism and, 241, 243; decision point mistake and, 88; fraternal ethics and, 300; hero of, 93–94; host failure and, 164; ideological stance of, 94–95; political security and, 44; sea voyages and ships and, 238; technology and, 96; unstructured disaster and, 93
On the Beach (Shute), 47
Operation Dark Winter, 100n7
optics, 280
Orwell, George, 102n18
Other: boundary blurring and, 293–94; Butler, Judith, and, 292; in colonial literature, 257; *Under the Dome* and, 296–97; ethics regarding, 292; exceptionalism and, 151–52; *Falling Man* and, 299; Levinas and, 293, 295, 299–300; monstrous, 244; narrator as, 260–61; perspective of, 299–300; reaching out to, 295–96; recognition of, 295; Self and, 26–27
The Overton Window (Beck), 96

Panarin, Igor, 117
The Passage (Cronin), 2, 6; abandonment theme in, 289; allochronism in, 214, 217; anarchy impulse and, 139; artifacts as desirable in, 250; automobiles in, 251; backward loop of progress in, *219*, 221; cannibalism and, 243; chains of logic in, 289–90; circular apocalypse and, 171–72, 177; contractual certainty/uncertainty and, 114; cultural conceit and, 68; decentering and, 206; fraternal ethics and, 301, 302; genetic code flaw and, 162; human relations in, 288; origins of, 134; overview about, 9, 11; secession in, 173; travel narrative elements in, 279
pathologist lens, 155–56
The Pentagon's New Map (Barnett), 199
Perkins, Bryan Ward, 233–34, 240–41
Perrow, Charles, 5–6
pessimism porn, 5
The Pesthouse (Crace), 6; artifacts as irrelevant in, 249; backward loop of progress in, *219*, 219–20, *220*, *221*; circular apocalypse and, 172; citizens and subjects and, 174; cultural objects and, 209–10; decentering and, 206; decisionism

INDEX

and, 132; displacement and, 297; enchantment in, 251; eschatological lens in, 156; human relations in, 288; illiteracy and, 50; last man and, 273, 275–76; narrator as powerless in, 275–76; nature as dominant in, 50–51; overview about, 9, 11, 26; political security and, 44; reaching out to Other in, 295–96; resources and, 210–11; sea voyages and ships and, 238; slavery and, 171; technological landscape in, 207; travel narrative elements in, 279

Pick, Daniel, 21

plausibility: catastrophe fiction and, 85–87, *128*; catastrophe *vs.* apocalyptic fiction, *128*; utopian/dystopian fiction and, 116–19

plausible events, 65–66, *66*

politics: beyond, 30; apocalyptic literature regarding, 207–8, 286–87; dystopian/utopian fiction regarding, 106–7, 286–87; *The Road* and, 286; *World Made by Hand* and, 44, 211, 286

political security: effects of loss of, *43*, 43–44, *45*; *One Second After* and, 44; *The Pesthouse* and, 44; real world threats to, *66*; *World Made by Hand* and, 44, 211

Pompeii, 225n40

Porter, Bernard, 187

positivism, 14

positivist framework, 91

possession, knowledge as, 279–80

possibility: catastrophe fiction and, 85, 87; utopian/dystopian fiction and, 116–19

possible worlds theory, 198–99

post-ideological society, 138–39

Precarious Life (Butler, Judith), 27–28, 292

prediction: apocalyptic literature and, 25–26; defined, 105; limits of, 91–95; methods of, 87–91; models for, 106

prevention: apocalypse and, 156–60; catastrophe fiction and, 157; intelligence gathering and, 100n7

probability: catastrophe fiction and, 85–87; utopian/dystopian fiction and, 116–19

progress. *See* backward loop, of progress

pronouns, 31

prophecy irreversibility, 157

The Prosperous Time: China 2013 (Chen), 123n11

Protestant Wind story, 151

Proteus organization, 100n1

proximity, 295

punitive destruction, 173–75

Al Qaeda, 152

quantitative analysis, 11, 33n24

realist approach, 92–93

reality, catastrophe and, 85–87

real world threats, *66*

rebirth, 172

reflexive security, 58–59

religious apocalyptics, 160–61, 182n34

religious apocalyptic literature, 9, 33n22; secular apocalyptic literature compared with, 167–68, 183n45. *See also* Biblical apocalypse

resources, 210–11, 244–45, 266–67

Rhodes, Cecil, 154–55
The Road (McCarthy): artifacts as desirable in, 250; automobiles in, 250–51; backward loop of progress in, *219, 220, 221*; bathtub and, 160; bleak worldview of, 211; cannibalism and, 241, 243; chains of events and, 159–60; cultural objects and, 208–9; enchantment in, 251; exceptionalism and, 137–38; fraternal ethics and, 302; geographic landscape in, 206; human relations in, 288; linear apocalypse in, 170–71; men as creedless shells in, 137–38; origins of, 134; overview about, 9, 10, 26; political details in, 286; resources and, 210–11; slavery and, 171; travel narrative elements in, 279
Robinson Crusoe (Defoe), 264, 265
Roman Empire, 45, 223n6, 233–34, 240–41
Ruggie, John, 153
Russian themes, 181n32

safety, 3–5
Sagan, Scott, 80
Said, Edward, 235
Salmon, Wesley, 85–86
satire, 259–60
Savage, Ian, 47–48
scatological humor, 268
scenarios: apocalyptic, 1, 100n7; catastrophe, 100n7; disaster assistance: assumptions of, 125–26; Centerville Flood, 126–27; Dark Winter, 131; myths contained in, 130–31; jihadist, 7
Schlozman, Steven, 34n47

Schroeder, Paul, 103n37
science fiction: cognitive estrangement and, 119–20; discussion and, 20, 34n47; foreign policy and, 223n9; machine/man boundaries and, 293; virtual worlds and, 14–15. See also *specific work*
sea voyages, 238
secession, 173
The Second Plane (Amis), 299; apocalyptic moment and, 64; overview about, 9, 11, 26
secular apocalypse, 42–43, 147–49
secular apocalyptic literature, 167–68, 183n45
security: absence of, *43*, 43–45, *45*; Biblical apocalypse and, 44–45, *45*; Crace on loss of, 44; economic, *43*, *43*, *45*, *66*; environmental, *43*, *43*, *45*, *66*; homeland security planners, 100n7; insecurity lens and, 60–62; IR theory and, 15–19, 58–59; literature of, 19–22; military, *43*, *43*, *66*; norms, 49–50; political, *43*, 43–44, *45*, *66*, 211; real world threats to, *66*; reflexive, 58–59; sectors, *43*, *43*; societal, *43*, *43*, *45*, *66*
Self, Other and, 26–27
self-aware narrator, 263–64, 273
self-centeredness, of exceptionalism, 186–87
September 11, 2001, 5; aesthetic representation and, 21, 35n53; Amis on, 60, 64; apocalyptic moment and, 63–65; Butler, Judith, on, 27–28; DeLillo on, 67; Erfani and, 36n66; hegemony

INDEX

backlash and, 59–60; identity shifting and, 257–58; reimagining and, 59. See also *Falling Man*; *The Second Plane*
ships, 238
Shivani, Anis, 60
Shute, Neville, 47
side by side human relations, 295
Silent Spring (Carson), 20, 24
Silent Vector, 100n7
slavery, 171
societal security: effects of loss of, 43, 43, 45; real world threats to, 66
society: dystopian and utopian fiction and, 121–23; modernist social construct, 173; post-ideological, 138–39
Soviet Union, 71n5, 182n36, 182n39, 223n10; apocalyptic moment and, 55
spatiality conception, 201–2
specialness: countering, 204–11; exceptionalism and, 194–95, 204–11; going native and, 230; U.S./Great Britain and, 194–95
speculative fiction: defined, 22; intelligence analysts and, 78–79; overview about, 23–28; themes and discourses in, *191*. See also *specific genre or work*
Spurr, David, 231, 232
Stanley, Henry Morton, 231, 232, 264
Star Trek, 112
state: dystopian fiction and, 111, 287–88; failed, 52–53; as imaginary, 287–88; smashing, 164–68; strengthening, 132–33; utopian fiction and, 111

Steadfast Resolve, 100n7
strategic interaction, 113–16
structural certainties, 109–10; *The Prosperous Time: China 2013* and, 123n11; strategic interaction and, 113–16
structured disasters, 93
subaltern perspective, 26
subjunctive conditional clauses, 84
Subramanian, Shankar, 259–60
substantive conditional clauses, 82–84, 103n23
survivalist narratives, 95, 104n44. *See also* narrator
Suvin, Darko, 79
Swift, Jonathan: scatological humor of, 268. See also *Gulliver's Travels*
Swiss Family Robinson (Wyss), 264

technology: in apocalyptic literature, 207; catastrophe fiction and, 96–97; disaster and, 4; exceptionalism and, 192, 224n11; *One Second After* and, 96; utopian and dystopian fiction and, 110–11; *World Made by Hand* and, 207
teleology: apocalyptic literature and, 148–53, 161; Biblical apocalypse and, 148–49, 160–61, 166–67, 182n34; eschatological narrative negating, 166–67; exceptionalism and, 149–50, 154–55; narrative types, 161; religious apocalyptics and, 160–61, 182n34
terrorism, 242–43
Tetlock, Philip, 118
theological apocalypse, 147–49
threats, real world, 66

time: apocalyptic moment resetting, 213–14; exceptionalism and, 212–13; travel, 256, 277–78

travel narrative, 279. See also *specific work*

trinkets. *See* artifacts

Twelfth Imam, 32n18

Uncouth Nation: Why Europe Hates America (Markovits), 226n45

Under the Dome (King), 296–97, 301

uniqueness: centrality and, 199–200; countering, 198–204; *Erewhon* and, 203, 225n31; exceptionalism and, 192–94, 198–204; *The First Men in the Moon* and, 203–4; *Gulliver's Travels* and, 202–3; U.S./Great Britain regarding, 192–94; utopian/dystopian novel and, 198

United States (U.S.): apocalyptic scenarios and, 1; challenges faced by, 1; dominating future and, 115; ethnocentrism of, 56–58; *Global Trends 2025* and, 106; hegemony backlash and, 59–60; luck and, 193; McCarthy on, 60; specialness regarding, 194–95; uniqueness regarding, 192–94; Victorian Britain and, 7–8. See also September 11, 2001

Unmaking the West (Tetlock), 102n16, 118

unstructured disaster, 93

U.S. *See* United States

utopia: definitions surrounding, 107; realistic *vs.* fantastical, 116–19

utopian fiction: allochronism and, 215–17; apocalyptic moment and, 74n58; author bias and, 112; catastrophe fiction compared with, 106; cognitive estrangement and, 119–20; consensus view and, 118–19; contractual certainty/uncertainty and, 113–14; decentering and, 206; defamiliarization and, 205; epistemology of, 119–21; Erfani and, 36n66; as forward looking, 108–9; gender roles and, 112; geography rewritten in, 286; maps related to, 200–201; maturity of civilization and, 213; *in medias res* and, 119–20; methodology of, 108–12; narrator as Other in, 260–61; origins of, 107; overview about, 24; political details in, 286–87; political scientists and, 106–7; production of, 121–23; realistic *vs.* fantastical, 116–19; as reflexivist, 119; society and, 121–23; spatiality conception and, 201–2; state and, 111; strategic interaction and, 113–16; structural certainties and, 109–10, 113–16; technology and, 110–11; themes and discourses in, *191*; vantage point of, 146; variables influencing, 111–12. See also *specific work*

Victorian novels: accomplishment of, 221–22; asymmetric warfare and, 99; chains of events in, *221*; foreign policy regarding, 223n9; hegemonic consensus and, 135; invasion fiction and, 97–98; IR and globalization lenses regarding, 189; loss and, 63; overview of, 12–13, *13*; purposes served by, 189–90, 223n9; themes

INDEX

and discourses in, *191*; travel narrative elements in, 279. See also *specific work*
Viehrig, Henrike, 52
virtual worlds, 14–15

Wagar, Warren, 22, 89
Walker, R. B. J., 56, 257
Wallender, Celeste, 71n5
Ward, Humphrey, 256
warfare, asymmetric, 99
weapons, 247
Weiner, Martin, 175–76
Wells, H. G.: on ground clearing, 135. See also *The First Men in the Moon*
Westernization process, 290–91
Winthrop, John, 150
world literature, cannibalism and, 239–40
World Made by Hand (Kunstler), 6; anarchy impulse and, 139; artifacts as desirable in, 249–50; autoimmune disorder and, 163; automobiles in, 250; backward loop of progress in, *219, 220, 221*; circular apocalypse and, 171, 176; colonial mentality in, 237–38; cultural objects and, 209; decisionism and, 132–33; empire erased in, 234; enchantment in, 251; fraternal ethics and, 300–301; human relations in, 288; last man and, 273, 274–77; linear apocalypse in, 169–70; "master of all I survey" trope and, 232–33; nostalgia and, 274–75; overview about, 9, 10–11, 26; political details in, 286; political security and, 44, 211; post-ideological society and, 138; powerless moment in, 298; property in, 208; sea voyages and ships and, 238; technological landscape in, 207; travel narrative elements in, 279
Wyss, Johan, 264

Yahoos, 123n10

Zemka, Sue, 235, 259, 263, 272
Zizek, Slavoj, 138, 161, 287
The Zombie Autopsy (Schlozman), 34n47
zombies, 10, 34n47

ABOUT THE AUTHOR

Mary Manjikian is assistant professor at the Robertson School of Government at Regent University in Virginia Beach, VA. She received a BA from Wellesley College, an M.Phil from St. Antony's College, Oxford University, and an MA and PhD from the University of Michigan. Her work has appeared in *International Studies Quarterly* and *Alternatives*. She is also the author of *Threat Talk: Comparative Politics of Internet Addiction* (2011). She is a former U.S. Foreign Service officer who has served in Bulgaria, Russia, and the Netherlands. She is currently working on a book about the securitization of property squatting in Western Europe.